INTRODUCTORY MICROECONOMICS:

Second Edition

MAURICE ARCHER, B.SC.(Econ.), M.A.
Professor of Business Management
Ryerson Polytechnical Institute

MAURICE ARCHER BOOKS
A Division of Maurice Archer Enterprises Incorporated
P.O. Box 244, Oakville, Ontario L6J 5A2

INTRODUCTORY MICROECONOMICS:
A Canadian Analysis
SECOND EDITION

Written, printed, and bound in Canada

First Edition published in 1974 by Macmillan of Canada

Canadian Cataloguing in Publication Data

Archer, Maurice
Introductory microeconomics

2nd ed.
Includes index.
ISBN 0-9691546-1-5

1. Microeconomics. 2. Canada - Economic conditions - 1945- . I. Title.

HB172.A67 1987 338.5 C87-093785-5

Designed and typeset in Times Roman by Accutext Limited
Printed by The Alger Press Limited
Cover by Brian Moore

Summary of Contents

Table of Contents

PART B: THE MARKET SYSTEM

PART C: THEORY OF THE FIRM

PART D: DISTRIBUTION OF INCOME

PART E: CANADIAN INDUSTRY

Preface

The purpose of this book is to provide the student of economics with a comprehensive, yet easy-to-read introductory account of *microeconomics* — the study of economic behaviour within society at the individual household, firm, or industry level (as contrasted with *macroeconomics* — the study of the economy as a whole or of basic sectors within it such as all households, all business firms, etc.).

In Part A of the book, we consider the nature and importance of economics; distinguish between different economic systems; and examine the tools of economic analysis. In Part B, we look at the market system, to understand how the interaction of demand and supply sets the market price of a good and helps allocate scarce resources. In Part C of the book, we consider how the individual firm operates within different market structures in its price and output decisions. Then, in Part D, we examine how the various factors of production are rewarded for their services. Finally, in Part E, we direct our attention at Canadian manufacturing and agriculture, including business organization and productivity.

Throughout the book, theoretical concepts have been explained and illustrated with the aid of tables and charts; mathematical treatment has been largely avoided. The examples, statistics, and viewpoints are Canadian and as up-to-date as possible.

Each chapter begins with a statement of objectives and an outline of its contents. This is followed by a straightforward description, explanation, and to some extent discussion of the topics presented. Numbered sub-headings (the principal ones in colour) help to guide the reader through the text material. At the end of each chapter, there are: a Summary of the key economic concepts that have been explained in the chapter; a list of the Key Terms used; and a series of Review Questions for class-room review and discussion.

MAURICE ARCHER

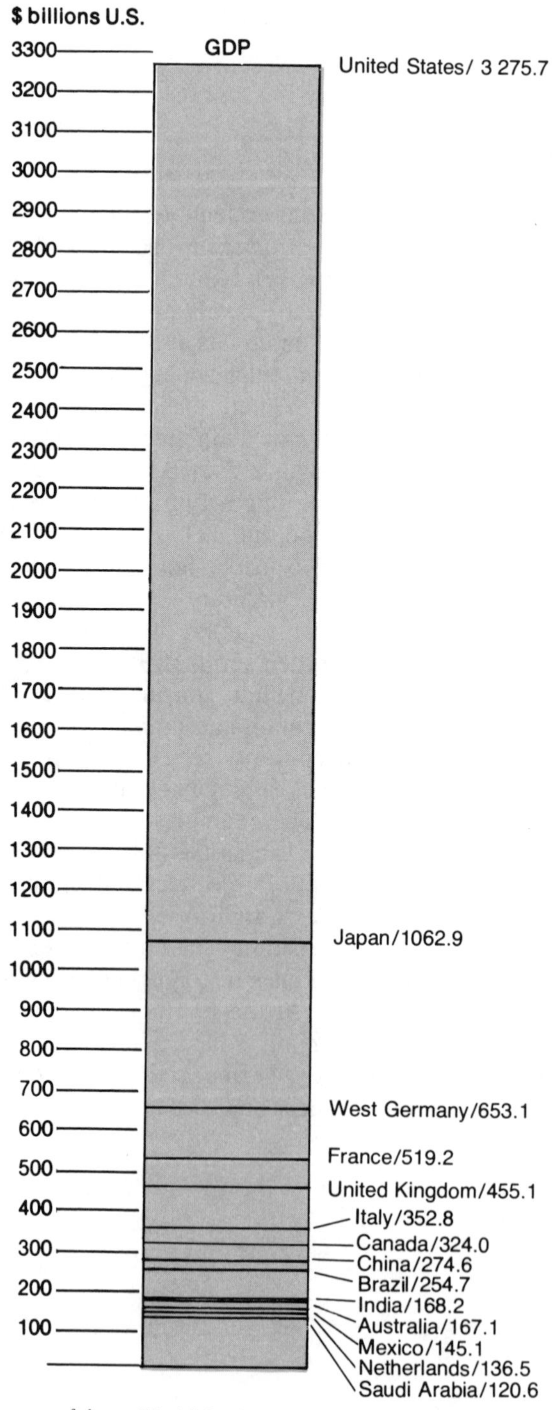

Source of data: World Bank, *World Development Report, 1985*
Note: Figures not available for the USSR, and most other East European Countries. GDP data is for 1983.

1. THE NATURE AND IMPORTANCE OF ECONOMICS

CHAPTER OBJECTIVES

A. To explain the meaning of the term "economics"
B. To emphasize the importance of economic understanding to individuals, business firms, and governments
C. To examine the various types of resources on which our economic prosperity depends
D. To emphasize the need for choice in the use of scarce resources, with the use of a production-possibility curve
E. To explain how in Canada we actually choose what to produce
F. To discuss Canada's economic goals

CHAPTER OUTLINE

1.1: ECONOMICS DEFINED

Economics is the study of the way in which society uses its scarce resources to satisfy its many different wants. Derived from the Greek words *oikos* (house) and *nemein* (to manage), "economics" means literally "the art of household management."

Two of the most famous definitions of economics are as follows:

Alfred Marshall, "Economics is a study of mankind in the ordinary business of life; it examines that part of individual and social action which is most closely connected with the attainment and with the use of the material requisites of well being," in *Principles of Economics* (Macmillan & Co. Ltd., London, 1930).

Lionel Robbins, "The science which studies human behaviour as a relationship between ends and scarce means which have alternative uses," in *An Essay on the Nature and Significance of Economic Science* (Macmillan & Co. Ltd., London 1935).

Macroeconomics and Microeconomics

Economics is now divided into two main areas: "macro" and "micro"—derived from the Greek words for "large" and "small." *Macroeconomics* is the study of the economic problems that face society as a whole—such as unemployment, inflation, economic growth, and international trade. *Microeconomics* is the study of the economic problems that face the various elements of society: (a) the individual units such as the consumer, the business firm, the government, the wage earner; and (b) the various groups within society such as the household sector, the business sector, and the government sector. Both areas of economics are closely related. Thus, for example, an increase in a country's money supply, as well as affecting the rate of inflation, can greatly affect the fortunes of the individual firm.

Economics: a Social Science

Economics is considered to be a social science because it involves the methodical study of the economic aspect of human behaviour. However, to understand economic behaviour, it also helps to have some knowledge of other social sciences such as psychology, sociology, geography, and politics. The study of many economic problems has also benefited from the rigorous application of mathematical and statistical techniques. In Chapter 3 (Economic Analysis), we examine how economists make use of the scientific method in analyzing economic problems and developing economic theories.

1.2: IMPORTANCE OF ECONOMICS

Today, economics is studied in schools, colleges, and universities throughout Canada. It is also an integral part of the curriculum of most professional associations. There are two basic reasons for this. First, economic reasoning helps one to develop a clear, logical way of thinking that is invaluable in practically any career. In particular, it emphasizes the constant need for choice in using scarce funds and the desirability of weighing rationally the pros and cons of each alternative before making a decision. As Lord Keynes (one of the world's greatest economists) once wrote, economics "is a method rather than a doctrine, an apparatus of the mind, a technique of thinking which helps its possessor to draw correct conclusions."

The second basic reason for studying economics is that it helps us to understand the economic system in which we live, so that, for instance, we can comprehend how economic events such as unemployment occur and how the economic situation of the country and the world at large can affect our personal, business, and government decisions.

From the personal point of view, economics helps us to plan our careers, decide when and where to seek work, make spending, savings, and investment decisions, and understand what is going on around us. The economic efficiency, or productivity, of Canadians (as discussed in more detail in Chapter 20) determines the standard of living that we enjoy. Of course, economic considerations only partly influence our decisions. We are also affected by social, moral and emotional factors—for example, the choice of a more interesting, but lower-paid job; or the decision to marry regardless of income. And even in the purely economic field, many economic events that affect our lives are largely beyond our personal control—for example, inflation, recession, unemployment, and high interest rates. However, we can, through the study of economics, understand why they are occurring and perhaps, through our choice of government, exert some influence on them.

Business firms, in their pursuit of profit, can also benefit from an understanding of the way the economy operates—in setting prices, making production and marketing plans, and making borrowing and investment decisions.

Every country, as one of its goals, tries to improve the economic well-being of its citizens. To do this, government must make a variety of economic policy decisions—for example, with regard to public spending, borrowing and taxation; and to changes in the money supply, in the level of interest rates, in the foreign exchange rate for the currency, and in a host of other economic matters. To do this wisely, requires a thorough understanding of economics, including Canadian and international economic institutions. And most governments are judged at election time on their success in dealing with the bread-and-butter issues of employment, income, and inflation, rather than on empty phrases.

If, in the future, Canadians are to enjoy a rising, rather than falling, standard of living, we must learn how to raise our productivity so as to compete successfully with the newly industrializing parts of the world, particularly S.E. Asia. This issue, perhaps the biggest economic issue for Canada in the 1980s, is discussed in detail in Chapter 20. If we do not resolve it, the extremely high unemployment levels that now exist in Canada will continue to haunt us.

Economic History

The economic system that we now take for granted did not develop overnight, nor will it remain unchanged in the years to come. Economic history—the study and analysis of past economic activities—helps us to understand more clearly our present economic system—its strengths and weaknesses, institutions, and directions for the future. We may not subscribe to the theory of economic evolution expressed by Karl Marx in *Das Kapital*—a required economics textbook in many countries of the world. Nevertheless, we can discern logical processes of economic change and development that have been at work over the years and which will continue in the years to come. In the nineteen eighties, as the technological impact of the silicon chip, the microtransistor, and the large-scale integrated circuit, spreads throughout the economy, a new industrial society, dubbed the "Third Wave" by Alvin Toffler, is expected to emerge, that will in one way or another, affect the economic life of us all. And before too long, we are expected to have the "fifth-generation" computers that can listen, see, think, speak and do all manner of industrial and other tasks.

1.3: LIMITED RESOURCES

A shipwrecked sailor, thrown up like Robinson Crusoe on a deserted island, obviously could not produce everything he would like to have with the limited resources available. He would have to determine: (a) what he could produce with these limited resources; and (b) what ranking, or priority, he would attach to his various wants.

First he would have to survey the resources: the land (what it would grow, the minerals and other raw materials it would yield, the fish to be caught along its shores); the labour (his own); and the capital (the tools salvaged from the wreck).

Canada too has a limited amount of resources with which to produce the goods and services that consumers, government, and business would like to have. Traditionally, these resources (referred to by economists as *the factors of production*) have been arbitrarily divided

"Well, Polly, what's it to be today: fish or goat, stockade or boat?"

into three categories—land, labour, and capital—in order to make the analysis of production as simple as possible. Two additional items, entrepreneurship and technology, are now often included among the factors of production. Just as important in our complex, modern society, as the factors of production, are the political and social environments in which our economic activity is carried out—something that we will say more about later in the chapter.

Land

This factor of production consists of natural (as distinct from people-made) resources such as farmland, building land, oil and other mineral deposits, forests, lakes, rivers, and neighbouring oceans, all of which can be used, directly or indirectly, for production and most of which this country possesses in abundance. Canada is, in fact, the second-largest country in the world, covering an area of just under 10 million square kilometres.

Labour

Labour, or human resources, comprises those members of the population who are able to work.

In Canada, this is almost 13 million persons out of a total population of over 25.5 millions (See Tables S.1 and S.2). The size of the labour force, although important, is only one part of the picture. Equally important are the skills and abilities of its members in performing the complex tasks of modern industrial society. Like Robinson Crusoe, society would be helpless without "technical know-how." Society would also be helpless without a variety of "leaders"—for example, business leaders to plan and organize the production of goods and services; government leaders to steer the economy; scientists, researchers and educators to expand our knowledge; professional leaders to pioneer new standards of service; and labour leaders to safeguard the welfare of the rank-and-file worker.

Capital

This factor of production (sometimes called *real* capital to distinguish it from money capital) is of two basic types: social capital and business capital. *Social capital* (also called the *economic infrastructure* of a country) includes electric-power plants and transmission lines, roads, railways, airports, harbours, and bridges; schools, hospitals, theatres, and

Table S.1
Canada's Population Growth, 1965-1986, thousands of persons

Year	Population at start of year	Total increase	Births	Deaths	Net Natural increase	Immi-gration	Residual (including emigration)	Annual rates per 1 000 pop. Births	Annual rates per 1 000 pop. Deaths	Annual growth rate of population
										%
1965	19 501	356	419	149	270	147	−60	21.5	7.6	1.8
1966	19 857	371	388	150	238	195	−62	19.5	7.5	1.9
1967	20 228	353	371	150	221	223	−90	18.3	7.4	1.7
1968	20 581	307	364	153	211	184	−88	17.7	7.4	1.5
1969	20 888	294	370	154	215	162	−83	17.7	7.4	1.4
1970	21 182	283	372	156	216	148	−81	17.6	7.4	1.3
1971	21 465	245	362	157	205	122	−82	16.9	7.3	1.1
1972	21 710	233	347	162	185	122	−74	16.0	7.5	1.1
1973	21 942	293	343	164	179	184	−71	15.6	7.5	1.3
1974	22 235	333	346	167	179	218	−64	15.5	7.5	1.5
1975	22 569	315	358	167	191	188	−64	15.9	7.4	1.4
1976	22 884	275	359	167	192	146	−64	15.7	7.3	1.1
1977	23 158	259	362	167	195	115	−51	15.6	7.2	1.1
1978	23 417	227	359	168	191	86	−50	15.3	7.2	1.0
1979	23 645	267	365	168	197	112	−42	15.5	7.1	1.1
1980	23 912	309	371	171	199	143	−33	15.5	7.2	1.3
1981	24 221	290	371	171	200	129	−38	15.3	7.1	1.2
1982	24 512	271	373	174	198	121	−49	15.2	7.1	1.1
1983	24 783	239	374	174	199	89	−50	15.1	7.0	1.0
1984	25 021	242	377	176	201	88	−47	15.1	7.0	1.0
1985	25 264	237	379	178	201	84	−48	15.0	7.1	0.9
1986	25 501									

Source: Statistics Canada, *Vital Statistics,* Cat. 84-201.

Table S.2
Canada's Labour Force, 1973-1986

Year	Civilian Population 15 and over	Civilian Labour force	Participation rate	Employed	Employment rate
	(000)	(000)	%	(000)	%
1973	15 526	9 276	59.7	8 761	94.4
1974	15 924	9 639	60.5	9 125	94.7
1975	16 323	9 974	61.1	9 284	93.1
1976	16 701	10 203	61.1	9 477	92.9
1977	17 051	10 500	61.6	9 651	91.9
1978	17 377	10 895	62.7	9 987	91.7
1979	17 702	11 231	63.4	10 395	92.6
1980	18 053	11 573	64.1	10 708	92.5
1981	18 375	11 904	64.8	11 006	92.5
1982	18 664	11 958	64.1	10 644	89.0
1983	18 917	12 183	64.4	10 734	88.1
1984	19 148	12 399	64.8	11 000	88.7
1985	19 372	12 639	65.2	11 311	89.5
1986	19 594	12 870	65.7	11 634	90.4
		(Percentage change)			
1973	2.6	3.9	1.3	4.2	0.3
1974	2.5	3.5	1.0	1.7	-1.7
1975	2.3	2.3	0.0	2.1	-0.2
1976	2.1	2.9	0.8	1.8	-1.1
1977	1.9	3.8	1.8	3.5	-0.2
1978	1.9	3.1	1.1	4.1	1.0
1979	2.0	3.0	1.1	3.0	-0.1
1980	1.8	2.9	1.1	2.8	0.0
1981	1.6	0.5	-1.1	-3.3	-3.8
1982	1.4	1.9	0.5	0.8	-1.0
1983	1.2	1.8	0.6	2.5	0.7
1984	1.2	1.9	0.6	2.8	0.9
1985	1.1	1.8	0.8	2.9	1.0

Source: Statistics Canada, *The Labour Force*, Cat. 71-001 museums; dwelling houses; and government buildings. *Business capital* includes fixed assets such as farm and factory buildings, warehouses, and retail stores and all the accompanying machinery, equipment, and furnishings, including vehicles.

To obtain more of these capital or investment goods, a country has to divert part of its resources away from the production of goods and services that are *consumed*—that is to say, used up immediately, or in a relatively short period of time. Canada also obtains capital goods through investment by foreigners in this country. When we acquire more of these capital goods, we are said to be *investing.*

Entrepreneurship

This term is used to describe the creative risk-taking efforts of enterprising businessmen and women, called *entrepreneurs*, willing and able to assess consumer demand, pioneer the development of new products, establish and manage small and large business enterprises, and produce and market a wide range of goods and services. Because of its vital importance to an economy, entrepreneurship is treated by some economists as a fourth factor of production, separate from labour.

Technology

Economically, a country would be almost powerless without its technology or "technical know-how." This is the expertise, or technical knowledge of how to produce goods and services. A country can have a good labour force and an adequate supply of capital but lack the technology to make the best use of its natural resources—for example, the problems in developing the Canadian oil sands or the Atlantic offshore oil and gas.

Over the years, the world has accumulated a vast amount of technical knowledge which can be passed on to each new generation. If we were to be plunged back into a new Dark Ages, it would take hundreds of years to develop the technical knowledge currently used in industry, medicine, communications, transportation, and so many other fields. That is why, in many eyes, technology ranks as a factor of production *par excellence.*

At one time, improvements in technical knowledge took place very gradually and were considered part of labour and capital. However, the extremely rapid pace of technological change in the twentieth century, much faster than the Industrial Revolution of the nineteenth century, has made economists give this input special attention. Technological change is now frequently cited as one of the most vital factors in a country's economic growth. The importance of technological change to society has been dramatized by Alvin Toffler in his book, *Future Shock*. By dividing the last 50000 years of our existence into lifetimes of approximately 62 years, he suggests that there have been 800 such lifetimes, of which some 650 were spent in caves. Only within the most recent lifetimes have human beings made their most important technological discoveries. Indeed, most of the material goods used by everyone today have been developed only in the present 800th lifetime. Radio, television, telephones, photography, steam engines, propeller-driven ships, electricity, electric-light bulbs, electric motors, internal combustion engines, cars, propeller-driven and jet aircraft, manned space rockets, computers, canned and frozen foods, electric household appliances, electric, atomic and digital clocks, industrial machinery of all kinds, automated manufacturing processes, plastic products, and synthetic fabrics are all examples of goods invented or developed in the last few lifetimes. Moreover, agriculture, not long ago the primary human occupation, has now been replaced in many countries by manufacturing and service industries as the chief source of income and employment.

Political and Social Environments

The contrast between the standard of living of the Western industrial democracies and that of most of the Communist countries of Eastern Europe emphasizes how important the political environment is in influencing economic activity. A government that tries to control almost completely the ownership and use of the means of production also destroys the personal freedom and economic initiative that are essential to rapid economic growth. And as we have seen in, for example, Central America and Lebanon, civil wars, resulting from political differences, can bring economic activity almost to a standstill.

Even within a democracy such as Canada, political decisions constantly interfere with and even overrule economic decisions—so much so that we have been said to have "politicized our economy"—for example, the political decisions in the nineteenth century to build the C.P.R., and later to institute a National Policy of tariff protection for Canadian manufacturers, and in more recent times, the emphasis in government legislation in Canada on income distribution rather than income creation, and the establishment of FIRA and the National Energy Program to promote economic nationalism perhaps at the expense of Canadian income and employment.

The social environment also greatly influences economic activity.

For example, one of the main factors contributing to Japan's economic success is considered to be its disciplined, co-operative labour force and system of life-time employment—both an outcome of the type of society. In Britain, by contrast, management and labour, broadly representing two different social classes, are natural adversaries. In other countries, particularly the Middle East, religion greatly affects business activity.

Scarcity

Land, labour, and capital, both on Crusoe's island and in society at large, are insufficient to produce everything that people want. As a result, economists call them *scarce resources*, even though the absolute quantities may be extremely large. The nature, quantity, and quality of these resources set limits or *constraints*, therefore, on what can be produced.

Alternative Use

Canada's resources, as well as being relatively scarce, are capable of alternative use. Sales reps can be employed to sell any one of a variety of product lines; farmland can be used to grow many different crops; and factories can be designed and equipped to make all kinds of products. We can build more houses if we build fewer schools; more hospitals if we build fewer houses. Or we can spread our resources and build some of each, but not as many as if we used all our resources to build just houses, just schools, or just hospitals.

1.4: THE PRODUCTION POSSIBILITY CURVE

The range of choice open to society is illustrated in economics by means of a *production possibility curve*, or PPC. This curve (also called a *boundary*, or *frontier*) shows, hypothetically, the possible combinations of two different goods that can be produced by society with a given amount of resources.

Let us assume, for simplicity, that society can produce only office desks (capital goods) and hockey sticks (consumer goods). Let us also assume that, by using all its resources, society can produce at the two extremes either 5000 office desks or 16 million hockey sticks. Table 1:1, entitled Alternative Production Possibilities, shows these two extremes, together with some of the various intermediate production combinations.

Table 1:1
Alternative Production Possibilities

	Office desks (thousands)	Hockey sticks (millions)
A	0	16
B	1	15
C	2	13
D	3	10
E	4	6
F	5	0

These various full-employment production possibilities can be plotted on a graph (see Figure 1:1). Along the horizontal axis, we show the number of office desks produced, and along the vertical axis the number of hockey sticks produced. Plotted in the body of the graph is a series of points, A to F, each of which denotes a full-employment production possibility. Thus, point A represents the extreme at which society could produce 16 million hockey sticks but no office desks. Point F represents the other extreme at which society could produce 5000 office desks but no hockey sticks. Points B, C, D, and E represent combinations in between. Thus point D indicates that society, using *all* its resources, could produce 3000 office desks and 10 million hockey sticks. To show that there are any number of possible production combinations, we can draw a smooth curve joining the various points already plotted. We can then read off, at any point along the curve, the number of office desks and hockey sticks that could together be produced.

In practice, many thousands of goods and services can be produced in many thousands of possible production combinations. It is impossible, however, to measure this real-life situation. To do so, we would need a multi-dimensional rather than a simple two-dimensional PPC. Nevertheless, the production possibility curve with just two goods does serve a very useful purpose. It helps drive home an important economic fact: if a society's resources are fully employed, the only way for society to obtain more of one good is by having less of another. To use our previous example, society can have more office desks only by having fewer hockey stocks. Every extra office desk "costs" society so many hockey sticks. For example, from Table 1:1, we can see that if society produces no office desks, it can have 16 million hockey sticks. If it wants 1000 office desks, however, it can have only 15 million hockey sticks. Each desk has "cost" society the opportunity of having 1000 hockey sticks. This is called the *opportunity cost*. It is the cost, in terms of alternative production possibilities, of producing a particular good.

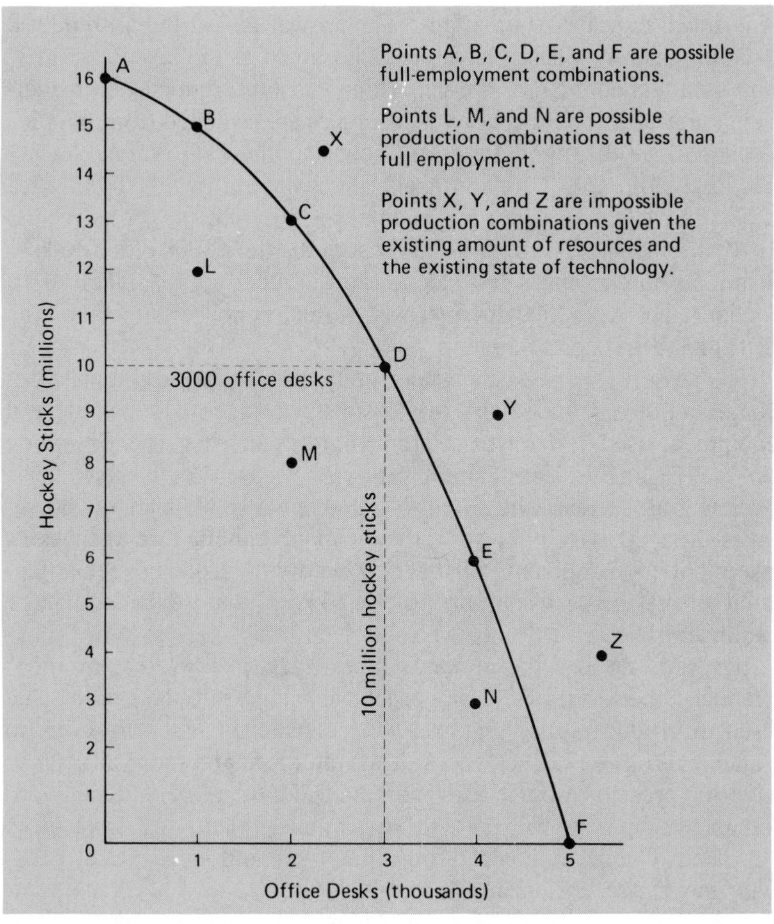
Points A, B, C, D, E, and F are possible full-employment combinations.
Points L, M, and N are possible production combinations at less than full employment.
Points X, Y, and Z are impossible production combinations given the existing amount of resources and the existing state of technology.
Hockey Sticks (millions)
Office Desks (thousands)
3000 office desks
10 million hockey sticks
A
B
C
D
E
F
L
M
N
X
Y
Z
0
1
2
3
4
5
6
7
8
9
10
11
12
13
14
15
16

Figure 1:1 The Production Possibility Curve

This need for choice is being demonstrated all the time. As one example, the Soviet Union has for many years had a deliberate policy of allocating economic resources predominantly towards the production of military and capital goods at the expense of consumer goods. There are not enough resources to produce sufficient of both. In Canada, as another example, if we want to use more of our resources to fight pollution, we must be prepared to use resources now unemployed or being used for something else.

Why does the PPC have the shape that it does? In other words, why is it drawn concave to its origin? The answer is that the arithmetical data on which it is based have been chosen so as to illustrate another important economic fact: the opportunity cost of producing each additional unit of a good increases as resources are switched from the production of another good. In terms of our hypothetical example, society has to give up only 1 million hockey sticks to get its first 1000 office desks, but it has to give up 2 million hockey sticks to get its second 1000 office desks. The opportunity cost of the third 1000 office desks is 3 million hockey sticks (a reduction in output from 13 million to 10 million). The next 1000 desks "costs" 4 million hockey sticks, and the fifth 1000 desks costs 6 million.

The reason for increasing opportunity cost is that it gradually becomes more and more difficult to substitute materials, labour, and equipment used in one type of production for another type. The wood or steel for office desks cannot very well be used for hockey sticks. Society must increase the output of suitable woods—which, of course, takes time. Management and other workers cannot turn their skills overnight to manufacturing the new product. Plant and equipment used for making desks cannot easily be converted to a different type of production.

If society decides that it wants more hockey sticks (or any other product), then the most easily adaptable of the resources now being used to produce something else will be switched first. However, to obtain even more hockey sticks, it will be more and more difficult to alter the present resource use. Workers will have to be retrained. Unsuitable equipment will have to be scrapped. Plants will have to be relocated. The per-unit cost of obtaining more and more hockey sticks will quickly rise, particularly in the short run.

Production possibility curves can be used to illustrate many different types of economic choice that face society—for example, between consumption goods and capital goods, between capital goods and military goods, and between private goods and public goods.

In practice, society's resources are not always fully employed. This means that the economy operates *within* the PPC rather than on it. Although able to produce up to 5000 office desks or 16 million hockey sticks, society with less than full employment might produce only 4000 office desks or 14 million hockey sticks. So long as it has sufficient unemployed resources, a country can undertake new projects, such as cancer research or a space program, without necessarily forfeiting something else. However, if all resources—land, labour, and capital—are fully employed, then society must do without something else. This is because the economy is operating on its production possibility curve, or boundary.

It should be noted that the production possibility curve is not static. If a country is enjoying rapid economic growth, its PPC will be constantly shifting outwards to the right. Each year, the country becomes able to produce more and more goods and services. However, if the economy is stagnant, the PPC will remain relatively unchanged. And if the country has an increasing population, the average standard of living may actually decline as the same amount of goods and services has to be shared among more people.

1.5: ECONOMIC CHOICE

How does society choose what is to be produced? Who determines what we are to have? What economic goals do our federal and provincial governments pursue? Choice is so fundamental in our economic system that economics is sometimes succinctly defined as the "science of choice".

Consumer Sovereignty

In Canada, the group with the most important say as to what is produced is the consumer sector (See Table S.3). A *consumer* is any private individual with money to spend. Every dollar that one has can be likened to a vote at an election. If one wants more of one good and less of another, one will cast one's dollar "vote" accordingly. In other words, one will purchase only those goods that one wants and in the quantities that one wants. The choice will reflect one's personal needs and desires. Because spending by consumers is still much greater in total than spending by busines firms or by government, we continue to talk about *consumer sovereignty*.

Although Canadian consumers may be said to be "sovereign," that sovereignty is by no means absolute. Advertising, for example, greatly influences how we spend our money. Indeed, it has been suggested that advertising has become so powerful that consumers are often manipulated to buy what business firms want them to buy rather than what they really want themselves.

Table S.3
Spending in Canada, 1965-1985

Year	Consumers	Government	Business	Total Spending	Consumers	Government	Business
		(millions of dollars)				(Percentage of total)	
1965	34 714	10 709	11 225	56 648	61.3	18.9	19.8
1966	37 952	12 484	13 081	63 517	59.8	19.7	20.6
1967	41 068	14 046	13 294	68 408	60.0	20.5	19.4
1968	44 842	15 668	13 509	74 019	60.6	21.2	18.3
1969	49,093	17 241	15 089	81 423	60.3	21.2	18.5
1970	51 853	19 621	15 838	87 312	59.4	22.5	18.1
1971	56 271	21 973	17 825	96 069	58.6	22.9	18.6
1972	63 021	24 088	19 926	107 035	58.9	22.5	18.6
1973	72 069	27 121	24 588	123 778	58.2	21.9	19.9
1974	84 231	32 890	30 370	147 491	57.1	22.3	20.6
1975	97 566	39 509	35 602	172 677	56.5	22.9	20.6
1976	111 500	44 519	40 462	196 481	56.7	22.7	20.6
1977	123 555	50 152	43 485	217 192	56.9	23.1	20.0
1978	137 427	54 469	47 496	239 392	57.4	22.8	19.8
1979	153 390	59 625	56 096	269 111	57.0	22.2	20.8
1980	172 416	67 473	64 065	303 954	56.7	22.2	21.1
1981	196 191	78 239	76 672	351 102	55.9	22.3	21.8
1982	212 468	88 351	71 067	371 886	57.1	23.8	19.1
1983	232 501	93 589	70 862	396 952	58.6	23.6	17.9
1984	251 353	100 527	73 034	424 914	59.2	23.7	17.2
1985	274 658	106 752	80 856	462 266	59.4	23.1	17.5

Source: Statistics Canada, *National Income and Expenditure Accounts*, Cat. 13-001.

There is no doubt that advertising is effective in introducing new products to consumers, but it is certainly not so effective in persuading them to continue to buy what they do not like. Business history is littered with products that consumers did not want. Nevertheless, advertising does exert a great influence. Lack of competition in certain industries can also restrict consumer sovereignty; new firms may be prevented from entering the field or existing firms from producing what consumers really want. And, of course, the government (by import duties, sales taxes, government monopolies, and various laws) places restrictions on what consumers may buy.

Consumer sovereignty has meant that the major part of Canada's resources are used to produce food, clothing, cars, housing, furniture, household appliances, and entertainment that are considered necessities by the average Canadian consumer. This method of allocating resources has, of course, led to anomalies—for example, more is spent on tobacco than on theatres, more on entertainment than on education. Nevertheless, it has meant that the wishes of the Canadian public (rather than of the government) are given the top priority in directing the use of the country's scarce economic resources.

Business Spending

Business firms purchase large quantities of materials and parts (or *intermediate goods*) in order to produce the finished products, and supply the services, that consumers, governments and other business firms, want. Such business spending reflects market demand. Thus, the larger the number of cars purchased, the more axles, wheels, tires, etc. the business firms will have to buy. The business firm's freedom of choice will be restricted to seeking the best value in materials and parts.

Business firms also spend money on *capital goods*, such as plant equipment, for the production of other goods. Their choice in this investment spending reflects their forecast of the production needed to meet expected sales and their view of the most efficient method of production.

Government Spending

Although consumers play the leading role in Canada in deciding what should be produced, our various governments—federal, provincial, and municipal—are also important spenders. Furthermore, they have in recent years shown the fastest rate of increase in spending. Indeed, one of the chief characteristics of the modern Canadian economy is the

"In the free market system, the consumer is always sovereign."

rapidly expanding role of government as a purchaser of goods and services.

Foreign Spending

Much of Canada's output is exported. Foreigners, therefore, greatly influence Canada's pattern of production. The growth of many of Canada's manufacturing industries, to say nothing of its more traditional resource industries, has depended as much on foreign markets, particularly the U.S. one, as on the Canadian one.

Other Government Tools for Allocating Resources

So far we have assumed that spending is the only method of determining how our economic resources are used. But the Canadian federal government, and to a much lesser extent the provincial and municipal governments, have various other tools at their disposal. Those available to the federal government, in addition to spending programs, include taxation, exchange rates, import duties, import quotas, and laws forbidding or encouraging certain business practices. It can use all of these to influence how Canada's resources are used and, equally important the degree of employment of these resources. In other words, it can influence not only Canada's position on the country's production possibility curve, but also whether Canada operates on it or within it—that is, whether Canada operates (see Figure 1:1) at point D (full employment) or at point M (less than full employment).

1.6: CANADA'S ECONOMIC GOALS AND POLICIES

Over the years, various federal governments have emphasized different economic goals for this country. In 1963, the Pearson government, in its terms of reference for the newly established Economic Council of Canada, indicated five basic economic and social goals for Canada: full employment, a high rate of economic growth, reasonable stability of prices, a viable balance of payments, and an equitable distribution of rising incomes. The choice of economic goals, and of the tools to achieve them (for example, tax incentives), by the government is known as *economic policy*.

Naturally, the goals set out by the Federal government in 1963 have been the subject of much discussion. Some years ago, the Economic Council of Canada, in its *Sixth Annual Review*, classified them as mainly *economic performance goals*, the attainment of which permits progress to other more fundamental *achievement goals*. The achievement goals specified by the Council included better education, better housing, the elimination of poverty, improvements in health, the maintenance of national security, increased international aid, rising standards of living and wider consumer choice, and an improved quality of life in a vastly changed and increasingly urban society. The Council also suggested that broader social, cultural, and political goals might also be included among these achievement goals. Since then, other possible achievement goals that have been suggested for Canada are protection of the environment, making cities more fit to live in, the preservation of national unity, and greater national economic independence.

Priorities and Tradeoffs

If a country does not have sufficient resources to achieve all its economic goals at once, it must obviously establish some priorities.In a country with authoritarian rule, these priorities are set by the government, often regardless of the public's wish. In a democracy, the priorities are set partly by the public (through its spending pattern) and partly by the government (through its spending, taxes, and laws). Frequently, a government must "trade-off" the pursuit of one economic or social goal against the pursuit of another. Thus policies designed to achieve a more equitable distribution of income may slow economic growth; and policies designed to combat inflation may increase unemployment.

Political goals may sometimes take priority over economic ones. Thus, the maintenance of law and order in a time of political crisis may cost money that could be used for regional economic development; and greater control over foreign investment in Canada may slow down growth in the economy. Canada, unlike many other countries of the world, needs to devote only a relatively small portion of its economic resources to national defence, because its immediate neighbour, the United States, is both militarily powerful and friendly, and willing to help defend Canada. In other words, Canada is able to devote most of its resources to *non-military goals*. In time of war, of course, many economic goals must be temporarily abandoned in an all-out effort to preserve a country's political identity.

In Canada, governments (like individuals) have found it impossible to pursue all their desired economic and social goals successfully at the same time. Consequently, governments at different times have stressed some goals more than others.

Evaluating Economic Performance

There are two basic ways of assessing a country's economic performance. One simple way is by wandering around the country, observing the people—how well-fed, dressed and housed they are—and the roads, buildings, and other private and public works. Another way is by collecting and monitoring statistical data in a variety of key areas, for example: Gross National Product; employment and unemployment; the rate of inflation (as shown by the Consumer Price Index); productivity; the standard of living (as shown by per capita real income); the balance of international trade and payments; the amount of foreign debt; and the foreign exchange rate for the currency.

The Federal Cabinet

The major economic policy-making body in Canada is the Federal Cabinet in Ottawa, a committee of Ministers headed by the Prime Minister. Particularly influential are the Minister of Finance and the Minister for Economic Development. All the Ministers are advised in their policy-making by Deputy-Ministers and their staff of the permanent Federal Public Service. For more effective performance, the cabinet has various sub-committees of which the Planning and Priorities Committee is the most important as regards economic policy.

Amongst the Ministries, the Department of Finance plays a key role in helping to formulate and implement the government's fiscal policy (changes in taxation and borrowing). Also, in consultation with the Bank of Canada (Canada's central bank), it helps to determine the government's monetary policy (changes in the country's money supply and interest rates) and its exchange-rate policy (the targetted foreign-exchange rate for the Canadian dollar). Another important Ministry is the Department of Regional Industrial Expansion, or DRIE, formed in 1983 from a merger of the Department of Regional Economic Expansion (DREE) and the Department of Industry, Trade, and Commerce (ITC). Also very important economically, as well as diplomatically, is the Department of External Affairs (DEA) which is now responsible for the federal government's export promotion efforts, including the Trade Commissioner service.

From time to time, the federal government also appoints special commissions to conduct investigations of particular economic problems and recommend solutions.

The Provincial Governments

Because Canada is a confederation, with ten provincial governments as well as a federal one, economic policy takes place at two different levels. The federal government has a unique role in monetary and exchange-rate policy but must share the fiscal policy field with its provincial counterparts—who can decide their own rates of income tax and sales tax and their own borrowing requirements. Ideally, the economic policies of the federal and provincial governments should be in harmony—for example, pay-restraint policies. In practice, unfortunately, this is not always so. And such lack of harmony is particularly serious if one or more of the three provincial economic heavyweights (Ontario, Quebec, and British Columbia) disagree with federal government policy.

Economic Council of Canada

Although it is the federal government's responsibility to establish economic policies for Canada, it receives advice not only from its own experts but also from various outside bodies. One of the most important of these is the Economic Council of Canada, established as an independent economic advisory body by the federal government in 1963. Its main functions are: (a) to define realistic five- to ten-year economic and social goals for Canada; (b) to recommend to government and industry the policies most likely to achieve these goals; and (c) to anticipate, as far as possible, Canada's economic and social problems and to advise on preventive or remedial measures. The Council consists of three full-time economists and 25 part-time members drawn from labour, business, finance, agriculture and other primary industries, and the public. It has a large research staff. The Council is required to publish every year "a review of medium- to long-term economic prospects" for Canada. It also publishes studies prepared by members of its staff on different economic problems. Furthermore, it undertakes special economic studies for the federal government.

Summary

1. *Economics* is the study of the way in which society uses its scarce resources to satisfy its many different wants. *Macroeconomics* is the study of the economic problems that face society as a whole.

Microeconomics is the study of the economic problems that face the various elements and sectors of society.

2. Economics is considered to be a social science because it involves the methodical study of the economic aspect of human behaviour.
3. Economics is important because economic reasoning is an invaluable training of the mind and because economic awareness helps improve personal, business, and government economic decisions.
4. *Economic history*—the study and analysis of past economic activities—helps us to understand better our present economic system and future economic trends.
5. Every society has limited economic resources capable of alternative use. Since people have many different wants, they must choose which goods and services to produce. Choice is the essence of economics.
6. A society's limited resources are classified under the broad headings of land, labour, and capital. Entrepreneurship is sometimes considered a fourth factor of production. And technology, a fifth. The political and social environments also affect a country's economic prosperity.
7. The range of choice open to society is illustrated by a production possibility curve, or PPC. Opportunity cost is the cost of producing a unit of one good in terms of the number of units of another good that could have been produced instead.
8. Various groups within society determine what is to be produced. The most important group is consumers—hence the term "consumer sovereignty". The three other main groups are business firms, governments, and foreigners.
9. Canada has many different economic goals. Since they cannot all be achieved at once, priorities must be established. Often, one goal must be traded off against another.
10. There are two basic ways of assessing a country's economic performance: observation and statistical analysis.
11. The Federal Cabinet is Canada's major economic policy-making body. Key economic ministries are the Department of Finance and the Department of Regional Industrial Expansion.
12. The provincial governments also have important economic powers.
13. The Economic Council of Canada is one of Canada's principal economic advisory bodies.

Key Terms

Review Questions

1. What is "economics"? Write a brief description, in your own words.
2. Distinguish between macroeconomics and microeconomics.
3. Why is economics considered to be a social science?
4. How can the study of economics benefit you, as an individual person? Give specific examples of the importance of economics to business firms and to governments.
5. What is economic history? Why study it?
6. Compare Alfred Marshall's definition of economics with Lionel Robbins' one.
7. "Economics is a method rather than a doctrine." Explain and discuss.
8. How do modern economists define economics? How do they differ? Why?
9. How can a person be both a Bachelor of Science and a Master of Arts in Economics? Does it make sense? If so, how?
10. Explain and comment on the following popular sayings:
    (a) "There's no such thing as a one-handed economist."
    (b) "Lock six economists in a room and they'll come up with a dozen answers."
    (c) "It's the economists who are running the country these days." Can you add to the list?

11. Economic history can explain the past, but not the present and the future. Discuss.
12. "Most empires have declined for economic rather than military, political, or social reasons." Discuss, with examples.
13. What are the factors of production? To what extent are they scarce?
14. Why is Canada said to be well-endowed with natural resources? What are our major resource deficiencies? What prevents Canada from fully utilizing many of its natural resources?
15. What are the chief characteristics of Canada's population? Size, sex, age, location, growth rate etc. What are its trends?
16. How big is Canada's labour force? How is it growing? Where is it located?
17. Distinguish between real capital and money capital.
18. Distinguish, with examples, betwen social capital and business capital.
19. What is meant by the term "investing"?
20. What is an "entrepreneur"? Why is entrepreneurship considered to be so important? Give some examples.
21. It has been recommended that Canada concentrate on high-technology industries for its future. What does this mean? Give some examples.
22. What difference has technology made to our lives compared with that of our grandparents?
23. How can political and social factors affect a country's standard of living? Give examples.
24. If our resources are so abundant, why do economists call them "scarce"?
25. What is a production possibility curve? What can it illustrate? Give some examples.
26. Why is the PPC drawn concave to the origin?
27. What is meant by "opportunity cost"? Why does it gradually increase?
28. "In Canada we are operating well within our PPC." Explain. Why is this so?
29. "The PPC is not static." Explain. Why not?
30. Canada imports most of its technology. How and why? Discuss.
31. Economics has been defined as the "science of choice". Explain and comment.
32. Explain the meaning and origin of the term "consumer sovereignty." How valid is the concept today?
33. "People buy what the ads tell them to." Discuss.

34. Consumers know what is best for them. Discuss.
35. Business firms buy mainly "intermediate goods" and "capital goods." Explain.
36. Business spending reflects market demand. Explain.
37. Business firms must also anticipate market demand. Why? What happens when their anticipations are wrong? Give examples.
38. How important a say do our governments have in the allocation of our economic resources? How has it changed over the years? Why?
39. How does foreign spending affect us?
40. How can our governments affect the allocation of our resources, other than by their spending programs?
41. Distinguish between economic performance goals and achievement goals. List, in order of priority, the economic goals that you think Canada should pursue.
42. Why do governments have to consider priorities and "tradeoffs"? What economic priorities does your federal government have?
43. Do your provincial and municipal governments have economic goals? What are they?
44. How can we assess a country's economic performance?
45. "Political goals sometimes take priority over economic goals." Explain, with examples.
46. Who decides economic policy for Canada? Which are the key Ministries, from the economic point of view?
47. What is the Economic Council of Canada? What is its role? What other economic advisory bodies exist in Canada?

2. *ECONOMIC SYSTEMS*

CHAPTER OBJECTIVES

A. To emphasize that every country, whatever its political system, has the same basic economic problems: what to produce, how to produce, and how to share what has been produced
B. To explain how the market system answers these basic economic questions
C. To describe the command system—the exact opposite of the market system
D. To explain how most countries have a mixed economic system that combines features of both the market and the command systems
E. To distinguish between economic systems and political systems
F. To discuss the weaknesses and strengths of Canada's economic system

CHAPTER OUTLINE

Every society, whatever its political complexion, has the same basic economic problems. These are: what to produce, how to produce, and for whom to produce (or, put in another way, how to share what has been produced). Countries differ, however, in the extent to which government intervenes in their solution. And this forms the basis of our classification of economic systems into three basic kinds: the market system, the command system, and the mixed economic system. Some economists also refer to a "traditional" economic system—in which economic decisions are made mainly on the basis of tradition and custom. However, all economic systems operate partly on tradition (why change something if it works well) and all economic systems, including those of highly traditional Third World countries, constantly undergo considerable economic change (e.g. depressed export prices, expensive oil imports, urbanization, and drought-hit agricultural production).

2.1: THE MARKET SYSTEM

Under this economic system (also known as *free enterprise*, or *laissez-faire*), the basic economic questions are decided in the marketplace. Demand and supply, free from government interference, are the determining forces.

As explained more fully in Chapter 5 (Supply, Demand, and Market Price), if the public wants more of a good, inventories of it will run low and the price of it will tend to rise. This will in turn encourage more production—requiring perhaps the use of additional resources. These may have previously been unemployed or used to produce other less desirable goods and services. If the public wants less of a product, the opposite process will occur.

The characteristics of the market system include the individual's rights: (a) to own property; (b) to earn profit; (c) to compete in business; (d) to decide what and how much to produce, (e) to decide how to produce; (f) as an employer to hire labour and other productive resources; (g) as an employee, to choose one's job and negotiate the terms of employment; and (h) as a consumer, to spend one's money as one sees fit.

Right to Own Property

For most people the right to own property is an important incentive to work hard, to save, and to invest part of one's income. This is because ownership of property can help provide a higher material standard of living and greater financial security, for the future as well as the present. In Canada, a person's property rights are protected by common and statute law, and by the existence of an efficient police force and judiciary. With this assurance, people have gone ahead and built up business firms of all types and sizes and for others the opportunity continues to exist.

Right to Earn Profit

Profit—the excess of revenue over expenses—is the reward that a person receives for assuming the risk of starting and operating a business. Without it, few people would be willing to invest their savings in the ownership of a business—for it is just as easy, if not more so, to make a loss rather than a profit. Unless businesspeople are rewarded for trying to bring new products on to the market and to produce existing ones more efficiently, they will direct their efforts elsewhere. And business investment and operations would have to be undertaken or directed by the government, with questionable results.

Right to Compete in Business

The market system would not operate efficiently if people were not free to start businesses and to close them, as necessary. If government permission were always required, resources would not be shifted into the production of the goods and services that the public wants. In Canada, as we discuss later in the book, competition is by no means perfect—with private oligopolies, government monopolies, production and marketing quotas, etc., all infringing on the businessperson's right to compete.

Right to Decide What and How Much to Produce

In the market system, the businessperson has the responsibility for anticipating consumer demand and deciding what goods to produce and in what quantity. In the command system, by contrast, this is done by planning commissions who seem inevitably, with the complexity of the task and the government bureaucracy involved, to bring about surpluses of some products and shortages of others, all at relatively high cost.

Right to Decide How to Produce

In the market system, the business firm strives constantly to produce and market its goods more efficiently. This is because, by lowering expenses, the firm can increase its profit. Without this freedom and incentive, we would not see the rapid technological change that now characterizes our industry.

Right to Employ Productive Resources

In order to produce the goods and services that the public wants, a business firm must be able to call upon productive resources: labour, land, capital, entrepreneurship, and technology.

In most communist countries, these resources are allocated to factories and farms by the various planning commissions. If a factory manager wishes to increase the labour force or obtain more equipment, he or she must obtain permission from the government. Furthermore the wage rates or equipment prices to be paid are prescribed by the authorities. In a market system, by contrast, a business firm hires its labour and other productive resources by bidding for them in the marketplace, in competition with other firms. And the firms for whose products the public demand is strongest, will be the ones best able to afford them.

Right to Choose One's Job

In a market system, the individual has the right to choose his or her job. Of course, this right is subject to the type of education, skills, etc. that the person has and the range of jobs available. This freedom means that people are able to move into industries for whose product public demand is increasing and out of those for whose product public demand is falling. The encouragement is, of course, different salaries and promotion opportunities. This freedom also means that people are encouraged to train for jobs for which there is a high demand.

In the market system, the individual has the right to negotiate with the employer the terms of his or her employment. A person is not just allocated a job by a government official and told how much he or she will be paid. A person has the right to decline the salary or wage, and, unlike Oliver Twist, to ask for more. This flexibility enables employees whose services are in greater demand to push up their wage rate and so encourage more people to enter that field—another example of the price mechanism at work, allocating society's resources according to public demand.

Consumer's Freedom of Choice

In the market economy, people are relatively free to spend their money on the goods or services they choose. This means that they can adjust their pattern of spending to suit their personal tastes. A person is not told what to buy, or rationed in the amounts that he or she can have—

"The wonderful thing about our economic system, George, is that everyone has an equal chance."

except by the size of his or her purse. The only government restrictions in Canada on this freedom of choice are the existence of government-operated or regulated monopolies and regulations relating to public health and morals, import restrictions, and varying levels of sales taxes.

Freedom of choice in spending has the important effect, for the economy as a whole, of helping to allocate the use of the country's available productive resources basically in accordance with the public's wishes. Through the working of the price mechanism, an increase in demand for a particular good or service will eventually cause business firms to increase their production of it. And a decrease in demand will cause the opposite effect.

One of the best-known exponents of the market system was the eighteenth-century Scottish economist, Adam Smith. He believed that if people were left alone by government and others to pursue their own private interests, this would result in the maximum benefit for society as a whole. An "invisible hand" would guide people's actions for the common good. Adam Smith's ideas are set out in his celebrated book, *An Inquiry into the Nature and Causes of the Wealth of Nations*, first published in 1776.

The term *private enterprise* is also used to describe this economic system, because most of the means of production and distribution are privately owned.

Advantages of the market system are:

1. The goods and services produced are of the type and quality demanded by the public, not ones ordered by some distant bureaucrat.
2. Entrepreneurs have freedom and incentive to use land, labour, capital, and technology, to produce the required goods and services as efficiently as possible.
3. Employees have freedom to choose and change their job and to negotiate the conditions of their employment.

Disadvantages of the market system are:

1. The public may not choose the goods and services that are best for it—for example, who will pay for schools, hospitals and roads? But governments usually undertake this task—however reluctant the public may be.
2. Business executives may treat labour and other resources in an inhuman or destructive way and may not pass on the benefits of

any efficiency to the public. However, labour unions and collective bargaining now help protect the interests of labour. And, in Canada, the Combines Investigation Act helps reduce unfair business practices.

3. There will tend to be great inequality of income and many people may have very little income to purchase what they need.

2.2: THE COMMAND SYSTEM

Under this system, the government rather than the public decides what is to be produced and how it is to be distributed. Economic plans are made by government planning boards who are also given the authority to carry them out. Such an economic system, operating under government command, is the direct opposite of the market system just discussed.

The characteristics of the command system are:

(a) public (i.e. state) ownership of the means of production (land, buildings, and equipment);

(b) central planning of all economic activity, including what and how much to produce, how to produce, and how to distribute;

(c) minor role of the consumer in deciding what is to be produced;

(d) minor role of the price mechanism;

(e) public rather than private investment in farms and factories;

(f) government assignment of jobs; and

(g) outlawing of "profits".

Possible *advantages* of the command system include:

1. A more logical choice of the goods and services to be produced—for example, sports facilities instead of cigarettes.

2. More efficient production methods—for example, no strikes or lockouts, no unemployment, and no labour exploitation.

3. A fairer distribution of the goods and services produced.

Possible *disadvantages* of the command system include:

1. A more illogical choice of the goods and services to be produced—for example, heavy spending on the armed forces instead of producing more consumer goods.

2. A government-directed manufacturing or service firm may be much less efficient than the highly motivated private entrepreneur. There may in fact be considerable "hidden unemployment"—for example, three persons doing the job of one.

3. A much smaller "national cake" to share out. Also, there

may still be economically privileged classes—for example, politicians, government officials, and military leaders—who receive a much larger slice than the others. So the distribution of goods and services, whatever the claims of the ruling political party, may still be inequitable.

2.3: MIXED ECONOMIC SYSTEMS

Very few countries operate today under a purely market system or a purely command one. In most private-enterprise countries, government control has been gradually increasing over the years. Thus, in Canada today the federal government, in addition to being the owner of several large commercial enterprises such as Air Canada and Canadian National Railways, regulates private business activity by a multiplicity of laws. These laws influence in various ways the answers to society's basic economic questions. As another example of government intervention, the federal government, through the Canadian Radio-Television and Telecommunications Commission, regulates and supervises all aspects of the Canadian broadcasting system, both public and private. By setting minimum standards, the federal government also influences the ways in which goods are produced and marketed. By taxes and subsidies, it alters the distribution of income. The provincial and municipal governments also intervene in the working of Canada's economic system by spending, taxing, and borrowing and by a variety of laws covering health, education, labour etc. Also, and very importantly, the government provides various "collectively used" goods such as roads, bridges, schools, hospitals, and services such as police and fire protection and military defence that the private sector would not adequately provide.

In many command or planned-economy countries, on the other hand, government economic control has declined in recent years. This has been particularly so in Hungary. Even in the Soviet Union, although most of the means of production are still owned by the state, the questions of what to produce and how to produce are being entrusted more and more to the managers of individual manufacturing plants and farming co-operatives. In turn, these managers are now attempting to supply what consumers want rather than what the central or regional government decides that they should have. Even the distribution of income, long a strictly controlled function of government, is becoming partly a matter of private decision. Plant managers and other employees, for example, receive bonuses that vary with the amount of profits made; and farm workers sell privately the produce from personally-owned small plots of land. However, central economic control remains the norm.

2.4: ECONOMIC VERSUS POLITICAL SYSTEMS

One must be careful not to confuse economic systems with political ones.

Political systems can be divided, at the most basic level, into two kinds: (a) those which permit the population, at reasonable intervals, to replace the government, if dissatisfied with it, by another group of persons, and (b) those which do not. In the first category would fall Canada, the U.S., Japan, Britain and other democratic countries. In the latter would fall the Soviet Union and other Communist countries, plus all the various military regimes—for example in South America and Africa.

Countries in the first category, including Canada, have a mixed economic system, with the emphasis towards a market rather than a command system. Countries in the second category also have mixed economic systems. But the communist countries have predominantly command economic systems whereas the military regimes have predominantly market economic systems.

To avoid confusion, there are some other terms that we should now define. These are the four "isms"—capitalism, socialism, communism, and fascism—that have both political and economic connotations.

Capitalism is a term used, often in a derogatory fashion, to describe the market, or private enterprise system that Canada enjoys, in which the "capitalists' (the private owners of the means of production) are supposed to be exploiting the workers. Such an interpretation ignores the fact that many large companies are owned by many small shareholders, that governments now closely regulate the activities of business firms, and that labour unions now often seem stronger than employers. Because the Western democracies have a predominantly market system, the term "capitalism" is also used as a derogatory synonym for "democracy".

Socialism is a political system in which: some or all of the means of production are owned by the state; there is a considerable degree of central economic and social planning; and the welfare of society generally is a prime concern of the government. Both democratic and non-democratic countries have professed to be socialist, at one time or another. Thus a distinction is usually made between *democratic social-*

ism, as has been practised, for example, by the Labour Party in Britain and authoritarian socialism as practised by the Soviet Union and other "socialist republics".

Communism is the ideal political system, preached by Lenin and other socialist writers, to which the socialist countries are supposed to be heading—in which each person gives of his or her best and receives according to his or her need. It is also the title assumed by the ruling political party in the one-party socialist states of, for example, Eastern Europe.

Fascism is the political system that originated in Italy and that was practised in that country under Mussolini during the period 1922 to 1943. The political regime in Germany under Hitler, during the period 1933 to 1945, officially called "national socialist", has also been labelled a fascist dictatorship. This is because it also subordinated the rights of the individual citizen to the will of the state and its supreme leader. Under fascism, private ownership of property, including the means of production, was permitted. However, the government reserved the right to intervene at any time in the national interest. In practice, fascism meant aggressively nationalistic policies, central regimentation of the economy, rigid censorship of the press, and the absence of elections and other democratic rights. Economically, fascism meant a mixed economic system, with a strong leaning towards a command system. Today, many of the military regimes throughout the world are labelled "fascist".

2.5: CANADA'S ECONOMIC SYSTEM

The type of economic system now prevailing in Canada can be called *mixed capitalism*, or *limited free enterprise*, because of the increasing economic intervention by government. In this market system, both private and public capital exist side by side and government exercises a considerable amount of control over private business activities.

The basic characteristics of Canada's economic system include (a) the right of individuals to choose their type of work and to bargain with their employer, either individually or collectively, as to the wage and fringe benefits that they will receive; (b) the right of individuals to establish and operate their own private businesses in pursuit of profit; (c) the right of individuals, both employers and employees, to accumulate property—*the institution of private property*; (d) the right of individuals, as consumers, to spend their money as they see fit, and (e) the right of government to intervene in this predominantly private-enterprise economic system, where appropriate, to achieve various economic and social goals.

Weaknesses of Canada's Economic System

The market system that exists in Canada seems to be preferred by most Canadians to a system in which the government tells everyone what job to do, what pay to receive, and what goods and services to produce. However, we have no reason to be complacent. As the system operates in Canada, it has major faults which we are only gradually—if at all—learning to overcome. These faults include: unemployment; inflation; regional economic disparities; poverty; poor labour-management relations; the divergence between private and social costs and benefits; insufficient competition between firms in certain industries operating in Canada; the manufacture abroad of goods for the Canadian market that might be better produced at home; relative low industrial productivity; and the possible misallocation of resources.

1. Unemployment. It is quite shocking and a reflection on our economic system that such a large percentage of Canada's civilian labour force is unemployed. Even more deplorable is the fact that the unemployment rate is highest among young people. Does the fault lie with a market system that does not create enough jobs? Or are people setting their sights too high and becoming unwilling to accept jobs their parents would have gladly taken? Is the work force becoming too highly educated or mistrained? Or is there insufficient emphasis in Canada on economic growth? Should the government supplement the market system, creating additional jobs through direct spending programs and subsidies to employers? Should people be willing to give up the freedom to choose their own jobs and careers, and to change jobs at will, in return for government-assured employment? Should Canada restrict its imports of manufactured goods to help protect local jobs?

2. Inflation. In our market system, business firms are free to set the prices for their products. Also, wage earners, represented in many cases by labour unions, are free to bargain with employers for wages and fringe benefits. As a result, price and wage levels are constantly being pushed upwards as business firms and labour unions compete to increase their share of the national income. Governments also, reeling under the interest burden of a large public debt, heavy unemployment and other social security payments, and the cost of new energy and job-creation programs, add their spending to already inflationary fires. And by borrowing money to finance deficit spending (i.e., spending more than is received from taxes and other revenue), our federal, provincial, and municipal governments force up interest rates and reduce the capital available for private business investment. People receiving relatively fixed money incomes (pensioners for instance) find that their real income—the goods and services they can buy with their money income—is constantly declining. And the continuation of inflation disrupts social harmony as each labour union and business firm struggles not to be left worse off. Again, we are faced with a variety of questions. Should firms be free to set their prices? Should workers be allowed to bargain collectively for higher wages? Should the federal and provincial governments impose wage and price controls? Should business firms and consumers receive protection from high interest rates?

3. Regional Income Disparities. Why is it, under the market system, that some parts of Canada are much better off than others? Why are Alberta, B.C., and southern Ontario, for example, relatively prosperous economically while most of the Atlantic provinces still find it hard to make ends meet? Why is it that the market system fails to spread economic prosperity evenly throughout the nation?

4. Poverty. How is it possible that poverty exists in an economically rich country like Canada? Why is it that Canada's market system fails to provide everyone with an adequate, if not comfortable standard of living? And what can be done to alleviate the problem?

5. Divergence Between Private and Social Costs and Benefits. By producing goods of the desired quality as cheaply as possible, business firms are helping society to make the best use of its limited resources. However, this has created a problem that many business firms until recently tended to ignore. This problem is the divergence between *private costs* and *social costs*, or, looked at in another way, between *private benefits* and *social benefits*.

Many business firms, seeking the lowest production and marketing costs, choose a course of action that often conflicts with the best interests of society—pollution of the environment is a good example. In the course of business activity, untreated waste products are often dumped into the nearest river, lake, or sea; various chemicals, such as sulphur, are emitted into the atmosphere in the form of smoke and drift down upon our lakes and forests as "acid rain"; large areas of the countryside are denuded by intensive logging of timber or strip mining of minerals; and natural scenery is masked by large billboards and so-called tourist attractions.

Fortunately, more and more firms, partly as a result of growing public indignation, are taking steps to reduce their pollution of the environment. These steps cost money, of course, and must be paid for either by a reduction in profits or by increased prices to the consumer. At the same time, governments are establishing new laws, increasing penalties, and enforcing existing laws more rigorously, to discourage industrial and human pollution.

6. Insufficient Competition. Competition among business firms in Canada to increase their share of the market comprises two basic forms: price competition and non-price competition. In Canada, the amount of price competition varies greatly from industry to industry. In most cases, business firms are extremely reluctant to reduce prices for fear of retaliatory action by competitors. A price war, business firms realize, benefits the public rather than themselves—an example of the divergence between private and social benefit. Advertising (a form of non-price competition) enables many firms to differentiate their products from those of competitors, even though the quality of the product may be the same. This means that consumers may remain loyal to a particular brand of product despite the fact that its price may be higher than that of similar products produced by other firms.

As we see later, the absence of price competition usually means that the public pays more for the goods and services they buy than they otherwise would. In Canada, the federal government, by means of the Combines Investigation Act, tries to discourage firms from restricting competition. On the other hand, through producer-managed marketing boards, liquor control boards, and air transport commissions, etc., it restricts competition in other fields.

7. The Exporting of Jobs. More and more manufacturing firms, often Canadian subsidiaries of U.S. multinational corporations, are reducing or closing down production in Canada, switching all or part of the work to their plants in the U.S., and exporting the finished goods to Canada. Other manufacturing firms, Canadian as well as foreign-owned, although continuing to produce in Canada, are now buying many of their parts and materials from countries such as Japan, South Korea, Malaysia, Taiwan, and Hong Kong, and thereby "exporting jobs" abroad. Other firms, unable to compete with foreign-made goods, have shut down completely, throwing their employees out of work and drastically affecting the economic health of many Canadian communities. At the same time, the federal government continues to reduce tariff and other barriers to foreign manufactured goods. By contrast, other countries such as Brazil, also with many resource-based exports, encourage local production of most of the manufactured goods that they need behind a heavily protected wall of import quotas and exchange controls. Japan, a leading exporter of manufactured goods, makes its local market almost impenetrable to foreign manufactured goods. And the Communist countries, long an advocate of protectionism, accept foreign goods by invitation only. Are Canadians, as some people suggest, becoming once more predominantly a nation of farmers, miners, lumberjacks, and fishermen—the traditional "hewers of wood and drawers of water"? And if so, what should be done about it?

8. Relatively Low Productivity. As we discuss in Chapter 20, Canada's rate of increase in industrial productivity over the last decade has been about the lowest in the Western world. And this is one important reason why manufacturing plants in Canada have been closing down or reducing production.

9. Possible Misallocation of Resources. There is, in theory, an optimum allocation of a society's scarce resources—a perfect "social balance." In practice such a balance is difficult to agree on, let alone achieve. For example, how much of its resources should a society devote to military as compared with civil purposes? What consumer goods and services should it provide? Should it train more doctors and fewer lawyers? More plumbers and fewer civil servants? Should we have less butter and more margarine? Should we pay to have our parks cleaned up rather than pay people to be idle while unemployed?

Canada, with its predominantly private-enterprise economy, has traditionally let the public, with its "dollar votes", have a large say in how our resources are allocated. Thus, spending on liquor and tobacco, for example, far outweighs spending on health. However, in recent years, our federal and provincial governments have been actively altering the way in which we allocate our resources—for example, by financing, with the taxpayers' money, medicare and higher education.

If we compare our society with that of other countries, the different allocation of our resources becomes more apparent. Many people do in fact think that we have achieved a satisfactory social balance in Canada.

Strengths of Canada's Economic System

Although we have just reviewed many apparent weaknesses of Canada's economic system, it is nevertheless true that many people would dearly love to come and live in Canada. Political freedom is one important attraction. But just as important, if not more so, for many people, are the economic benefits.

1. High Average Level of Income. As the result of an impressive output of goods and services, encouraged by our predominantly private-enterprise economic system, Canadians enjoy one of the highest material standards of living in the world. In fact Canada is now considered by the World Bank, which makes international statistical comparisons, to have the seventh highest standard in the world. Even though Canada's international ranking has slipped somewhat since the end of World War II, when it was fourth, the actual level is still impressive. Good food, clothing, education, health care, housing, cars, appliances, annual vacations at home and abroad, are the lot of most Canadians. (The decline in ranking has been due partly to the instant wealth, since 1970, of the oil-exporting countries and partly to our own economic neglect. If world oil prices stay down, Canada's ranking should improve).

The standard of living of Canadians now ranks seventh in the world.

Country	GNP Per Capita in U.S. Dollars	Country	GNP Per Capita in U.S. Dollars
1. United Arab Emirates	22 870	16. Austria	9 250
2. Kuwait	17 880	17. United Kingdom	9 200
3. Switzerland	16 290	18. Belgium	9 150
4. United States	14 110	19. Libya	8 480
5. Norway	14 020	20. New Zealand	7 730
6. Sweden	12 470	21. Singapore	6 620
7. Canada	12 310	22. Italy	6 400
8. Saudi Arabia	12 230	23. Oman	6 250
9. Denmark	11 570	24. Hong Kong	6 000
10. Australia	11 490	25. Israel	5 370
11. W. Germany	11 430	26. Ireland	5 000
12. Finland	10 740	27. Spain	4 780
13. France	10 500	28. Greece	3 920
14. Japan	10 120	29. Venezuela	3 840
15. Netherlands	9 890	30. Yugoslavia	2 570

Source of data: World Bank, *World Development Report 1985*
Note: Data are for 1983

2. Limited Economic Bureaucracy. Most Canadians believe that the country has more bureaucrats than it needs, particularly tax collectors. However, it is nothing compared with the economic as well as political and other types of bureaucracy that exist in most command economies such as the Soviet Union. So we should perhaps count our blessings.

3. Personal Economic Freedom. In Canada, people have the freedom to change jobs and the town or part of the country in which they live and work. They also have the right to start a business and work for themselves if they choose. They can also own land, buildings, and other means of production and hire other people to work for them. And they can accumulate capital, to spend later, on whatever they see fit. All these economic freedoms, usually taken for granted in Canada, are non-existent in many other countries of the world.

4. Incentive to Innovate. Because of the right to earn profit and to undertake business, a person has every incentive to innovate whether it be a new product or a new production method. As a result, Canada and other private enterprise economic systems continue to remain in the forefront of technological change.

Summary

1. Every society, whatever its political system, has the same economic problems: what to produce, how to produce and for whom to produce.
2. With the market system (also known as free enterprise or "laissez-faire"), the basic economic questions are decided in the marketplace, through the interaction of demand and supply free from government interference.
3. Under the command system, government, rather than the public, decides what is to be produced, how, and for whom.
4. Most countries have a mixed economic system—that is, a market economy with a certain amount of government intervention or a command system with a certain amount of market freedom.
5. Economic systems should not be confused with political systems. However, market systems are more characteristic of political democracies, and command systems of totalitarian, or one-party political regimes.
6. Canada's economic system is a mixed one, with government intervention gradually increasing.

7. Weaknesses of Canada's economic system include: a high level of unemployment; inflation; regional income disparities; poverty for some; poor labour-management relations; the divergence between private and social costs and benefits with environmental pollution and other results; insufficient competition in certain industries; the incentive to produce abroad goods that might better be produced at home; and the possible misallocation of resources—e.g., entertainment rather than health care or, in other countries, "guns rather than butter".
8. Strengths of Canada's economic system include: a high average level of income for Canadians; limited economic bureaucracy; personal economic freedom; and incentive to innovate.

Key Terms

Market system 30
Laissez-faire 30
Private enterprise 34
Command system 35
Mixed economic system 36
Political system 37
Capitalism 37
Canada's economic system 38
Unemployment 39
Inflation 39
Regional income disparities 40
Poverty 40
Private and social costs 40
Competition 41
Exporting of jobs 41
Low productivity 42
Misallocation of resources 42
High material standard of living 42
Limited economic bureaucracy 44
Personal economic freedom 44
Incentive to innovate 44

Review Questions

1. What is a "market system"?
2. Who was Adam Smith? And what was his "invisible hand"?
3. What other terms are used to describe the free market system?
4. What are the possible advantages for society of the market system?
5. What are the possible disadvantages? How might it be possible to have the advantages without the disadvantages?
6. What are the characteristics of a command system?

7. What are the possible advantages of a command system?
8. What are the possible disadvantages?
9. Distinguish between capitalism, socialism, and communism.
10. Choose five countries from different regions of the world and indicate which type of economic system they use.
11. Why have some communist countries granted more economic freedom to their people in recent years?
12. Economic systems are closely linked to political systems. Discuss.
13. What economic system exists in Canada? How has it changed in recent years? Give reasons for the change.
14. One major weakness of Canada's economic system is the high rate of unemployment. How high is it? How does it vary by age and location of the persons involved?
15. How might Canada's unemployment problem be resolved?
16. What is "inflation"? What are its disadvantages? Does it have any advantages?
17. Why are some parts of Canada better off than others?
18. Who are Canada's poor? Why are they poor?
19. Explain, with an example, the possible discrepancy between private costs and benefits and social ones.
20. Why do most people favour competition yet resent foreign goods replacing Canadian ones, particularly in Canada?
21. Give some examples of lack of competition in Canada. Who tries to ensure that competition takes place? How?
22. What is meant by the phrase: "exporting jobs"? How does it occur? Why is it taking place?
23. Should foreign goods have unrestricted access to the Canadian market? Explain and discuss the pros and cons. What is the present situation?
24. How is Canada moving, if at all, towards a better "social balance" in the allocation of its economic resources?
25. Why do many people in other countries consider that they would be "better off" living in Canada?

3. *ECONOMIC ANALYSIS*

CHAPTER OBJECTIVES

A. To explain how economic research is usually conducted
B. To explain how an economic theory is developed and tested
C. To discuss cost-benefit analysis—a practical, everyday application of economic reasoning
D. To indicate that one area of economics is the study of our various economic institutions e.g., the banking system
E. To explain what economists do
F. To offer some tips for clearer thinking about economic problems.

CHAPTER OUTLINE

Unless we can properly diagnose our economic troubles and prescribe the correct remedies, we will continue to be plagued with high unemployment, inflation, income insecurity, and other economic woes. Economic research and the economic theories that result are our best attempt to understand and explain the workings of our economic system and the ways in which we can adjust it to our needs. Obviously, we have far to go and probably will never arrive.

3.1: ECONOMIC RESEARCH

Over the years, a great deal of research into the working of our economic system has been carried out in Britain, the United States, and other countries, including Canada, and the names of Ricardo, Marshall, Keynes, as well as of many leading contemporary economists such as Samuelson, Galbraith, and Friedman have become known even to the general public. This research has resulted in the formulation of *economic theories* that describe and explain the various cause-effect relationships that exist in our economy—for example, the relationship between national income and employment.

Economic research usually follows a definite scientific pattern: (a) the collection and analysis of relevant data; (b) the formulation of an economic theory or a modification of an existing one; and (c) the testing of the economic theory.

Collection and Analysis of Relevant Data

Sometimes economists or other economic researchers must conduct statistical and other surveys of their own. However, statistical data about a wide variety of economic topics is collected, summarized, and published by Statistics Canada, the federal government's statistical agency. The most important statistical compilation that it undertakes is the census, prepared every ten years. In addition, Statistics Canada publishes an official statistical annual called the *Canada Year Book* and a more concise annual statistical handbook. It also publishes, on a more frequent basis, many other statistical reports, notably the *Daily Bulletin* (with the latest weekly, monthly, and quarterly statistics and details of any new publications), and the monthly *Canadian Statistical Review*. The latter contains key economic indicators, often going back many years, and various graphs and tables. The Bank of Canada also publishes a monthly statistical review, with an emphasis on financial data such as the money supply. Also, the Federal Department of Finance publishes its *Quarterly Economic Review* containing a review of the previous quarter's economic events and, on an annual basis, a variety of key economic statistics, including federal, provincial, and municipal government revenues and expenditures. Furthermore, such bodies as the Economic Council of Canada, the Conference Board in Canada, the Private Planning Association, the Fraser Institute, the Canadian Foundation for Economic Education, and various temporary, *ad hoc* commissions provide a steady flow of economic studies of different aspects of the Canadian economy.

And then there are the professional economic journals such as *The Canadian Journal of Economics,* published four times a year, by the Canadian Economics Association—an organization of Canadian economists, mainly academics. Newspaper and magazine articles also provide topical economic information and analysis. The economist has to sift this great mass of statistical data and verbal description and abstract what is relevant to the study being undertaken.

3.2: ECONOMIC THEORIES

After a study of the data, the economist suggests the existence of certain relationships—for example, between the money supply and the rate of inflation. This economic hypothesis—a concise statement of the presumed relationship between various economic variables—is called an *economic theory.*

Simplifying Assumptions

Because of the great complexity of most economic problems, arising from the many variables involved, economists are forced, in developing a hypothesis, to make a number of simplifying assumptions—for example, that the supply of a product remains unchanged. In this way, they can concentrate their attention on the relationships that exist among other economic variables. By assuming the money supply and other factors to be constant, for example, they can focus attention on the relationship between government spending and employment.

In addition, since economists must generalize about the economic behaviour of countless consumers and business firms, they must make certain basic assumptions about them—for example, that consumers always act rationally or that business firms always try to maximize profits. In practice, of course, this is not universally or constantly true. Thus, for example, a consumer may buy a poor-quality article for a high price rather than a low price; an investor may be unaware of certain profit opportunities and invest in the wrong company; a businessperson may, for charitable reasons, give away some of his goods rather than sell them for a profit; and a government may, for political reasons, subsidize an economically inefficient plant.

Inductive and Deductive Economic Reasoning

The identification of various economic relationships is achieved by either inductive or deductive reasoning. In *inductive reasoning*, economists infer certain principles from the observation and study of a large number of economic facts. For example, they may infer from a survey of the working habits of a large number of factory workers that the average person works more effectively if given many short work-breaks rather than one or two long ones. In *deductive reasoning*, economists conclude from the study of an established relationship that another relationship logically exists. For example, if they know that a consumer will get less satisfaction from each additional unit that he or she consumes of the same good (the principle of "diminishing marginal utility"), they can deduce that the consumer will not be willing to pay as much for each additional unit as for each previous one. This can have economic significance for a company in deciding its pricing policies. Economic theories are often based on both types of reasoning. Thus, the deduction, based on a knowledge of human nature, that individually-owned and managed business firms usually try to maximize long-run profits can also be inferred empirically from a study of actual business behaviour.

Once the economist has established an hypothesis, or theory, about the relationship between different economic variables, he or she can then predict economic events—for example, that if the government increases its spending when the economy is operating at the full-employment level, this will cause an increase in the general price level. This type of prediction is not, of course, the forecasting of actual events. It is a prediction of what will happen *if* certain events take place and *if* various other economic variables (such as household and business spending) remain unchanged. That is why economists often qualify any statement of an economic relationship with the phrase: "other things being equal".

Most economic theories have been described verbally. However, because most of the variables involved (for example, income, employment, demand, and prices) are quantitative in nature, mathematical symbols have been increasingly employed. Also, as we have already seen, graphs are frequently used to illustrate many of the cause-effect relationships. Sometimes an economic theory is described verbally and then restated in purely mathematical terms. This mathematical treatment has the disadvantage that it renders the theory unintelligible to anyone who does not possess sufficient knowledge of basic algebra. However, it has the advantage that it makes the treatment of the economic problem much more rigorous—definitions, relationships, and assumptions must be explicitly stated; and the limitations of the theory are starkly revealed.

"Other things being equal, you should do well in this course."

Testing the Economic Theory

An economic theory is of doubtful value if it cannot be verified in practice. Consequently, the final step in economic theorizing is to test the predictions that have been made on the basis of the theory. Thus, for example, we could predict, on the basis of exchange-rate theory, that a fall in the foreign exchange value of the Canadian dollar would cause Canada's imports to decrease and its exports to increase. To confirm this prediction we would then need to check exactly what did happen to Canada's international trade when the foreign exchange rate of the Canadian dollar decreased. Of course, we must be careful to watch for any other factors (such as changes in import duties, export subsidies, new trade relations) that might also affect the trade picture.

If the facts confirm the prediction, we can say that the economic theory is valid. Over the years, some economic theories, such as the "sun-spot" theory of business cycles, have become discredited. Others have never got off the ground. However, there are many other economic theories, such as the division-of-labour principle, whose validity continues unscathed despite many years of critical examination.

Empirical testing of economic theories, we should note, has become commonplace only in this century. Indeed, many economic theorists in the past felt that the presentation of an economic theory, based on logical reasoning, was sufficient in itself. Facts were used more as illustrations than controls. This attitude was encouraged by the absence of statistical data about most economic phenomena (the census, for example, was introduced only in the mid-nineteenth century) and by the problem of handling these data even when they were available.

Today, with the regular holding of the census and various other kinds of economic survey, and the preparation and publication of statistical reports, much more data are available. Furthermore, the invention and refinement of electronic computers has made it possible to handle statistical data much more quickly, cheaply, and flexibly than in the past. As a result, the testing of economic theories is now enjoying a boom after several centuries of relative neglect. Over the last forty years in fact, the practice of formulating economic theories in mathematical terms and testing them by statistical techniques has become so widespread that it has come to be recognized as a specialized field of economics, called *econometrics*.

In econometrics, an economic theory is called an *economic model*. A model can consist of a single mathematical equation or a set of simultaneous mathematical equations that set out the assumed relationships between the various economic variables. A model, like the economic theory that it represents, is an abstraction of reality that highlights the relationships to be considered. Because of its relative simplicity, the model enables economists to analyze more easily the possible effects of changes in any key element. From a model of the Canadian economic system, they could estimate, for example, the effects of a change in the country's foreign exchange rate, of a reduction in federal and provincial personal income tax, or of an unusually high rate of immigration.

To visualize the effect of changes in one of the key elements, it is assumed, in simple models, that all the other elements remain constant—in other words, "other things being equal". In practice, of course, they continue to change. Thus, a tax increase may be offset in its revenue effects by a decline in business activity. More advanced economic models, made possible by the advent of more sophisticated electronic computers, have more variables. By systematically changing key elements in a model, economists can draw conclusions about the economic situation—for example, how the levels of income and employment in a country can be affected by changes in the supply of money. The Bank of Canada and several Canadian universities now have sophisticated, computer-programmed models of the Canadian economy that can supply relatively quick answers as to the effects of deliberate changes in one or more of the variables involved.

3.3: COST-BENEFIT ANALYSIS

Since economic resources are: (a) scarce and (b) capable of alternative use, the way in which they are deployed requires careful thought. In our own personal spending, for example, we usually think twice about what we are going to buy, and the larger the amount involved, the greater the deliberation. Thus many people will spend weeks and months shopping for a car or a house. The process of evaluating the costs and benefits of alternative uses of scarce resources is called *cost-benefit analysis*. Its purpose is to improve our choice among these alternatives. Since this type of analysis is used to help solve actual problems, it is also known as *applied economics*.

Cost-benefit analysis involves, first of all, a clear statement of the various alternative possibilities. Thus, an increase in a province's electric power supply, for example, can be obtained by investment in a hydroelectric plant, a thermal plant, an atomic plant, a nuclear plant, or by purchase from an outside producer. Cost-benefit analysis also involves, second, an evaluation of the costs and benefit of each alternative. The costs, in the case of electricity, will depend on relative fuel prices and the capital expenditures involved. Costs, it should be noted, can be very broad in scope, particularly when account is taken of social as well as private costs. Thus, some thermal plants in Canada now use more expensive coal (with a lower sulphur content) than they used to do, in order to reduce environmental pollution. They deliberately incur, in other words, higher private costs to obtain lower social costs. Of course, it is easier for a government-owned enterprise to follow such a policy than for a private business firm, which must justify its actions to its shareholders.

The cost of using resources in one particular way is just one side of the cost/benefit equation. For the use to be worthwhile, the benefits must exceed the costs. Often, of course, it is difficult to measure benefits. In a business firm, expected sales and profits can be given a dollar value. A government goal such as high employment can be expressed as a percentage of the labour force. However, a goal such as greater national unity is impossible to quantify. So also is an individual's goal of pleasure from ownership of a new car or from dining out. Nevertheless, some attempt to measure the benefits is usually undertaken. Often, this measurement is in the form of a comparison with the benefits to be derived from other possible uses of the same money. In devoting money (and thereby resources) to the pursuit of one goal, a government, firm, or individual is, of course, forfeiting the opportunity of doing something else. For example, by spending more on public transportation, a government will have less to spend on, say, public health. In other words, for each course of action, there is an "opportunity cost".

3.4: INSTITUTIONAL ECONOMICS

Another important type of economic analysis is the study of the growth, structure, and operations of Canada's various economic institutions, such as manufacturing, mining, agriculture, banking, other financial intermediaries, and government financial institutions. It also includes the study of the various international economic institutions and systems in which Canada participates. Without this type of analysis and description, our knowledge of the working of Canada's economic system, as well as the international one, would remain incomplete, as well as out of date. Also, the effects of proposed government economic measures, as well as the impact of changes in private spending at home and abroad, would be more difficult to predict than they already are. Furthermore, such study and analysis can point the way to improvements in the country's institutional framework so that the country can operate more efficiently. Thus, for example, a study of Canadian agriculture by a federal task force might suggest more efficient ways of providing government financial aid. Or a study of Canada's capital market might provide a better understanding of the past growth and future prospects of the various Canadian financial intermediaries and thereby help improve the shape of future Bank Acts and other financial legislation. This area of economics is sometimes called *descriptive economics.*

3.5: THE ECONOMIST

An *economist* is a professionally-qualified person who earns his or her living by specializing in the study of economic problems. Both government and industry find it worth while to employ such specialists, full-time and part-time, to undertake analytical research and to provide economic policy advice. In the federal government, for example, economists are required to advise the Minister of Finance on the implications of proposals for tax changes. In an oil company, as another example, the economist must prepare long-range forecasts of the demand for petroleum products and analyze the implications of actions by competitors and by government. Economic policies, public or private, are very much the end-product of the economist. Professional economists working in private industry sometimes describe themselves as *business economists*. Also, not to be overlooked, are the many economists who combine economic teaching and research at our universities with consulting for the private and public sectors.

An economist, if he or she is to be efficient in the job, must understand how the economy operates; be able to recognize and understand the causes of the economic problems that occur; and be able to foresee, in all their ramifications, the likely effects of the measures recommended or undertaken—for example, the effects on the supply of mortgage money of an increase in government borrowing.

Perhaps the most valuable contribution that an economist can make in government, business, or education, is to apply the problem-solving technique of economic analysis to each problem, as it comes along. As we saw previously, this technique involves, first of all, setting out quite explicitly the nature and dimensions of the problem. Second, it involves clear delineation of the various possible courses of action. And third, it involves careful evaluation of the probable benefits and cost of each alternative course. This requires, of course, considerable research. Only then is the economist in a position to make a worth-while policy recommendation.

"What I want you to do, Mario, is to forecast the demand for our product ten years from now."

3.6: ECONOMIC PITFALLS

The study of economic problems can be fascinating. However, clear thinking is essential. For the average student, there are several pitfalls. However, if they are recognized from the start, their ability to hinder is reduced. These pitfalls can be listed under the following headings: preconceptions; self-interest; problems of definition; fallacy of composition; and false analogy.

Economic Preconceptions

Whereas a person begins the study of such subjects as mathematics, physics, or astronomy with little or no background knowledge, the student of economics often has many preconceived ideas or biases about the subject-matter. These are obtained from listening to casual conversation at home and among friends, from reading newspapers, magazines, and books, from listening to radio, and from watching television. Some examples are: "It's always better to buy goods made in Canada."; "Management always tries to exploit the worker"; "We should get rid of foreign capital"; "Workers always try to do the least work for the most money"; "Unions are opposed to technological progress"; "A business always charges the highest price possible for its product"; "The consumer is always being exploited"; "Advertising is an economic waste"; "Saving is a virtue"; "What's good for the company is good for everyone in it."

Economic Self-Interest

In studying economics, a person can easily start looking for economic facts or arguments to fit his or her own particular situation. Thus, the college student quickly appreciates that governments should spend more on education, for the good of the economy; the taxpayer quickly appreciates that high taxes for education and other purposes are destroying private initiative, to the detriment of the economy; the farmer easily believes that farm subsidies should be increased, for the good of the economy; and the federal government realizes that taxes should be increased, perhaps to dampen inflation, again for the good of the economy. To think clearly about economics, a person should, therefore, first recognize where his or her own self-interest lies and consciously try to prevent it from interfering with his or her reasoning.

Problems of Economic Definition

A common source of misunderstanding and disagreement in economics, as well as in other fields, is the fact that different people use the same term to mean different things. Thus a cool weekend can mean one thing to one person and something else to another. In economics, unlike many other disciplines, many of the terms used are also widely used in everyday language. Unfortunately, from the viewpoint of clear economic thinking, the everyday meaning is usually different from the economic one. For example, the verb "to demand" in everyday language means to insist strongly on having something. In economics it means to have not only a desire for a product but also the ability to pay for it. Obviously, then, persons who wish to reason clearly about an economic problem must define carefully what they and others are talking or thinking about. Then, for example, when talking about foreign exchange rates, they would not confuse the "depreciation" of a currency with a "devaluation"; or glibly compare U.S. food prices with Canadian ones, without taking into account the exchange rate differential.

Fallacy of Composition

By fallacy of composition we mean the mistake of assuming that what is true for part of a group must necessarily be true for the group as a whole. Thus, whereas an individual farmer may be better off by increasing his or her production, farmers, as a whole, by increasing their production, may be worse off. This is because the increased supply of goods would probably depress market prices. The same applies to oil-producing and wheat-producing countries.

False Economic Analogy

An analogy is a situation that is similar to, but not identical with, the situation that is being discussed. Thus, in explaining the public finances of a country, a person may use the behaviour of the individual household for purpose of comparison and illustration. In many respects this analogy is useful. However, in some respects—for example, in savings policy—it may be a false analogy. While it may be desirable for an individual household to balance its budget, it may not always, or even usually, be desirable for a government to do likewise. This is because a government must, at different times, increase or decrease consumer demand to keep the economy at high levels of income and employment without runaway inflation. Only by spending more than it receives can a government cause an increase in consumer-demand. And, conversely, only by spending less than it receives, can it cause a reduction in consumer demand.

Summary

1. Research into the working of our economic system has, over the years, resulted in the formulation of economic theories that describe and explain the various cause-effect relationships that exist in the economy.
2. Large amounts of statistical data about the Canadian economy are published by Statistics Canada, the Bank of Canada, and others. These must be sifted and analyzed by the economist or other economic researcher.
3. An economic theory is a concise statement of a presumed relationship between various economic variables. Because so many variables are involved, the economist is forced to make various simplifying assumptions—for example, that consumers always act rationally.
4. The economist in identifying various economic relationships, uses either inductive or deductive reasoning.
5. Once the economist has established an hypothesis, or theory, about the relationship between different economic variables, he or she can predict economic events.
6. Economic theories can be stated verbally and mathematically and illustrated diagrammatically.
7. The final step in economic theorizing is to test the predictions that have been made on the basis of the theory.
8. The process of evaluating the costs and benefits of alternative uses of scarce resources is called *cost-benefit analysis*. This type of analysis is also called *applied economics*.
9. *Institutional economics* is the study of the growth, structure, and operations of various economic institutions. It is also sometimes called *descriptive economics*.
10. An economist is a professionally-qualified person who earns his or her living by specializing in the study of economic problems in government, business, or educational institutions.

Key Terms

Economic research 48
Economic theory 48
Census 48
Economic variables 49
Inductive reasoning 49
Deductive reasoning 50
Economic hypothesis 50
Empirical testing 52
Econometrics 52
Economic model 52
Cost-benefit analysis 53
Institutional economics 54
Economist 55
Business economist 55
Economic preconceptions 57
Economic self-interest 57
Problems of economic definition 58
Fallacy of composition 58
False economic analogy 58

Review Questions

1. Who conducts economic research in Canada and why?
2. What is the usual pattern of economic research?
3. What are the main sources of economic data in Canada?
4. Why is it necessary for the economist, in developing an economic theory, to make simplifying assumptions? What basic assumptions are made in economics about consumers and business firms?
5. Distinguish between inductive and deductive reasoning. Give an example of each.
6. What is meant by economic prediction?
7. What are the merits of describing economic theories in mathematical terms?
8. Why was empirical testing of economic theories so long neglected? What is the situation today?
9. Give an example (of your own) to explain the usefulness of cost-benefit analysis.
10. Distinguish between private and social costs and benefits. Show, with examples, how they can easily diverge.
11. Provide three examples of published studies that would fall into the category of institutional economics.
12. What is an economist? What services does he or she provide?
13. Amongst the pitfalls facing the student of economics are economic preconceptions, economic self-interest, and problems of economic definition. Explain each of these with an example.
14. What is meant by fallacy of composition and by false economic analogy? Give an example of each.

Part B:
THE MARKET SYSTEM

Here we examine how the economic force of public demand, modified by government intervention, operates through the price mechanism to direct society's scarce resources into the production of the chosen goods and services.

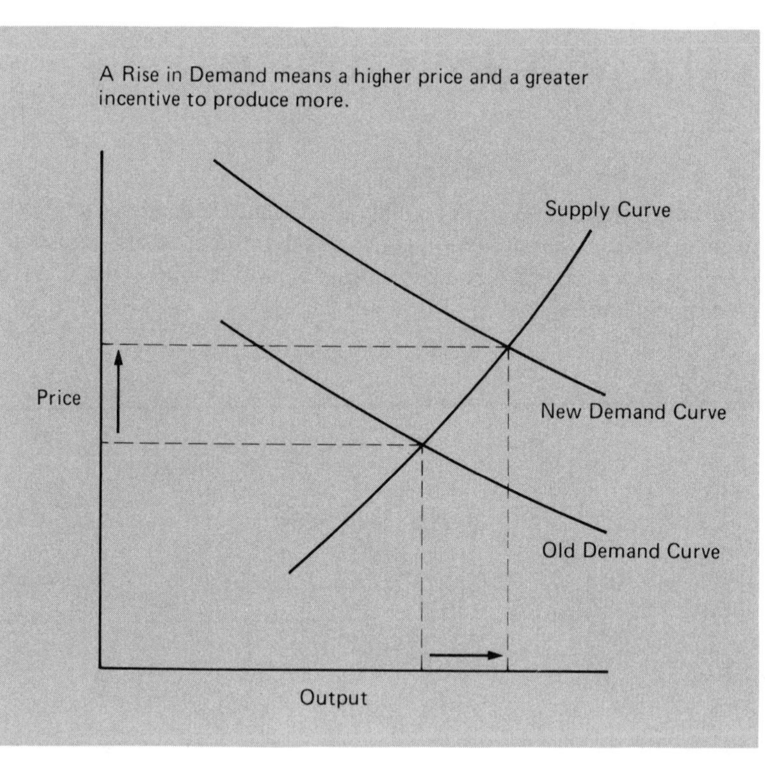
A Rise in Demand means a higher price and a greater incentive to produce more.
Supply Curve
Price
New Demand Curve
Old Demand Curve
Output

4. THEORY OF DEMAND

CHAPTER OBJECTIVES

A. To indicate how a market demand schedule and a market demand curve are constructed
B. To explain the "law of demand"
C. to explain the concept of marginal utility and how it helps determine a person's equilibrium expenditure
D. To distinguish between a change in demand and a change in the quantity demanded of a good
E. To distinguish between price-elasticity and income-elasticity of demand

CHAPTER OUTLINE

4.1 Market Demand Schedule
4.2 Market Demand Curve
4.3 Marginal Utility
4.4 Change in Demand versus Change in Quantity Demanded
4.5 Price-Elasticity of Demand
4.6 Income-Elasticity of Demand
4-A Appendix—Indifference Curve Analysis

The term *demand* is used in economics to signify the quantity of a good or service that consumers will buy at various prices during a given period of time. Demand, it should be noted, is not necessarily the same as desire since a person must have money to translate desire into demand. Many poor families, for example, would be overjoyed to have more and better food. However, the demand for a certain type of food at any time is the amount that people, with both desire *and* the money, would actually be willing to purchase at various prices. Sometimes, to distinguish demand from desire, the term *effective demand* is used.

Example of a market demand schedule

Price	Fred	Sue	Jim	Liz	Rick	Bill	Tina	Total
$10	1	0	0	1	0	2	0	4
$9	2	0	1	1	0	4	2	10
$8	3	1	3	2	1	7	2	19
$7	4	2	5	2	1	9	3	26
$6	5	4	7	2	2	10	3	33
$5	6	6	9	3	2	12	5	43

* Number of units of the product that would be bought at different prices

Example of a market demand curve (based on the above data)

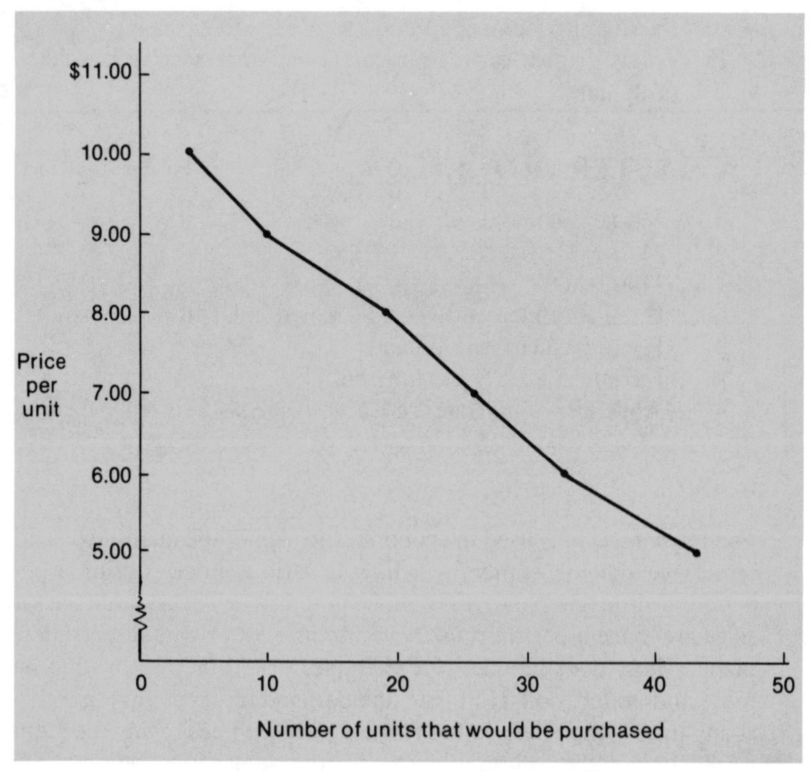

4.1: MARKET DEMAND SCHEDULE

At any one time, all the consumers in a particular area are willing and able to purchase a certain quantity of each good or service at the current market price. This *market demand* is the result of all individual consumers seeking to maximize their total satisfaction (or *utility*) within the constraints imposed by their tastes, the prices of similar goods, and the amount of their incomes.

To describe more fully the demand for a good, it is customary in economics to draw up a *market demand schedule*. This is a numerical statement, usually in column form, of the quantity of a good that would be sold in, say, a week, at each of a series of prices. It is a summation of the individual consumer demand schedules.

For purposes of illustration, we can use a hypothetical example of the demand for lettuce at a supermarket during a given week. At one extreme, $1.00 each, the store would sell hardly any lettuce. Consumers would either go without or substitute something else. At the other extreme, 10 cents each, practically all the lettuce would be sold. At other prices, the number of lettuces sold would vary from almost all to almost none. This is shown in Table 4:1. An imaginary market demand schedule can easily be drawn up. However, without successively charging a variety of prices within a short space of time, it is impossible to ascertain what the demand schedule for a good actually is.

4.2: MARKET DEMAND CURVE

The information contained in a market demand schedule can be illustrated graphically. Thus, in Figure 4:1 the price per lettuce is shown on the vertical axis and the number of lettuces that would be purchased on the horizontal axis. Each point in the body of the chart indicates how many lettuces would be bought at a particular price. Thus, point A indicates that 250 lettuces would be bought at a price of 30 cents each. These points can be joined to form a *market demand curve*. Such a curve, although depicting exactly the same price-quantity relationship as the market demand schedule, is much easier to understand.

Law of Demand

Most demand curves, including the one for lettuce, slope downward to the right. This means that, so long as the other determinants of demand remain unchanged, the lower the price of a good, the more of it will be bought. Conversely, the higher the price, the less will be

Table 4:1
Demand for Lettuce at Store X

Price per Lettuce	Number of Lettuce That Would Be Bought per Week
$1.00	5
0.80	20
0.60	50
0.50	100
0.40	150
0.30	250
0.20	500
0.10	750

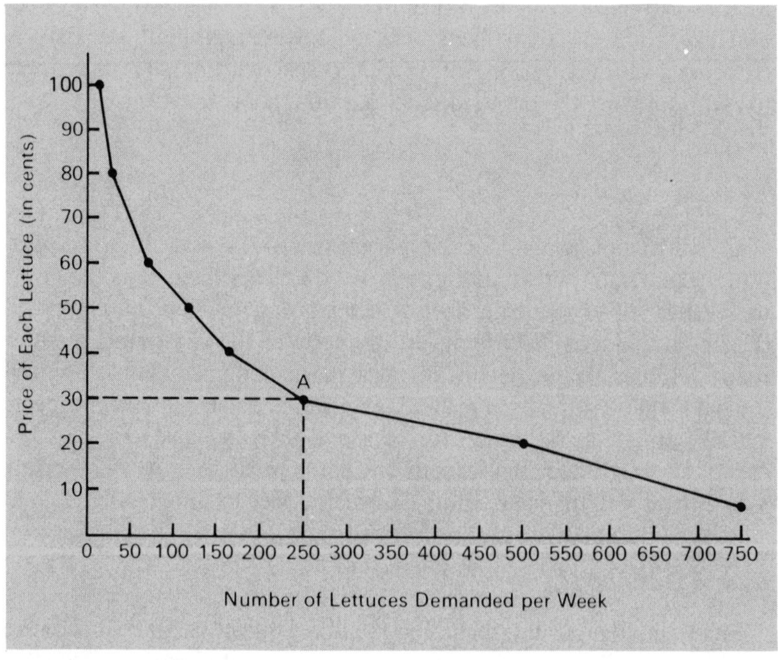

Figure 4:1 Demand Curve for Lettuce at Store X

bought. In other words, there is an inverse relationship between the price of a good and the quantity demanded of it. This inverse relationship is called the *law of demand.*

More of a good is bought at a lower price for two basic reasons. First, there is the *income effect*: persons who had previously bought the good at the higher price can now buy more with the same amount of money. Second, there is the *substitution effect*: consumers will, whenever possible, substitute these goods for other relatively higher-priced goods.

Exceptional Demand Curves

Usually, a demand curve slopes downward from left to right, indicating that more of a good will be bought at a lower price than at a higher price. Occasionally, however, a demand curve slopes upward from left to right, over part of its length, indicating just the opposite. Several possible reasons account for such exceptional demand curves.

1. Fear of future higher prices. If people believe, as in a period of rapid inflation, that prices may rise extremely fast in the future, they may increase their purchases now, even though prices have already gone up. This type of situation occurs, for instance, at the outbreak of war.

2. Ostentatious goods. Some goods occasionally sell better if their price is raised. This is because people tend to assume that a high price signifies high quality. Examples of such goods include jewellery, fashionable clothes, and country club memberships.

4.3: MARGINAL UTILITY

The satisfaction that a person derives from the last unit consumed of a good is called *marginal utility*. It is the difference in total utility obtained from drinking, say, three cups of coffee instead of two. The more a person consumes of a good, the smaller becomes this additional, or marginal utility.

Law of Diminishing Marginal Utility

The relationship between the quantity consumed of a good and the marginal utility that it provides was formulated as an economic theory, or "law" in England and Austria in 1871. The *law of diminishing marginal utility* states that, *as a person increases his or her consumption of a good, the additional satisfaction (or marginal utility) derived from each extra unit of that good will gradually diminish.*

The law of diminishing marginal utility helps us to understand the nature of the demand for a good. Since marginal utility declines as consumption increases, a person will obviously not be willing to pay as much for each successive unit of a good as for the previous ones. Thus, at a particular time, a person might be willing to pay $2.00 for a kilogram of grapes,$1.00 for a second kilo, 80 cents for a third, 50 cents for a fourth, 30 cents for a fifth, 15 cents for a sixth, and 10 cents for a seventh. These figures are shown in Table 4:2 and represent that person's demand for grapes.

Table 4:2
Marginal Utility and Demand

Price of Grapes per kilogram	Quantity Purchased (kilogram)
$2.00	1
1.00	2
0.80	3
0.50	4
0.30	5
0.15	6
0.10	7

The key fact to be noted here is that a person will buy an additional unit of a good only if that person considers its marginal utility to be greater than its price. Thus, if a person considers the marginal utility of the fifth kilogram of grapes to be equivalent only to 20 cents, that person will not pay a market price of 30 cents for it. This is because the marginal utility of the money itself exceeds the marginal utility of the grapes. In other words, a person can be happier by keeping his or her money.

Consumer's Surplus

In the previous example, a person would pay $2.00 for a kilogram of grapes, but less and less for additional kilograms. Now suppose that the market price of grapes is 20 cents per kilo. For the first kilo, our person *would have paid* $2.00, but only paid 20 cents. For the second kilo, the person would have paid $1.00, but again only paid 20 cents. For the third kilo the person would have paid 80 cents, but once more paid only 20 cents. For the fourth kilo, the person was willing to pay 50 cents, but only paid 20 cents. For the fifth kilo, the person would have paid 30 cents, but only paid 20 cents. Altogether, therefore, the person would have paid $4.60 (see Table 4:3), but in fact paid only $1.00. *Consumer's surplus* is the difference between the amount the consumer would have paid for a good and the amount the consumer actually paid. In the example, the difference was $3.60.

Table 4:3
Consumer's Surplus

Kilograms of Grapes Purchased	Total Amount the Customer Would Have Paid	Total Amount the Consumer Actually Paid	Total Consumer's Surplus
1	$2.00	$0.20	$1.80
2	3.00	0.40	2.60
3	3.80	0.60	3.20
4	4.30	0.80	3.50
5	4.60	1.00	3.60

This economic concept emphasizes the fact that consumers often get much more utility from a good than its market price would suggest. The last or marginal unit that they purchase is just worth its price to them, but units that they have purchased before may, in terms of satisfaction, be worth much more. Business firms, in their pricing policies, sometimes try to take advantage of this fact—for example, with regard to new books and movies.

Equilibrium Distribution of Personal Expenditure

A person will distribute his or her money among the various goods and services available so that the marginal utility from the last dollar spent on each item is equal. For, with a given amount of money and current set of tastes, a consumer will have maximized total utility only when he or she no longer has any incentive to switch a dollar from the purchase of one good to that of another. Although we cannot measure marginal utility in absolute terms, we can nevertheless measure it in relative terms. We know whether we can gain more satisfaction by spending more on product A and less on product B, or vice versa.

By concentrating spending on, say, product A, a consumer would find that his or her total utility would increase less with each additional dollar spent. This is because the marginal utility from buying that good is getting smaller all the time. A consumer would be far better off to purchase other goods, B, C, and D, each of which would give him or her a larger marginal utility for each dollar spent.

At first, the marginal utility from purchasing these other goods would be very great. But the more of them the consumer purchases, the smaller it becomes. Conversely, as a person reduces the purchases of product A, he or she will get a larger marginal utility from the last dollar spent on that product. Eventually, a person would reach the equilibrium situation at which the marginal utility from the last dollar spent on each good is equal. Of course, perfect equilibrium can be achieved only if each good is divisible into very small units.

This equilibrium situation is not, of course, one in which a person spends an equal amount on each good. A person's spending pattern also reflects his or her priority of tastes, or scale of preferences. Thus if a person likes product A more than product B, he or she will be able to buy more of A than B before the marginal utilities of the two products are the same.

It is sometimes argued that many people do not bother to weigh carefully the marginal utilities of the various goods and services that they buy. Consumers tend, in other words, to buy impulsively. Obviously, the cheaper the product involved, the less the amount of thought given at the time of purchase. Conversely, however, people tend to deliberate very much when buying a house, car, or other important item. Of course, not every consumer is consistently rational in his or her buying behaviour. Generally speaking, however, the vast majority of consumers do normally try to get the most for their money. If we believe that we will be better off by altering our pattern of spending, we will do so.

Another criticism of marginal utility theory is that a consumer's knowledge of the market is by no means perfect. A person often does not know exactly what he or she is getting for the money spent, nor the range of products available for choice. Nevertheless, within the consumer's field of knowledge, he or she is usually rational enough.

Another criticism is that it is often impossible to switch just one dollar from, say, product A to product B. We cannot, for example, buy one dollar's worth less of an airplane ticket and buy one dollar's worth more of a chair. But the fact that many goods are "indivisible" means only that a consumer's allocation of his money will be more "lumpy" than would otherwise be the case. The average consumer will still try, nevertheless, to maximize his or her total utility.

Paradox of Value

Because the marginal utility of a good falls as more of it is consumed, market price will have to be reduced if more of the good is to be sold. Otherwise, consumers will prefer to spend their money on something else. Consequently, the more abundant a good is, the lower its market price will tend to be. In other words, it is the utility of the *last* unit that is important in determining price, not the utility of *all* the units. This explains why water is so cheap in comparison with diamonds, despite the fact that the world's water supply is more useful than the world's supply of diamonds.

4.4: CHANGE IN DEMAND VERSUS CHANGE IN QUANTITY DEMANDED

It is important not to confuse a change in demand with a change in the quantity demanded as a result of a change in price. A change or shift in demand caused by a change in tastes, income, or other reasons, means a change in the demand schedule and a shift in the accompanying demand curve. Thus, the demand by college students for beefburgers might fall drastically if tuition fees are substantially increased. A new demand schedule, and a new demand curve (see Figure 4:2), would have emerged. A *change in demand* means, in other words, a different quantity of a good being demanded at each of the previous prices.

A *change in quantity demanded* caused by a price change would, on the contrary, leave the demand schedule and demand curve unchanged. For example, people might double their consumption of beefburgers as a result of a reduction in their subsidized price from, say, 50 cents to 40 cents. In this case, there has only been a movement along the demand curve to a new equilibrium position further to the right where more is purchased at a lower price.

Reasons for Changes in Demand

A change in the demand for a good or service may occur for any one of a variety of reasons. Let us briefly consider the most important of them.

1. Change in tastes. People's tastes in food, clothing, shelter, entertainment, and other items gradually change over the years. Education, income, and advertising are all factors influencing a person's tastes. Some tastes, such as for clothing, can change annually as new fashions appear. Others, such as for leisure pursuits, change more gradually.

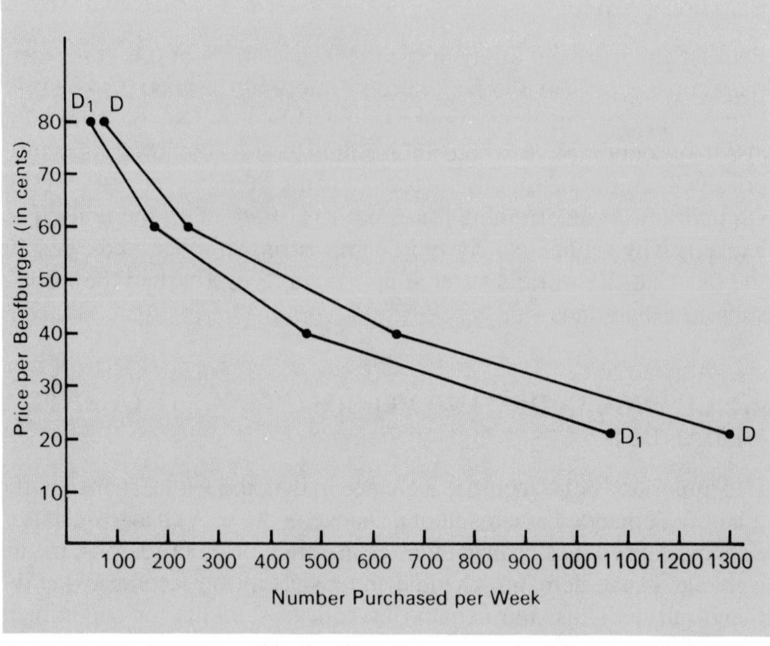

Note: **DD is the previous demand curve; D_1D_1 is the new demand curve.**

Figure 4:2 Change in the Demand for Beefburgers, as a Result of a Reduction in Student Income

2. Change in income. If a person has a larger money income than before, he or she will buy more of the various goods—assuming, of course, that the increase in income is greater than any increase in the prices of the goods to be purchased. Otherwise, purchases, in terms of quantity, will actually decline. A change in the distribution of a country's income, by increasing some people's income and reducing that of others, will also cause changes in the demand for various goods.
3. Change in relative prices. If the prices of other goods increase or decrease, the demand for a particular good will change because of the income and substitution effects discussed earlier in this book.
4. New goods replacing old. As new goods are invented, the demand for old ones often declines. Thus, the automobile has replaced the horse and buggy; the jet airliner, the transatlantic passenger ship.
5. Change in population. A change in the size of the population and in

its age distribution will cause changes in the demand for various goods. For example, the larger the population, the greater the demand for homes; and the younger the population, the greater the demand for schools.

6. Change in expectations. If business managers predict an upturn or a slowdown in consumer demand, their demand for raw materials, parts, and machines will change accordingly. Or if consumers predict shortages, they will want to stock up.

Interrelated Demand

The demand for some goods is related to the demand for others. In some cases, an increase in the demand for one good brings about an *increase* in the demand for another. In other cases, an increase in the demand for one good brings about a *decrease* in the demand for another.

1. Complementary or joint demand. Some goods are used together, like cups and saucers. Consequently, an increase in the demand for cups inevitably means an increase in the demand for saucers.

2. Derived demand. The demand for labour, machinery, parts, and raw materials, depends on the demand for the final goods which they help to produce. A change in demand for such final goods means, therefore, a corresponding change in demand for the various inputs.

3. Competitive demand. Some goods can be fairly easily substituted for each other—for example, margarine and butter. Consequently, if people increase their demand for one, they usually decrease their demand for the other.

4.5: PRICE-ELASTICITY OF DEMAND

The concept of price-elasticity of demand has been devised as a simple means of describing the responsiveness of the quantity demanded of a good or service to a small change in its price. It is defined as the effect of a change in the price of a good on the quantity sold of that good. Numerically, it can be expressed as the percentage change in the quantity sold divided by the percentage change in the price (see Table 4:4). For example, if the price of milkshakes were reduced 25 per cent and if the number sold consequently doubled, then the elasticity of demand for milkshakes over that part of the demand curve would be 4. Also since total revenue is equal to prices times quantity sold, we can determine price-elasticity by considering how total revenue has changed following an increase or decrease in the price of a product (see Table 4:5).

Table 4:4
Measuring the Elasticity of Demand

Formula for measuring the price-elasticity of demand:

$$ed = \frac{\% \triangle qd}{\% \triangle p}$$

where ed = price-elasticity of demand
$\% \triangle qd$ = percentage change in quantity demanded
$\% \triangle p$ = percentage change in the price of the good

Examples (*n* is the unknown number):

1. What is the elasticity of demand if a business firm increases the price of one of its products by 10% and finds that the quantity sold drops by 16%?

   Answer: $ed = \frac{16\%}{10\%} = 1.6$

2. If the elasticity of demand for a firm's product is 2, what will happen if the price is reduced by 5%?

   Answer: The quantity sold will increase by 10%.

   $$2 = \frac{n}{5\%} \therefore n = 2 \times 5\% = 10$$

3. If the elasticity of demand for a firm's product is 0.5, what will happen if the price is reduced by 8%?

   Answer: The quantity sold will increase by 4%.

   $$0.5 = \frac{n}{8\%} \therefore n = 0.5 \times 8\% = 4\%$$

4. If the elasticity of demand is 1.2, what reduction in price would be necessary to increase the quantity sold by 20%?

   Answer: 16.7%

   $$1.2 = \frac{20\%}{n} \therefore n = \frac{20\%}{1.2} = 16.7$$

Demand for a good or service can be classified, on the basis of its price-elasticity, into one of three main types: elastic demand, inelastic demand, and demand of unitary-elasticity. Over the length of the demand curve for a particular good or service, all three types of price-elasticity may be present.

Table 4:5
Example of the Relationship between Price-Elasticity of Demand and Total Revenue

1. A business is selling 10 000 units of each of two products, A and B, at a price of $5.00 each, for a total revenue for each product of $50 000. Manager X believes the firm would be better off by raising the price of each of the two products to $6.00.
   In fact, the elasticity of demand for each product is different:

   for A, it is 2.0
   for B, it is 0.5

   What would happen to the total revenue from each product, if Manager X has his way?

   Answer (*n* is the % change in quantity sold):

   Product A $2.0 = \frac{n}{20\%} \therefore n = 40\%$

   Total revenue = $6.00 × 6000 = $36 000

   Product B $0.5 = \frac{n}{20\%} \therefore n = 10\%$

   Total revenue = $6.00 × 9000 = $54 000

   Conclusion: If demand is elastic, total revenue will decrease; if demand is inelastic, total revenue will increase.

   Manager X should have been more selective. Give X a second chance. What other factor should we take into account in determining whether the firm will be better or worse off?

Elastic Demand

The demand for a good is said to be *price-elastic* if the elasticity of demand is greater than one. This would be the case if, for example, a reduction in the price of a good caused a more than proportionate increase in the quantity demanded. Thus, in Figure 4:3, a reduction in price from $5.00 to $4.00 per unit has caused an increase in the quantity demanded from 5000 units at point A to 10000 units at point B. Numerically, the elasticity of demand is 100% ÷ 20% = 5. Total revenue, it should be noted, has increased. If the demand for a good were perfectly elastic, the demand curve would be a straight horizontal line and elasticity would be equal to infinity.

The demand for a good or service tends to be price-elastic if one or more of the following circumstances exists:

1. There are close substitutes. Thus, if the price of pears goes up, consumers can buy apples or other fruit instead. Conversely, if the price of pears goes down, consumers can substitute them for other relatively higher-priced fruits. Demand for an individual fruit, it should be noted, may be highly price-elastic, even though demand for fruit as a whole may be relatively price-inelastic.

2. The price of the good absorbs a significant part of the consumer's total expenditure. Thus, a 50 per cent increase in the price of houses may cause a large reduction in the quantity demanded, whereas the same percentage increase in the price of table salt may have little effect.

3. The good is a luxury rather than a necessity. Thus, a rise in the price of sports cars may severely reduce the quantity demanded, whereas a rise in the price of beer (a "necessity" for many consumers) may not cause any reduction in purchases.

Inelastic Demand

The demand for a good or service is said to be *price-inelastic* if the elasticity of demand is less than one. This would be the case if a reduction in the price of a good caused a less than proportionate increase in the quantity demanded. In Figure 4:4, for example, a reduction in price from $5.00 to $4.00 per unit has caused an increase in the quantity demanded from 5000 units at point A to 5500 units at point B. The elasticity of demand over this part of the demand curve is 10% ÷ 20% = 0.5; and total revenue has fallen. If demand were perfectly inelastic, the demand curve would be a straight vertical line and the elasticity would be zero.

Demand for a good or service tends to be price-inelastic if one or more of the following circumstances is present:

1. There is no close substitute. A different painting, movie or book can rarely replace the specific one desired.

2. The money spent on the good is only a small part of a consumer's total expenditure. Thus, consumers will tend to go on buying matches, razor blades, or elecric light bulbs even though their price may have increased substantially.

3. The good is a necessity rather than a luxury. Thus, the demand for salt is quite inelastic.

4. The good is needed to accompany some other higher-value good that consumers wish to have. Thus, consumers must have tapes for their tape recorders and diskettes for their microcomputers.

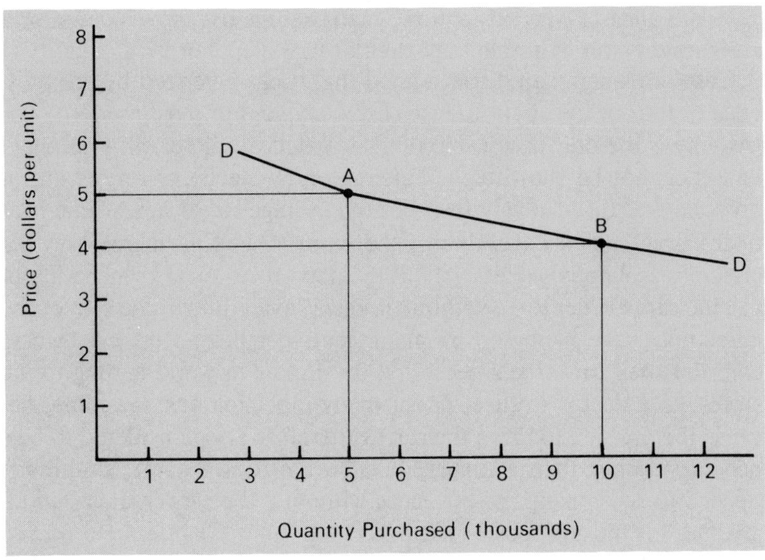

Figure 4:3 Example of Elastic Demand

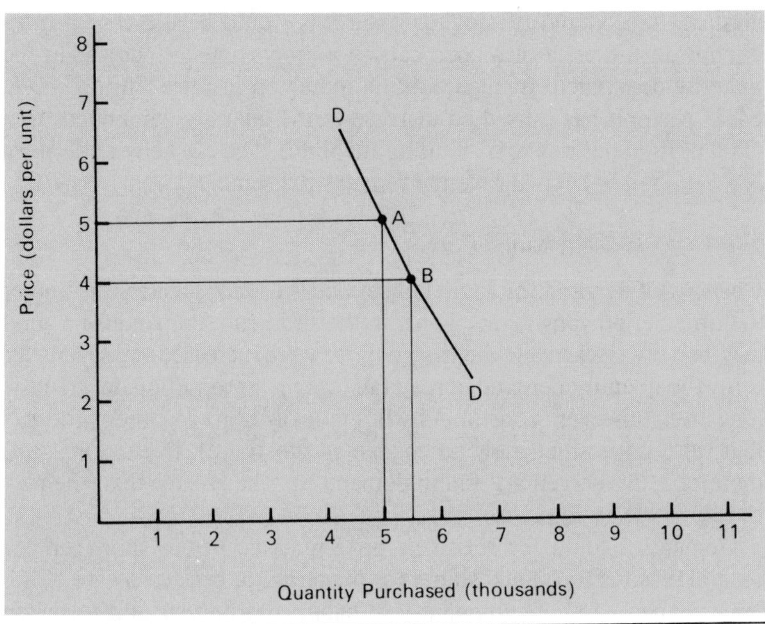

Figure 4:4 Example of Inelastic Demand

5. It is a good to which consumers, after some use, develop a strong attachment—for example, a particular newspaper or magazine.

Gasoline is an example of a good that is characterized by the presence of four of the circumstances listed above. For most modern cars, gasoline is the only acceptable fuel—wood, coal, diesel oil, electricity, or gas cannot be substituted. Cars driven by electricity, diesel oil, or propane are still relatively few. For the average car owner, with a relatively large capital expenditure, the extra cost of an increase in the price of gasoline is of relatively little importance. A car owner will not sell the car in order to do without gasoline, even though the cost of the latter may have increased by many cents per litre. Most car owners consider their car to be a necessity, for driving to work, getting to the stores, to a doctor's office, or for many other reasons. Gasoline, because it is needed to drive the car, is therefore also considered to be a necessity rather than a luxury. Finally, the fourth point, gasoline is needed to accompany the car, since without it the car remains stationary and, for most purposes, useless.

Demand of Unitary Elasticity

The demand for a good is said to be of *unitary elasticity* if the price-elasticity of demand is equal to one. This would be the case if a reduction in the price of a good caused a proportionate increase in the quantity demanded. In Figure 4:5, a reduction in price from $5.00 to $4.75 per unit has caused an increase in the quantity demanded from 5000 units at point A to 5250 units at point B. The elasticity of demand is 5% ÷ 5% = 1. Total revenue remains the same.

Short versus Long Run

Elasticity of demand for a good or service is usually greater, the longer the time period considered. Thus, in the short run, demand for a good may be very inelastic. If the market price were increased by, say 50 per cent, the quantity demanded may fall less than proportionately. In the long run, however, consumers will gradually shift to other products that were not immediately acceptable as substitutes. In the long run, therefore, the percentage fall in demand may be greater than the percentage increase in price.

Demand tends to be relatively price-inelastic in the short run for several reasons: (a) it takes time for the public to become aware of the price change; (b) consumers, out of habit, may be reluctant to switch to or from other products; (c) consumers, anticipating further price changes in a good, may hesitate to change the quantity bought; and (d)

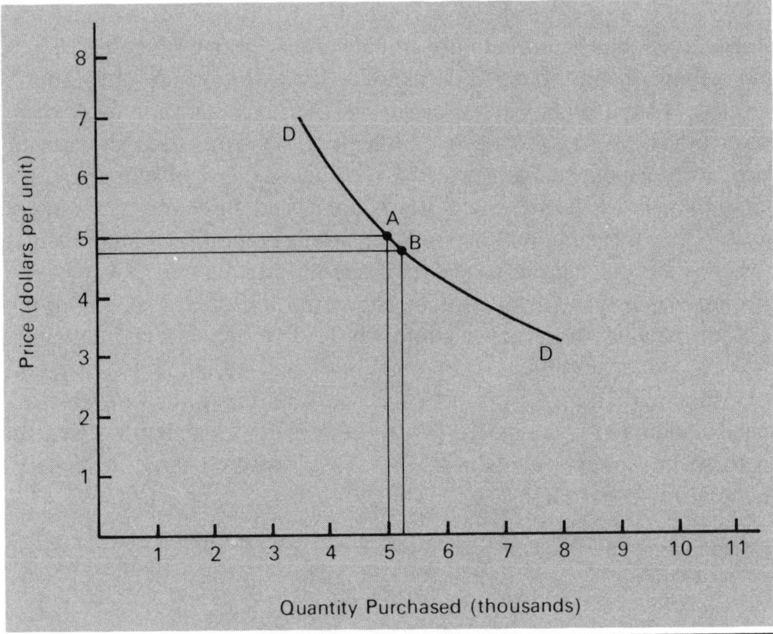

Figure 4:5 Example of Unitary-Elasticity of Demand

because of the durability of some goods, consumers will not replace them immediately.

Cross-Elasticity

Where two goods are in competitive demand, a change in the price of one will not only affect the quantity demanded of that good, but also the quantity demanded of the other. *Cross-elasticity* is the term used to describe the relationship between a change in the price of one good and the corresponding change in the quantity demanded of the other. Income-elasticity of demand, considered next, is considered to be a special case of cross-elasticity.

4.6: INCOME-ELASTICITY OF DEMAND

This is the term used to describe the way in which a person's demand for a good changes as a result of a change in his or her income. Applied to a market as a whole, *income-elasticity of demand* is the change in the quantity consumed of a good following a small change in consumer income.

For most goods, the income-elasticity of demand is considered to be positive; that is, an increase in consumers' money income causes an increase in the quantity demanded. However, where consumers, because of their higher incomes, switch their consumption away from lower-priced to higher-priced goods, such as from cheaper cuts of meat to more expensive ones, the income-elasticity of demand for a good may be negative. Such items are called in economics *inferior goods*—the normal condition for such goods being that demand shifts inversely to a change in a person's income. For food as a whole, the income-elasticity of demand is considered to be quite low, signifying that an increase in money income will lead to only a relatively small increase in consumption. For consumer durables, such as television sets, cars, and kitchen appliances, on the other hand, the income-elasticity of demand is considered to be quite high. This signifies that an increase in money income will result in a relatively large increase in the quantity demanded.

Summary

1. A *market demand schedule* is a numerical statement, usually in column form, of the quantity of a good that would be sold in a certain period of time at each of a series of prices. It is a summation of the individual consumer demand schedules.
2. A *market demand curve*, shown on a two-dimensional graph, illustrates the price-quantity relationship contained in the market demand schedule.
3. An *exceptional demand curve* is one that slopes upwards from left to right. One possible reason for this is ostentation value—people buy more of a good if it is higher priced, equating value with price.
4. Usually, the lower the price of a good, the more of it will be bought; the higher the price, the less of it will be bought. This inverse relationship between market price and the quantity purchased, called the *law of demand*, is illustrated by the downward-sloping demand curve. It is due to the income and substitution effects.
5. *Marginal utility* is the satisfaction that a person derives from the last unit consumed of a good. The *law of diminishing marginal utility* states that as a person increases consumption of a good, its marginal utility will gradually diminish. Consequently, a person will buy more of a good only if its price is lowered. For, if the price remains unchanged, the marginal utility of holding money will exceed the

marginal utility of the good. It is the marginal utility of a good, rather than its total utility, that helps determine how much a person will buy of it—hence the "paradox of value".

6. *Consumer's surplus* is the difference between the amount that a consumer would have paid for a good and the amount actually paid.
7. The *equilibrium distribution* of a person's expenditure is achieved when the marginal utility from the last dollar spent on each good is equal. Perfect equilibrium assumes that the consumer is completely rational; that he or she has a complete knowledge of the market; and that all goods are highly divisible.
8. A *change in demand* caused by a change in tastes, income, or other reasons, means a change in the demand schedule and a shift in the accompanying demand curve. A *change in the quantity demanded* caused by a change in price would, however, leave the demand schedule and demand curve unchanged.
9. The possible reasons for a change in consumer demand for a good include: a change in tastes, perhaps caused by advertising; a change in income; a change in relative prices; new goods replacing old; a change in the size of the population; and a change in consumer expectations.
10. The demand for some goods is related to the demand for others. Thus there is complementary or joint demand; derived demand; and competitive demand.
11. *Price-elasticity of demand* is the effect of a change in the price of a good on the quantity sold of that good. Numerically, it can be expressed as the percentage change in the quantity sold divided by the percentage change in the price.
12. The demand for a good is said to be *price-elastic* if the elasticity of demand is greater than one; *price-inelastic* if the elasticity of demand is less than one; and *unitary-elastic* if the price-elasticity is equal to one. The possible reasons for demand being price-elastic include: the existence of close substitutes; the price of the good absorbing a significant part of a consumer's total expenditures; and the good being a luxury rather than a necessity. Elasticity of demand is usually greater in the long run than in the short run.
13. *Cross-elasticity* is the term used to describe the relationship between a change in the price of one good and the corresponding change in the quantity demanded of the other. *Income-elasticity*, a special case of cross-elasticity, indicates how the demand for a good varies with changes in a person's money income.

Key Terms

Demand 63
Effective demand 63
Market demand 65
Utility 65
Market demand schedule 65
Market demand curve 65
Law of demand 65
Exceptional demand curve 67
Income effect 67
Substitution effect 67
Marginal utility 67
Law of diminishing marginal utility 67
Consumer's surplus 68
Equilibrium distribution of personal expenditure 69
Paradox of value 71
Change in demand 71
Change in quantity demanded 71
Interrelated demand 73
Complementary or joint demand 73
Derived demand 73
Competitive demand 73
Price-elasticity of demand 73
Elastic demand 75
Inelastic demand 76
Demand of unitary-elasticity 78
Short-run elasticity of demand 78
Long-run elasticity of demand 78
Income-elasticity of demand 79
Inferior goods 80

Review Questions

1. What is a market demand schedule? A market demand curve?
2. What is the law of demand? Explain the income effect and the substitution effect as reasons for downward-sloping demand curves.
3. What is an exceptional demand curve? Why does it occur?
4. Distinguish between a change in demand and a change in the quantity demanded.
5. What are the possible reasons for a change in demand?
6. What are the various types of interrelated demand? Give examples of your own.
7. What is price-elasticity of demand? How is it measured?
8. Distinguish between elastic-demand, inelastic demand, and demand of unitary-elasticity.
9. What causes demand to be price-elastic?
10. What causes demand to be price-inelastic?
11. How does the time period affect the elasticity of demand?
12. What is cross-elasticity of demand?

13. What is income-elasticity of demand? Why is it considered positive for most goods?
14. There is an inverse relationship between the price of a good and the quantity demanded of it. Explain this relationship and the reasons for it.
15. Illustrate the law of diminishing marginal utility with an example of your own. Illustrate also an exception to this law.
16. Explain how business firms take advantage of the existence of "consumer's surplus."
17. How does a person achieve an equilibrium distribution of his or her expenditure? Why is a perfect equilibrium rarely achieved?
18. Suppose that the price of a good is reduced by 5 per cent and the quantity demanded increases by 10 per cent. What is the elasticity of demand?
19. Suppose that the price of a good is raised by 8 per cent and the quantity demanded falls by 5 per cent. What is the elasticity of demand?
20. Suppose that the elasticity of demand for a good is 0.4 and that the government imposes an import duty that raises the price by 12 per cent. What would happen to the quantity purchased?
21. Why is the concept of price-elasticity of demand useful for governments as well as for business firms?
22. List three products for which demand is price-elastic and three for which it is price-inelastic. Explain why the products fall into the two different categories.
23. Give two examples of products for which demand might be (a) perfectly elastic, and (b) perfectly inelastic.
24. Explain, with an example, how price-elasticity of demand affects a firm's total revenue.
25. Give two examples of goods that are characterized by cross-elasticity of demand.
26. Suppose a person's income increases by 12 per cent and the person's demand for entertainment, as a result of overwork, rises by 20 per cent. What is the income-elasticity of demand?
27. Give an example of an "inferior good" and explain how it earned that label.
28. Why is the admission price to a new movie usually so high compared with regular prices? What economic concept does this illustrate?
29. Why are diamonds "a girl's best friend"?
30. How does the existence of substitutes affect the demand for a

product? Give examples.

31. Suppose your parents won $100 000 in a provincial lottery. How do you think it would affect their pattern of spending? For which goods and services would their demand increase and for which would it decrease? Suppose you won the money instead. How would your answers be different? Why?
32. What is the purpose of a demand curve if, in practice, few people ever try to draw them for actual products?
33. The demand for a firm's product may go up, even though demand for the product of the industry as a whole may go down. Explain, with reasons.
34. If poor people demanded more, they would be better off. Comment.
35. What happens in a communist country, if the demand for a product increases?
36. List three products for which the demand has increased in recent years. Explain why.
37. List three products for which demand has decreased in recent years. Give the reasons for this decrease.
38. Look at the stock page of a daily newspaper. How have stock prices changed recently? What causes an increase or decrease in demand for corporation shares?
39. Explain, with a product example, what each of the following demand curves signifies.

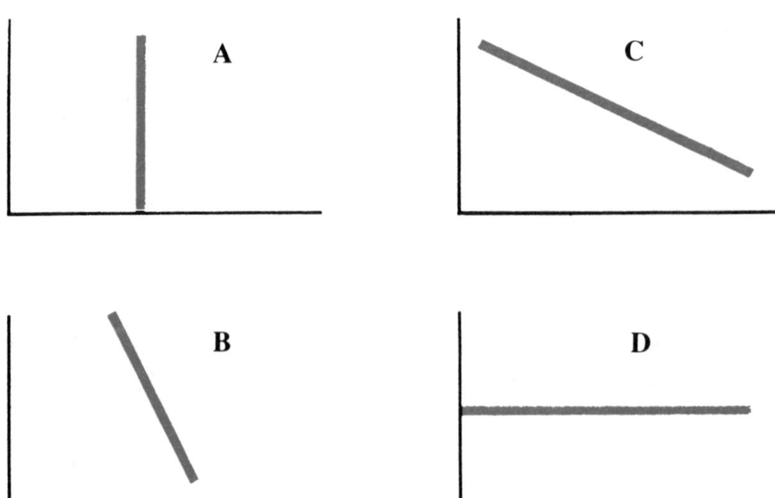

APPENDIX 4-A: INDIFFERENCE CURVE ANALYSIS

So far in this Chapter we have used the theory of marginal utility to explain the nature of demand. Another approach is that of indifference curve analysis. It starts with two suppositions: (a) that there are many different combinations of the various goods available that will provide a person with maximum total satisfaction; and (b) that consumer behaviour involves a choice between different alternative combinations of goods and services rather than, as in the marginal utility approach, an evaluation of the effects of a little more or a little less of each item.

THE INDIFFERENCE CURVE

Suppose, for instance, that a person can spend his or her money on only two different goods, A and B. We can then plot on a two-dimensional graph (See Figure A.1) the various combinations of these two goods that would make that person equally content. At the extremes, he or she would be just as happy to have 10 units of A and no units of B as to have 8 units of B and no units of A. By joining in the graph all the points which indicate such combinations, we obtain an *indifference curve*. The person is "indifferent" as to his or her position on the curve, since all combinations afford equal total satisfaction. The shape of the curve (convex to the origin) indicates that as a person reduces the consumption of one good, he or she requires larger amounts of the other as compensation. The term, *the marginal rate of substitution*, is used to indicate the amount of product A that must be given up in exchange for an extra unit of product B. Instead of just two goods, one axis of the chart can be used for one good and the other axis for all other goods.

MAP OF INDIFFERENCE CURVES

Instead of just one indifference curve, we can draw for each person a whole series, or "map," of them (see Figure A.2). Each curve represents a different total combined quantity of goods. The larger a person's real income, the higher his or her actual indifference curve. The rational person will try to reach the highest possible indifference curve.

THE BUDGET LINE

The combination of goods that a consumer can actually obtain will depend on his or her money income and the relative prices of the

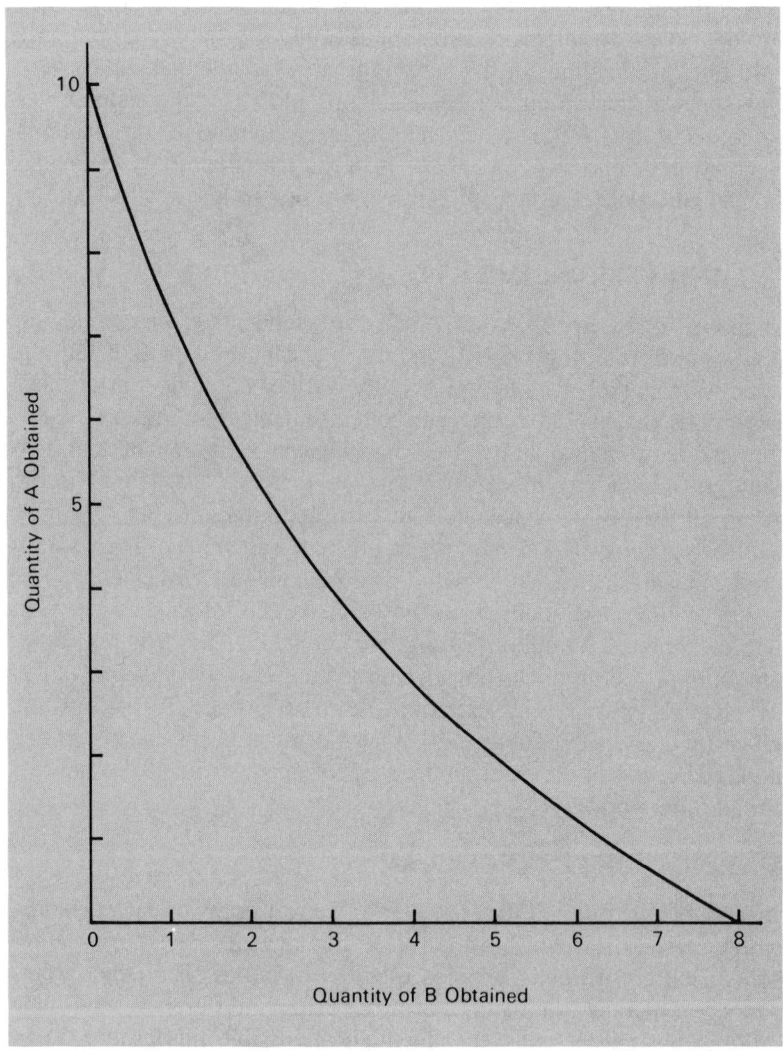

Figure A:1 Indifference Curve

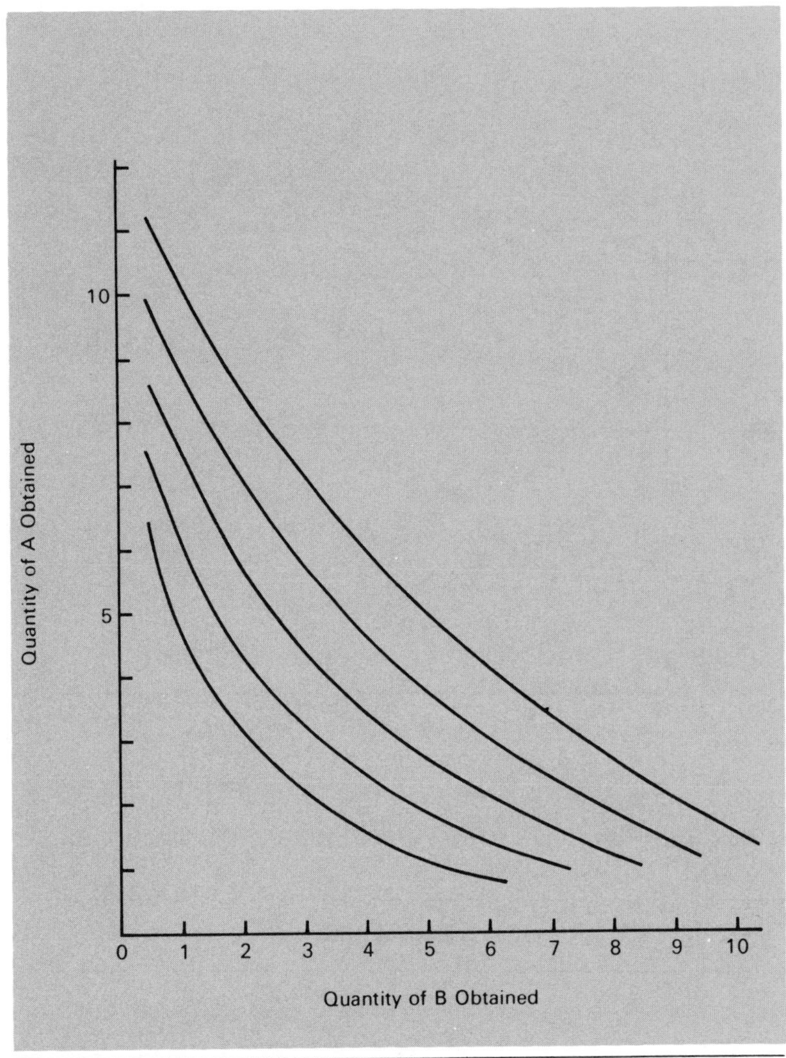

Figure A:2 Map of Indifference Curves

various goods. Let us assume, for example, that a consumer has a monthly income of $500 which is spent entirely on two goods, X and Y, costing $10.00 and $5.00 per unit respectively. The possible combinations of X and Y that can be obtained are depicted in Figure A.3 by the straight line AB. This is known as a *budget line*.

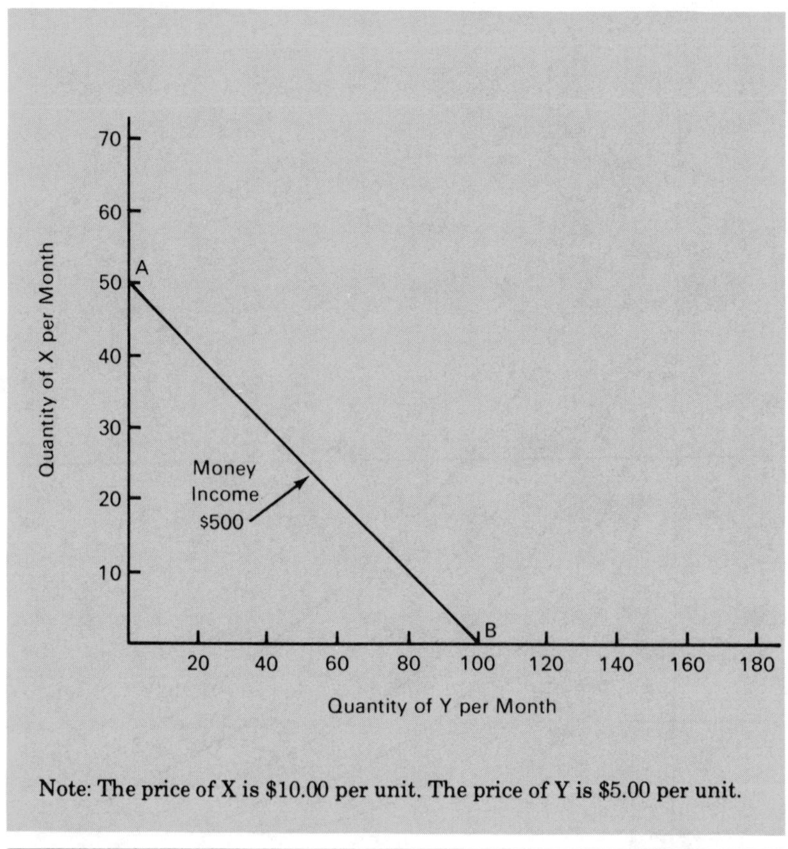

Note: The price of X is $10.00 per unit. The price of Y is $5.00 per unit.

Figure A:3 The Consumer's Budget Line

COMBINING THE BUDGET LINE AND INDIFFERENCE MAP

By combining a consumer's budget line and his or her map of indifference curves (see Figure A.4), we can show theoretically what amount of each good a consumer will purchase, given his or her tastes, income, and the relative prices of the goods shown. This preferred combination of goods is indicated by the point at which the budget line is at a tangent to one of the indifference curves (point P in Figure A.4). At this point, the consumer has attained the highest indifference curve that his or her budget allows and has thereby achieved maximum total satisfaction.

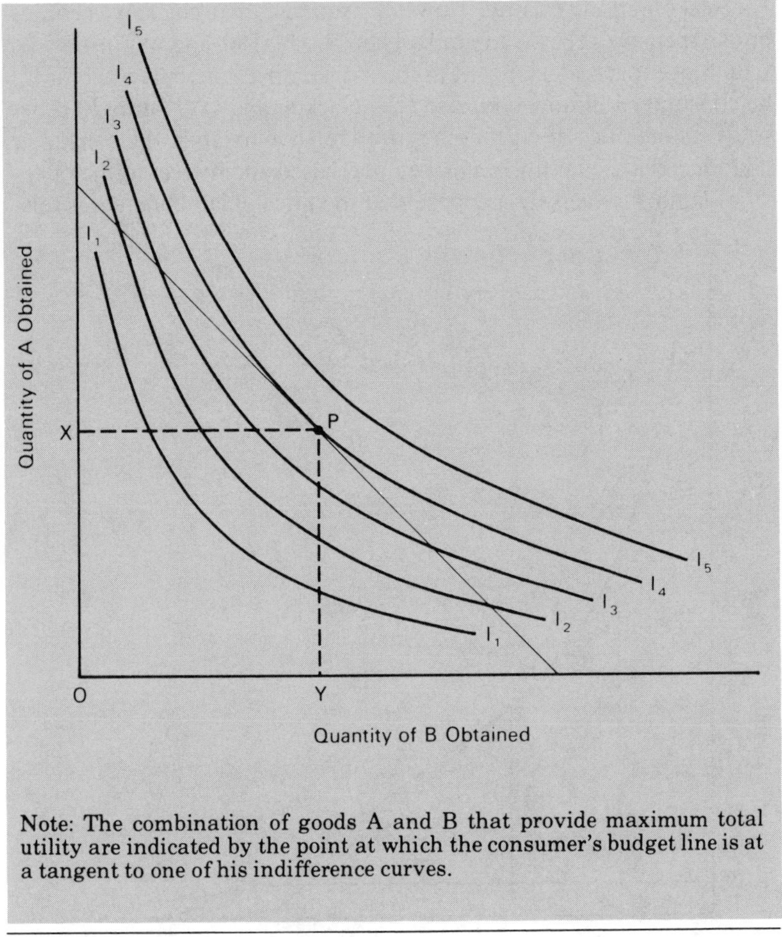

Note: The combination of goods A and B that provide maximum total utility are indicated by the point at which the consumer's budget line is at a tangent to one of his indifference curves.

Figure A:4 How a Consumer Obtains Maximum Total Utility

1 Since the indifference map contains an infinite number of indifference curves, the budget line must be at a tangent to one of them.

CHANGES IN RELATIVE PRICES

We can also make use of the budget line and indifference map to show what happens when the relative prices of goods change.

Let us assume in Figure A.5 that the relative prices of chicken and lamb are indicated by the budget line AB. Since this line is at a tangent to the indifference curve I_1I_1 at the point P, the consumer will purchase OX chicken and OY lamb. However, suppose that chicken becomes more expensive relative to lamb. Then the budget line might now be A_1B_1. Since this is at a tangent to the indifference curve at the point P_1, the consumer will now purchase OX_1 chicken and OY_1 lamb. In other words, as the price of chicken has risen relative to lamb, the consumer has reduced the quantity of chicken purchased and increased the quantity of lamb. Conversely, suppose that the price of lamb increases rela-

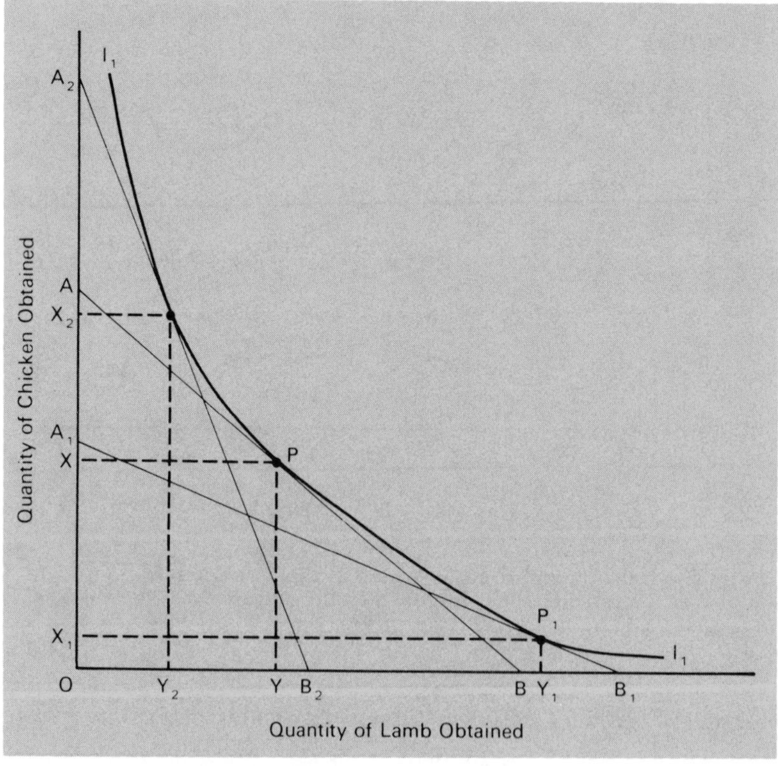

Figure A:5 Effect of a Change in Relative Prices on a Consumer's Expenditure Pattern tive to the price of chicken. The budget line, indicating the possible combinations of chicken and lamb with a given income, might now be A_2B_2, and the quantities consumed, OX_2 chicken and OY_2 lamb. The consumer now purchases more chicken and less lamb. In conclusion, we can see that as a good becomes relatively cheaper, a consumer will purchase more; and as a good becomes relatively more expensive, a consumer will purchase less. This pattern of consumer behaviour assumes that all other things remain equal—notably consumer tastes and income.

CHANGE IN CONSUMER INCOME

What happens to a person's pattern of expenditure when his or her income changes? As Figure A.6 indicates, an increase in money income (assuming that absolute prices remain the same) means a movement of the budget line away from the point of origin. A decrease in

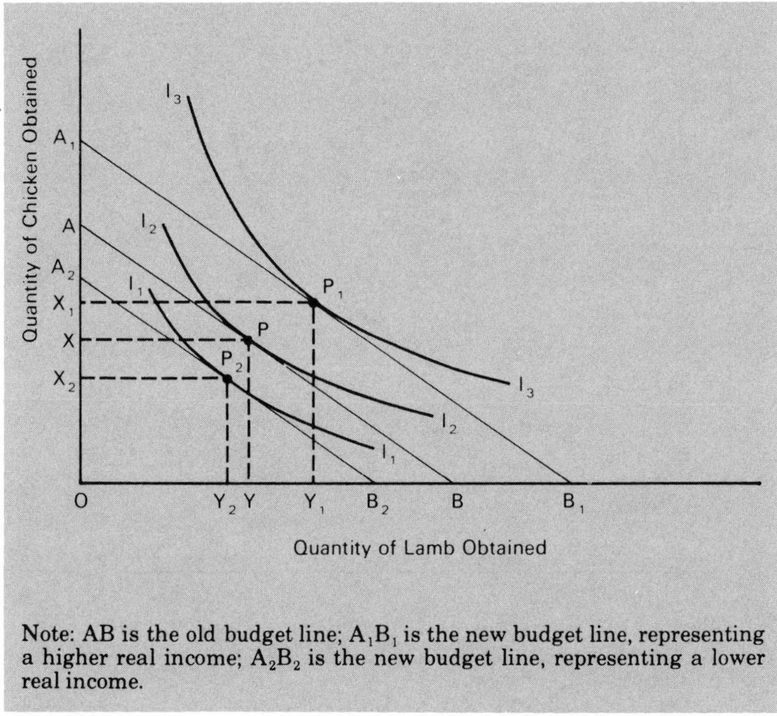

Note: AB is the old budget line; A_1B_1 is the new budget line, representing a higher real income; A_2B_2 is the new budget line, representing a lower real income.

Figure A:6 A Change in Real Income Means a New Budget Line income means a movement toward the point of origin. This illustrates that, at a higher income, a person can buy more of each good; and at a lower income he or she can buy less. So long as relative prices are unchanged, the pattern of expenditure will remain the same. Only the total amount will have altered. If absolute prices rise, the increase in real income will be less than the increase in money income. Usually, an increase in income causes an increase in consumption. The goods that are bought in greater quantity are called *normal goods*. Sometimes, however, an increase in income may cause a fall in the consumption of a particular good. This occurs when people, because of their larger income, switch to other more expensive goods. The goods that experience a fall in consumption when income rises are called *inferior goods*.

The relationship between a consumer's money income and his or her consumption of a good (over the same period of time) is expressed graphically by what is known as an *Engel curve*. In Figure A.7, the Engel curve indicates that as a consumer's money income (shown on

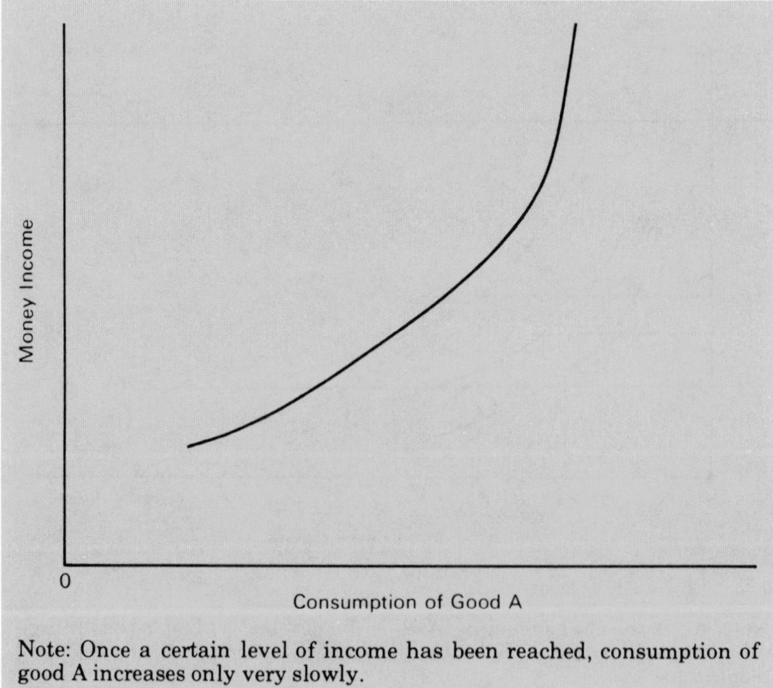

Note: Once a certain level of income has been reached, consumption of good A increases only very slowly.

Figure A:7 Engel Curve for Good A

the vertical axis) increases, his or her consumption of good A rises, but only at a declining rate. This could well hold true for a man's consumption of clothing. Once he has been adequately attired, he may not purchase much more for some time even though his income continues to increase. In the case of other goods—for example, golf balls—consumption may rise even more rapidly than income. Once a certain income level has been reached, the Engel curve would, therefore, tend to flatten out horizontally. This is shown in Figure A.8.

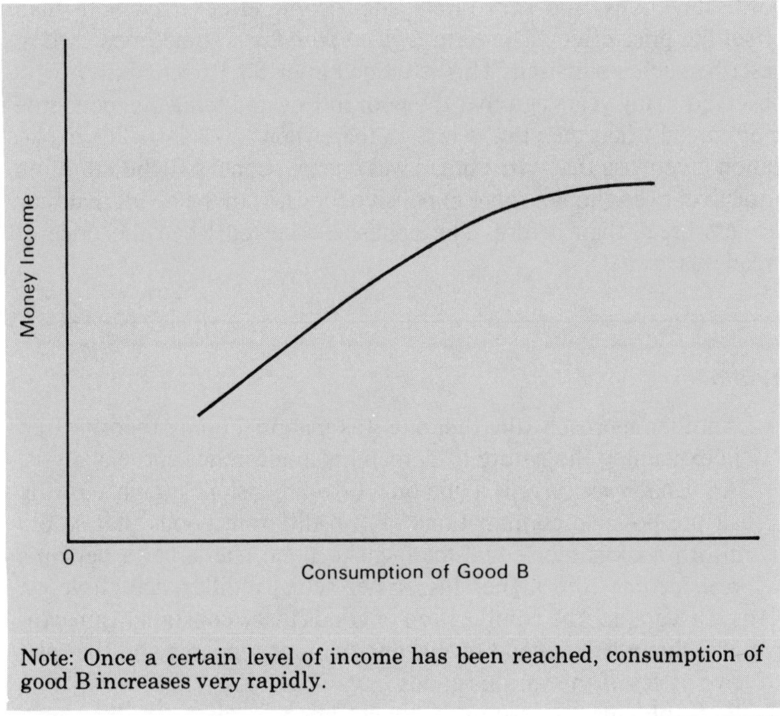

Note: Once a certain level of income has been reached, consumption of good B increases very rapidly.

Figure A:8 Engel Curve for Good B

DETERMINANTS OF CONSUMPTION

In conclusion, we can say that, given a person's tastes, there are two major features that determine his or her consumption of a good: the relative price of the good, and the level of the person's income. If the price of the good, relative to that of other goods, changes, the individual will increase or decrease his or her consumption of that particular good. Similarly, if the individual's real income (the goods and services that can be purchased with the money income) changes, he or she will increase or decrease consumption of all goods. In practice, of course, both factors are at work at the same time, and they usually work in the same direction. Thus, a reduction in the price of lamb will normally cause an increase in its consumption for two reasons: (a) because it is now cheaper relative to other goods; and (b) because the individual now has a larger real income.

Sometimes, however, the price and income effects will work in opposite directions, and very rarely, the income effect may more than offset the price effect. The term *Giffen's paradox* is sometimes used to describe such a situation. This is named after Sir Robert Giffen who observed many years ago that the poor in England tended to consume more bread when the price was high than when it was low. The explanation given was that when bread was cheap, people switched to more attractive, even though more expensive foods, with the result that they ate less bread than before. The opposite occurred when the price of bread was low.

Summary

1. Another approach (the first one was marginal utility theory) used in explaining the nature of demand is indifference curve analysis. An *indifference curve* is a line on a two-dimensional graph showing all the possible combinations of two different goods that would afford a consumer equal total satisfaction. The larger a person's real income, the higher his or her actual indifference curve on such a graph. The combination of goods that a consumer can actually obtain will depend on his or her money income and the relative prices of the various goods.
2. By combining a consumer's budget line and map of indifference curves, we can show theoretically what amount of each good a consumer will purchase, given his or her tastes, income, and the relative prices of the goods shown on the graph. This preferred combination of goods is indicated by the point at which the budget line is at a tangent to one of the indifference curves. We can also make use of the budget line and indifference map to show what happens when the relative prices of goods change.
3. An increase in money income (assuming that absolute prices remain the same) means a movement of the budget line away from the point of origin and hence an increase in consumption. A de-

crease in money income means the opposite. The relationship between a consumer's money income and his or her consumption of a good, over the same period of time, is expressed graphically by an *Engel curve*.

4. Given a person's tastes, there are two major determinants of his or her consumption of a good: the relative price of the good, and the level of that person's income.

Key Terms

Indifference curve 85
Marginal rate of substitution 85
Map of indifference curves 85
Budget line 86
Change in relative prices 90
Change in consumer income 91
Normal goods 92
Inferior goods 92
Engel curve 92
Determinants of consumption 93
Giffen's paradox 94

Review Questions

1. What is an indifference curve? Why is it convex in shape? What is a map of indifference curves?
2. The rational person will try to reach the highest possible indifference curve. Explain.
3. What is a budget line? What is its use in indifference curve analysis?
4. What happens to the budget line when relative prices change? How does this affect a person's expenditure?
5. What happens to a person's pattern of expenditure when his or her income changes?
6. Distinguish between normal goods and inferior goods.
7. What is an Engel curve? What does it illustrate?
8. What are the major factors that determine a person's consumption of the various goods and services?
9. What is meant by the term "Giffen's paradox"?

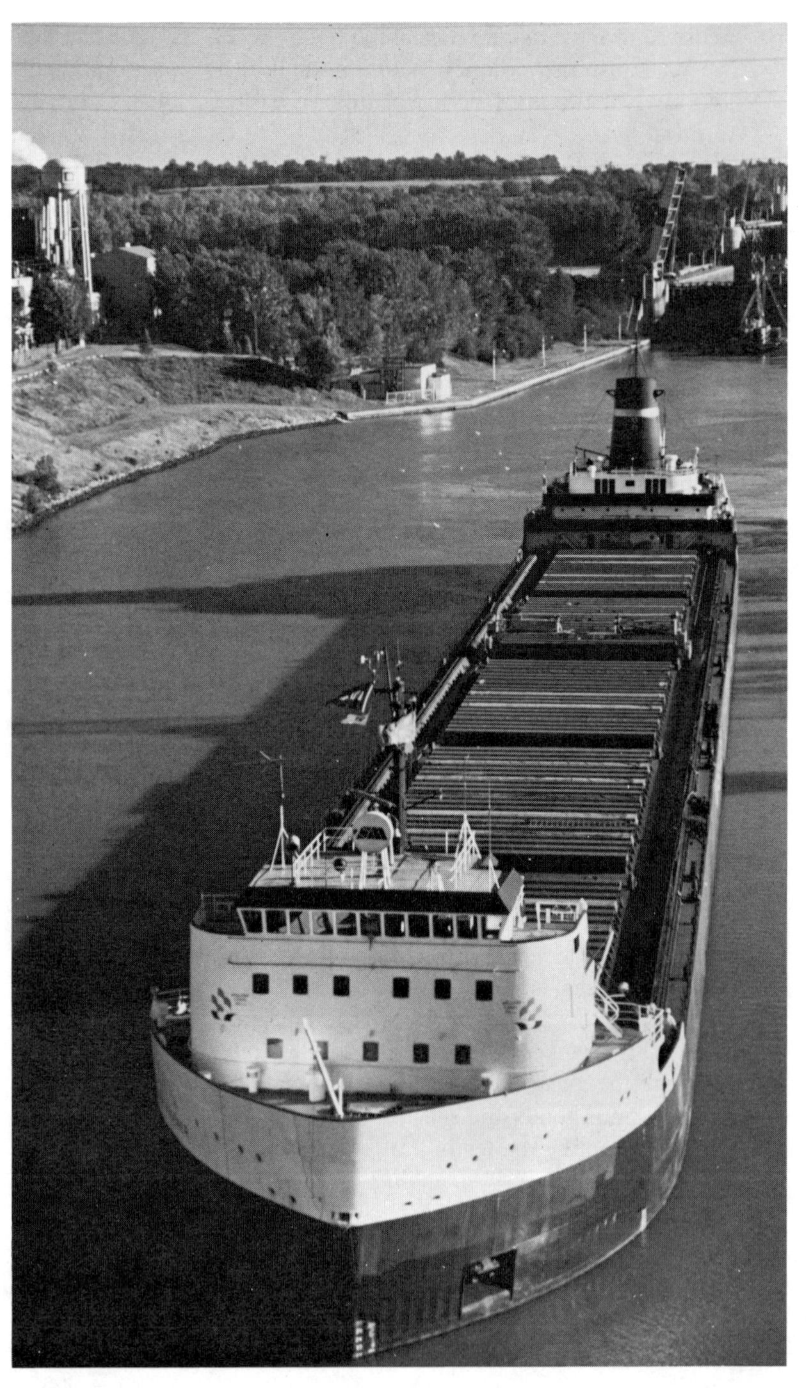

5. SUPPLY, DEMAND, AND MARKET PRICE

CHAPTER OBJECTIVES

A. To explain how a market supply schedule and a market supply curve for a product are constructed
B. To distinguish between between a change in supply and a change in the quantity supplied of a product
C. To explain the concept of price-elasticity of supply
D. To show how changes in market price bring about an equilibrium between the supply and demand for a product
E. To indicate what can happen when government intervenes in the working of the market system by, for example, price control

CHAPTER OUTLINE

5.1 Market Supply
5.2 Change in Supply versus Change in Quantity Supplied
5.3 Elasticity of Supply
5.4 Determination of Market Price and Amount Sold
5.5 The Price Mechanism
5.6 Government Intervention

We have just looked at demand, which is the quantity of a good or service that consumers will buy at various prices during a certain period of time. Now let us look at *supply*, which can be defined as the quantity of a good or service that producers are willing to sell at various prices during a certain period of time. Afterwards, we can consider how supply and demand interact to determine the market price and amount sold of a good, and how the price mechanism helps to allocate productive resources.

5.1: MARKET SUPPLY

For every good or service, we can, in theory, prepare a market supply schedule showing how much of the item will be offered for sale during a certain period of time at each different market price. Market supply, it should be noted, is not the total stock of a good at any one time, but only the amount that is actually offered for sale at each price.

Market Supply Schedule

A hypothetical market supply schedule for oats (comprising all the individual farmers' supply schedules) is shown in Table 5:1. It shows that the higher the market price, the larger the quantity of oats that farmers would be willing to offer for sale. In any one crop year, once the land is seeded, the supply of oats is largely set. However, in the following season, if a rise in the market price of oats has occurred, land can be switched from other crops. If the price of oats has fallen, compared with the price of other alternative crops, land can be switched out of oats. This supply schedule illustrates what is sometimes called the *law of supply* which can be stated as: *the higher the price of a good, the larger the quantity that will be supplied.* Conversely, of course, the lower the price, the smaller the quantity that will be supplied.

Market Supply Curve

The information contained in a market supply schedule can be shown diagrammatically in the form of a market supply curve. Figure 5:1, for example, is the market supply curve that accompanies the market supply schedule for oats shown in Table 5:1. Price in cents per kilogram is shown on the vertical axis, and the quantity of oats, in thousands of tonnes, supplied by farmers, is shown on the horizontal axis. Usually, as in our example, the supply curve slopes upward from left to right. This indicates that more of a good will be supplied at a higher price than at a lower price; and, conversely, less at a lower price than at a higher price.

In the short run, the supply of most goods is relatively fixed, since it takes time (as with our example of oats) to switch resources from the production of other goods. Consequently, in the short run, the supply curve for most goods will slope quite steeply upward from left to right, signifying that even a large increase in price cannot induce much of an increase in supply. For some goods, such as original works of art, there may be no way of increasing the supply at all. The supply curve, in such instances, would be a vertical line.

Table 5:1
Hypothetical Supply Schedule of Oats

Price (¢/kg)	Quantity Supplied by all Farmers (thousands of tonnes)
70	200
72	210
74	220
76	230
78	240
80	250
82	260
84	270
86	280

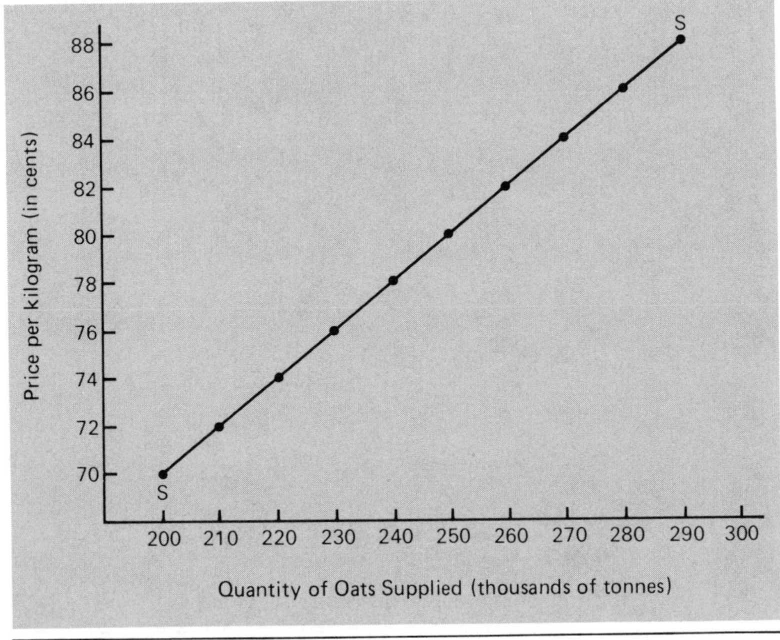

Figure 5:1 Supply Curve for Oats

We saw earlier that there are exceptional demand curves. So also are there exceptional or *regressive supply curves*. Instead of more of a good or service being offered for sale at a higher price, less is offered. Such a situation might occur in a manufacturing plant where the workers, after receiving a substantial increase in their hourly rate of pay, may prefer to work fewer hours. An increase in the price of labour has, in other words, caused a reduction in its supply.

5.2: CHANGE IN SUPPLY VERSUS CHANGE IN QUANTITY SUPPLIED

As with changes in demand, we must be careful to distinguish between a change in supply and a change in the quantity supplied. A *change in supply* means that producers will supply more or less of a good in a certain period of time than they did before at each price. Such a change causes a shift of the supply curve to the right if supply has increased, and a shift to the left if it has decreased. A *change in the quantity supplied* is the terminology used to indicate that supply conditions are unaltered. What has happened is that, as a result of a change in market price, there has been a movement along the existing supply curve.

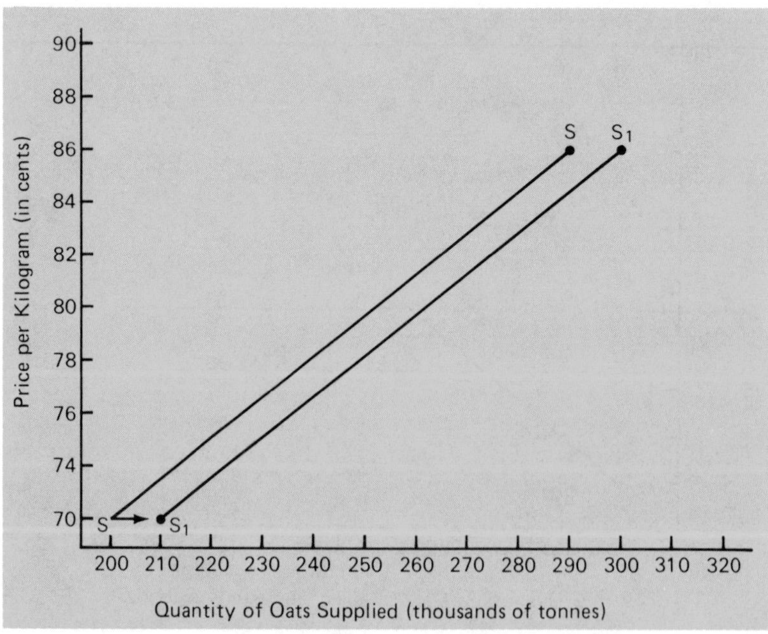

Figure 5:2 Shift in the Supply Curve of Oats, from SS to S_1S_1

In Figure 5:2, for example, we show that the supply curve has changed from SS to S_1S_1. This means that, at the same market price, farmers are now willing to supply more oats than they were before—for example, 210000t at 70 cents per kg rather than 200000t. In Figure 5:3, however, supply has increased from 240000t to 250000t because of an increase in market price from 78 cents to 80 cents per kilogram. In this case, the supply curve, SS, and the supply schedule on which it is based, have remained unchanged.

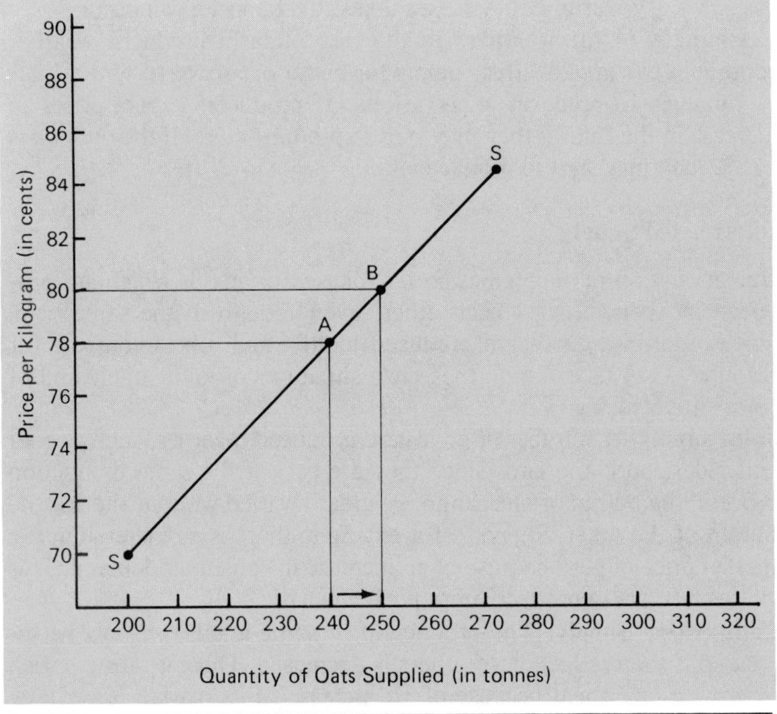

Figure 5:3 Increase in the Quantity of Oats Supplied, with the Same Supply Curve, and an Increase in Market Price

Reasons For Changes in Supply

What causes producers to supply more or less of a good now at each particular price than they did previously? Let us consider the various possible reasons.

1. Changes in technology. If the state of technology improves to permit cheaper production, more can be supplied at each price. The supply curve will have shifted to the right. An example would be the micro-computer.

2. Changes in production and marketing costs. If the per unit costs of production have increased through, for example, a higher wage or raw-material bill, less of the good will be supplied at each price. The supply curve will have shifted to the left. An example would be houses.

3. Changes in taxation. If the government reduces corporation income taxes and sales taxes, producers will tend to supply more at each price. If the government increases taxes, the opposite will occur.

4. Changes in the weather. In the case of farm products, weather conditions can greatly affect supply for better or for worse.

5. Changes in producer expectations. If producers expect prices to increase in the future, they may start to produce more. If the outlook is bleak, they may start to produce less.

Interrelated Supply

Our discussion of supply has so far focused on goods which are produced independently of each other, even though in the same firm. However, some goods are produced jointly, and others compete for resources. Let us examine these two situations of joint supply and of competitive supply.

Joint supply. A number of goods are produced together, such as beef and hides, pork and lard. Since they are part of the same production process, the output of one cannot be greatly varied without altering the output of the other. Suppose, for example, there is an increase in the market price of pork because of an increase in consumer demand. This causes farmers to produce more pork *and* lard.

Competitive Supply. The production of some goods can only be increased if the production of others is decreased. Thus, if farmers wish to grow more wheat because of an increase in its market price, they must grow less of the various other crops. This assumes, of course, that they have no idle land.

5.3: PRICE-ELASTICITY OF SUPPLY

Price-elasticity of supply is the concept used to describe the responsiveness of supply to changes in market price.

Elastic Supply

Supply is considered to be *price-elastic* if an increase in the price of a good or service causes a more than proportionate increase in the quantity supplied of it.

In Figure 5:4, for example, an increase in price from $1.00 to $1.20 results in an increase in supply from 5000 units to 10000 units. In other words, a 20 per cent increase in price has led to a 100 per cent increase in the quantity supplied.

The elasticity of supply is 5, obtained by dividing the percentage increase in quantity supplied (100 per cent) by the percentage increase in price (20 per cent). A formula for measuring the elasticity of supply is given in Table 5:2.

Supply is considered to be price-elastic whenever its elasticity is greater than 1. The higher the number, the greater is the elasticity. Supply is said to be perfectly elastic if producers are willing to supply as much of the good as is required at the existing price. In the case of a perfectly elastic supply, the supply curve is horizontal throughout its length and the elasticity is equal to infinity. The easier it is for firms to increase or decrease production, the more elastic is the supply.

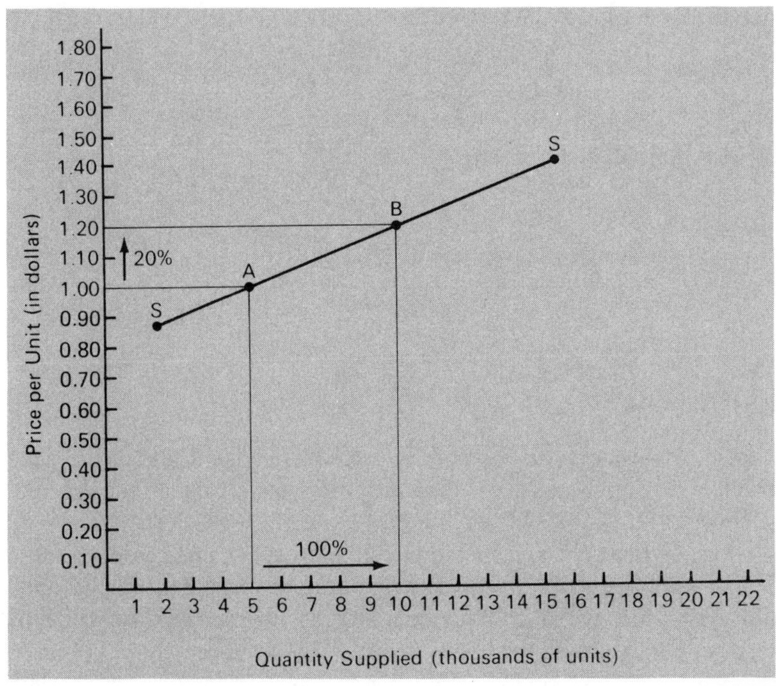

Figure 5:4 Elastic Supply of Product X

Table 5:2
Measuring the Elasticity of Supply

Formula for calculating the price-elasticity of supply:

$$es = \frac{\% \triangle qs}{\% \triangle p}$$

where es = price-elasticity of supply
$\% \triangle qs$ = percentage change in quantity supplied
$\% \triangle p$ = percentage change in the price of the good

Examples (*n* is the unknown number):

1. What is the elasticity of supply if a business firm increases its supply of a good by 30%, following an increase in the price of the good by 10%?

   Answer: $es = \frac{30}{10} = 3$

2. What will be the effect on the industry supply of a good if price is lowered by 5%?
   (a) if the elasticity of supply is 1.8

   Answer: $1.8 = \frac{n}{5} \therefore n = 1.8 \times 5 = 9$
   Supply will decrease by 9%.

   (b) if the elasticity of supply is 0.6

   Answer: $0.6 = \frac{n}{5} \therefore n = 0.6 \times 5 = 3$
   Supply will decrease by 3%.

Inelastic Supply

Supply is considered to be *price-inelastic* if a change in the price of the good or service causes a less than proportionate change in the quantity supplied of it.

Thus, in Figure 5:5, for example, an increase in price from $1.00 to $1.20 would result in an increase in supply from 5000 units to 5500 units. This means that a 20 per cent increase in price would cause only a 10 per cent increase in supply.

The elasticity of supply in this example is 0.5, obtained by dividing the percentage increase in quantity supplied (10 per cent) by the percentage increase in price (20 per cent).

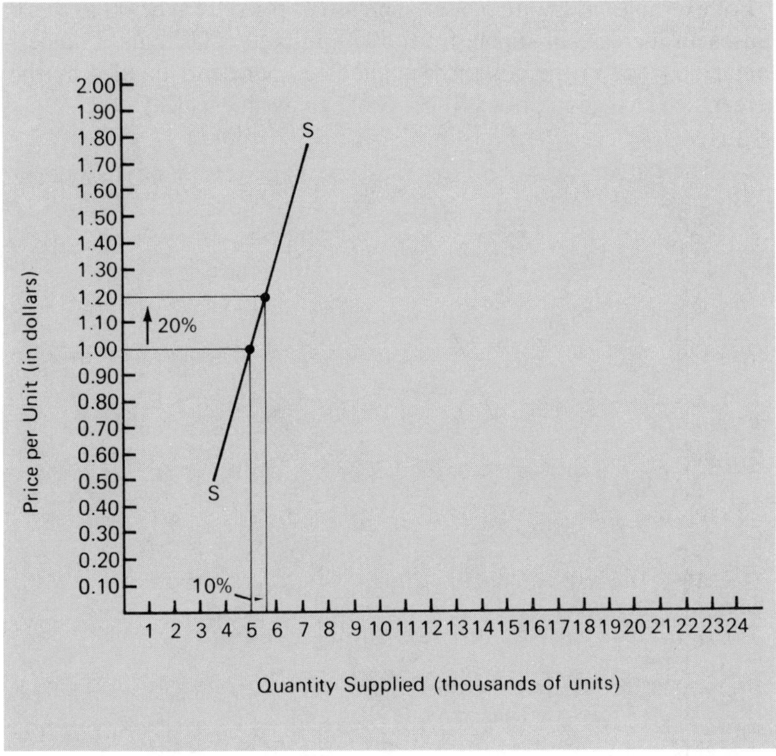

Figure 5:5 Inelastic Supply of Product Y

Supply is considered to be inelastic if its elasticity is less than 1. The smaller the fraction of 1, the more inelastic is the supply. Supply is said to be perfectly inelastic if producers will supply no more of a good or service whatever its market price. A perfectly inelastic supply is represented by a vertical line on the supply chart, and the elasticity is equal to zero.

If it is difficult for a firm to increase or decrease production (often because of considerable fixed investment), supply will tend to be inelastic, particularly in the short run.

Unitary Elasticity

Supply is considered to be of *unitary elasticity* when a percentage change in the price of a good or service is accompanied by an equal percentage change in the quantity supplied of it.

For example, in Figure 5:6, an increase in price from $1.00 to $1.20 causes an increase in supply from 5000 units to 6000 units. The percentage change in the quantity supplied (20 per cent) divided by the percentage change in price (20 per cent) gives an elasticity of 1.

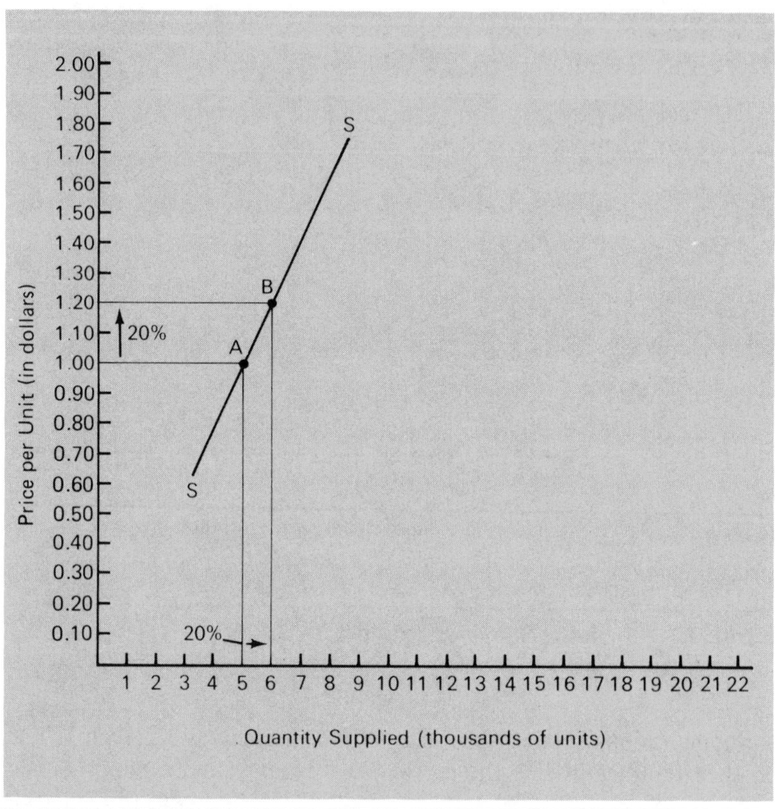

Figure 5:6 Supply of Unitary Elasticity

Short versus Long Run

Because of the fixed nature of business plants and equipment, supply responds much more sluggishly to a change in market price than does demand. In fact, economists have found it useful to distinguish between three different types of equilibria: (a) *momentary*—when output is fixed; (b) *short run*—when output has increased or decreased from existing plants; and (c) *long run*—when output has increased or decreased by firms entering or leaving the industry.

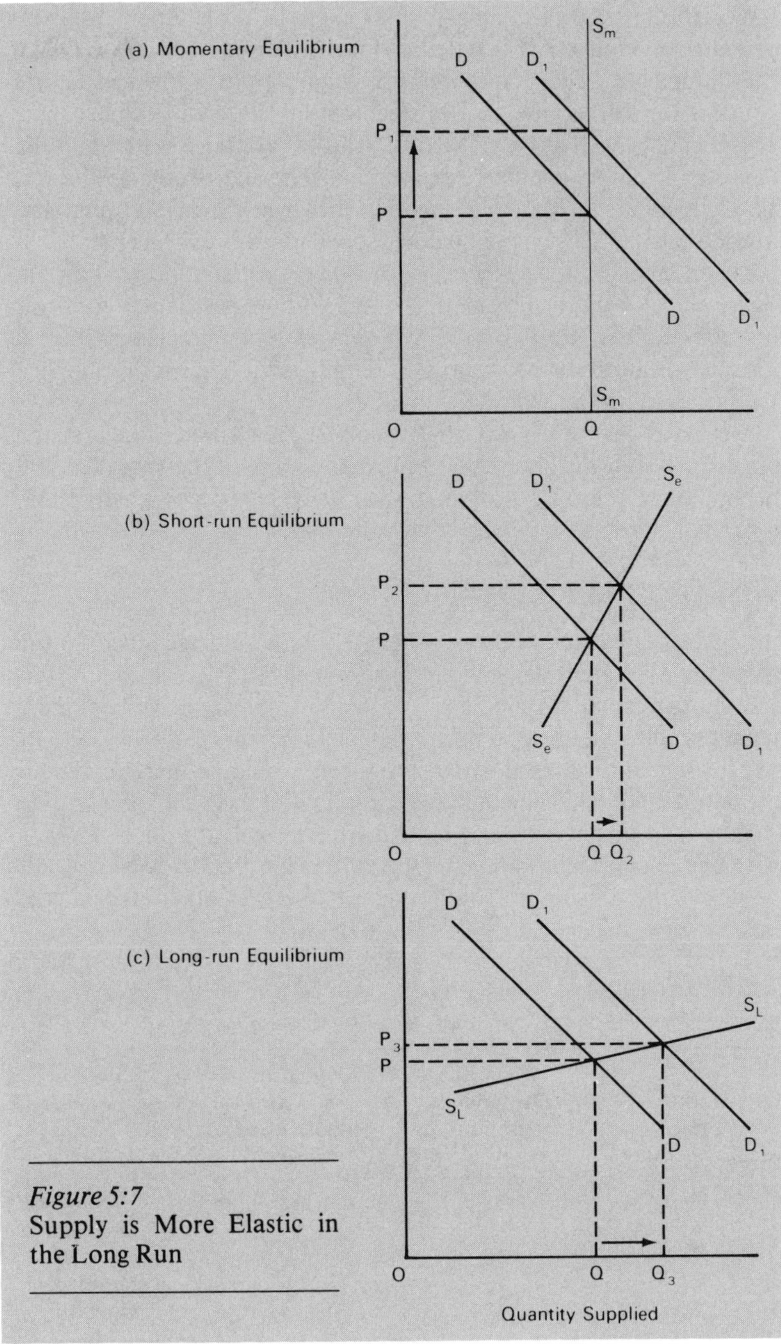

Figure 5:7
Supply is More Elastic in the Long Run

We can illustrate how supply varies over the three time periods by assuming (in Figure 5:7) that demand has increased from DD to D_1D_1. The immediate effect, or momentary equilibrium, shown in Figure 5:7(a), is for market price to rise steeply from OP to OP_1, while supply remains unchanged at OQ. The effect of the high price is to ration the fixed supply among would-be consumers. The short-run equilibrium, shown in Figure 5:7(b), is a situation in which the market price has dropped back to OP_2 as the quantity supplied from existing plants has increased from OQ to OQ_2. Finally, the long-run equilibrium, shown in Figure 5:7(c), reflects the fact that sufficient time has elapsed for firms to move into the industry and build new production facilities. Market price has dropped further from OP_2 to OP_3; and the quantity supplied has increased further from OQ_2 to OQ_3.

In conclusion, we can say that supply is much more elastic in the long run than in the short run. And supply in both the short run and the long run is more elastic than in the immediate or momentary situation in which supply is perfectly price-inelastic.

5.4: MARKET EQUILIBRIUM

The market price and amount sold of a good are determined by the interaction of market demand and market supply. We can see how this is so by combining (in Table 5:3) a market demand schedule and a market supply schedule, both for product A. At a price of $5.00, supply exceeds demand. Consequently, producers would be under competitive pressure to reduce the market price in order to sell all their output. There is also supply pressure, for the same reason, at a price of $4.00.

At a price of $1.00, however, the demand for product A far exceeds the supply. As consumers would compete with each other to obtain the

Table 5:3
Market Demand and Supply Schedules for Product A

Market Price (dollars per unit)	Quantity Demanded (thousand units per week)	Quantity Supplied (thousand units per week)	Pressure on Market Price
5	10	27	Downward
4	13	25	Downward
3	20	20	Neutral
2	30	15	Upward
1	45	5	Upward

limited supply, producers could sell all their output even if they were to charge more. There would consequently be upward pressure on market price. The same thing applies at a price of $2.00. Only at a market price of $3.00 would demand be equal to supply, with therefore no upward or downward pressure on price. This would be a state of *competitive market equilibrium* in which the quantity demanded is equal to the quantity supplied, with no tendency for price to change up or down. In other words, $3.00 is the *equilibrium market price* for product A. The amount sold at this price is 20 000 units per week. This situation can be illustrated by combining the market demand and supply curves that we can plot (see Figure 5:8) from the data contained in Table 5:3. The equilibrium market price and the amount sold are where the two curves intersect.

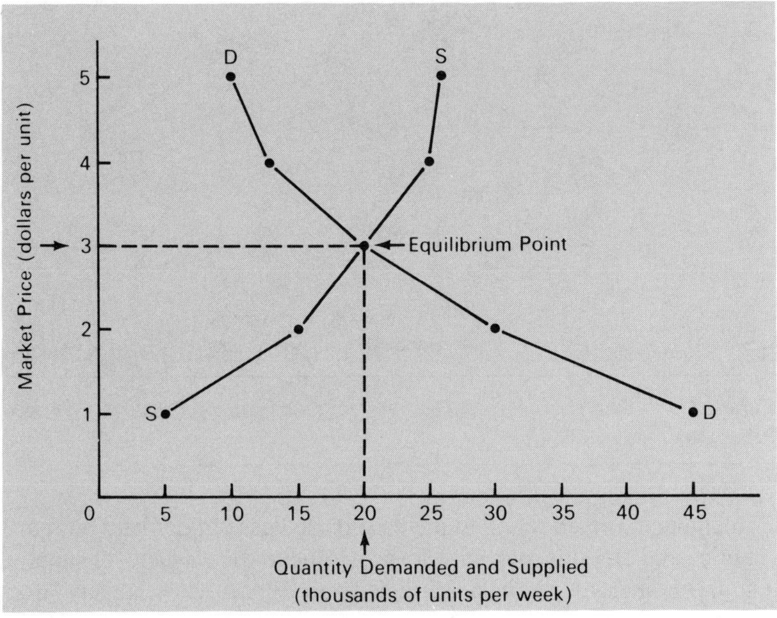

Figure 5:8 Market Demand and Supply Curves for Product A Combined to Show Equilibrium Market Price

Effect of a Change in Demand

What happens to the market price and amount sold of a good if there is a change in the demand for it? Let us assume that the demand for product A has increased because of a change in consumers' tastes. At each price, consumers are now willing and able to purchase more, and a new demand curve D_1D_1 now replaces the old demand curve DD. This new demand curve (see Figure 5:9) now intersects the supply curve SS at point B, so that market price is now $4.00 and the amount sold 25 000 units. The effect of the increase in demand has been to increase both the market price and the amount sold of the good.

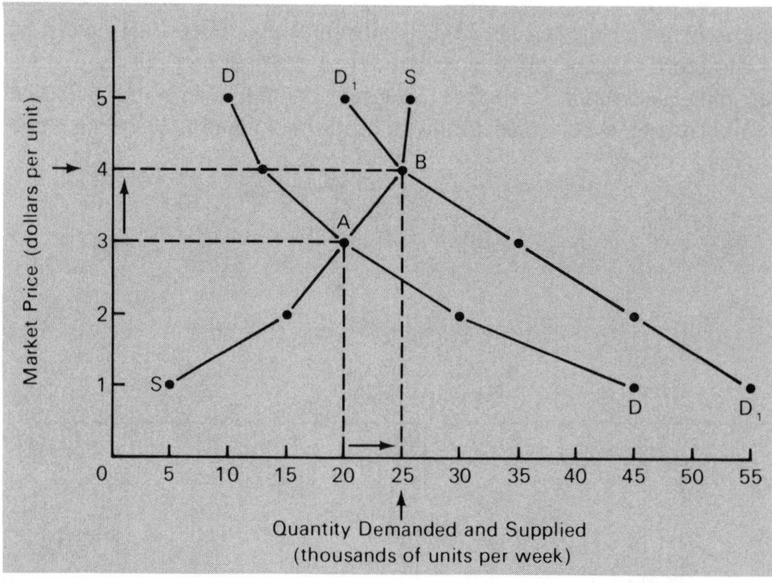

Figure 5:9 An Increase in Demand Causes an Increase in Market Price and Amount Sold

In practice, the effect of an increase or decrease in demand on market price and amount sold will vary according to the elasticity of supply. If supply is inelastic, an increase in demand will cause a relatively large increase in market price and a relatively small increase in the amount sold. If supply is elastic, an increase in demand will cause a relatively small increase in market price and a relatively large increase in the amount sold. This difference is illustrated in Figure 5:10, where S_iS_i is the inelastic supply curve and S_eS_e is the elastic one.

Effect of a Change in Supply

How does a change in supply affect the market price and amount sold

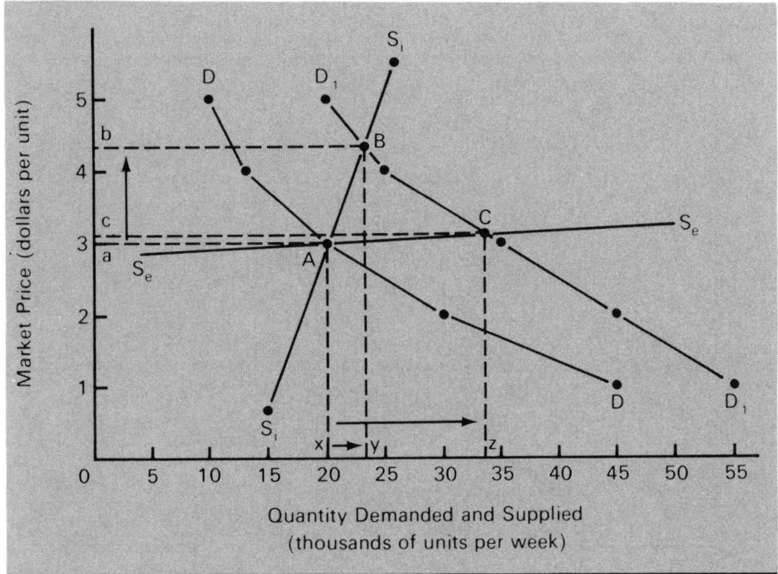

Figure 5:10 Elasticity of Supply Helps Determine the Effect of a Change in Demand

Note: Demand has increased from DD to D_1D_1. With an inelastic supply curve S_iS_i, market price increases from O_a to O_b and the amount sold from Ox to Oy.

With an elastic supply curve S_eS_e, market price increases from Oa to Oc and the amount sold from Ox to Oz.

---

of a good? Suppose that new technology has lowered the unit cost of production of product A. Producers are now willing and able to supply more at each price. As a result, a new supply curve S_1S_1 replaces the old supply curve SS. The new supply curve (see Figure 5:11) now intersects the demand curve DD at point B, so that market price is now about $2.25 and the amount sold about 27000 units. The increase in supply has caused a *reduction* in the market price and an *increase* in the amount sold.

The actual effect of any increase in supply on market price and amount sold will depend considerably on the nature of demand. If demand is inelastic, an increase in supply will cause a relatively large fall in market price, but only a relatively small increase in the amount sold. If, however, demand is elastic, an increase in supply will cause a relatively small reduction in market price and a relatively large increase in the amount sold. The way in which demand elasticity affects the outcome of an increase in supply is illustrated in Figure 5:12, where D_iD_i

is the inelastic demand curve and D_eD_e is the elastic one.

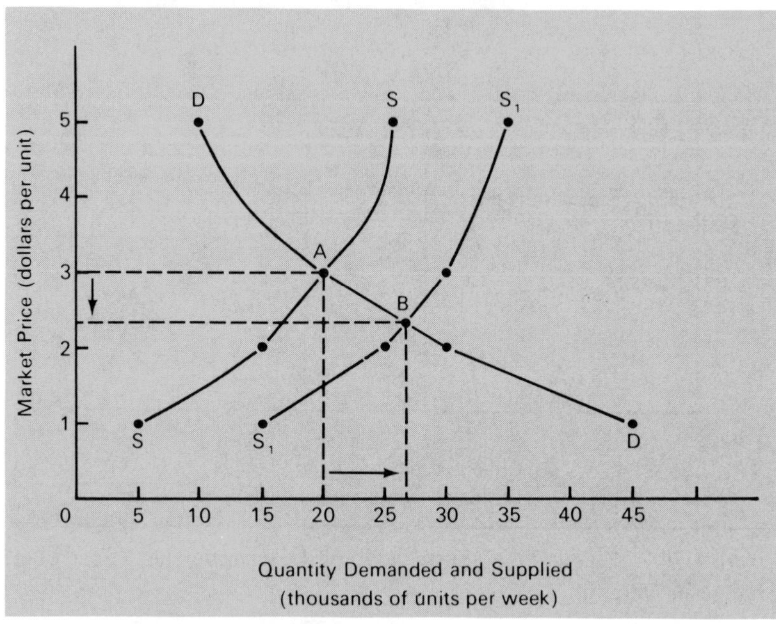

Figure 5:11 An Increase in Supply Causes a Decrease in Market Price and an Increase in Amount Sold

5.5: THE PRICE MECHANISM

Market price, as well as equating the demand for a product with its supply, plays a very important role in our economy in ensuring that business firms produce what the public wants to buy. If, for example, Canadians decide to purchase more tennis racquets, present stocks will be quickly depleted. Retailers will then place more orders with wholesalers and manufacturers. However, if domestic manufacturers and importers are unable to supply enough to meet the increased demand, the price of tennis racquets will rise, for producers will find that they can charge a higher price and still sell all they can supply. However, the higher price, combined with the same expenses, means a larger profit. This larger per unit profit will in turn encourage greater production of tennis racquets; present producers will enlarge their productive capacity and new firms will enter the industry. As a result, we have the situation in which a permanent increase in public demand for tennis racquets has led to an increase in market price. This, in turn, has

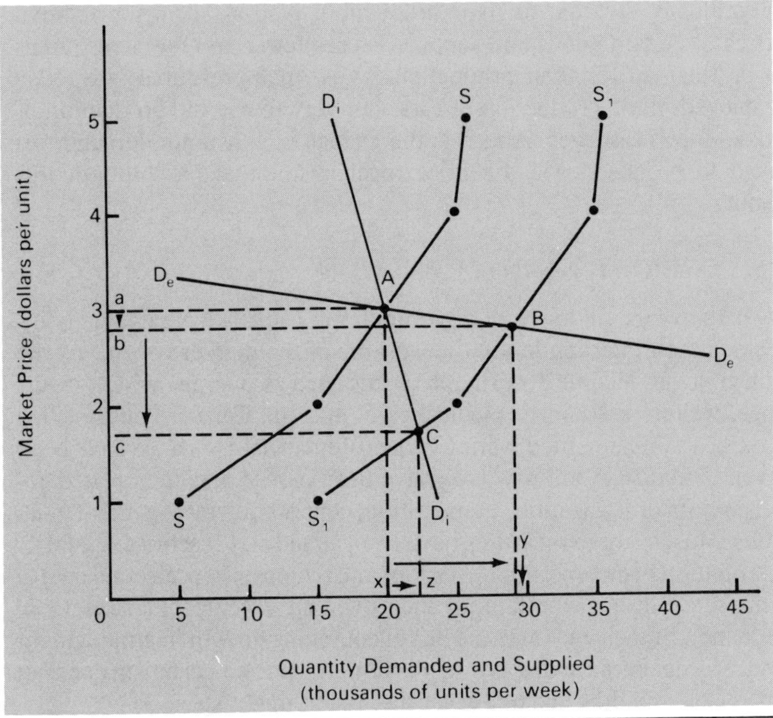

Note: Supply has increased from SS to S_1S_1. With an inelastic demand curve D_iD_i, market price decreases from O_a to O_c and the amount sold increases from O_x to O_z.

With an elastic demand curve D_eD_e, market price decreases from O_a to O_b and the amount sold increases from O_x to O_y.

Figure 5:12 Elasticity of Demand Helps Determine the Effect of a Change in Supply

induced an increase in the quantity supplied by more intensive use of existing productive capacity and by diverting resources from the production of other goods or from any unemployment pool. Conversely, if the public decides permanently to reduce their purchases of tennis racquets, the exact opposite will occur. And if the reduction in demand is sufficiently large, the fall in the market price and in profits will force firms out of the industry.

The action of market price in allocating the use of a country's resources is called the *price mechanism.* A rise in the price of certain goods and services relative to the prices of others, causes resources to be gradually diverted to their production. And a fall in the relative prices of certain goods and services causes fewer and fewer resources to be retained for their production. Thus, many resources are today employed in the production of cars, but very few in the production of horse-drawn carriages. And it is the change in consumer demand, relayed to producers via the price mechanism, that has brought this about.

5.6: GOVERNMENT INTERVENTION

Over the years, all levels of government in Canada have gradually increased their intervention in the working of the market system. At the federal level, income-security programs such as unemployment insurance, welfare assistance, medical care, and the Canada Pension Plan have been implemented; various types of financial assistance have been given to industry; and new laws have been passed or contemplated governing income taxation, competition, and labour-management relations. Most of these measures have been aimed at: (a) achieving a fairer distribution of income among persons and regions; (b) protecting people who, often through no fault of their own, are faced with a substantial reduction in their income; and (c) encouraging growth in employment and income. Because of this intervention, the price mechanism does not operate as smoothly as the earlier discussion might suggest.

Price Control

One important type of government invervention in the working of our economic system is price control. It is usually undertaken as part of a comprehensive prices and incomes policy designed to combat inflation. Sometimes, however, it is aimed at a particular product—for example, rental accommodation. What are its economic effects? Suppose, for example, that (a) the present market price of product A is $5.00 per unit; (b) the market demand and supply curves, DD and SS, are as shown in Figure 5:13; and (c) the government forbids any increase in the price for, say, a year. The price control in such a case does not create any immediate problem. The quantity supplied, OQ, at this price and the quantity demanded, OQ, are both equal. There is no surplus or shortage. However, suppose that two months later the demand curve (reflecting an increase in demand) has shifted to D_1D_1 while the supply curve has remained unchanged. Then, at the controlled price of $5.00 per unit, the quantity supplied would still be OQ, whereas the quantity demanded will have increased to OQ_1. In other words, demand at the controlled price exceeds supply with the result that shortages occur.

This gap between demand and supply is shown in Figure 5:13, as the distance AB.

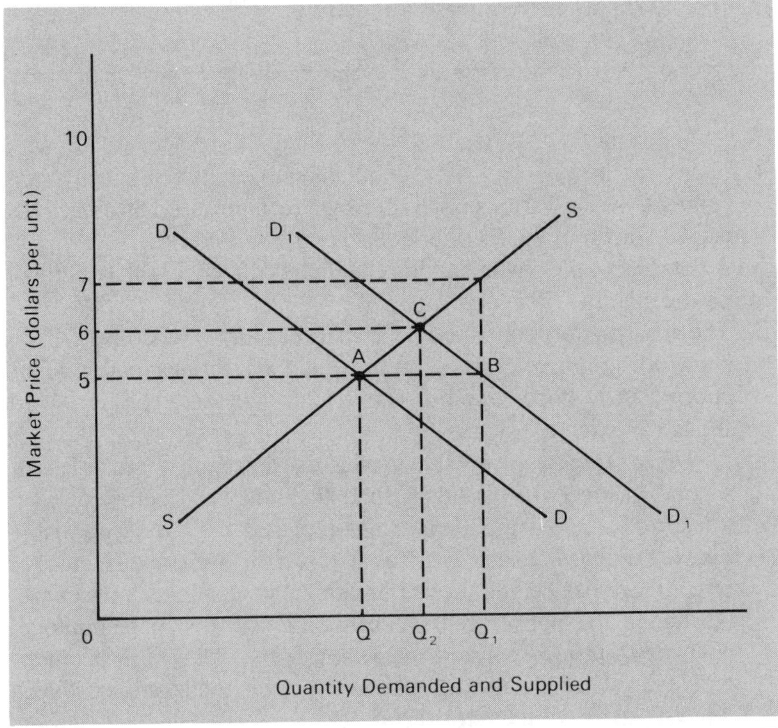

Figure 5:13 The Effects of Price Control on Market Supply and Demand

The economic effect of the price control is therefore to create a shortage of the product. This means that some consumers will go empty-handed or, if the government adopts a rationing scheme, receive a little of the product, but not as much as they would like, (or alternatively, be able to buy it on a lottery basis). The government has been successful in preventing the price of the product rising (a socially desirable goal), but at the expense of thwarting consumers' demand. Only if producers can obtain a market price of $7.00 per unit will they supply enough of the product to satisfy consumer demand. If the government wishes to control the price at $5.00 per unit and see supply increased to OQ_1 it will have to give producers a subsidy of $2.00 per unit. Without price control, the market equilibrium, with the new demand curve D_1D_1 would be a price of $6.00 per unit and a quantity demanded and supplied equivalent to OQ_2. The new demand curve and the old supply curve intersect at point C.

Summary

1. *Supply* is the quantity of a good or service that producers are willing to sell at various prices during a certain period of time. This can be shown in the form of a *market supply schedule*.
2. According to the law of supply, the higher the price, the larger will be the quantity of a good supplied.
3. The information contained in a market supply schedule can be shown diagrammatically in the form of a *market supply curve*. This curve usually slopes upward from left to right, in accordance with the law of supply.
4. A *change in supply* means that producers will supply more or less of a good in a certain period of time than they did before at each price; and a new supply curve has replaced the old. A *change in quantity supplied* means that, as a result of a change in market price, there has been a movement along an existing supply curve.
5. A change in supply occurs because of changes in technology, changes in production and marketing costs, changes in taxation, and even changes in the weather. Some goods are produced jointly; others compete for resources.
6. Supply is considered to be *elastic* if a change in the price of a good or service causes a more than proportionate change in the quantity supplied of it. It is considered to be *inelastic* if a change in price causes a less than proportionate change in the quantity supplied. Supply is considered to be of *unitary-elasticity* if a change in the price of a good causes an equal percentage change in the quantity supplied. Supply is much more elastic in the long run than in the short run.
7. The market price and amount sold of a good are determined by the interaction of market demand and market supply. *Competitive market equilibrium* exists when the quantity demanded is equal to the quantity supplied and there is no tendency for market price to move up or down.
8. If *supply* is *inelastic*, an increase in demand will cause a relatively large increase in market price and a relatively small increase in the amount sold. If *supply* is *elastic*, an increase in demand will cause a

relatively small increase in market price and a relatively large increase in the amount sold.

9. If *demand* is *inelastic*, an increase in supply will cause a relatively large fall in market price, but only a relatively small increase in the amount sold. If *demand* is *elastic*, an increase in supply will cause a relatively small reduction in market price and a relatively large increase in the amount sold.
10. The action of market price in allocating the use of a country's resources is called the *price mechanism*. A rise in the price of certain goods and services relative to the price of others causes resources to be gradually diverted to their production. And a fall in the relative prices of certain goods and services causes fewer resources to be retained for their production.
11. Over the years, all levels of government in Canada have gradually increased their intervention in the working of the market system: one important type of intervention is *price control*. Its main economic effect, apart from holding down prices, is to create a shortage of the product.

Key Terms

Market supply 98
Market supply schedule 98
Law of supply 98
Market supply curve 98
Regressive supply curve 100
Change in supply 100
Change in quantity supplied 100
Joint supply 102
Competitive supply 102
Elasticity of supply 102
Elastic supply 102
Inelastic supply 104
Unitary elasticity of supply 105
Competitive market equilibrium 109
Equilibrium market price 109
Price mechanism 112
Government intervention 114
Price control 114

Review Questions

1. How is supply defined in Economics?
2. What is the law of supply?
3. What is a supply curve? Why does it slope quite steeply in the short run?
4. What is an exceptional, or regressive, supply curve? Give an example of your own.

5. Distinguish between a change in supply and a change in the quantity supplied.
6. What reasons might account for a change in the supply of a good?
7. Distinguish between joint supply and competitive supply.
8. When is the supply of a good considered to be elastic? When is it considered to be inelastic?
9. How does the time period affect the elasticity of a supply of a good?
10. What determines the market price and amount sold of a good?
11. What is competitive market equilibrium?
12. What happens to the market price and amount sold of a good if there is a change in the demand for it? What significance does the elasticity of supply have?
13. How does a change in supply affect the market price and amount sold of a good?
14. What is the price mechanism? How does it help determine the allocation of a country's resources?
15. How does government intervene in the economy?
16. What are the economic effects of price controls?
17. According to the "law of supply," the higher the price, the larger the quantity supplied. Is this always true? Answer, with examples.
18. What happens to the supply curve, if manufacturers decide to produce less of a good even though its price remains unchanged?
19. What can happen to the supply curve of a product if business firms become more optimistic about the future?
20. Suppose that the price of a good rises by 30 per cent and output also increases by 30 per cent. What is the elasticity of supply?
21. Suppose that the price of a good increases by 20 per cent and the output increases by 10 per cent. What is the elasticity of supply?
22. Suppose that the price of a good increases by 8 per cent and that the elasticity of supply is 0.5. How would the supply change? What would be the answer if the elasticity were 2.0?
23. Give an example of a good for which the supply might be (a) perfectly elastic, and (b) perfectly inelastic. Explain.
24. Supply is more elastic in the long run. Explain.
25. Competitive market equilibrium is a notion rather than a fact. Explain.
26. Elasticity of supply helps determine the effect of a change in demand. Explain.
27. "If people weren't so hooked on coffee, we wouldn't have to pay so much for it." Discuss.
28. How have rent controls affected the supply of rental accommoda-

tion in Canada?

29. Show on a graph how the price of gold has changed in recent years. Explain what has happened to demand and supply.
30. How and why has the price of crude petroleum increased so much since 1973?
31. Indicate the typical price range in your district for the following types of home:
    (a) condominium apartment
    (b) townhouse
    (c) semi-detached house
    (d) detached house.
    What determines the price of a home? Why are they so expensive?
32. Explain, with a product example, what each of the following supply curves signifies.

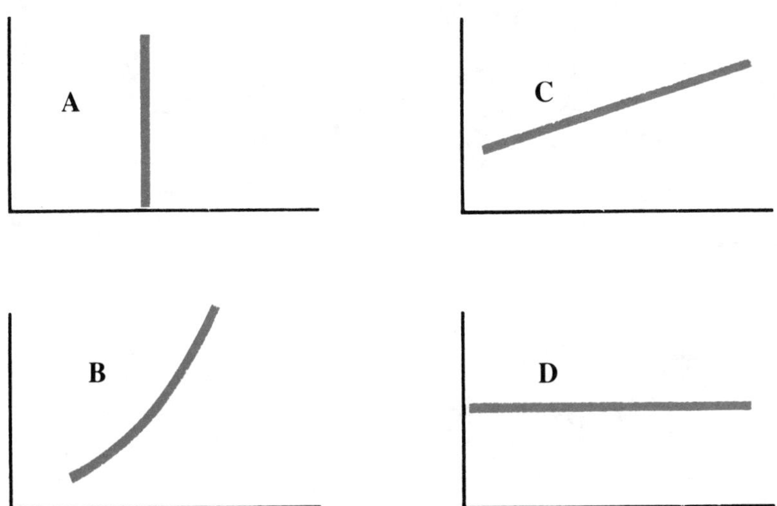

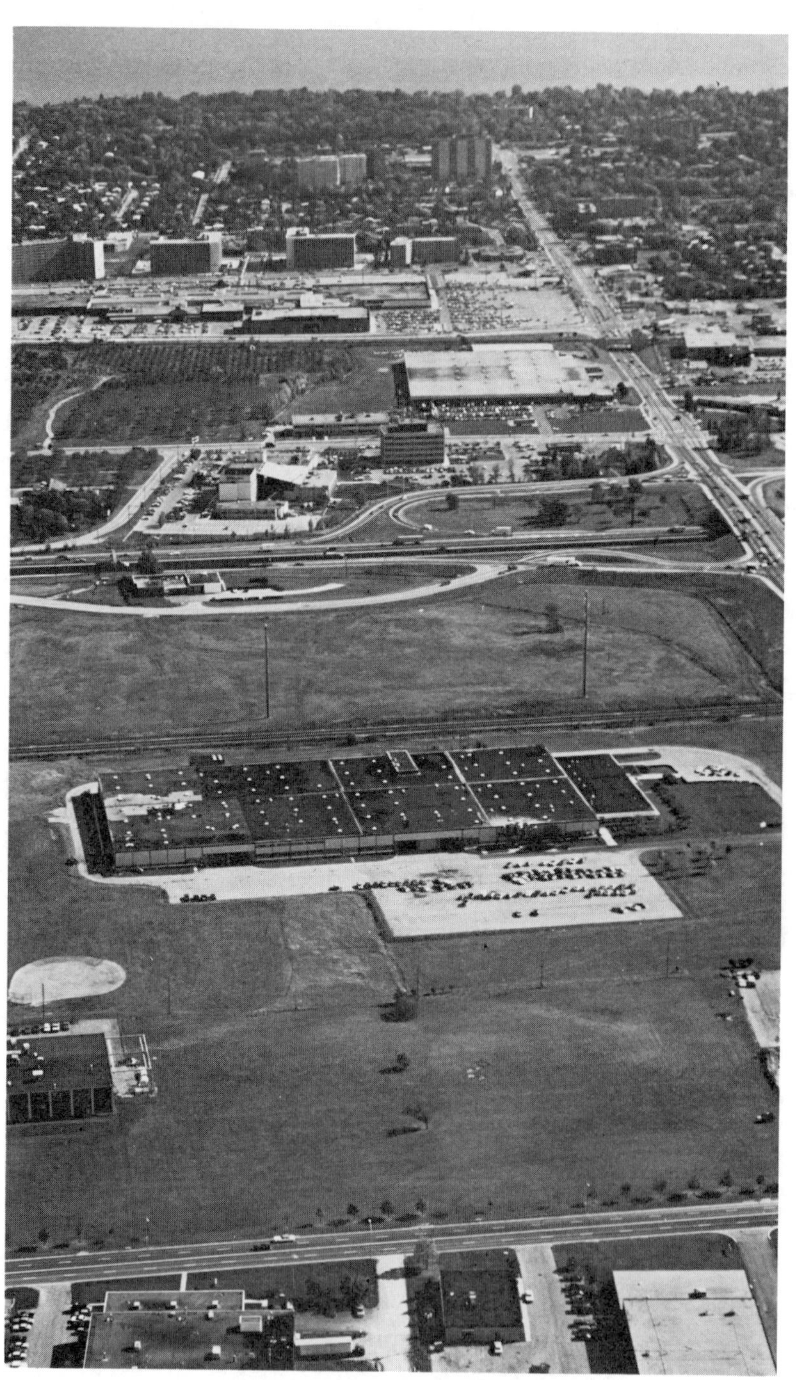

Part C:
THEORY OF THE FIRM

In this third part of the book, we look first at the various costs involved in the production of goods and services and how a firm decides how much to produce. We then consider the different possible market structures in which firms operate in Canada, ranging from the extremes of perfect competition and pure monopoly to the more usual, in-between situations of monopolistic competition and oligopoly.

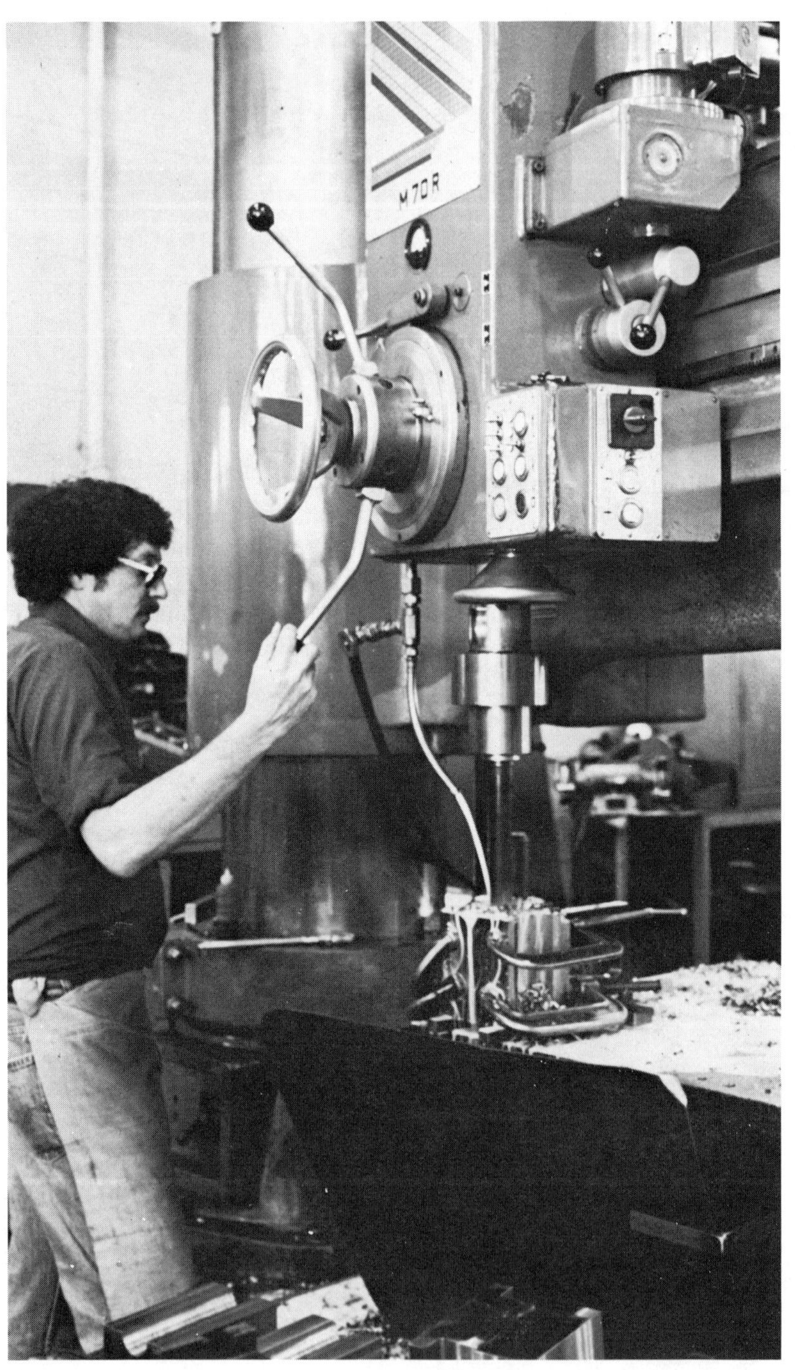
M70R

6. THE COSTS OF PRODUCTION

CHAPTER OBJECTIVES

A. To distinguish between the explicit and implicit costs of production
B. To show how the difference between private costs and social costs can often result in harm to society
C. To distinguish between fixed and variable costs and to examine how they vary as production increases
D. To explain the concepts of average and marginal cost and the relationship between them at different levels of output
E. To discuss the use of cost analysis in business decision-making

CHAPTER OUTLINE

A business firm's main objective is to make a profit. To do this, management must try to increase sales revenue and hold down costs. The larger the difference between the two, the greater is the profit—for revenue minus expenses equals profit.

In business, expenses, as shown in the income, or profit and loss statement, include only items on which money has been spent. However, from the economist's point of view, this is not always logical—because there are certain implicit costs that business firms tend to ignore with the use of conventional accounting procedure.

6.1: EXPLICIT AND IMPLICIT COSTS

The costs of production, as defined in economics, include both explicit costs and implicit costs. *Explicit costs* are expenses such as payment for materials, wages for labour, and rent for a building, that are actually paid out. The items included are the same as those shown under the heading "Expenses" in a business firm's income statement. Also included is depreciation, which is the allocation of the past cost of a capital item such as machinery over the expected years of its use. *Implicit costs* are costs not included among expenses in the income statement, but which are nevertheless incurred.

One important implicit cost can be the amount of owner's time devoted to the business. In many cases, the owners of a business *do* pay themselves a salary and this may even be more than the "going rate" for their services elsewhere. Often, particularly in a new business struggling to get established, or in an old one struggling to survive, this salary may be considerably less than what the owner could earn elsewhere. In some cases, no salary is paid at all. Obviously, to get a truer picture of production costs, a reasonable salary (paid or not) should be included among expenses.

The money that the owners have invested in a business must also not be overlooked. This money could, if employed elsewhere, earn at least the rate of interest currently being paid by the banks. Sometimes the owners will provide part of the capital of the business in the form of a loan. If this is interest-bearing, an interest cost is included among the firm's expenses. However, the equity, or ownership capital, does not receive interest. Therefore, to give a truer picture of the costs of production of a business, we should also include as a cost the return which this equity capital could have earned if invested elsewhere. In economics, this cost is called *normal profit*—the payment required to keep capital in a particular line of business.

6.2: SOCIAL VERSUS PRIVATE COSTS

In the past, the explicit and implicit costs considered by economists have been purely *private*, or *internal costs*. Recently, however, *social* or *external costs* are also being taken into account. These are the costs to society that result from business production. The most important of these are air and water pollution. More and more firms are, of course, taking steps to reduce pollution. If, for example, a business firm builds a taller smokestack or installs special treatment and recycling equipment for liquid wastes, its costs of production are thereby increased. These additional costs are part of its total costs and are therefore included in our analysis of a firm's production behaviour. However, many social or "external" costs, such as draining liquid wastes into a nearby stream or polluting the local air, are ignored.

6.3: FIXED AND VARIABLE COSTS

Some costs of production, such as materials, labour, fuel and power, can be altered relatively quickly. More materials can be purchased or orders cancelled; an extra shift can be worked or some employees laid off. But other costs, such as the wages of plant-maintenance and security staff, the heating costs of an office or factory building, or the implicit annual cost of equity capital tied up, can often be changed only after months or years. In some cases, it may be practically impossible to change them at all, and the plant or store may keep operating until there is no return whatsoever on the capital invested or on the owner's talents employed. Obviously, the longer the time that elapses, the greater the possibility of adjustment.

Short and Long Run

In analyzing a firm's production behaviour, we therefore find it useful to distinguish between the short and the long run. The *short run* is a period of time too short to allow a firm to alter its plant capacity, but long enough to permit it to vary the degree to which this capacity is utilized—for example, by adding or dropping a shift, or by setting up or abolishing a production line. The *long run*, conversely, is a period of time long enough to permit a firm to vary the capacity of the plant as well as the degree of its use. In the short run, the capacity of the plant is fixed; in the long run, it is variable. A short-run adjustment for a firm would be working on Saturday when the normal practice is a five-day week. A long-run adjustment would be building and equipping an addition to the plant. Obviously, the short run is different for each firm; some firms can add to their plant or move to a larger one more quickly than others.

The fixed capacity of a manufacturing plant or a retail store in the short run means that certain of a firm's costs are fixed. For example, so long as the owner's capital is tied up in the land, buildings, and equipment, there is a continuing implicit cost of, say, at least 12 per cent per annum if not more on the equity capital invested. There are also other fixed costs such as interest on borrowed capital; depreciation of capital assets; the wages of management, clerical staff, maintenance and security personnel; rent; insurance premiums; plant and equipment maintenance; and property taxes. These costs would be incurred even if output were nil. *Fixed costs*, therefore, are costs that remain unchanged whatever the level of output.

In business, fixed costs are usually called *overhead*. They can be divided into three parts. The first is *factory overhead*, or *factory burden*, comprising indirect labour costs such as salaries of the plant manager, supervisors, production and inspection clerks, and security staff; indirect material costs such as cleaning supplies; and insurance, rent, and taxes. The second is *administrative overhead*, comprising salaries to general management and "front office" staff such as accounting, personnel, and research. And the third is *sales overhead*, comprising salaries, commissions, and expenses; advertising; and promotion.

Many costs can, of course, be varied in the short run. As output is increased or decreased, payments for materials, labour, power, fuel, and transportation can also be changed. If a firm has not sufficient orders for its goods, it can perhaps lay off some of its workers and reduce the amount of materials purchased. If it is prospering, it can expand its labour force and purchase more materials. It will also use

Table 6:1
A Firm's Fixed, Variable, and Total Costs of Production

Units of Output	Total Fixed Cost (in dollars)	Total Variable Cost (in dollars)	Total Cost (in dollars)
0	100	0	100
1	100	60	160
2	100	110	210
3	100	150	250
4	100	180	280
5	100	220	320
6	100	280	380
7	100	360	460
8	100	470	570
9	100	620	720
10	100	820	920

more fuel, power, and other production inputs. These costs are called *variable costs*, because they vary according to the level of output.

How do costs vary as a firm's output increases? The term *cost function* is used to describe the relationship between costs and the rate of output. Obviously, in the short run, fixed costs are the same whatever the output. The fixed-cost function is shown in Table 6:1 and illustrated in Figure 6:1.

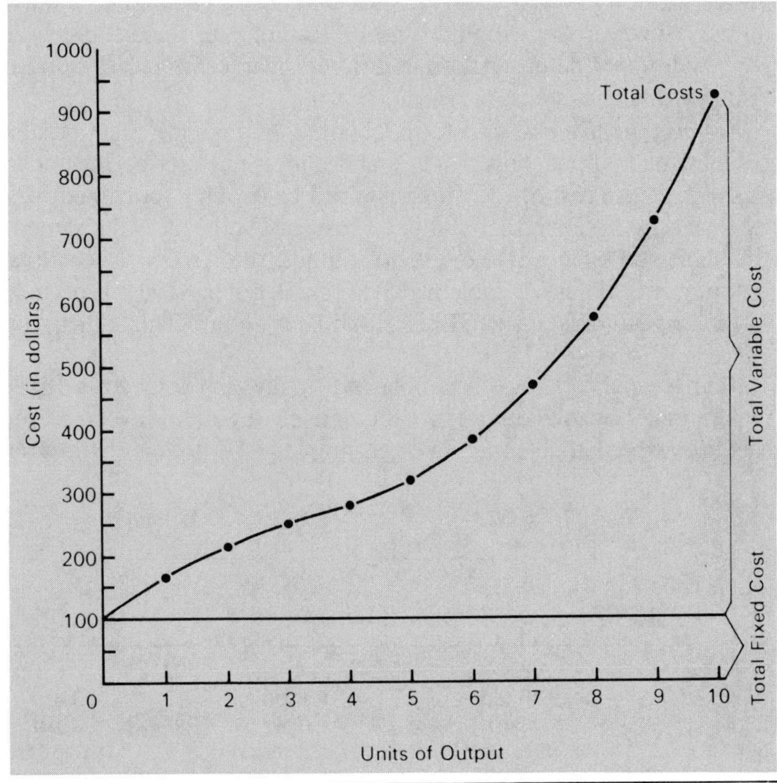

Figure 6:1 Total Cost Comprises Fixed and Variable Costs

But how do variable costs increase? Is it in strict proportion to the increase in output? The answer is no. In fact, up to a certain level of output, the increase in total variable costs will usually be at a decreasing rate. After that, it will be at an increasing rate. The variable-cost function, illustrating this situation, is also shown in Table 6:1 and Figure 6:1, where we can see the relationship between variable costs, fixed costs, and total costs. For simplicity, we have kept the numbers in our example quite small. They can, if desired, be multiplied by hundreds or thousands.

In practice, not all costs fit neatly into one category or the other.

6.4: AVERAGE COST

So far we have looked solely at total production costs in relation to output. However, we will find it useful for our later understanding of price and output determination in different market structures to think also in terms of average, or per unit, costs.

Average variable cost (AVC) is obtained by dividing total variable costs by total output. This cost at first declines, but later begins to rise.

Average fixed cost or (AFC) is obtained by dividing total fixed costs by total output. Since the total fixed cost, or overhead, is the same in the short run whatever the level of output, the AFC will decline as output grows. Thus, in Table 6:2, AFC starts out at $100 but declines as production increases to $10 at 10 units of output. The falling AFC curve is illustrated in Figure 6:2.

Average total cost (ATC) is obtained by dividing total costs (fixed plus variable) by total output, or, alternatively, by adding average fixed cost to average variable cost. In our example, ATC declines from $160

Table 6:2
A Firm's Average Costs of Production

Units of Output	Average Fixed Cost (in dollars)	Average Variable Cost (in dollars)	Average Total Cost (in dollars)
1	100.00	60.00	160.00
2	50.00	55.00	105.00
3	33.33	50.00	83.33
4	25.00	45.00	70.00
5	20.00	44.00	64.00
6	16.67	46.67	63.34
7	14.29	51.43	65.72
8	12.50	58.75	71.25
9	11.11	68.89	80.00
10	10.00	82.00	92.00

at 1 unit of output to $92 at 10 units of output. The ATC curve is also shown in Figure 6:2

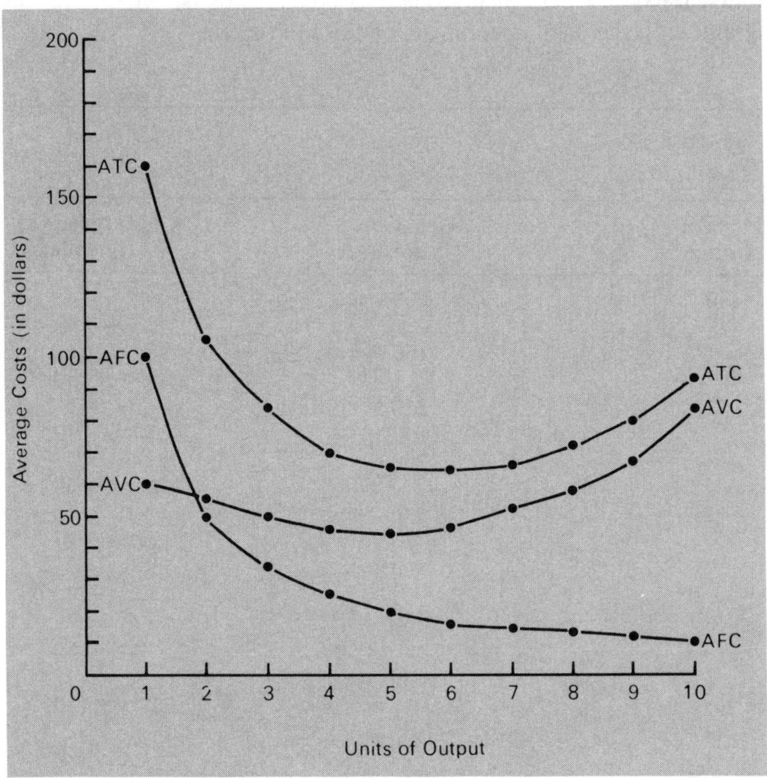

Figure 6:2 The Short-Run Average-Cost Curves

6.5: MARGINAL COST

The term *marginal cost* is used to denote the extra cost of increasing output by one unit. The concept of marginal cost is important because it is the cost that a business manager tends to consider above all when deciding to reduce or increase output. The expected additional revenue from a proposed increase in output must be weighed against the additional marginal cost involved. If the expected marginal revenue is less than the expected marginal cost, the manager will be reluctant to produce more.

In practice, marginal cost at first declines (see Table 6:3) then begins to rise as a firm reaches its optimum production level. Eventually, marginal cost may rise very steeply as overtime rates of pay and other unusual expenses are incurred and as breakdowns become more frequent, with the plant operating at or close to full capacity.

Table 6:3
Marginal Cost

Units of Output	Total Cost (in dollars)	Marginal Cost (in dollars)
0	100	
		60
1	160	
		50
2	210	
		40
3	250	
		30
4	280	
		40
5	320	
		60
6	380	
		80
7	460	
		110
8	570	
		150
9	720	
		200
10	920	

6.6: RELATIONSHIP BETWEEN AVERAGE COST AND MARGINAL COST

If we look at Table 6:4, we can see that when AVC is falling, AVC exceeds MC. And when AVC is rising, MC exceeds AVC. Also, we can see that when ATC is falling, ATC exceeds MC. And when ATC is rising, MC exceeds ATC. This means (see Figure 6:3) that the MC curve intersects the AVC and ATC curves at their lowest points.

The reason for this relationship between average cost and marginal cost is that marginal cost represents the amount by which total variable costs and total costs (fixed and variable) change with an extra unit of output. So long as marginal cost is less than average variable cost and average total cost, the AVC and ATC curves respectively must be sloping downward. Once marginal cost exceeds AVC and ATC, those curves must be sloping upward to represent the fact that the amounts are increasing. Only when marginal cost has stopped declining and has begun to rise would it be equal to AVC and ATC. And this is the point at which the MC curve intersects the AVC and ATC curves.

Firms incur marginal cost as they expand output. If the marginal cost is less than the average cost, the average cost falls. When the marginal cost equals the average cost, the average cost remains the same. When marginal cost exceeds average cost, the average cost rises. Of course, marginal cost only bears this relationship to average variable cost and average total cost. It does not bear it to average fixed cost because fixed cost remains the same whatever the level of output and is unaffected by marginal cost.

Table 6:4
The Relationship between Average Cost and Marginal Cost

Units of Output	Total Cost (in dollars)	Average Variable Cost (in dollars)	Average Total Cost (in dollars)	Marginal Cost (in dollars)
0	100			
1	160	60.00	160.00	60
2	210	55.00	105.00	50
3	250	50.00	83.33	40
4	280	45.00	70.00	30
5	320	44.00	64.00	40
6	380	46.67	63.34	60
7	460	51.43	65.72	80
8	570	58.75	71.25	110
9	720	68.89	80.00	150
10	920	82.00	92.00	200

6.7: SCALE OF PRODUCTION

As a business increases the scale of its production, from say the tens of thousands of units to many hundreds of thousands, its average costs of production per unit of output will decline. This is in addition to the decline in average total costs because of the spreading of fixed overhead among more units of output. Eventually, however, average costs will start to rise.

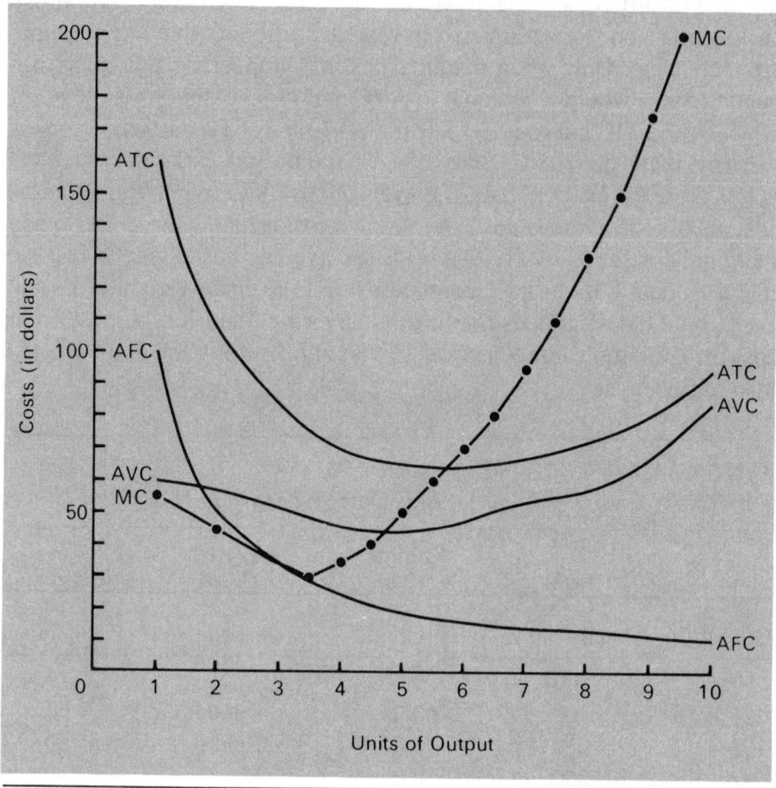

Figure 6:3 The Marginal Cost Curve Intersects the ATC and AVC Curves at their Minimum Points

Economies of Scale

The additional fall in average total costs occurs because of what are called the "economies of scale". These economies, or "savings" arise in several different ways.

1. Greater specialization of labour and equipment. In a mass-production plant—for example, a car manufacturer—the division of labour is extremely great. The work is broken down into small steps and each worker performs a highly specialized task. This specialization often creates boredom and frustration. However, because of greater labour proficiency, it also greatly increases output per worker and so lowers per unit production costs.

Specialization also extends to equipment. With a large quantity of the same good being produced, it is possible to use special-purpose rather than general-purpose machines. Highly specialized machine tools, including industrial robots, although expensive, more than pay for themselves in lower per unit production costs—so long as the production runs are long.

2.More efficient use of common services. There are many common services in a plant, or among branch plants of a single firm, such as production planning and control, research and development, personnel recruitment and training, financing, electronic data processing, advertising, purchasing, and warehousing. Usually, the cost of such services does not increase in proportion to output. Consequently, it is often possible to obtain a reduction in the cost of these services per unit of output as production increases. The larger the output, the wider these costs are spread.

3. Quantity buying. Large-scale production means large purchases of materials and parts. This enables the firm's purchasing managers to obtain quantity price discounts from suppliers and so reduce the cost of materials and parts.

4. Mechanized handling. Long production runs means that workers and machines can be grouped along a production or assembly line. Since the materials and parts always travel the same path, highly mechanized materials-handling methods such as chain-conveyor systems can be used. Mechanized handling lowers per unit costs of handling materials, parts, and finished products.

5. Better use of by-products. In a small firm, by-products are often discarded because the amount is small. With large-scale production, there is an incentive to devise a use for them. With large firms, these by-products, such as wood shavings from sawmills, can be made into a product that can provide a useful source of revenue and so help offset the costs of production.

Diseconomies of Scale

Once production in a plant becomes extremely large, inefficiencies start to arise. These are called the *diseconomies of scale*.

The most important of these diseconomies is the difficulty in managing such a large operation. Up to a certain point, large-scale production can enable a firm to "stretch" its managers further. However, once a firm becomes too large, and there is no proper decentralization of authority, management can become a nightmare, with the whole firm

DIRECTOR
OF
RED TAPE

entangled in red tape. A second diseconomy is the growing number of mechanical breakdowns that seem to arise with very large-scale production. A third one is the likely worsening of labour-management relations and its effect on labour productivity. These diseconomies are one reason why some manufacturers prefer to have several medium-sized plants widely dispersed, rather than just one large-sized plant. The other reason for decentralized operations is the greater competitive effectiveness that comes from being close to one's markets.

Finally, we must remember that, whatever the economies or diseconomies, there must be sufficient demand to justify large-scale production. The *extent of the market* is, in fact, the key to obtaining benefit from large-scale production. If a firm cannot sell all its output, the benefit of any cost reduction obviously disappears.

6.8: COST ANALYSIS AND BUSINESS DECISION-MAKING

In conclusion to this chapter, we should emphasize that business managers are very much concerned with their production costs—because the higher the average cost of each unit produced compared with the factory selling price, the lower a firm's profit margin. Also, in deciding whether to increase output (either by working overtime or by enlarging the plant), managers need to know how average production costs will decline with a larger volume of production. Such information is also essential in making pricing decisions—for cost is one important factor that is considered in setting the price of a product. (Others are management's analysis of consumer demand and the prices of competing products). Also, as explained in the next chapter, an estimate of a firm's total production costs at different levels of output is required if a firm's managers are to make use of break-even analysis in evaluating a new business venture—whether it be a new product, a new machine, or a new branch plant.

By contrast, the concepts of marginal cost and marginal revenue are less generally applied, usually because of the difficulty of actual measurement, except historically, and because of the usual impracticability of varying output in small quantities.

Summary

1. A firm's *total costs* comprise explicit and implicit costs. *Explicit costs* are expenses, such as payments for materials, wages or labour, and rent for a building, that are actually paid out. *Implicit costs* are costs, such as the owner's time, that may not be included

among expenses in the income statement, but which are nevertheless incurred. In the past, the explicit and implicit costs considered by economists have been purely *private* or *"internal"* ones. Nowadays, however, *social* or *"external"* costs are also being taken into account.

2. A firm's total costs, looked at in another way, comprise fixed and variable costs. *Fixed costs* are items such as rent of buildings and management salaries that are fixed, at least in the short run. *Variable costs* are items such as payments for materials that will vary in the short run.
3. In considering price and output determination, we find it useful to calculate *average fixed cost* (total fixed costs divided by total output), *average variable cost* (total variable cost divided by total output), and *average total cost.*
4. The term *marginal cost* is used to denote the extra cost of increasing output by one unit.
5. The *marginal cost curve* intersects the average variable cost curve and the average total cost curve at their lowest points.
6. If there is an increase in the scale of a firm's production, average total costs may fall even faster than usual. This is because of the *economies of scale*—that is, the savings from greater specialization of labour and equipment, more efficient use of common services, quantity buying, mechanized handling, and better use of by-products. However, average total costs eventually rise more and more sharply because of the *diseconomies of scale*—that is, the extra costs of managing a very large operation, even despite attempts at decentralization.
7. The extent of the market is the key to obtaining the benefits of large-scale production.
8. Business managers are vitally concerned, in their decision-making, with production costs. However, the emphasis is usually on total costs (compared with total revenue) rather than marginal costs (compared with marginal revenue).

Key Terms

Profit 123
Explicit costs 124
Implicit costs 124
Normal profit 124
Private (or internal) costs 124
Administrative overhead 126
Sales overhead 126
Variable costs 127
Average cost 128
AFC 128

Review Questions

1. Why do economists include implicit costs among total costs, even though they may not appear in a firm's income statement? What are such implicit costs?
2. What are social or external costs? Why do economists argue that they should be included among a firm's total costs?
3. Distinguish between fixed and variable costs. What is the significance of the time period?
4. How do costs vary as a firm's output increases?
5. What are the various types of average cost? How are they calculated?
6. What is marginal cost? What is its significance?
7. What is the relationship between marginal cost and total cost?
8. What is the relationship between average cost and marginal cost?
9. What are the various economies of scale? What are the eventual diseconomies?
10. The extent of the market is the key to obtaining benefit from large-scale production. Explain.
11. Why, in practice, do business firms neglect to include social costs when making investment and other decisions? Why should they be included?
12. In the long run, there is no such thing as fixed costs. Explain.
13. What are the various categories of business "overhead"? What is the purpose of such a classification?
14. To what extent do business firms use marginal cost analysis in their production decisions?
15. The average cost of production invariably declines as output increases. Comment.
16. Explain why some busines firms are large and others small. Is there an optimum size for each type of production?
17. How does geographical location affect the optimum scale of production?
18. How does government policy affect the optimum scale of production?

19. Many large firms are the result of market power rather than of economies of large-scale production. Discuss.
20. Government transportation subsidies help large-scale Ontario manufacturers at the expense of smaller local firms in other parts of Canada. Discuss.
21. The small size of the Canadian market is no excuse for failure to take advantage of the economies of large-scale production. Discuss, in the light of Canada's export opportunities.
22. Canadian manufacturing costs are too high to permit unrestricted competition by foreign manufacturers in Canada's domestic market. Discuss.
23. Nowadays it makes sense for many Canadian retailers to have most of their goods manufactured abroad. Discuss.
24. Government policies (e.g. minimum wages, unemployment insurance) are making Canadian manufacturing less and less competitive. Discuss.
25. Japan produced its first car only a few years ago. Now it is outselling everyone else. Discuss, with particular reference to relative costs.
26. Canada should have only one car manufacturer. Discuss, with reference to production and marketing costs.

7. *REVENUE, COSTS, AND PROFIT*

CHAPTER OBJECTIVES

A. To distinguish between total revenue, average revenue, and marginal revenue
B. To indicate how a firm determines its best-profit output
C. To explain the use of the break-even concept in business
D. To explain why a firm may continue to produce even though its total costs may exceed its total revenue
E. To indicate when a firm reaches its shut-down point
F. To define briefly the basic market structures that exist in Canada, as an introduction to the following chapters

CHAPTER OUTLINE

7.1: SALES REVENUE

The money that a firm receives in exchange for its products is called its *sales revenue*. Thus, if a firm sells 5000 units of product X for $10.00 each, its total sales revenue is $50 000.

Average Revenue

The total sales revenue, when divided by the number of units of the good sold, gives us the firm's *average revenue*. Thus, if a firm sells 5000 units of its product for a total sales revenue of $50 000 its average revenue is $10.00—the same as the price.

Marginal Revenue

If the selling price of the firm's product is $10.00, the sale of one additional unit will increase the firm's total sales revenue by $10.00. If the product is sold only by the thousand, the sale of an extra thousand units will increase sales revenue by $10000. This extra amount of money is called the *marginal revenue.*

In certain types of industry, a firm will always be able to sell more goods at the same price. Consequently, marginal revenue will remain constant—in our example at $10.00

In other situations, more can be sold only at a lower price. If the extra units can be sold to a separate market (for example, a foreign country), the lower price may apply only to the extra units sold. Suppose, however, the firm is selling the extra units to the same market; then the price at which all the firm's output is sold will have to be reduced to increase the number of units sold. The firm's marginal revenue in such a case will be the extra revenue from the sale of the extra unit or units, *minus* the reduction in price on the units already being sold. Thus if a firm can sell an extra 1000 units by reducing its price for all its units to $9.50 each, its marginal revenue would be only $7000. This amount is obtained by subtracting the $2500 no longer received on the other 5000 units from the $9500 received for the extra 1000 units, because of the reduction in price from $10.00 to $9.50 each. If the firm can avoid reducing the $10.00 price for existing sales and sell the extra 1000 units in some other market, even for only $8.00 each, its marginal revenue would be greater—$8000 as compared with $7000.

7.2: BEST-PROFIT OUTPUT

One method of theoretically determining a firm's most desirable output is by comparing marginal revenue and marginal cost. So long as marginal revenue exceeds marginal cost, it will be profitable for a firm to produce and sell more goods. Conversely, if marginal cost exceeds marginal revenue, it would be more profitable for a firm to produce and sell less. A firm would be in an equilibrium situation, with optimum output and sales and with maximum profit, when its marginal revenue equals its marginal cost. This concept is elaborated and illustrated in the following chapters.

Total Revenue and Total Costs

In business, because of the difficulty of measuring marginal revenue and marginal costs, particularly on a current rather than historical basis, management usually concentrates its attention on a comparison of total revenue and total costs. And if a firm's primary goal is to maximize profit (as it often is), it will try to make its total revenue as large as possible and its total costs as small as possible. A firm will therefore usually try to produce and sell that output at which total revenue exceeds total costs by the widest possible margin. In economics, we assume that total costs include "normal profit."

Break-Even Point

Business firms vary greatly in their efficiency and their profits differ accordingly. The more efficient firms make considerably more than "normal profit," while their less efficient rivals may find that their total revenue is only equal to their total costs. Since their total cost includes a normal profit, they are content to stay in the industry rather than look elsewhere. Such firms are operating at a break-even point.

The concept of break-even analysis is widely used in business to decide not only whether to stay in business but also whether to launch a new product, buy new equipment, open a new plant, etc. In the latter case, the first step is to estimate total costs (fixed and variable) at different levels of output. The second step is to estimate the total revenue that these different levels of output would bring. The third step is to compare total revenue and total costs at different levels of output to ascertain the break-even point—the level of output and sales at which total revenue equals total costs. Then, after market research, a management decision can be made on the likelihood of the firm's achieving such a level of sales and the time period required to do so. Of course, a firm would want to do better than just break even. But the break-even point is the minimum goal. If the sales prospects look grim, the investment can be cancelled and little money lost. An example of break-even analysis is illustrated in Table 7:1 and Figure 7:1.

7.3: LEAST-LOSS OUTPUT

A firm may find, perhaps because of increased competition or higher wages, that it is no longer breaking even—in other words, its total revenue is now less than its total costs. Obviously, this may be only a temporary situation and may be remedied by changes within the firm (for example, a more determined marketing effort or a reduction in production costs) or by external factors such as an improvement in the economy or a quota on imports.

Once a firm has invested time and money in equipping a factory and training a labour force, it may continue to operate for some time even though its total costs exceed its total revenue. This is because it has certain fixed costs (such as depreciation of the equipment) that will be incurred whether or not the firm produces.

Thus, even if the less than break-even situation continues more or less permanently, a firm may find it worthwhile to continue to produce so long as its revenue covers its variable costs of production. Ideally,

Table 7:1
Example of Break-even Analysis

Situation: XYZ Enterprise Ltd. is contemplating the introduction of a new product. Fixed and variable costs have been estimated for different levels of output. Variable costs are estimated at an average of $5.00 per unit over the expected range of production and includes an allowance for units scrapped. An analysis of demand and of prices charged by competitors for similar products suggests a factory selling price of $10.00 per unit. *Question:* What volume of sales would be required to break even? *Answer:* 10 000 units per month, determined as follows:

Output per month (1000s of units)	Fixed Costs (share of overhead) (in $1000s)	Variable Costs (in $1000s)	Total Costs (in $1000s)	Total Revenue (in $1000s)	Profit or Loss (in $1000s)
1	50	5	55	10	−45
2	50	10	60	20	−40
3	50	15	65	30	−35
4	50	20	70	40	−30
5	50	25	75	50	−25
6	50	30	80	60	−20
7	50	35	85	70	−15
8	50	40	90	80	−10
9	50	45	95	90	− 5
B.E.P. 10	50	50	100	100	0
11	50	55	105	110	+ 5
12	50	60	110	120	+10
13	50	65	115	130	+15
14	50	70	120	140	+20
15	50	75	125	150	+25
16	50	80	130	160	+30
17	50	85	135	170	+35
18	50	90	140	180	+40
19	50	95	145	190	+45
20	50	100	150	200	+50

the revenue should also make some contribution towards covering the firm's fixed costs (ones that would be incurred whether the firm produces or not). It will have to decide at what level of output its losses are minimized. This will be the output at which marginal revenue equals marginal cost, even though total costs at this output exceed total revenue.

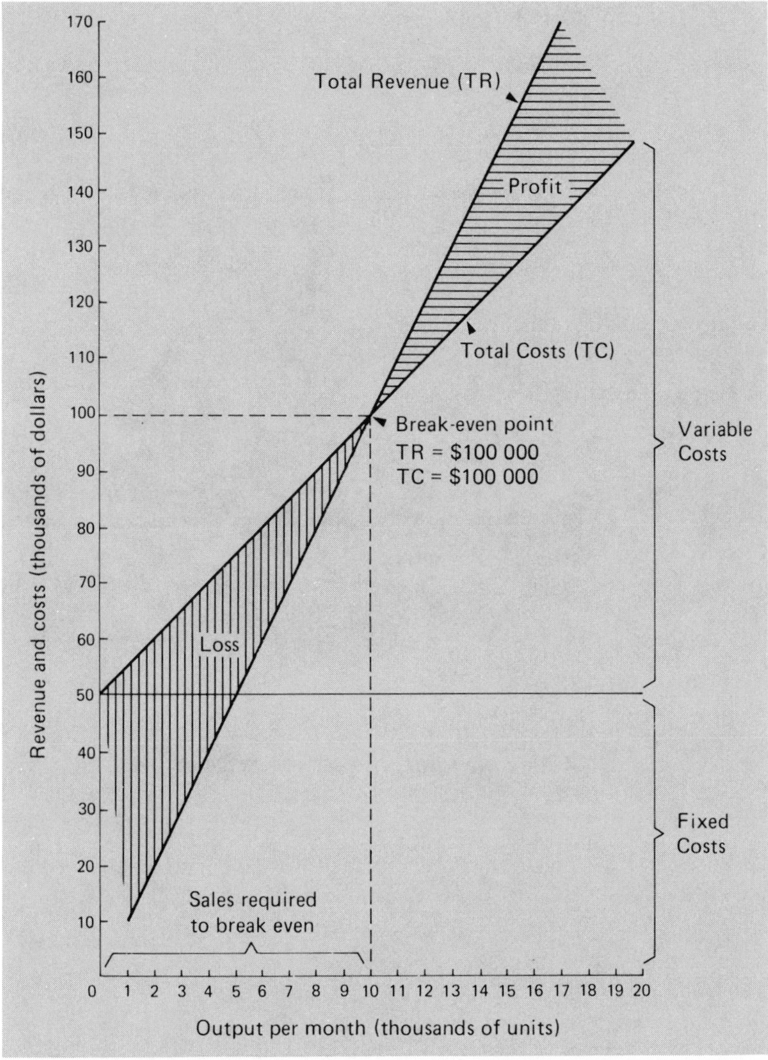

Figure 7:1 The Break-Even Point

"Who's the idiot who set our price below cost?"

7.4: SHUT-DOWN POINT

Only when a firm's total revenue fails to cover its variable costs of production will it be forced to close down—through lack of funds to buy materials and parts and pay wages, utilities, etc. This would be its *shut-down point*. Shut down may be postponed, of course, by borrowing or drawing on financial reserves.

7.5: DIFFERENT MARKET STRUCTURES

We said earlier that consumer demand largely determines what is produced in our economy. Thus, if consumers want more of a good, the increase in their demand will cause inventories to decline and the market price to rise and so induce profit-seeking firms to produce more. Conversely, a reduction in demand will cause stocks to rise, the market price to fall, and so cause firms to produce less. But this use of market price as a mechanism for allocating the use of a country's resources assumes that firms compete effectively with each other in supplying goods. It also assumes that firms may freely enter or leave an industry.

In practice, the degree of competition varies considerably from industry to industry and from place to place. There may be many snack bars in a town, each competing fiercely with others, but only one post office, one liquor store, or one funeral parlour. There may be no doctors in the country, but many in the towns; and even if there are many, they may not wish or be allowed to compete. In some industries, one or a few firms can influence the market price; in other industries, the member firms have no such control. Thus, a provincial electricity commission can set the price for electric power; the chartered banks, the price for the use of their cheques. But the individual rancher has no say as to the market price of beef. In many industries, a firm can make its product appear different from that of competing firms, even though it is basically the same. A firm "differentiates" its product from that of other firms by using a brand name and intensive advertising.

In the face of such diversity, how can we attempt to explain how price and output are actually determined? For many years, economists used only two models for their market analysis: perfect competition and pure monopoly.

Perfect competition was defined as a market in which many firms compete; each produces the same product and each, because of its limited output, cannot influence market price. *Pure monopoly* was defined as a market with only one firm, which can, therefore, set market price. Many economists and other people realized, however, that most business activity fitted into neither category, but fell somewhere in between. Consequently, in the 1920s and 1930s, a new concept, that of *imperfect competition,* was advanced to explain this middle ground. Imperfect competition was divided into two main types: (a) *monopolistic competition*—a market in which many firms sell differentiated products; and (b) *oligopoly*— a market in which just a few firms sell either the same or differentiated products. Economists now therefore make use of four basic models for market analysis, as summarized in Table 7:2.

In the following chapters, we consider how a firm can theoretically determine its best-profit output, least-loss output, and shut-down point in each of these market structures.

Table 7:2
The Four Basic Market Structures

Characteristic	Perfect Competition	Pure Monopoly	Monopolistic Competition	Oligopoly
Number of firms	Many	One	Many	Few
Kind of good	Same	Unique	Differentiated	Same or differentiated
Control over price	None	Considerable	Some	Very much
Condition of entry	Easy	Restricted	Quite easy	Difficult
Non-price competition	None	Advertising Public relations	Advertising Brand names Packaging	Advertising Brand names Packaging
Examples	Agriculture	Local utilities Post Office Telephone	Retail trade Dresses Shoes	Steel Cars Farm implements Household appliances

Summary

1. *Sales revenue* is the money that a firm receives in exchange for its product.

2. *Average revenue* is sales revenue divided by the number of units sold.
3. *Marginal revenue* is the extra revenue received by a firm from the sale of one more unit of the product.
4. Depending on the type of industry, marginal revenue will remain constant or decline.
5. A business firm usually tries to produce that output at which total revenue exceeds total cost by the widest possible margin.
6. The concept of "break-even" point is used to decide not only whether a firm should remain in business but to evaluate new investment opportunities.
7. A firm which has fixed costs may continue to produce, at least temporarily, even though total costs exceed total revenue, so long as it can cover its variable costs and some part of its fixed costs.
8. Shut-down point occurs when a firm's total revenue fails to cover even its variable costs.
9. Economists make use of *three basic market structures* to analyze the economic behaviour of the firm. These are: *perfect competition, imperfect competition* (itself divided into monopolistic competition and oligopoly), and *monopoly*.

Key Terms

Sales revenue 139
Average revenue 139
Marginal revenue 140
Best-profit output 140
Total revenue 145
Total costs 140
Breakeven point 141
Least-loss output 141
Shut-down point 145
Perfect competition 145
Pure monopoly 145
Imperfect competition 146
Monopolistic competition 146
Oligopoly 146

Review Questions

1. Distinguish between total revenue, average revenue and marginal revenue.
2. What is profit? How is it determined? Why should a firm try to maximize its profit?
3. How can a firm determine its optimum or best-profit output?
4. What is a firm's break-even point? Do all firms in an industry operate at this point? Explain.

5. What practical application does break-even analysis have in business?
6. What is meant by a firm's "least-loss output"?
7. What is a firm's shut-down point? How is it determined? What is its significance?
8. Distinguish between perfect competition and monopoly.
9. How does monopolistic competition differ from oligopoly?
10. "Marginal revenue is always the same as the price of the product." Discuss.
11. "Most business firms pay little attention in practice to marginal revenue and marginal cost." Discuss.
12. "Break-even analysis is only as sound as the assumptions on which it is based." Explain and comment.
13. "Today it costs about $500 000 to set up a 24-track recording studio, which must then be booked for about 2500 h every year at $150/h to break even." What is the price, marginal revenue, and total cost? If the studio is booked for 300 h, what would be the rate of return on total capital? State any assumptions that you make.
14. What are the various market structures that economists use to help analyze the economic behaviour of the business firm?

8. PERFECT COMPETITION: MANY FIRMS WITH THE SAME PRODUCT

CHAPTER OBJECTIVES

A. To explain what is meant by "perfect competition" and the purpose of the concept
B. To explain how a firm determines its most profitable level of output, using first the marginal revenue and marginal cost approach and then the total cost and total revenue approach
C. To show how market supply schedules and curves can be constructed for a firm and an industry
D. To explain how each firm and industry arrives at an equilibrium market situation in both the short run and the long run
E. To indicate the effects of increasing costs on market equilibrium

CHAPTER OUTLINE

The term "competition" is commonly used in business to describe a market situation in which two or more firms strive in various ways to secure the consumer's dollar. In economics, however, the term *perfect competition* (or *pure competition*) is used in a much narrower sense.

8.1: PERFECT COMPETITION DEFINED

Perfect competition is said to exist in an industry if the following conditions occur:

1. The industry consists of many independent firms. In this way, there is no possibility of collusion among firms to fix prices or restrict output.

2. Every firm produces exactly the same product. This means not only the same physical characteristics, but also such intangibles as product availability and service. Consequently, this excludes industries producing such items as breakfast cereals, toiletries, cosmetics and fast foods, as the member firms "differentiate" their products by advertising and sales promotion.

3. Each firm's output is so small that the firm's output behaviour cannot affect market price. By contrast, if one or just a few firms exist in an industry, they can easily influence industry output or market price.

4. Resources are completely mobile. Workers must be easily able, in the long run, to move from job to job, or from place to place. New firms must be able to enter an industry; old ones, to leave it. Existing production facilities must be capable of being switched from one type of production to another.

5. Firms and consumers must be fully informed. Every firm should be aware of the latest methods of production, the cost of each input, and the state of the market for its products. Workers should know what they can earn in different jobs and in different places. Landowners and financial investors should be fully informed as to possible financial returns on their resources in alternative uses. Consumers should be fully aware of the products available and their relative prices.

Purpose of the Concept

Some industries in Canada—perhaps for example, the production of wheat and other farm products—would, without government intervention, satisfy the first three conditions. These are the closest examples that we have of industries operating under perfect competition. But even in these cases, the existence of government price-support programs and marketing boards means that the third and fourth conditions of perfect competition—no control over market price and no restriction on the movement of resources—are not met.

If no industries operate under perfect competition, as we define it, what is the usefulness of such an economic model? The answer is that the analysis of perfect competition as a market structure reveals how resources would be allocated and market prices set without various market "imperfections," such as product differentiation, resource immobility, poor consumer knowledge, and restrictions on production. It reveals, in other words, what would be the most efficient allocation of resources under perfect conditions. It is particularly useful in helping to understand how output and price are determined in agriculture. It also enables us to see, in the simplest possible setting, how revenue and cost help determine output and even price.

Would perfect competition be the ideal or optimum market situation for a country? Certainly, resource allocation would, under such a market structure, more closely follow the dictates of the consumer as expressed by the price system. Firms would also be under great pressure to use the most efficient methods of production, for high-cost producers would in the long run be forced out of an industry. However, perfect competition would also mean that business firms would be much more vulnerable to competition and that workers at all levels would consequently have much less job security.

8.2: PROFIT MAXIMIZATION

When a firm operates under perfect competition, it can sell all it can produce at the current market price. In other words, demand for its product is perfectly elastic. Whether it produces more or produces less has no effect on market price—because the individual firm's output is too small, compared with that of the industry as a whole, to make any significant impression. Total revenue for such a firm is the number of units produced multiplied by the market price for the industry's product as a whole.

Since the market price is given, all that a firm can do under perfect competition to maximize profit is to alter the amount of its output. The question to answer, therefore, is, "How could such a firm determine its most profitable level of output?"

Marginal Revenue and Marginal Cost

Under perfect competition, marginal revenue is always the same as market price because the price of the good cannot be affected by changes in the individual firm's output. Marginal cost will at first decline. Before long, however, it will rise more and more steeply as the increase in average variable cost more than offsets the decline in average fixed cost, as explained in Chapter 6.

Best-Profit Output

The output at which a firm's profit will be maximized will be that at which marginal revenue equals marginal cost. This best profit level is shown in Table 8:1—at an output of 8 units. At lower levels of production, marginal revenue will be greater than marginal cost. Therefore, the firm can increase its profit by increasing output. Beyond 8 units, marginal cost exceeds marginal revenue. It is more profitable, therefore, to reduce output. The equilibrium position is the output of 8 units where marginal revenue is equal to marginal cost. The best-profit level can also be shown graphically (Figure 8:1).

Table 8:1
Best-Profit Output for a Firm Operating under Perfect Competition

Units of Output	Average Fixed Cost (in dollars)	Average Variable Cost (in dollars)	Average Total Cost (in dollars)	Marginal Cost (in dollars)	Marginal Revenue (price = $90)
0				60	MR > MC
1	100.00	60.00	160.00	55	
				50	
2	50.00	55.00	105.00	45	
				40	
3	33.33	50.00	83.33	35	
				30	
4	25.00	45.00	70.00	35	
				40	
5	20.00	44.00	64.00	45	
				50	
6	16.67	45.00	61.67	55	
				60	
7	14.29	47.14	61.43	70	
				80	↓
8	12.50	51.25	63.75	90	MR = MC
				100	↑
9	11.11	56.67	67.78	115	
				130	
10	10.00	64.00	74.00	145	MR < MC

Note: Average and marginal cost figures are based on total cost data shown in Table 8:3.

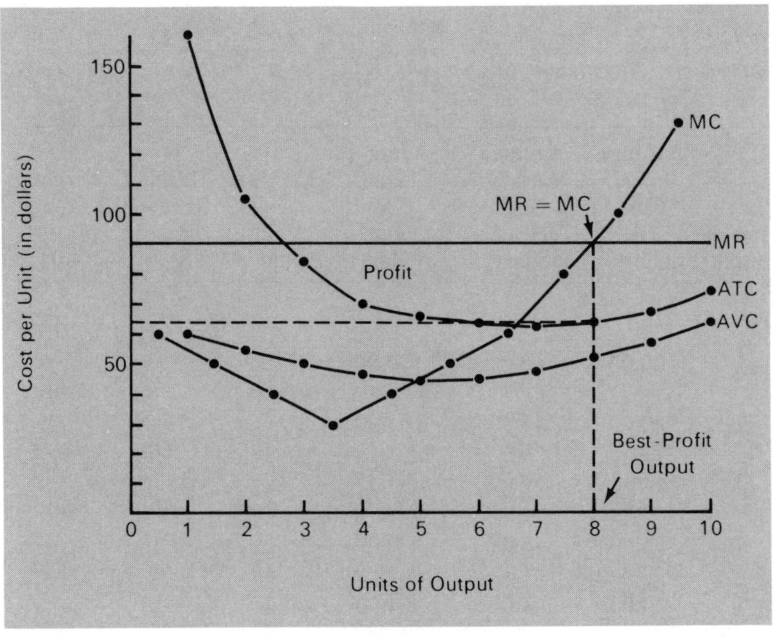

Figure 8:1 Best-Profit Output for a Firm Operating under Perfect Competition

Least-Loss Output

Let us suppose that the market price is reduced. How, by using the marginal revenue and marginal cost method, can we determine the output at which a firm's losses would be minimized? If we look at Table 8:2, we can see that at a market price of $60, the marginal revenue from the first unit of output would only just cover the $60 of marginal cost. However, on each succeeding unit up to 6 units, marginal revenue will exceed marginal cost. At 7 units, marginal revenue will equal marginal cost. And at 8 units and beyond, marginal cost will exceed marginal revenue. Consequently, the firm should produce only 7 units—where MR = MC. At this output, total revenue is $420 (7 × $60); total cost, $430 (7 × $61.43); and total loss, $10. Obviously, in the short run, it is better to produce 7 units for a total loss of $10 than to close down production and incur a loss of $100 (the total fixed cost).

Table 8:2
Least-Loss Output and Shut-down Point for a Firm Operating under Perfect Competition

Units of Output	Average Fixed Cost (in dollars)	Average Variable Cost (in dollars)	Average Total Cost (in dollars)	Marginal Cost (in dollars)	Marginal Revenue (price = $60)	Marginal Revenue (price = $40)
0						
				60	60	40
1	100.00	60.00	160.00			
				50	60	40
2	50.00	55.00	105.00			
				40	60	40
3	33.33	50.00	83.33			
				30	60	40
4	25.00	45.00	70.00			
				40	60	40
5	20.00	44.00	64.00			
				50	60	40
6	16.67	45.00	61.67			
				60	60	40
7	14.29	47.14	61.43			
				80	60	40
8	12.50	51.25	63.75			
				100	60	40
9	11.11	56.67	67.78			
				130	60	40
10	10.00	64.00	74.00			

Shut-Down Point

Suppose that the market price drops even further to $40. If we look at Table 8:2 again, we can see that the average variable cost, whatever the level of output, is always greater than the price per unit. In other words, the price is never sufficient to cover average variable cost, let alone the average fixed cost. It would, therefore, be better for the firm, on purely financial grounds, to halt production. This would be the case at any price less than $44 (the lowest average variable cost). This shut-down situation means that we must slightly modify our previous rule that the optimum output for a firm is where MR = MC. Now we should say that, under perfect competition, a firm will maximize its profit or minimize its loss in the short run by producing that level of output at which price (or marginal revenue) is equal to marginal cost, *so long as the price exceeds the average variable cost.* The shut-down point is, therefore, the point at which P = AVC = MC, as shown in Figure 8:2

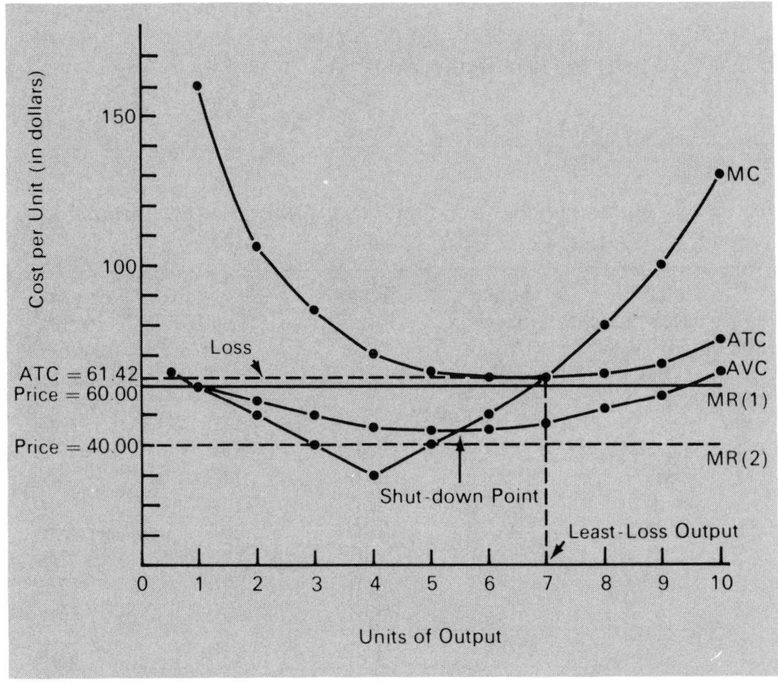

Note: At a price of $60, the least-loss output is 7 units. At this output, total revenue is $420 (7 × $60.00); total cost is $430 (7 × $61.43); and total loss is $10. The price of $60 is greater than the average variable cost ($47.14). The difference of $12.86 goes to help cover the average fixed cost of $14.29. At a price of $40, the firm is financially better off to shut down production. The price cannot even cover the average variable cost. In the chart, the MR line is always below the AVC curve.

Figure 8:2 Shut-Down Point for a Firm Operating under Perfect Competition

8.3: TOTAL-REVENUE AND TOTAL-COST APPROACH

So far in this chapter we have used the marginal-revenue and marginal-cost approach to determine theoretically the output at which a business firm achieves its best profit or least loss, or the point at which it shuts down production. However, the same conclusions can be reached by comparing total revenue and total costs at different levels of output. Thus, in Table 8:3, as an example, we give a hypothetical example of a firm's total revenue and total cost at different levels of output. The total revenue figures are obtained by multiplying the number of units of output by a market price of $90. The total cost figures include normal profit—that is, a rate of return on the owner's time and capital just sufficient to keep the firm in the industry.

Table 8:3
Best-Profit Output for a Firm Operating under Perfect Competition (Total-Revenue and Total-Cost Approach)

Units of Output	Total Revenue (price = $90)	Total Fixed Cost (in dollars)	Total Variable Cost (in dollars)	Total Cost (in dollars)	Economic Profit or Loss (in dollars)
0	0	100	0	100	−100
1	90	100	60	160	− 70
2	180	100	110	210	− 30
3	270	100	150	250	+ 20
4	360	100	180	280	+ 80
5	450	100	220	320	+130
6	540	100	270	370	+170
7	630	100	330	430	+200
8	720	100	410	510	+210
9	810	100	510	610	+200
10	900	100	640	740	+160

Best-Profit Output

We can readily see that profit, using the total revenue and total cost approach, is maximized at an output of 8 units—where total revenue is $720, total cost $510, and profit $210. At a larger or smaller output, the profit would be less.

8.4: MARKET SUPPLY CURVES

Now that we have seen how a firm, operating under perfect competition, can determine its optimum output at the given market price, we can construct hypothetical market supply schedules and curves for the firm and industry.

The Individual Firm

Given its pattern of production costs, which include normal profit, each individual firm will have a best-profit (or least-loss) output for each different possible market price. An example is given in Table 8:4. These different amounts of a product that a firm would be willing to supply at different prices can be set out in the form of a supply schedule (see Table 8:5). As the price falls, so does the quantity that the firm is willing to supply. Finally, when the price drops below $50, the firm finds it better to produce nothing at all.

Seen from the marginal point of view, a firm will produce up to the point at which marginal revenue equals marginal cost. Since, under perfect competition, marginal revenue is the same as price, an individual firm's marginal cost curve will therefore be its supply curve. There

Table 8:4
Best-Profit or Least-Loss Output at Different Market Prices for a Firm Operating under Perfect Competition

Units of Output	Economic Profit or Loss in Dollars at the Following Different Market Prices							
	$100	$90	$80	$70	$60	$50	$40	$30
0	−100	−100	−100	−100	−100	−100	−100	−100
1	− 60	− 70	− 80	− 90	−100	−110	−120	−130
2	− 10	− 30	− 50	− 70	− 90	−110	−130	−150
3	+ 50	+ 20	− 10	− 40	− 70	−100	−130	−160
4	+120	+ 80	+ 40	0	− 40	− 80	−120	−160
5	+180	+130	+ 80	+ 30	− 20	− 70	−120	−170
6	+230	+170	+110	+ 50	− 10	− 70	−130	−190
7	+270	+200	+130	+ 60	− 10	− 80	−150	−220
8	+290	+210	+130	+ 50	− 30	−110	−190	−270
9	+290	+200	+110	+ 20	− 70	−160	−250	−340
10	+260	+160	+ 60	− 40	−140	−240	−340	−440

Note: Obtained by subtracting total cost from total revenue at the different market prices. Total cost is obtained from Table 8:3. Total revenue is the number of units of output multiplied by each different price.

is one qualification to be made, however. This observation is only true for that part of the MC curve that is above the AVC curve. For, as we saw earlier, once the marginal revenue is less than the average variable cost, a firm will be better off to shut down rather than to continue producing. The short-run supply curve, based on the MC curve, is shown in Figure 8:3. This curve slopes upward from left to right to show that the firm will supply more of the good at a higher price than it will at a low price.

Table 8:5
The Individual Firm's Supply Schedule

Market Price	Units of Output
100	8.5
90	8
80	7.5
70	7
60	6.5
50	5.5
40	0
30	0
20	0
10	0
0	0

Source: Based on data in Table 8:4.

The Industry

To obtain the industry's short-run supply curve, all we need to do is to combine the supply data for each individual firm. Thus in Table 8:6, we show the amount of a good that would be supplied at different prices by one individual firm and the amount that would be supplied by one hundred individual firms put together.

8.5: FIRM AND INDUSTRY EQUILIBRIUM

We know that under perfect competition an individual firm's output has no influence on market price. But the industry's output as a whole can, of course, affect it. What can happen to market price and output in the short and long run? What is the equilibrium situation?

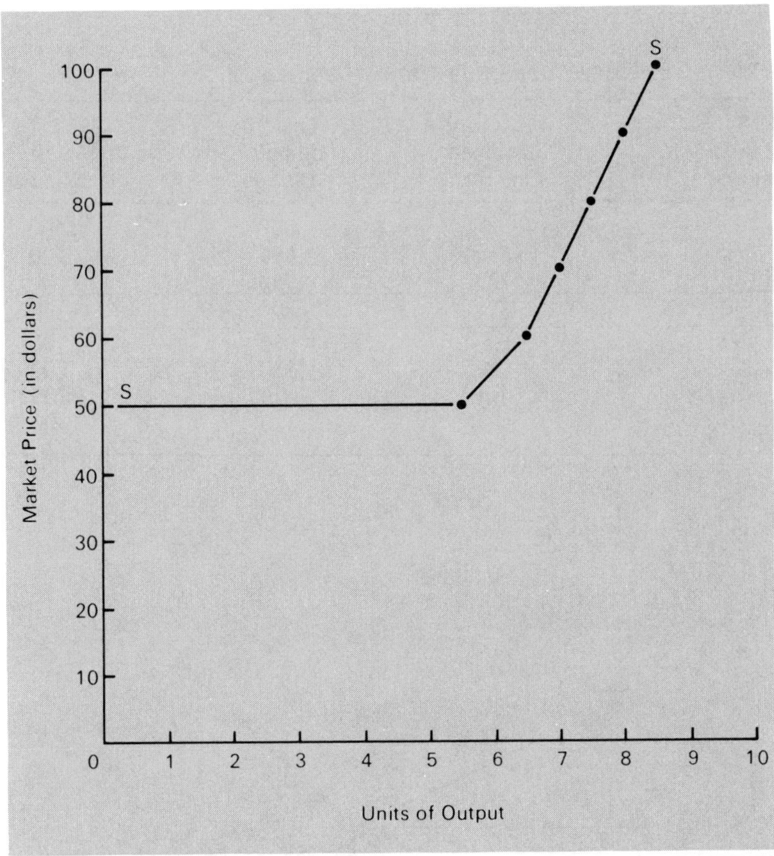

Note: At a market price of less than $50, output will be zero since the price will be less than average variable cost.

Source: Based on data from Table 8:5.

Figure 8:3 The Individual Firm's Supply Curve

Short Run

In the short run, every firm in the industry has fixed production costs. A firm can, it is true, shut down production and thereby eliminate variable costs, but it cannot escape its fixed costs. The equilibrium output and price will therefore be where the industry's supply curve and the market demand curve for that product intersect. This is shown in Table 8:6 and Figure 8:4 at a price of $70 and an output of 700 units.

Table 8:6
Firm and Industry Supply and Market Demand

Market Price	Quantity Supplied One Firm	Quantity Supplied 100 Firms	Quantity Demanded
100	8.5	850	400
90	8	800	500
80	7.5	750	600
70	7	700	700
60	6.5	650	800
50	5.5	550	900
40	0	0	1100
30	0	0	1300

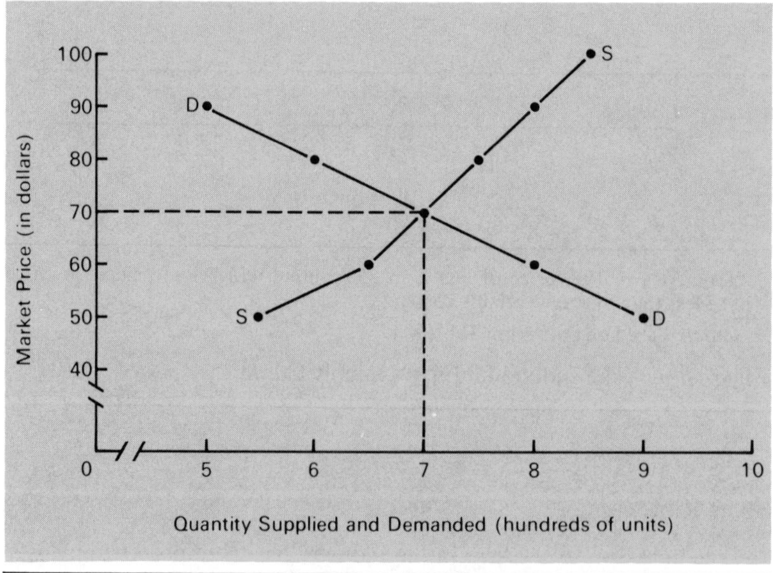

Note: The short-run equilibrium price and output for the industry are $70 and 700 units respectively. The individual firm produces the best-profit (or least-loss) output possible with this market price.

Figure 8:4 Industry Short-Run Equilibrium Output and Price

Long Run

In the long run, a firm can reorganize or re-equip its plan to reduce its costs or switch to the production of something else. Sometimes this will be done by a new owner. In the long run, therefore, no firm has fixed costs. All production costs are variable. If a firm does not find it profitable to produce, it will have had sufficient time to leave the industry. In the long run also, other firms, armed with a lower cost structure, will have had time to enter the industry.

This complete mobility of resources (one of the characteristics of perfect competition) has important implications for our discussion of long-run equilibrium. Combined with the fact that business firms seek to maximize economic profit (or minimize loss), it means that eventually, as a result of all this movement in and out of the industry, every firm that remains will produce up to the point at which its marginal revenue (price) is equal not only to its marginal cost but also to minimum average total cost. If this were not so, firms in the industry would still make a loss and other firms outside could still enter and make a normal profit.

Here we should remind ourselves that, in economics, total cost includes normal profit. The surplus of total revenue over this total cost is called *pure profit*. In the long-run equilibrium situation, there will be no pure profit. The entry of new firms, each competing for a share of the market, will have eliminated it. Conversely, if market demand were to fall, causing a drop in market price, firms which could not make a normal profit would either leave the industry or reduce their output capacity. The long-run equilibrium would once more be the situation in which each individual firm earns only normal profit.

Constant Versus Increasing Costs

We have said previously that the equilibrium market price would be re-established at its former level. This assumes, however, that the entry of new firms into an industry, or the departure of old ones from it, would have no effect on cost structures—in other words, that the industry enjoys constant costs.

If this is the case (and it is quite possible if the industry does not use a large portion of total available resources), the long-run industry supply curve would be perfectly elastic and would appear as a horizontal line. A change in demand would not alter the market price.

In most cases, however, an industry cannot indefinitely increase supply without bidding up the price of its inputs. Consequently, an industry usually has an upward-sloping long-run supply curve. This means that a change in demand will cause a change in the equilibrium market price even after firms have entered or left the industry.

Summary

1. Perfect competition exists when: (a) an industry consists of many independent firms; (b) every firm produces exactly the same product; (c) each firm believes that it cannot affect market price because its output is so small; (d) resources are completely mobile; and (e) firms and consumers are fully informed.
2. The main value of analyzing perfect competition as a market structure is that it reveals how resources would be allocated and market prices set without various market "imperfections," such as product differentiation, resource immobility, poor knowledge, and restrictions on production. It is questionable whether perfect competition would be a desirable market structure for a country.
3. Since the market price is given, all a firm can do under perfect competition to maximize pure profit is to alter the amount of its output.
4. A firm can theoretically determine its best profit output, its least-loss output, or its shut-down point by comparing its marginal revenue with its marginal cost. Under perfect competition, a firm will maximize its pure profit (or minimize its loss) in the short run by producing that level of output at which price (marginal revenue) is equal to marginal cost—as long as the market price exceeds the firm's average variable cost of production. Total revenue can also be compared with total costs.
5. Given its pattern of production costs, which include normal profit, each individual firm will have a best-profit (or least-loss) output for each different possible market price. Since a firm will produce up to the point at which marginal revenue (price) equals marginal cost, the individual firm's marginal cost curve will in effect be its supply curve. The supply data for each individual firm can be combined to obtain the industry's short-run supply curve.
6. Although the individual firm's output has no influence on market price, the industry's output can affect it. The industry's output and price are in equilibrium when the industry's supply curve and the market demand curve for the product intersect. In the long run, since movement in and out of an industry is possible, no firm will earn more than normal profit. Each firm will produce up to the

point at which marginal revenue (price) is equal not only to marginal cost but also to minimum average total cost.

7. If market demand increases, pure profit may be earned until the entry of new firms and the enlargement of existing ones eliminate it. The long-run equilibrium would once more be where each individual firm earns only normal profit.

Key Terms

Perfect competition 149
Marginal revenue 151
Marginal cost 151
Best-profit output 152
Least-loss output 153
Shut-down point 154
Total revenue 155
Total costs 156
Short-run supply 159
Equilibrium output 159
Mobility of resources 161
Pure profit 161
Constant costs 161
Increasing costs 161

Review Questions

1. What is the significance of each of the following conditions of perfect competition?
   (a) many independent firms
   (b) exactly the same product
   (c) each firm's output is small
   (d) completely mobile resources
   (e) full information.
2. To what extent does perfect competition exist in Canada?
3. What is the purpose of the concept of perfect competition?
4. Is perfect competition a desirable situation for a country? Justify your answer.
5. Since the market price is given, what can a firm operating under perfect competition do to maximize its profit?
6. How can a firm theoretically determine its most profitable level of output?
7. In economics, a firm's total cost figures include normal profit. Explain.
8. Why would a firm operate at a loss?
9. What is meant by a firm's shut-down point? When does this occur?
10. The output at which a firm's profit is maximized is where the

marginal revenue equals marginal cost. Explain.

11. A firm's shut-down point is where P = AVC = MC. Explain,
12. Since, under perfect competition, marginal revenue is the same as price, an individual firm's marginal cost curve will in effect be its supply curve. Explain.
13. What will be the equilibrium output and price for an industry as a whole?
14. What implications does the assumption of complete mobility of resources have for the long-run equilibrium of an industry?
15. What is the significance, in our discussion of long-run industry equilibrium, of the assumption of constant costs?

9. *PURE MONOPOLY: THE SOLE SUPPLIER*

CHAPTER OBJECTIVES

A. To explain what is a "pure monopoly"
B. To identify the reasons why monopolies exist
C. To examine the nature of the demand for a monopolist's product
D. To indicate how a monopolist decides how much to produce
E. To explain why a monopolist may engage in price discrimination
F. To discuss how monopoly power can be abused
G. To show what can happen when government regulates a private monopoly

CHAPTER OUTLINE

The economic model of the marketplace that we have just examined (perfect competition) was characterized by one very important fact. The firms in an industry are so many in number and so small in relative size that each by itself is powerless to influence market price. Our present task is to consider the opposite case—a situation in which there is only one firm instead of many and in which the market price, as a consequence, is directly influenced by changes in that firm's output.

The name given to this situation is *pure monopoly*. By first examining the two market extremes—perfect competition and pure monopoly—we shall be in a much better position to understand, in the next two chapters, the type of market structure in which most businesses in Canada actually operate.

9.1: MONOPOLY DEFINED

A *pure monopoly* (also called *complete, absolute*, or *exclusive monopoly*) exists where there is only one firm supplying a product and where there are no close substitutes for this product. By close substitute, we mean a product that a consumer could easily use instead of the one supplied by the single firm. Thus, if one firm produced and supplied all refrigerators, this would be a pure monopoly, for there is no close substitute except perhaps the long-forgotten icebox. The single firm that enjoys this monopoly power is known as a *monopolist*—from the Greek words *mono* for "one" and *polist* for "seller."

In Canada, numerous examples of pure monopolists are to be found, often in key industries. Thus, for instance, there are the provincial and municipal public utility commissions supplying electricity and water, and privately owned firms supplying natural gas, cable television, and telephone services.

Monopoly power, as the previous examples suggest, has its limitations. Even though we may consider that the supplier of electricity has an absolute monopoly, there could come a point (if the price of electricity were raised high enough) when consumers would either do without or turn to something else (such as candles or gas mantles for lighting) that we do not normally regard as a close substitute. Even the post office, which has a legal monopoly on mail delivery, can lose business if its prices are too high or its service too inefficient. Some firms may find it cheaper (if permitted by law) to deliver their own mail, contract the work out to hand-delivery firms, or switch to other forms of data transmission.

9.2: REASONS FOR MONOPOLY

There are several different reasons why monopolies come into existence. These are now discussed in turn.

Ownership of Key Raw Materials

One firm may own or control the supply of an essential raw material used in a manufacturing process. Thus the International Nickel Company of Canada once owned most of the world's known nickel ore reserves. However, new mines in Australia, Central America and Indonesia have changed this picture. More recently the OPEC oil cartel has acted in monopoly fashion.

Government Decree

In return for a substantial fee, or for reasons of public policy, including the raising of additional revenue, governments sometimes grant an exclusive franchise to a private firm or government agency to operate a particular business or to import a certain type of good. It thereby becomes illegal for any other firm to carry on the same business in that area, which often extends over a whole country. Thus the Hudson's Bay Company was given the exclusive right by the British monarch to carry on the fur trade in a substantial portion of Canada. In modern times, the retailing of liquor in most of Canada is governed in this way. Historically such monopolies, like the fur trade, were the monarch's way of rewarding his or her courtiers or a way of raising funds for the monarch's use. Today, the usual justification for the award of monopoly powers is that only one firm can logically provide such a service—for example, a municipal transit system. Competition by several firms would be a wasteful duplication of facilities. Usually, if the firm is not government-owned, the government specifies the area to be served and regulates the rates to be charged. It can no longer be said that monopolies are usually goverment-run to protect the public from being overcharged for a good or service—as many Crown corporations and other government agencies such as Canada Post or Air Canada now charge the public just as much, if not more, than privately owned firms for the goods or services provided. And in the case of wine, beer, and liquor retailing, such monopolies are an important source of provincial revenue.

Sales Franchise

An exclusive franchise may also be conferred by one private firm on another—as with a fast-food sales franchise, which gives the franchisee the exclusive right to use a particular firm's name, logo, techniques etc. in a given geographical area. A popular example is McDonald's.

Patent Rights

A third possible reason for the existence of a monopoly is that a firm may have the patent rights on a particular product or manufacturing process—for example, certain pharmaceutical drugs. Copyrights on books may also be considered to grant a monopoly to the publisher.

Economies of Scale

A fourth and very important reason for the existence of monopolies is the reduction in the average cost of production per unit of output that results from large-scale or "mass" production. These "economies of scale," explained earlier, may be so great that a firm can afford, by price undercutting, to put all its competitors out of business. This battle for "survival of the fittest" leaves only one firm in the industry. Also, the lower average production costs of the survivor may effectively deter any new competitors.

There must, of course, be sufficient demand to justify large-scale production. If a firm cannot sell all of its output, the benefit of any cost reduction disappears.

9.3: DEMAND FOR A MONOPOLIST'S PRODUCT

We saw that, under perfect competition, the demand for an individual firm's output is perfectly elastic. In other words, the individual firm can supply as much of the product as it likes without affecting the market price. Such a firm's marginal revenue is, therefore, the same as the market price. Only changes in the output of the industry as a whole can disturb the equilibrium market price.

For a monopolist, the situation is quite different. The individual firm is in such a case the entire industry. And the demand curve for its products is therefore also the market-demand curve. As such, it is downward-sloping rather than horizontal. This means that the monopolist will be able to sell more of its product only by charging a lower price. Demand is no longer perfectly elastic.

9.4: BEST-PROFIT OUTPUT

How does a monopolist, faced with a downward-sloping demand curve, determine the best-profit output? Less can be charged and more sold, or more can be charged and less sold. But the monopolist cannot have the best of both worlds: price and output cannot *both* be set, because market demand for the product imposes constraints.

Thus, as in Figure 9:1. the monopolist may decide to charge $4.00 for the product, but only 50 000 units can be sold. Or the monopolist may decide to sell 100 000 units, but must therefore accept a market price of $2.00 each for them. Given the nature of market demand, 100 000 units cannot be sold at $4.00 each.

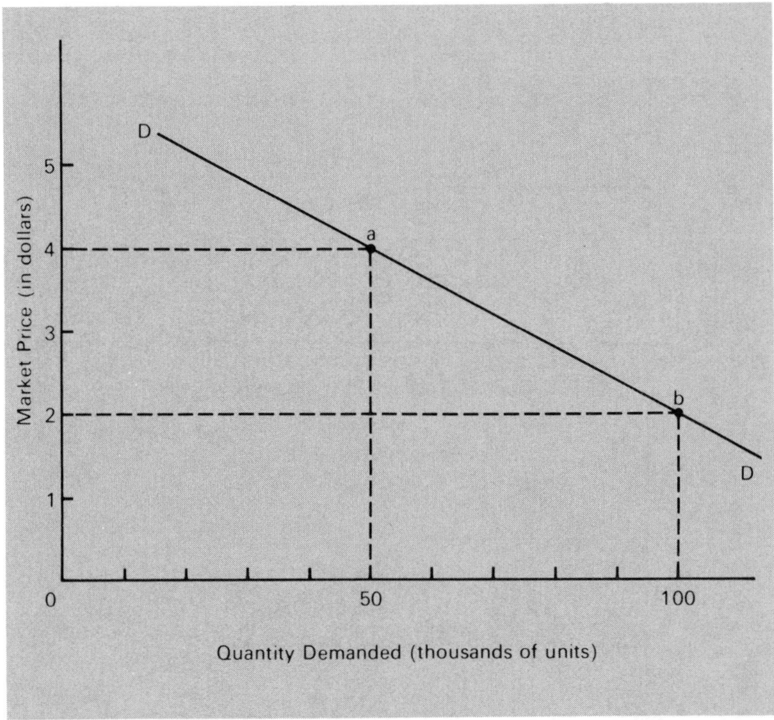

Figure 9:1 The Monopolist Can Set Either Price or Output, but not Both

Elasticity of Demand

Being the sole supplier of a product, the monopolist can, if it so desires, restrict output. However, whether it can gain a monopoly profit (in addition to normal profit) by doing so, will depend partly on the price-elasticity of demand for the product. The more inelastic that demand is, the greater the chance of such a profit—for an inelastic demand means that a reduction in supply will cause a more than proportionate increase in market price and therefore an increase in total revenue. Conversely, an elastic demand means that a reduction in supply will cause a less than proportionate increase in price and therefore a decrease in total revenue.

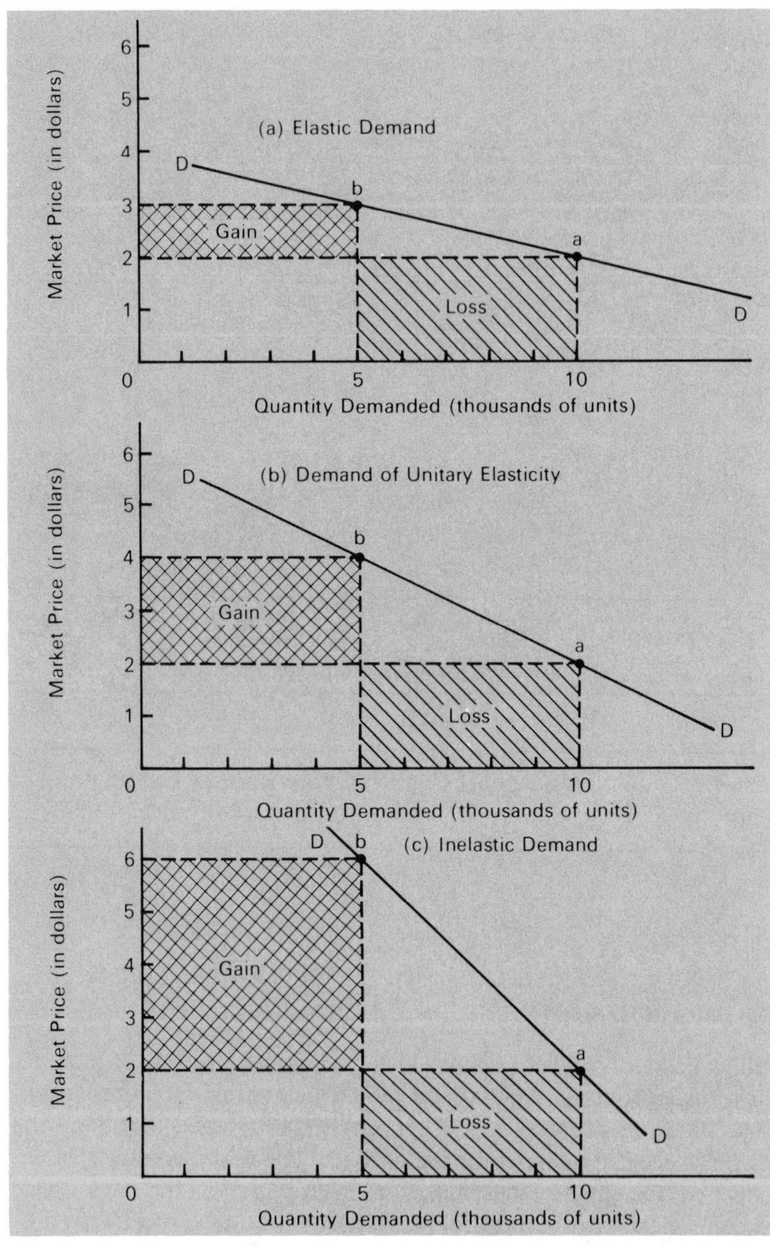

Figure 9:2 How Elasticity of Demand Affects a Monopolist's Total Revenue

Let us suppose, for example, that a monopolist now supplies 10000 units of product A at a market price of $2.00 each. In Figure 9:2 we show three different market demand curves for the same product. Now suppose that the monopolist reduces output by 5000 units. In Figure 9:2(a) where demand is elastic, the price will rise only to $3.00. Total revenue will decline from $20000 ($2 × 10000 units) to $15000 ($3 × 5000 units). In Figure 9:2(b) where demand is of unitary-elasticity, the price will rise to $4.00. As a result, total revenue will remain at $20000 ($4 × 5000 units). In Figure 9:2(c) where demand is inelastic, the reduction in output by 5000 units will cause the price to rise to $6.00.

Demand, we have seen, determines the market price that a monopolist can obtain for its product at different levels of output. Depending on the elasticity of this demand, total revenue may be greater at a higher or lower price. However, before deciding how much to produce, a monopolist must also take into account the costs of production. With enough knowledge of market demand and costs of production, a monopolist could compare total revenue with total cost or marginal revenue with marginal cost to determine its best-profit output.

Total-Revenue and Total-Cost Approach

Using the total-revenue and total-cost approach, the monopolist would, in our example (Table 9:1), gain maximum profit at an output of 6 units, at which total revenue is $540 and total cost is $370.

Table 9:1
Determining the Monopolist's Best-Profit Output (Total-Revenue and Total-Cost Approach)

Units of Output	Market Price (in dollars)	Total Revenue (in dollars)	Total Cost (in dollars)	Economic Profit or Loss (in dollars)
0		0	100	−100
1	115	115	160	− 45
2	110	220	210	+ 10
3	105	315	250	+ 65
4	100	400	280	+120
5	95	475	320	+155
6	90	540	370	+170
7	85	595	430	+165
8	80	640	510	+130
9	75	675	610	+ 65
10	70	700	740	− 40

Marginal-Revenue and Marginal-Cost Approach

The monopolist can also determine the best-profit output by comparzing marginal revenue with marginal cost. Since the monopolist can only sell more by charging a lower price, it follows that marginal revenue (unlike the situation in pure competition) is *not* the same as market price. The marginal revenue will, in fact, be the price received for the last unit of output *minus* the reduction in revenue on all the other units, which are now sold for less. Therefore, the marginal revenue curve will diverge from the demand curve. The demand curve for the monopolist's output (see Figure 9:3) will also be the average revenue curve.

The monopolist, just like a firm in a competitive market structure, will attempt to maximize profit by producing extra units of output so long as the additional revenue exceeds the additional cost. We can see, therefore, in Table 9:2, that the monopolist's best-profit position (where MR = MC) is 6 units. At any other level of output, there will

Table 9:2
Determining the Monopolist's Best-Profit Output
(Marginal-Revenue and Marginal-Cost Approach)

Units of Output	Market Price	Average Variable Cost (in dollars)	Average Total Cost (in dollars)	Marginal Revenue (in dollars)	Marginal Cost (in dollars)	MR : MC
1	115	60.00	160.00	115	60	MR > MC
2	110	55.00	105.00	105	50	↓
3	105	50.00	83.33	95	40	
4	100	45.00	70.00	85	30	
5	95	44.00	64.00	75	40	
6	90	45.00	61.67	65	50	
7	85	47.14	61.43	55	60	↑
8	80	51.25	63.75	45	80	
9	75	56.67	67.78	35	100	
10	70	64.00	74.00	25	130	MR < MC

Note: Because of the indivisibility of units of output, marginal revenue exceeds marginal cost at best-profit output.

Source: Marginal-revenue and marginal-cost data are derived from Table 9:1.

be less profit, or even a loss. This situation can also be shown graphically. Thus, in Figure 9:3, we can see that the nearest complete unit of additional output at which marginal revenue equals marginal cost is 6. If we were to have used fractions of units in Table 9:2, the best-profit output would have been slightly more.

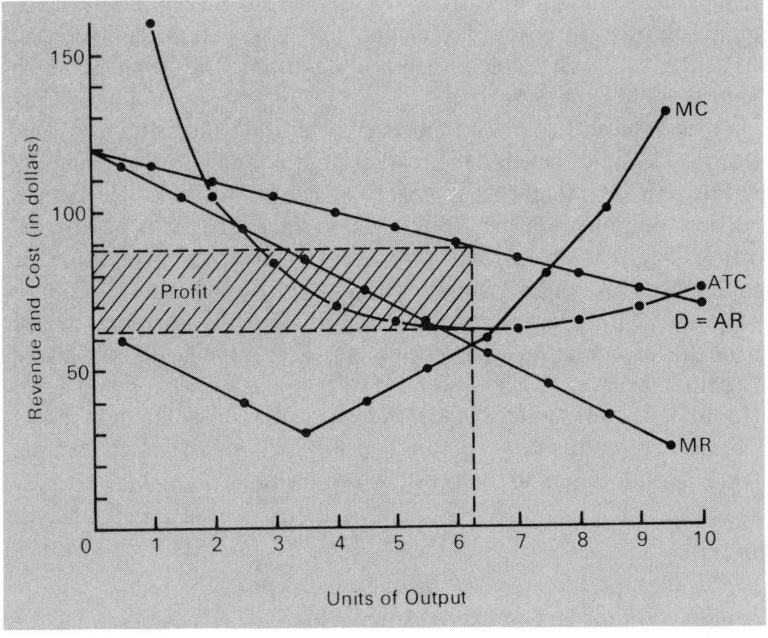

Figure 9:3 Determining the Monopolist's Best-Profit Output by the Marginal-Revenue and Marginal-Cost Approach

9.5: LEAST-LOSS OUTPUT

Although it may enjoy a monopoly position, a firm has no guarantee that it will make a profit. Perhaps consumers are not interested in the product. Or perhaps the item costs too much to produce compared with the price at which it can be sold. There are patents on many new products and processes in Canada for which there is no worthwhile demand. Obviously, in such cases, a firm does not even begin production. It is only worthwhile to enter into production if average revenue is expected permanently to exceed average total cost.

But let us suppose that a monopolist has been supplying a product for some time and is starting to make a loss. The reason for this could be that labour and material costs have increased or that market demand, because of a change in consumer tastes, has declined. What should the monopolist do? In the short run, just like the competitive firm, the monopolist is saddled with the fixed cost of plant and equipment. Thus, it has an incentive in the short run to keep producing so long as the variable cost of production and some part of the fixed cost can be covered. The problem then is to determine the output at which the loss would be minimized.

Let us assume that the monopolist's costs are the same as in our previous example, but that the market price is much lower. Using the total-revenue and total-cost approach, we can see in Table 9:3, that the least-loss output would be 4 units: where total revenue is $220; total cost, $280; and total loss, $60. Obviously, it is financially better for the monopolist to produce 4 units for a total loss of $60 than to produce nothing at all for a loss (the fixed cost) of $100. This situation can also be illustrated in Figure 9:3 by having the ATC curve lie entirely above the demand curve.

In the long run, rather than continue to make a loss, the monopolist would cease production. To continue production, the total revenue must at least be equal to total cost (which includes normal profit).

Table 9:3
Determining the Monopolist's Least-Loss Output
(Total-Revenue and Total-Cost Approach)

Units of Output	Market Price (in dollars)	Total Revenue (in dollars)	Total Cost (in dollars)	Profit or Loss (in dollars)
0	75	0	100	−100
1	70	70	160	− 90
2	65	130	210	− 80
3	60	180	250	− 70
4	55	220	280	− 60
5	50	250	320	− 70
6	45	270	370	−100
7	40	280	430	−150
8	35	280	510	−230
9	30	270	610	−340
10	25	250	740	−490

9.6: PRICE DISCRIMINATION

Usually, a monopolist will charge everyone the same price for the product. However, in certain circumstances, the monopolist may engage in *price discrimination*, charging different prices to different groups of consumers for exactly the same product. Thus, for example, a movie theatre may charge $8.00 for a seat for the first week's showing of a new film and only half that amount later on. The two markets are separated by time. Airline, bus, and railway fares, railway freight rates, and utility charges, may also vary according to time or user. A monopoly firm which practises price discrimination, is called in economics a *discriminating monopolist.*

What are the circumstances that might encourage a monopolist to become a *discriminating monopolist*? First, buyers of the product must consist of separate groups—for example, different income groups. Second, buyers of the product should not be able to transfer it easily from one group to the other; otherwise, members of the group that buy the product at the lower price might sell it to those being charged a higher price and so make it impossible for the monopolist to maintain a price differential. Third, each group of buyers (because of different incomes, different tastes, or different availability of substitutes) should have a different elasticity of demand for the product.

Let us now see, with an example, how a monopolist can benefit from

Table 9:4
A Monopolist's Total Revenue and Total Costs

Units of Output	Market Price (in dollars)	Total Revenue (in dollars)	Total Cost (in dollars)	Pure Profit or Loss (in dollars)
1	115	115	170	−55
2	110	220	240	−20
3	105	315	280	+35
4	100	400	350	+50
5	95	475	415	+60
6	90	540	470	+70
7	85	595	555	+40
8	80	640	630	+10
9	75	675	695	−20
10	70	700	740	−40

price discrimination. Table 9:4 shows how a monopolist's revenue and costs might vary with changes in output. The best-profit output would be 6 units sold at a market price of $90 each. Pure profit at this point would be $70. To sell 10 units instead of 6, the price would have to be reduced to $70. This means that total revenue would increase by $160, while total cost would increase by $270. As a result, pure profit would decline by $110, and the monopolist would be worse off.

Suppose, however, that the monopolist continued to sell 6 units in the first market for $90 each (the best-profit output), but sold 4 additional units in another market. Then, so long as more revenue than the additional cost of producing the 4 units can be obtained, total profit has increased. Since this additional cost is $270, each unit must be sold at more than $67.50. If a price of $75 can be obtained, our discriminating monopolist will have increased the total profit to $100 from the original $70. Whereas total revenue is now $840 (6 units at $90 = $540, plus 4 units at $75 = $300), total cost is only $740.

The monopolist's optimum allocation of output between the two (or more) markets will be where marginal revenue in each market is equal to marginal cost. Until this situation exists, it would be profitable for the monopolist to alter the allocation. Supply will in fact be smaller and the price higher in the market in which demand is more inelastic.

By price discrimination, a monopolist is able to increase profit at the expense of the "consumer's surplus". Thus if, for example, some people are willing to pay $8.00 to see a new movie, the monopolist can charge this price until those people have seen the film. Then $4.00 can be charged to the people who would only be willing to pay this lower amount. By not charging $4.00 from the start, the monopolist has prevented people who would have paid $8.00 from paying only $4.00.

One important example of price discrimination between different markets is the sale of a product in the home (or domestic) market at one price and the sale of the product abroad at a lower one. So long as the foreign price exceeds the variable cost of production, a manufacturer who sells mainly to the home market can profit by this practice. The monopolist has already incurred the fixed costs of production, such as plant and equipment, administration, and research and development, and any extra sales will help pay for them. If the price abroad is less than the home market price, the foreign countries which receive the goods may label such export sales as "dumping" and impose anti-dumping import duties to bring the foreign price up to the Canadian price. Often, to make price discrimination less apparent, a monopolist will try to differentiate the product by name, packaging, or other means.

9.7: POSSIBLE ABUSES OF MONOPOLY POWER

Being the sole supplier of a product, a monopolist has considerable economic power. Just how great this power is will depend on the nature of market demand. If demand is very inelastic (that is to say, a change in price will cause little change in the quantity demanded), the monopolist is in a position to charge a high price for the product. This is the case in Canada with sales of liquor by provincially-owned liquor boards. Unlike a firm operating under conditions of perfect competition, the monopolist is able, by restricting the supply, to obtain pure profit, even in the long run.

Of course, for many products, there is a limit beyond which the monopolist cannot push the price. If the price becomes too high or the supply becomes too small, other products that were not previously considered close substitutes will start to be used instead.

If demand is very elastic (because consumers, rather than pay a high price, would prefer to do without or substitute something else), the monopolist's power is much more limited.

There are other reasons, too, why a monopolist does not have a completely free hand in its pricing and output behaviour. It may, for example, be anxious to avoid adverse publicity. Also, if it abuses its monopoly power by raising prices exorbitantly, it may cause so much public uproar that the government may be tempted to step in. Of course, in Canada, most monopolies providing essential services to the public are already government-owned or regulated. This does, to some extent, help prevent the consumer from being exploited, except by government. Another factor that may help persuade a monopolist to seek less than maximum profit is the possibility of encouraging possible rivals. If, for example, a firm which controls the major sources of a particular mineral ore raises its price too much, mining exploration to find alternative sources of supply will be intensified. In the long run, if the incentive is sufficiently great, most monopolies can be overcome. One classic example was the development of synthetic rubber to replace high-cost natural rubber. Another was the replacement of natural pearls by Japanese cultured pearls.

From society's point of view, the major criticism of monopoly, compared with perfect competition, is that it leads to inefficient allocation of resources. Consumers are prevented from having as much of the monopoly product as they would like. Also, they usually have to pay more for it. This is because average production costs are higher than they would otherwise be and because monopoly profit (in addition to normal profit) is obtained by the monopolist.

Another serious criticism of monopolies is the misplaced political power that can accompany the concentration of economic power.

9.8: REGULATED MONOPOLY

We have seen that a monopolist will charge a higher price and produce less than if subject to competition. Thus, in Figure 9:4 monopoly price and output (determined by the intersection of the MR and MC curves) are OP_1 and OQ_1 respectively. If there were perfect competition, output would increase up to the point at which market price equals marginal cost. In Figure 9:4, this would be where output is OQ_2 and price OP_2. Consequently, to ensure that a monopolist supplies more of the product and to improve the allocation of a country's resources, government could impose a maximum price of OP_2. This would, in effect, make the monopolist's demand curve P_2AD rather than DD. Unfortunately, however, this government-regulated maximum price would cause the monopolist a loss since average cost per unit at OQ_2 output exceeds

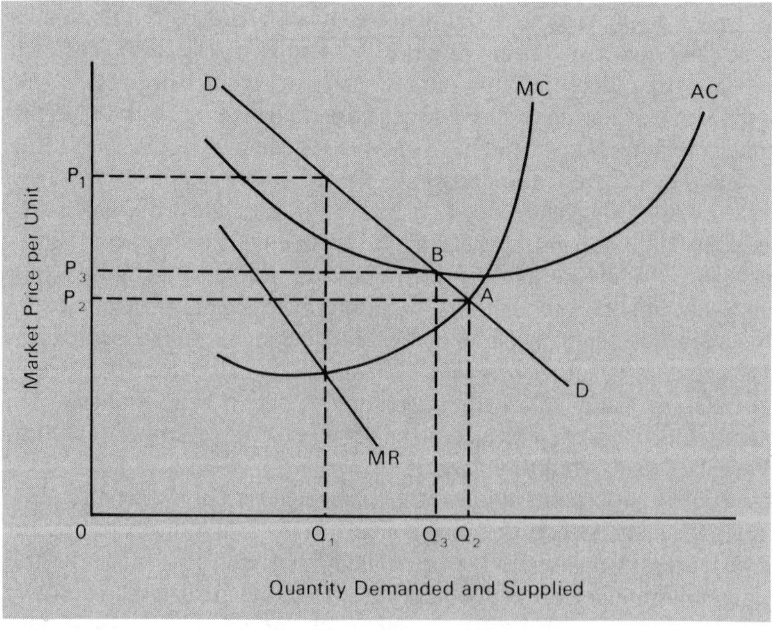

Figure 9:4 Regulated Monopoly and a "Fair Return" Price

market price. To be fair to the monopolist (for example, a public utility) and provide normal profit, the maximum price should cover the average cost. Therefore, the desirable government-regulated price should be OP_3. At this "fair return" price, output will be OQ_3, which is still much more than if the monopolist were left unregulated. As an alternative, the government may insist that the monopolist charge no more than the price OP_2, but make up the difference in the form of a subsidy, as is often done, for example, with government-controlled ferry services.

Summary

1. A *pure monopoly* exists when: (a) there is only one firm supplying a good; and (b) there are no close substitutes for it. The firm is called a *monopolist.*
2. Most of the monopolies in Canada are government-owned or government-regulated.
3. The basic reason for the existence of a monopoly is that no other firms are able to enter the industry. Barriers to entry include: (a) ownership of key raw materials; (b) government decree (c) sales franchise; (d) patent rights; and (e) economies of scale already achieved by the monopolist.
4. With a monopoly, the individual firm is the entire industry. Therefore, the demand curve for the monopolist's product is downward-sloping—rather than horizontal as with perfect competition—indicating that the monopolist can sell more only if the monopolist lowers the price of the good.
5. The monopolist can set *either* market price *or* the amount sold, but not both price *and* output because constraints are imposed by the market demand for the product.
6. Whether a monopolist can gain a *monopoly profit* (in addition to normal profit) by restricting output will depend partly on the price-elasticity of demand for the product. The more inelastic is the demand, the greater the chance of such profit.
7. The monopolist can theoretically determine its best-profit output by comparing total revenue with total cost, or marginal revenue with marginal cost. Unlike perfect competition, where marginal revenue equals market price, the *marginal revenue of the monopolist* is the price received for the last unit of output *minus* the reduction in revenue on all the other units, which are now sold for less.
8. In the short run, a monopolist may continue operating at a loss, so

long as the variable costs of production as well as some part of the fixed cost can be covered. In the long run, to continue production, the total revenue must at least be equal to total cost (which includes normal profit).

9. Sometimes, a monopolist will charge different prices to different groups of consumers for exactly the same product. A *discriminating monopolist* is most likely to exist if: (a) buyers consist of clearly separate groups; (b) the product cannot be easily transferred from one group to another; and (c) each group has a different elasticity of demand for the product. The discriminating monopolist's optimum allocation of output between the various markets will be where marginal revenue in each market is equal to marginal cost. By price discrimination, a monopolist is able to increase profit at the expense of the consumer's surplus.
10. A monopolist is restricted in its ability to abuse its economic position. In addition to the elasticity of market demand, there is government ownership and regulation. The major economic criticism of monopoly is that it leads to inefficient allocation of a country's resources.
11. To ensure greater output by a monopolist and so improve the allocation of a country's resources, government could impose a maximum price for the monopolist's product. This maximum should be set at a level that would enable the monopolist to cover the average cost per unit and so earn normal profit.

Key Terms

Pure monopoly 166
Monopolist 166
Key raw materials 166
Government monopoly 167
Sales franchise 167
Patent rights 167
Economies of scale 168
Best-profit output 168
Elasticity of demand 169
Least-loss output 173
Price discrimination 175
Discriminating monopolist 175
Consumer's surplus 176
Dumping 176
Abuses of monopoly power 177
Regulated monopoly 178

Review Questions

1. What are the characteristics of a pure monopoly?
2. To what extent do monopolies exist in Canada? Give three examples.

3. How do monopolies originate?
4. Describe and explain the nature of the demand curve for a monopolist's product.
5. What control does a monopolist have over the price and amount sold of the product?
6. How does the elasticity of demand for a product help determine the opportunity for monopoly profit?
7. What factors must a monopolist take into account when determining best-profit output?
8. What is the relationship in pure monopoly, between marginal revenue and market price?
9. A monopoly position automatically ensures that a firm makes a profit. Comment.
10. Explain how a monopolist might benefit from price discrimination.
11. What controls exist to prevent the abuse of monopoly power?
12. What are the major criticisms of monopoly power?
13. In regulating a monopoly, government should set a maximum market price for the product that will ensure the same output as under perfect competition. Comment.
14. Why might a government subsidize a monopolist?

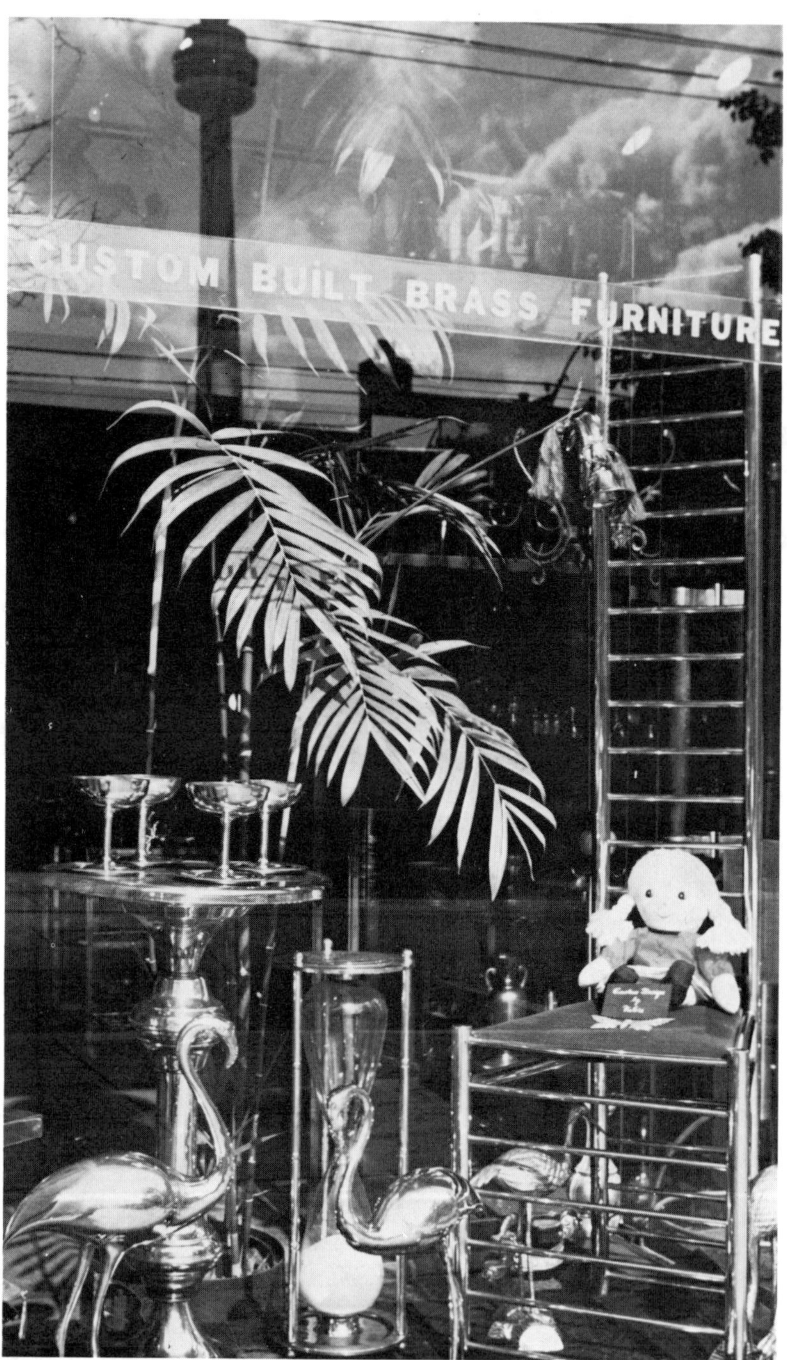
CUSTOM BUILT BRASS FURNITURE

10. MONOPOLISTIC COMPETITION: MANY FIRMS BUT DIFFERENTIATED PRODUCTS

CHAPTER OBJECTIVES

A. To explain what is meant by product differentiation
B. To define monopolistic competition
C. To analyze the nature of demand for a monopolistic competitor's product, as compared with perfect competition and pure monopoly
D. To explain how output and price are determined in the short run and long run
E. To indicate how non-price competition affects the previous analysis
F. To examine the effects of product differentiation from the consumer's point of view

CHAPTER OUTLINE

So far we have looked at the two extreme forms of market structure—perfect competition and pure monopoly. In practice, most firms are neither perfectly competitive nor purely monopolistic.

10.1: PRODUCT DIFFERENTIATION

Most industries, it is true, consist of many firms in competition with each other. However, although the various firms may produce basically the same good or service (for example, cameras or the services of a travel agent) the product is not exactly the same, which is one of the conditions of perfect competition. Consumers will, for example, prefer one make of camera or one firm of travel agent over another, even though they may cost the same. The reason for this is that most firms, although making basically the same product as their competitors, try to make their own product distinctive—for example, by differences in packaging, by use of brand-name advertising, by better service, and so on. All these efforts are aimed at achieving what is called *product differentiation.*

There is a limit, nevertheless, beyond which a firm cannot go in trying to make its product "unique" and so confer on itself monopoly power. Whatever the amount of product differentiation, consumers will usually switch to another similar product made by a rival firm if the price of the original product is raised too much. Thus, no firm can create for itself conditions of pure monopoly. However, successful product differentiation can make the demand curve for a firm's product more inelastic than it would otherwise be. And in, say, the case of a plastic surgeon or other person with special skills who has devoted customers, the demand curve may be almost vertical—meaning that practically any price may be charged without loss of customers.

To provide a better explanation of how most firms actually behave than do the theories of perfect competition and pure monopoly, a new theory—that of monopolistic competition—was advanced in the 1930s.

10.2: MONOPOLISTIC COMPETITION DEFINED

Monopolistic competition is a market situation in which the following conditions are present.

1. There are many firms, each of which is responsible for only a relatively small part of total supply. This means that each firm can act without much fear of retaliation by other rival firms, in the form either of price-cutting or of non-price competition.

2. Each firm's product, although basically the same, is not identical to that of the other firms in the industry. If some measure of monopolistic power is to be obtained, a firm must be able to differentiate its product from that of its competitors. The firm can achieve this in many ways: for example, by use of a brand, distinctive packaging, effective advertising, good sales techniques, availability of credit, good location of sales outlets, and satisfactory after-sales service.

3. Each firm has only a limited ability to raise the price of its product without losing sales. Through product differentiation, each firm can build its own loyal clientele. But if the price is raised too much, customers will eventually switch to another, cheaper brand.

A *brand* is a general term which includes any name, symbol, design, or combination of these, used to identify some or all of the goods of a particular manufacturer or retailer. The term *brand name* refers to any word or letters contained in the brand and which can be vocalized. *Brand mark* or *trademark* is another name for the symbol used in the brand.

4. New firms can enter the industry. However, entry is more difficult than under perfect competition because the new firm has to compete with firms that have already built brand or store loyalties among the buying public. The new firm will have to spend a great deal on advertising, samples, and other forms of sales promotion to entice consumers away from existing firms. It may also have to invest considerably in research and development to ensure that its product will have a competitive edge over similar products already on the market.

The most important example of monopolistic competition in Canada is the retailing industry. Although there are many firms in each particular line—drug stores, gift shops, flower shops, dry cleaners, restaurants, travel agents, and so on—consumers usually have a definite preference for one store or firm rather than another. This may be because of price differences, but more often because of convenience of location, credit and delivery facilities, or quality of service. And each firm, through advertising, store appearance, and customer service, constantly tries to make itself even more distinct from its competitors.

10.3: DEMAND FOR A MONOPOLISTIC COMPETITOR'S OUTPUT

As we saw in Chapter 8, demand for a firm's output is perfectly elastic when the firm is operating under conditions of perfect competition. A firm can sell as much as it wants without affecting the price. The demand curve is perfectly horizontal. Under pure monopoly, however, the firm *is* the industry and the demand for its products is the aggregate or market demand. So the amount that the monopolist supplies of its product will directly influence the market price. The monopolist can only sell substantially more of its product if it lowers the price significantly. The demand curve for the product is, in other words, downward-sloping from left to right.

By comparison, the demand curve for the product of a firm operating under monopolistic competition is certainly not perfectly elastic. This is because such a firm will have to lower its price to draw customers away from competitors. However, since such a firm is still only one among many suppliers, it does not have to reduce the price drastically (as would a pure monopolist) to encourage consumers to buy more. Conversely, if such a firm were to raise its price, it would soon lose its customers.

In conclusion, we can say that the demand for the product of a firm operating under conditions of monopolistic competition is quite price elastic—not perfectly elastic as under perfect competition but more elastic than under pure monopoly. We can also say that the smaller the number of competing firms and the greater the degree of product differentiation, the closer a firm will be to a pure monopolist's situation. Conversely, the greater the number of competing firms and the smaller the degree of product differentiation, the closer a firm will be to a perfect competitor's situation.

10.4: SHORT-RUN OUTPUT AND PRICE

A firm operating under conditions of monopolistic competition will, the same as any other privately-owned firm, try to maximize its profit or minimize its loss. In the short run, it will attempt to produce that output at which the surplus of total revenue over total cost is greatest. This output, seen from the marginal point of view, is where marginal revenue equals marginal cost. The firm will increase output, therefore, so long as the additional revenue from each extra unit exceeds the additional cost. This marginal revenue, we should remember, is not the same as price. Because the demand curve is downward-sloping, more can be sold only at a lower price. Marginal revenue is, therefore, the price received for the additional unit minus the reduction in price on all the other units. Marginal cost will at first fall but, because of increasing variable costs as the firm approaches full capacity, it will begin to rise steeply. In the short run, a firm operating under conditions of monopolistic competition may make an economic profit, an economic loss, or just break even. These three possible situations are shown in Figure 10:1.

Since, under monopolistic competition, marginal revenue is less than market price, a firm will produce less than it would under perfect

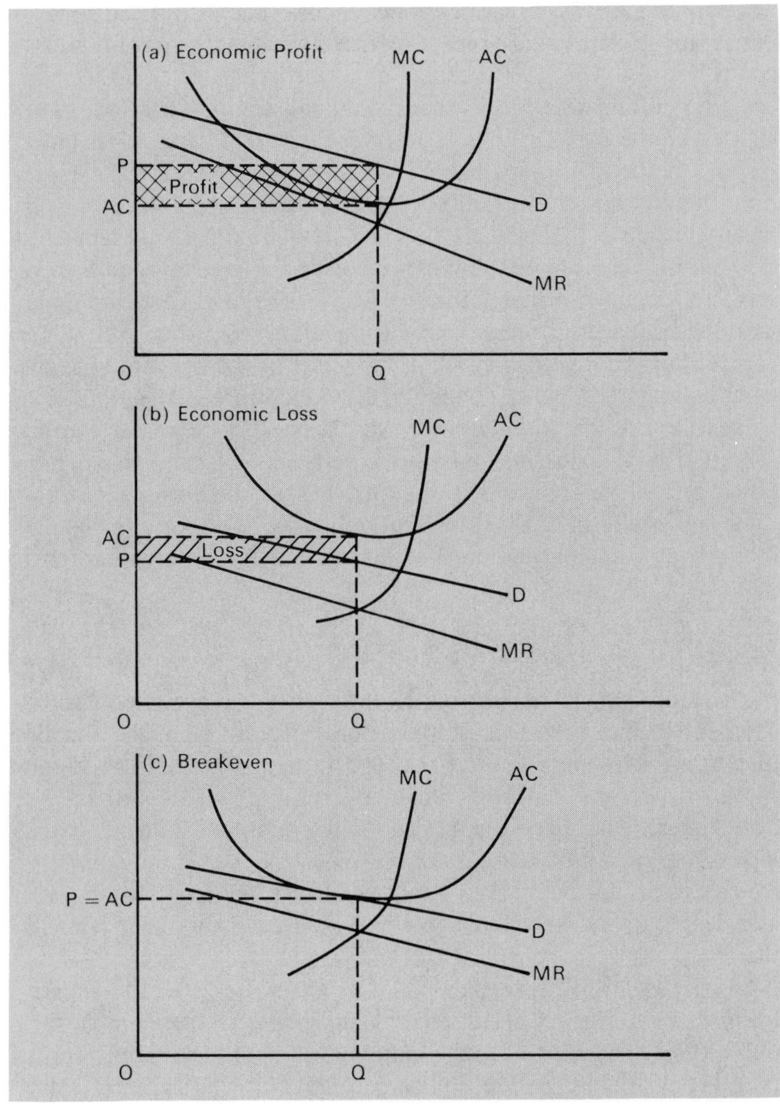

Note: Each firm produces that output (OQ) at which marginal revenue (MR) equals marginal cost (MC). In situation (a), market price (P) exceeds average cost (AC), resulting in a profit for the firm. In situation (b), average cost exceeds market price, resulting in a loss. In situation (c), price equals average cost and the firm merely breaks even.

Figure 10:1 Possible Short-Run Positions of the Monopolistically Competitive Firm competition. Also, because of the heavy cost of advertising, distinctive design and packaging, after-sales service, and other forms of non-price competition, it will have to charge more for its product. Furthermore, the splintered market means that each manufacturing firm will have a shorter production run than it otherwise would. Therefore, it cannot obtain, and pass on to the public, any benefit from large-scale production. In addition, product differentiation, particularly in retailing, can mean considerable duplication of facilities—one glaring example, at least until recently, was the presence of two, three, or even four gas stations or bank branches at many road intersections. These are important disadvantages of monopolistic competition compared with perfect competition. However, they are partly offset by the benefit to the public of a greater variety of goods and services offered. Also, it is by no means certain that the resources displaced (for example, the gas-station or bank managers and other employees) will find employment elsewhere. There are also strong arguments for the encouragement in Canada of small business firms, not only as a source of employment, but also as a training ground for entrepreneurs and as a bastion of democracy.

10.5: LONG-RUN OUTPUT AND PRICE

In the long run, firms are free to leave or enter a monopolistically competitive industry. This is completely different from the situation under pure monopoly where no other firm can get in. This freedom of movement means that firms which are sustaining a loss—those with average total cost greater than price—will tend to switch to some other type of production or close down completely. It also means that firms which can produce at a profit—those with average total cost the same as or less than price—will tend to enter the industry or stay in if already there.

So long as a firm can keep its ATC no greater than price, it will earn a normal profit. The net effect, in the long run, of all these countervailing forces is that all firms in the industry will tend to earn only normal profit—the situation in which price equals ATC. This situation is illustrated in Figure 10:1(c). Pure or economic profit will tend to disappear because the entry of new firms into the industry will mean that each firm will now obtain a smaller share of the market and be faced with a larger number of close substitutes for its products. And this in turn means that the demand curve for each firm's product will shift to the left and become more elastic.

However, there are several reasons why, in practice, some firms may for some time continue to make more or less than normal profit. First, some firms will be more successful than others in differentiating their product. To the extent that they are able to build strong customer loyalty to their particular brand or store, these firms may be able to earn an economic profit. This profit, although attractive to would-be competitors, may nevertheless continue to be earned by some firms for the simple reason that nobody can entice their customers away. A second reason for some firms earning economic profit, even in the long run, is that it is often very expensive for a new firm to enter an industry. Also, for various reasons, some firms may not, in the long run, move out of an industry even though they are making a loss. The owner of a small grocery store or restaurant may hang on even though little or no return is received for the capital or time expended. The owner may not be able to find a buyer for the business or may not be willing to risk or be able to afford any other type of life.

10.6: NON-PRICE COMPETITION

Let us now look more closely at competition among firms other than by price. In order to increase its sales, a firm operating under monopolistic competition may do more than just lower its price. It may redesign its product, advertise more, increase its selling effort, or offer better after-sales service. How does this affect our previous analysis? Basically, a change in price means a change in the quantity demanded as a result of a shift along an existing demand curve. A change in the amount of non-price competition is really an attempt to alter the demand curve so that consumers will demand more at each given price. Of course, this additional non-price competition will also alter a firm's cost structure. So, as well as a new pattern of marginal revenue, we would have a new pattern of marginal cost. Equilibrium would, nevertheless, still be at the point at which MR = MC. In practice, the ideal combination of price, output, and promotional expenditure will only be found, if at all, on the basis of trial and error.

10.7: PRODUCT DIFFERENTIATION AND THE CONSUMER

Product differentiation, as the key element in non-price competition, helps a firm secure its own loyal band of customers, and there is nothing like having a stable core of demand in a fiercely competitive market. But does product differentiation help the consumer? The answer to this question is highly subjective. Nevertheless, it is possible to claim as a benefit: the variety of product styles and qualities; the attempt by most firms to make their own products more satisfying and attractive to the consumer; the urge felt by a firm to inform consumers about its products; and even the availability of customer credit.

The biggest possible disadvantage to the consumer of product differentiation is that it sometimes helps to perpetuate the existence of many small firms rather than just a few large ones. This can mean, for certain types of product, that the consumer is prevented from obtaining the benefits of large-scale production and merchandising. Thus, many small retail stores may continue to exist even though the public might be better served, from the cost point of view, by fewer, larger units. However, experience indicates that, for many products, the personal service of the small store is still essential.

Some people criticize product differentiation for confusing the consumer with so many similar products. According to this point of view, life would be simpler for a woman, for instance, if she had only one style of dress from which to choose. But for many women, on the other hand, life would be much less interesting. Would we be happier buying only one make and model of car year in and year out, even though the price were less? No one can disagree, however, that changing the appearance of a product just to make the previous ones appear obsolete is economically very wasteful. On the other hand, planned obsolescence helps promote sales and thereby increases national income and employment.

Summary

1. Most firms, even though producing basically the same product as that of their competitors, try to make their own product distinctive. This *product differentiation* is achieved by such means as differences in product design, differences in customer service, differences in packaging, and use of brand-name advertising.
2. To provide a more direct explanation than the theories of perfect competition and pure monopoly of how most firms actually behave, a new theory—that of monopolistic competition—was advanced in the 1930s. *Monopolistic competition* exists when: (a) there are many firms, each of which is responsible for only a relatively small part of total supply; (b) each firm's product, although basically the same, is not identical to that of the other firms in the industry; (c) each firm has only a limited ability to raise the price of its product without losing sales; and (d) new firms can enter the industry. The most important example of monopolistic competition in Canada is the retailing industry.

3. The demand for the product of a firm operating under conditions of monopolistic competition is quite price-elastic—not perfectly elastic as under perfect competition, but more elastic than under pure monopoly.
4. A firm operating under monopolistic competition will attempt to produce that output at which marginal revenue equals marginal cost. However, marginal revenue is not the same as price; it is the price received for the additional unit *minus* the reduction in price on all the other units. This is because the demand curve for the firm's products is downward-sloping; that is, more can be sold only at a lower price.
5. Under monopolistic competition, a firm will produce less than it would under perfect competition. Also, because of the heavy cost of non-price competition, it will have to charge more for its product. However, a greater variety of goods and services will be offered.
6. Because of freedom of movement in and out of an industry operating under monopolistic competition, all firms will, in the long run, tend to earn only normal profit—the situation in which price equals ATC. However, there are several reasons why, in practice, some firms may for some time continue to make more or less than normal profit.
7. A change in the amount of non-price competition is really an attempt to alter the demand curve so that consumers will demand more at each given price. Product differentiation, the key element in non-price competition, provides the consumer with variety of choice, better product design, greater product information, and other customer services. However, by helping to perpetuate the existence of many small firms rather than just a few large ones, product differentiation makes it more difficult for the consumer to obtain the benefits of large-scale production and merchandising. However, for many goods and services, the personal service of the small store is still essential.

Key Terms

Product differentiation 184
Monopolistic competition 184
Brand 185
Brand name 185
Brand mark 185
Trademark 185
Non-price competition 189

Review Questions

1. What is meant by product differentiation? How is it achieved? What is its purpose?
2. Despite product differentiation, no firm can create for itself conditions of pure monopoly. Explain.
3. What are the characteristics of monopolistic competition?
4. Why is retailing considered to be a prime example of monopolistic competition?
5. Explain the nature of the demand for the product of a firm operating under monopolistic competition.
6. What is the optimum output, in the short run, for a firm operating under monopolistic competition? How does this compare with the optimum output under perfect competition?
7. How does freedom of movement in and out of a monopolistically competitive industry theoretically affect long-run profits? What exceptions exist in practice?
8. Explain the nature and purpose of non-price competition.
9. From the viewpoint of the consumer, what are the advantages and disadvantages of product differentiation?

11. OLIGOPOLY: COMPETITION AMONG THE FEW

CHAPTER OBJECTIVES

A. To explain the nature and origin of oligopolies
B. To analyze an oligopolist's marketing and production behaviour
C. To examine the various forms of collusive oligopoly
D. To explain how prices are set in an oligopoly
E. To discuss non-price competition, particularly advertising
F. To examine how oligopolies affect the public
G. To review government competition policy, including the Combines Investigation Act
H. To compare the advantages and disadvantages of competition, from the public's point of view, as a conclusion to our analysis of the different market structures

CHAPTER OUTLINE

11.1 Oligopoly Defined
11.2 Reasons for Existence of Oligopoly
11.3 Oligopolist's Production and Marketing Behaviour
11.4 Price and Output
11.5 Cartels, Unwritten Agreements, and Trusts
11.6 Price Leadership
11.7 Resale Price Maintenance
11.8 Non-Price Competition
11.9 Advertising
11.10 Oligopoly: Friend or Foe?
11.11 Oligopoly versus Monopoly
11.12 Government Competition Policy
11.13 Advantages and Disadvantages of Competition

In our discussion of monopolistic competition, we stipulated that the number of firms in an industry must be quite large. The implication was that a firm could act with little or no fear of retaliation by its competitors. But what if there are only a few firms in an industry? This situation of competition among the few is called *oligopoly*—from the Greek *oligos*, meaning "few," and *poly*, meaning "sellers."

11.1: OLIGOPOLY DEFINED

An oligopoly is considered to exist if there are only a few firms in an industry and each firm is interdependent in its price and output policy. By a few firms we mean any number from two (sometimes called a *duopoly*) to, say, ten or twenty, depending on the industry. There is, in fact, no generally accepted maximum number. The criterion as to whether a firm is operating under oligopoly or monopolistic competition is whether the firm's price and promotional decisions may cause changes in the other firms' behaviour. If there are so few firms in an industry that, say, a cut in price by one firm causes a retaliatory cut in price by the others, then we are dealing with oligopoly. If there are so many firms that each one can act quite independently, then we are talking of monopolistic competition. The reason for this distinction should by now be obvious: an *oligopolist* (unlike a monopolistic competitor) will have to think twice before cutting price, launching a new promotional campaign, or otherwise disturbing the current market situation. If not careful, the oligopolist may spark a price or other type of competitive war that may leave it worse off than before.

Oligopoly, in its various forms, is a very common form of market structure in Canada. Most of the things we buy, ranging from soap to newspapers, are produced or marketed by a relatively small number of large firms.

It should be emphasized, however, that not all oligopolies are the same. In some industries there are just one or two firms, whereas in others there may be ten, twenty, or more. In some industries, firms produce exactly the same product, whereas in other industries they have a differentiated one. In some industries, member firms enter into "gentlemen's agreements" and other forms of price collusion; in others, they act in strict independence. In some industries, it is relatively easy for new firms to enter; in others, it is not. In some industries, firms are highly interdependent, whereas in others they are much less so.

11.2: REASONS FOR EXISTENCE OF OLIGOPOLY

There are four basic reasons for the existence of oligopolies. First, economies can be obtained from manufacturing or marketing on a large scale. Second, business firms, through advertising and other means, can create artificial barriers to competition. Third, many firms pursue a deliberate policy of acquiring other firms. Fourth, despite the Combines Investigation Act, the federal government encourages some industrial mergers and takeovers.

11.3: PRODUCTION AND MARKETING BEHAVIOUR

When there are only a few firms in an industry, as with oligopoly, the probable behaviour of competing firms becomes of crucial importance. The fewer the firms, the more important this behaviour becomes. A firm must not only try to predict what competitors will do if it pursues a certain course of action, it must also be able to react swiftly to anything that they actually do. If it reacts too slowly, it may already have lost many of its previous customers.

An oligopolist's production and marketing behaviour will also vary according to whether the product is exactly the same as that of rival firms or whether the monopolist is able by various means to differentiate it. That is why it is usual to divide oligopolies into two basic types. The first of these, *pure oligopoly*, is where a few firms produce an identical product, such as steel, cement, or sugar. The second, *differentiated oligopoly*, is where a few firms produce a similar but differentiated product, such as cheese, cars, or television sets.

The most distinctive characteristic of oligopoly, from the viewpoint of economic analysis, is the air of uncertainty that surrounds a firm's possible behaviour. It is impossible for a firm to predict with any degree of certainty how other firms will react if it reduces its price or changes any aspect of its non-price competition. This last fact has given rise to what is called the "Theory of Games," in which as in a poker game, one player (or firm) tries to outwit the others.[1]

11.4: PRICE AND OUTPUT

Because of the many possible combinations of oligopolistic situations (as well as the air of uncertainty as to how other firms will react to, say, a change in price by firm A), no general economic theory of price and output determination under oligopoly has been established. How can we say, for example, that a firm will sell 10000 more units of output if it reduces the price of its product by $1.00, when one or more rival firms may or may not also cut their prices or undertake a retaliatory advertising campaign?

Undoubtedly, an oligopolistic firm will ideally go on producing and selling more up to the point at which marginal revenue equals marginal cost. Just like a firm in any other market structure, it wishes to maximize its profit. And, certainly like any other firm, it will have a definite pattern of production costs. The big question that arises with oligopoly, however, is the nature of the demand for a firm's product. But how can a firm foresee what it can sell at different prices if it does not know how its competitors will react?

Of course, we can build economic models based on a variety of assumptions—for example, that if firm A cuts its price, firms B and C will not. Models of this sort have been in existence since the early nineteenth century. The one that carries most weight today is that advanced by Edward Chamberlin in 1933[2]. This is a model in which there are two firms, each producing the same product. According to Chamberlin's theory, the two firms will reach a tacit agreement to produce between them the output which affords a large measure of monopoly profit. Both firms would recognize that price-cutting, in an attempt to capture each other's share of the market, would be detrimental to both, unless total demand for the industry's product is very price-elastic. Instead, they would both tend to restrict output, even without collusion, and share the market and the monopoly profit between them. Once this understanding has been reached, the price would be reasonably stable as each firm would know that a price cut by one would trigger retaliation by the other. Of course, one firm might undertake such a battle in order to destroy its opponent and, in the long run, capture the whole market for itself.

11.5: CARTELS, UNWRITTEN AGREEMENTS, AND TRUSTS

Two facts—the small number of firms and their mutual interdependence— make it both relatively easy and advantageous for oligopolistic firms to engage in some form of price and output collusion. In this way, they can avoid painful price wars, reduce competitive uncertainty, maintain stable output levels, deter possible new entrants to the industry, and even implement industry-wide price increases.

There are various forms of *collusive oligopoly*. When a formal written agreement is entered into to restrict output and fix prices, the participating firms are described as a *cartel.* Thus, for example, most airlines, including Air Canada and CP Air, are members of IATA (the International Association of Airlines), a cartel that sets air-travel prices. Unwritten arrangements between firms, or even countries, usually with regard only to the price to be charged, are known as *gentlemen's agreements.* Cartels and gentlemen's agreements, since they are voluntary associations of independent manufacturing firms often located in different countries, are by no means always successful in restricting output and keeping up prices. Occasionally, there are disputes among members as well as outside competition. A good example of this has been the Organization of Petroleum Exporting Countries, or OPEC, which after a few years of spectacularly successful price and output regulation, became bitterly divided once the world oil supply began to exceed demand at the current OPEC price.

To ensure better control over firms producing the same product than could a voluntary association, a different form of organization, the *trust*, was devised in the United States in the nineteenth century. This was an amalgamation of a number of different firms, the shareholders of which were given trust certificates in exchange for their shares.

Another method of securing control over a number of previously independent business firms is to establish a *holding company.* This is a firm which is set up purely for the purpose of acquiring the controlling interest in other firms. The firms are acquired either by *merger* (where the owners of the firm being acquired are quite willing to exchange control for shares in the holding company) or by *takeover* (where a controlling interest is obtained by buying up enough shares in the market against the will of the present controlling group of shareholders). The firms acquired in this way usually retain their previous name, but the management is often changed. Together, the holding company and its subsidiaries are known as a *conglomerate* or *group.*

Conglomerates are often highly diversified in their operations because of the desire of the entrepreneurs involved to reduce financial risk or to seize any profit opportunity that becomes available. Conglomerates enable a person with relatively little investment capital to acquire control over business assets worth many times the investor's own. This is because control of other companies can be obtained by ownership of a substantial block of the voting common shares of a company—and not necessarily 51 per cent, if share ownership is widely scattered. The assets of these other companies can, in turn, be used to acquire control of other companies. This practice is known as *leverage* or *pyramiding.*

"And before you could say Dun & Bradstreet, I'd been taken over."

11.6: PRICE LEADERSHIP

Oligopolistic firms, instead of participating in a cartel or unwritten agreement, will often adopt a "follow-my-leader" pricing policy. This is a policy whereby all or most firms in an industry follow the prices set by one large firm—the industry's unofficial price leader. Most firms are forced to follow the leader if it cuts its prices; otherwise, they will suffer a considerable reduction in sales, depending on how strong their customers' loyalty is. Most firms willingly follow the leader in raising prices since they know that the rise will be industry-wide and no firms will be at a competitive disadvantage. They also know that it can mean more profit for all—the actual amount varying according to the price-elasticity of market demand for the industry's product. Furthermore, it eliminates a great deal of the uncertainty from doing business. Often such a follow-my-leader policy becomes a matter of habit.

11.7: RESALE PRICE MAINTENANCE

An oligopolist spends a great deal of time and money in building up the brand image of its products and the distribution network that brings them to the consumer. By ensuring that the product is sold at the recommended retail price, the oligopolist knows that the retailer also obtains a good financial return and can therefore afford to give good customer service. If one store cuts the price of the product, the oligopolist will receive angry complaints from other retailers who sell at the suggested retail price. Also the image of the product in the eyes of the public may suffer. A recent example of this in Canada has been the retailing of art books.

For many years, oligopolists in Canada exerted pressure on retailers to sell only at the manufacturer's recommended retail price. They did this by threatening to discontinue, or actually discontinuing, supplies to the offending retailer. This practice of maintaining retail prices at the manufacturer's desired level is called *resale price maintenance.* It had the result, in practice, of enabling relatively inefficient retailers to survive and preventing more efficient price discounters from growing.

In Canada, resale price maintenance is now illegal. All that manufacturers may now do is to "suggest" the retail price. They may not legally enforce it. However, by owning retail outlets (such as service stations), it has been possible for some oligopolists (e.g., the oil companies) to continue control over the retail price of their products. And there are still occasional reports in the newspapers of attempts by suppliers to force retailers not to charge less than a certain price.

11.8: NON-PRICE COMPETITION

Although oligopolistic firms may be reluctant to engage in price-cutting because of its possibly dangerous consequences, this does not prevent them from competing in other ways. New styles or models of the product, more conveniently located sales outlets, brand name advertising, sponsorship of sporting events, intriguing sales promotional campaigns—all these various forms of non-price competition can together help expand a firm's sales.

If it is successful in its promotional efforts, a firm will have (a) made the demand for its product more price-inelastic (the demand curve falling more steeply from left to right) and (b) caused the demand curve for its products to shift to the right—meaning that consumers will buy more at each possible price than before.

Since these promotional efforts will have increased the firm's share of the market (assuming that total market demand remains the same), rival firms will also intensify their non-price competition. The final result may well be that the market shares enjoyed by each firm remain much the same, but that all firms, because of this extra non-price competition, have incurred higher total costs. Nevertheless, despite this possibility, heavy expenditure on advertising, selling, and other forms of non-price competition, is still a characteristic feature of firms operating under oligopolistic and monopolistic competition. In the case of perfect competition, by contrast, there would be little purpose in such non-price competition, for the product is the same, consumers are fully informed, and a firm can sell all it wishes to produce.

11.9: ADVERTISING

Perhaps the strongest claim that oligopolistic competition is wasteful is directed at the money (and therefore society's resources) spent on advertising. Advertising, formally defined, is the presentation of ideas, goods, or services to customers and prospective customers in a non-personal way by use of such media as newspapers, television, and direct mail. Part of this advertising is purely informative in nature—for example, details about product price and availability. However, another large part consists of subjective claims as to the product's performance and desirability. These claims about the quality of the product are really nothing more than a matter of personal opinion. Occasionally, there may even be misrepresentation, though this is against the law.

It is against the persuasive type of advertising that charges of waste are laid. Instead of spending so much money on this type of advertising, critics argue, why not just reduce the price of the product? Also, critics ask, why should consumers have to submit, when watching a television show or reading a newspaper or magazine, to being brainwashed with advertisements that repeat over and over again the brand name of the product and very little else? Indeed, the advertisements that inform or even amuse are considered to be few and far between. Or why, some people would complain, should the countryside and even city streets be disfigured by a wild variety of billboards and illuminated signs?

Critics also argue that advertising often does not even achieve its goals. If all rival firms advertise their products then the advertising of one firm is largely offset in its impact and persuasive effect by the advertising of the others. If all firms were to spend less on advertising, money would be saved and all firms would still have the same chance of attracting customers. It is also argued that the heavy cost of advertising required to get a brand name established is a deterrent to new firms which contemplate entering an industry.

Another strong criticism of advertising is that it leads to *social imbalance*. By this is meant an unreasonable allocation of a society's resources between private goods, such as cars, dishwashers, and snowmobiles, and social goods, such as hospitals, schools, and roads, and the maintenance of law and order. Because of advertising, it is argued, consumers place a higher priority on, say, entertainment than they do on cleaning up their environment or eliminating disease.

Another criticism is that most of a country's news media depend on advertising as their principal source of revenue. This means, therefore, that large business firms often exert a direct or indirect censorship over program content. This, of course, may be considered a better alternative than government financing of the news media and the possibility of government censorship. But it may not be a better alternative to no censorship at all. Again, it is a matter of opinion.

Another criticism of advertising in recent years is the use by governments in Canada of large sums of the taxpayers' money to advertise the virtues of various government programs. However, the governments argue that the public needs to be better informed and also not just receive the private sector point of view.

What are some of the arguments in favour of advertising? Certainly the need to inform consumers of new products, as well as of new features in existing products, is a necessary task. Even in communist countries, "commercials" abound on state television programs. Thus, advertising keeps the consumer informed about the possible range of choice. Another argument is that advertising encourages consumers to buy and thereby helps bring about production. Without a high level of consumer demand, production in our type of private-enterprise society would tend to stagnate, unemployment rise, and incomes fall. In other words, advertising, both informative and persuasive, is one of the engines of economic prosperity. Also, it is argued, advertising enables a firm to increase its sales and thereby reduce its average costs of production by manufacturing on a larger scale. Consumers will therefore obtain the product at a lower price than would otherwise be the case. However, as we have already indicated, some people question the efficiency of competitive advertising in enlarging demand. Also, critics question whether any reduction in cost would be passed on to consumers, especially if the firm now has fewer competitors. It is also argued that advertising enables the public to enjoy their newspapers and televised hockey games at little or no cost. However, it may also be argued that the public pays for the advertising in the form of higher prices for the products. The alternative, say, for television, would be, as in many other countries, to pay an annual fee to the company (often government-owned) that provides television broadcasting.

11.10: OLIGOPOLY: FRIEND OR FOE?

Is oligopoly, as a market structure, beneficial to society? One point of view is that, since the entry of new firms is restricted in an oligopoly, output is less and price is higher than they would be under perfect competition. In other words, because there is less competition in such an industry, society gets less output and pays more for it than would otherwise be the case. Firms operating under oligopoly, as well as under monopolistic competition and pure monopoly, are guilty, so to speak, of failing to produce up to the point at which marginal cost equals price. The fewer firms there are and the more difficult it is to enter the industry, the further away the industry gets from the purely competitive situation. Also, part of the advertising by such firms is considered by many to be socially wasteful.

In practice, it has been noted that many oligopolistic firms such as car makers, airlines, and radio, television, camera, watch manufacturers and so on have constantly improved the quality of their product and kept price increases relatively small compared with those of other products and the country's rate of inflation. They have also expanded output to take full advantage, wherever possible, of the economies of large-scale production. In some countries, such as Britain, France and Japan, governments have in fact openly or discreetly encouraged oligopolies as a means of promoting the orderly growth of industry and the necessary technological research for product development. According to this point of view, a few firms are more beneficial to society than many.

11.11: OLIGOPOLY VERSUS MONOPOLY

From the public's point of view, any agreement to restrict competition means that product prices are kept abnormally high and output restricted. In fact, there are several good reasons for concluding that the effects of a collusive oligopoly are more detrimental to consumers than the effects of even a pure monopoly. First, a pure monopoly is so apparent that its prices are usually regulated by government, as, for example, with Bell Canada. Second, a pure monopolist will not need to undertake the expensive advertising and sales promotion that is essential to oligopolistic firms if they wish to expand or maintain their share of the market or to differentiate their products. Third, it can also be argued, but with less assurance, that a pure monopolist will take better advantage of the economies of large-scale production than a number of oligopolistic firms each with a limited share of the market.

11.12: GOVERNMENT COMPETITION POLICY

At one time, collusion among oligopolistic firms, with regard to product price and market shares, was considered quite respectable among business people and politicians. However, by the 1930s, meetings of cartel members were being held more and more discreetly. Also, the names of the cartels were being changed to more innocent-sounding ones. After World War II, efforts were made by the authorities in many Western European countries to break up cartels. In the United States, trusts had been outlawed as long ago as 1890 by the Sherman Act. Nevertheless, attempts by firms to enlarge their control over the market by buying control of rival firms continue and anti-trust legislation still has to be invoked. However, in some countries (even those concerned with eliminating international cartels) firms in certain industries were encouraged to merge, sometimes with government financial aid. The governments concerned—for example, the British—felt that larger-sized firms might better be able to lower per unit production and marketing costs, undertake expensive research and development, and compete better abroad. Thus, mergers for purposes of "rationalization" were sometimes considered desirable. In Japan, cartels have for many years been officially encouraged as a means of ensuring large-scale production, a high level of research and development, and the more orderly development of industry—promoting thereby a favourable balance of payments, with a high level of exports of manufactured goods providing jobs and income for the country's labour force.

Combines Investigation Act

In Canada, as far back as 1923, the federal Parliament passed a *Combines Investigation Act* authorizing the government to investigate and prosecute firms combining to restrain trade. Under the terms of the Act, a Director of Investigation and Research is responsible for investigating alleged offences and a Restrictive Trade Practices Commission for reviewing the evidence and recommending action by the Registrar General of Canada. An inquiry into alleged offences can be held (a) following an application by six Canadian citizens, (b) on the initiative of the Director, or (c) at the direction of the Registrar General of Canada.

The most important practice outlawed by the Act is the formation of mergers or monopolies. A *merger*, as we have seen, is where one firm gains control of a competitor and thereby reduces competition. A *monopoly* is where a firm gains complete or almost complete control of a certain type of business in a particular area and thereby reduces competition. Such a monopoly is legal only if the monopoly right is conferred by the Patent Act or by any other Act of the federal Parliament.

Pricing practices outlawed by the Act are: (a) *price fixing*—an agreement by business firms, often unwritten, to charge the same price for similar products; (b) *price discrimination*—the practice of selling goods more cheaply to one firm than to another; (c) *predatory pricing*—the practice of charging abnormally low prices in order to reduce or eliminate competition; (d) *price misrepresentation*—the practice by a firm of misrepresenting the price at which it sells its goods; and (e) *resale price maintenance*—the practice by a manufacturer of setting the price at which wholesalers and retailers may sell the product and ensuring that these prices are observed by the actual or threatened cutting off of supplies. All these practices limit competition and prevent the public from being able to buy the goods involved at the lowest price. Such practices interfere, in other words, with the free play of the market forces of supply and demand. The prevention of such practices has, therefore, long been considered to be in the public interest. There are, of course, at the same time, many government-run or government-regulated monopolies in Canada.

Although the Act seems positive enough, particularly with the various amendments made in 1949, 1952 and 1960, its enforcement has always suffered from lack of staff. Various ways have also been devised—for example, consignment selling by oil companies—to avoid prosecution under the Act. In addition, any fines imposed under the

Act have been considered too low to have had any real deterrent effect.

In 1971, because of the inadequacies of the Combines Investigation Act, the federal government proposed new legislation in this area. However, Bill C256, as it was called, provoked a great deal of criticism, particularly from business and was subsequently withdrawn.

In 1973, the federal government decided to implement changes in competition policy in two stages. The first stage, Bill C-2, was passed by Parliament in October 1975 and came into force on January 1, 1976. Stage I greatly increased the powers of the Restrictive Trade Practices Commission, giving it review power over such trade arrangements as refusal to sell, consignment selling, exclusive dealing, tied sales, market restriction, and trade practices detrimental to small business firms and the public at large. A second major change was the extension of the coverage of the Combines Investigation Act to all service industries except electric power, rail transportation, telephone service, and bona fide trade union activities. Previously, only industries producing, transporting, storing, distributing, or selling physical goods were included. A third important change was the abolition of the need to prove "complete or virtual elimination" of competition.

In June, 1986, the federal government proclaimed a new *Competition Act* designed to modernize Canada's competition law and ensure greater competition in the Canadian marketplace. Under the Act, a Competition Tribunal is empowered to block or dissolve combinations (including mergers, acquisitions, or joint ventures) that are considered likely to cause a substantial reduction of competition in a market. However, the Act does recognize that for purposes of efficiency, large-scale production and distribution are often required. But the onus is on the firms involved to demonstrate that these economies could not be otherwise achieved. For firms defined as "dominant" in an industry, the Act prohibits all strategies designed to prevent the entry of new competitors, eliminate existing competitors, or restrict the degree of price competition in a market.

11.13: ADVANTAGES AND DISADVANTAGES OF COMPETITION

Let us now conclude our analysis of different market structures and this part of the book by setting out the pros and cons of competition in the market-place.

Advantages

The first advantage of competition, from the viewpoint of the economy as a whole, is the more efficient use of a country's resources. At present, many Canadian manufacturing industries are inefficient because of small plant size, short production runs, and multiplicity of product lines. More competition tends to reduce the number of firms in an industry and enables the remaining firms to achieve economies of scale, such as mechanized materials handling, greater specialization of labour and equipment, and more effective use of their marketing organizations. So long as the displaced labour and equipment can be usefully employed in other production, this rationalization of an industry is beneficial for the economy as per unit production and marketing costs are less. The scope for achieving such economies of scale is even greater if the number of models, styles, or designs offered to consumers is substantially reduced. The continued existence of many small firms, because of government subsidies or resale price maintenance, for instance, may prevent a firm from reaching a size that would permit it to achieve major economies of scale and to spend substantial sums on research and development, which is a vital ingredient of future growth in practically all industries, not just "high-tech" manufacturing. This is why governments in countries such as Japan, Britain, Italy, and Germany have at various times deliberately encouraged the merger of small and medium-sized companies. Such a policy of rationalization not only offers production and marketing benefits at home, but also economies in exporting goods abroad. Thus, the optimum size of firm in certain industries such as steel manufacture, telephone service, and newspapers may in some countries be just one or two firms rather than many. Even without government encouragement, the industry would gradually reduce the number of firms by mergers and takeovers.

At the retailing level, competition has meant the development of supermarkets that can merchandise food more economically than the small corner store. However, we once again encounter the question of social cost. Some people argue that the social cost of the elimination of many small retail stores has outweighed the economic benefits of mass food merchandising.

The second advantage of competition is that it forces business firms to pass part or all of the benefits of improved efficiency on to consumers. These benefits are passed on in the form of lower prices or, at least, prices that do not increase as rapidly as the general price level. Thus, the price of many manufactured goods in Canada has risen relatively slowly because of continuing improvements in plant efficiency and the price of some goods such as ball point pens, electronic calculators, and microcomputers, has even declined.

A third advantage of competition is that it keeps business firms alert. It makes them constantly seek ways to lower production and marketing costs and encourages them to develop new products, all of which ultimately benefit the consumer.

Disadvantages

What are the possible disadvantages of competition? First of all, there is the social and economic disruption caused to a community when a firm is forced to reduce or stop production and lay off its employees. Even though a firm may not be as efficient as a newer firm located elsewhere, this is not necessarily a justification for closing it down completely and depriving its employees of jobs they may have held for many years. This would not be a rational use of a country's human resources, especially when chances of employment elsewhere, particularly for the older worker, may be very poor. Also, the buildings and equipment may not, in fact, be used to produce something else; they may just lie idle. The mobility of human and capital resources is not in practice very great. If it has taken two or three generations to build a firm, should that firm be banished overnight?

A second disadvantage of competition relates to imports. Although imports of goods manufactured abroad—for example, Japanese television sets—can mean lower prices for the Canadian public, it can also mean cutbacks in domestic production of similar items and a reduction in Canadian employment and income. Foreign competition, it is true, can help keep many Canadian producers on their toes, but it can also mean their gradual elimination.

Summary

1. An *oligopoly* is considered to exist if there are only a few firms in an industry, and each firm is interdependent in its price and output policy. *Pure oligopoly* is where a few firms produce an identical product, such as steel, cement, or sugar. *Differentiated oligopoly* is where a few firms produce a similar, but differentiated, product, such as cheese, cars, or television sets. Oligopoly, in its various forms, is the most common form of market structure in Canada.
2. Because of the many different types of oligopolistic situations (as well as the air of uncertainty as to how other firms will react to,

say, a change in price by firm A), no general economic theory of price and output determination under oligopoly has been established.

3. There are various forms of *collusive oligopoly*. When firms in an industry sign a formal, written agreement to restrict output and fix prices, the participating firms are described as a *cartel*. Less formal arrangements between firms, usually with regard only to the price to be charged, are known as *gentlemen's agreements*. Being voluntary, such agreements were not always successful in their aims. Consequently, a different form of organization, the *trust*, was devised. This is an amalgamation of a number of different firms, the shareholders of which are given trust certificates in exchange for their shares. Another method of securing control over a number of previously independent firms is to establish a *holding company* which purchases a controlling interest in other firms. Together, the holding company and its subsidiaries are known as a *conglomerate* or a *group*.
4. Very often, oligopolistic firms, instead of participating in a cartel or gentlemen's agreement, will adopt a "follow-my-leader" price policy whereby all or most firms in an industry follow the prices set by one large firm.
5. For many years, oligopolists in Canada exerted pressure on retailers to sell only at the manufacturer's recommended retail price. They did this by threatening to discontinue, or actually discontinuing, supplies to the offending retailer. This practice of *resale price maintenance* is now illegal in Canada.
6. Oligopolistic firms, although reluctant to engage in price competition, aggressively undertake many forms of non-price competition, notably brand-name advertising. If successful, a firm will shift the demand curve for its products to the right.
7. Perhaps the strongest claim that oligopolistic competition is wasteful is directed at the money (and therefore society's resources) spent on persuasive-type advertising.
8. There are differing views as to whether oligopoly, as a market structure, is beneficial to society.
9. There are several good reasons for concluding that the effects of a collusive oligopoly are more detrimental to consumers than the effects of even a pure monopoly.
10. In Canada, any agreement to fix prices or otherwise reduce or eliminate competition is illegal under the terms of the Combines Investigation Act. However, most agreements, being oral rather than written, are not easy to detect.

Key Terms

Oligopoly 194
Duopoly 194
Oligopolist 194
Pure oligopoly 195
Differentiated oligopoly 195
Collusive oligopoly 196
Cartel 197
Gentlemen's agreement 197
OPEC 197
Trust 197
Holding company 197
Merger 197
Takeover 197
Conglomerate 197
Group 197
Leverage 197
Follow-my-leader pricing 199
Resale price maintenance 199
Non-price competition 200
Advertising 200
Social imbalance 201
Competition policy 203
Rationalization 203
Combines Investigation Act 204
Monopoly 204
Price fixing 204
Price discrimination 204
Predatory pricing 204
Price misrepresentation 204
Competition advantages 206
Competition disadvantages 207
Pyramiding 197

Review Questions

1. What is an oligopoly? A duopoly?
2. Distinguish between pure oligopoly and differentiated oligopoly.
3. Give three examples of oligopoly in Canada. Why do oligopolies exist?
4. What is an oligopolist's best-profit output? What is the main difficulty in determining an oligopolist's price and output behaviour?
5. What is the essence of Chamberlin's theory concerning the optimum output of an oligopolist?
6. Why do oligopolists find it both relatively easy and advantageous to engage in some form of price and output collusion? What forms does this collusion take?
7. Distinguish between a cartel and a conglomerate.
8. Why do governments of some countries discourage mergers and takeovers, while governments of other countries encourage them? What is the situation in Canada?
9. What is price leadership? Why does it exist?
10. What is resale price maintenance? What are the arguments for and against it?
11. Why do oligopolistic firms fear price competition, but aggressively engage in non-price competition?
12. Why is the persuasive-type advertising used by oligopolistic firms

considered to be wasteful? What are the arguments in favour of it?

13. From society's point of view, does oligopoly seem to be a desirable market structure?
14. What has the federal government done to promote competition in Canada? How effective have its efforts been?
15. What advantages does competition have for society? What disadvantages?
16. How has competition affected the retailing of food in recent years?
17. How has competition affected the supply of manufactured goods in recent years?
18. How do business firms view competition?
19. Most competition in Canada takes the form of non-price competition. Why is this so?
20. What steps can business firms take to reduce competition?

References

1 See, for example, John Von Neumann and Oskar Morgenstern, *Theory of Games and Economic Behaviour*, Princeton University Press, Princeton, N.J., 1944.

2 Edward Chamberlin, *The Theory of Monopolistic Competition*, Harvard University Press, Cambridge, Mass., 1933.

Part D: DISTRIBUTION OF INCOME

Here we examine the various basic types of remuneration (wages, rent, interest, or profit) that the factors of production receive in our society and why some factors, including people, receive more and others less.

"Okay, Reg, you win. A $1 million signing bonus, $500,000 a year for five years, and your mom gets to travel with the team."

12. DEMAND FOR THE FACTORS OF PRODUCTION

CHAPTER OBJECTIVES

A. To emphasize how the demand for labour and other factors of production is derived from the demand for a firm's product

B. To explain how the productivity of one factor may decline if more of it is used with the same amount of the other factors

C. To indicate how, in certain industries, an increase in the amount of all the factors may increase productivity

D. To analyze how the demand for a factor is determined under different market structures for the product

E. To explain how a firm decides on the best combination to use of the various factors of production

CHAPTER OUTLINE

The various factors of production (as described in Chapter 1, Unit 1.2) are land, labour, capital, entrepreneurship, and technology.

12.1: DERIVED DEMAND

A business firm is willing to employ the various factors of production for one reason only—namely, to help produce the goods and services that households, business firms, and governments want to buy. If a firm cannot sell its output, it will not want to hire more factors of production or even retain those that it already has. Conversely, the more goods a firm can sell, the bigger its demand for labour and the other factor inputs. That is why the demand for the factors of production is called a *derived demand.*

Because of its derived nature, the demand for one factor compared with another will depend, first, on that factor's *productivity*—that is, the amount of output that results from the services of each unit of that factor; and, second, on the market value of the output which that factor helps to produce. Thus, a leading hockey player is in great demand not only because of his skill as a hockey player (high productivity) but also, just as important, because the public is willing to pay a large sum of money to watch him perform (market value of output).

12.2: DIMINISHING MARGINAL RETURNS

The demand for a factor of production is influenced by the fact that output does not increase in proportion to the amount of the factor used. This fact was formulated as an economic principle, the *law of diminishing marginal returns*, by the English economist, David Ricardo, in the early nineteenth century. The law states that: *when the amount of one factor of production is increased relative to other factors that are fixed in amount, the extra output (or marginal return) from each additional unit of the variable factor may at first increase but will eventually decrease.* In other words, there will at first be *increasing marginal returns* as more of the variable factor is used, but eventually there will be *diminishing marginal returns.* These diminishing marginal returns may even become negative. This is because the extra units of the variable factor may cause so much confusion, and hamper production so greatly, that total output may actually decline.

Let us illustrate the law of diminishing marginal returns with a simple, hypothetical example. Assume, for example, that a farmer owns a tractor, plough, and other farm machinery, plus a hundred acres of land that he uses to grow wheat. In Table 12:1, we show how many bushels of wheat would be produced as the number of workers is increased (assuming all the workers are equally efficient). The farm machinery and the land are the fixed factors, and the number of workers the variable factor. With the farm machinery and one hundred acres of land and no workers, the output of wheat would be nil. With the same amount of land and machinery and one worker, output is 1000 bushels. With two workers, output is 2500 bushels. With three workers, it is 3500 bushels. With four workers, it is 4000. And, finally, with five workers, it is 3800 bushels. What has happened? At first, there were increasing marginal returns—the extra output from employing one extra worker rose from 1000 bushels to 1500 bushels. But then diminishing marginal returns set in. The extra output from employing a third worker is only 1000 bushels; that from the fourth worker only 500 bushels; and the fifth worker, instead of adding to production, causes total output to decline by 200 bushels.

Table 12:1
An Example of Diminishing Returns
Extra Units of Labour Combined with a Fixed Amount of Land

Number of Workers	*Total Output (bushels of wheat)*	*Extra Output from Each Additional Worker*
0	0	
1	1,000	1,000
2	2,500	1,500
3	3,500	1,000
4	4,000	500
5	3,800	−200

12.3: ECONOMIES OF SCALE

We have considered what can happen to output if the amount of one factor of production is increased relative to the other factors. But what happens to output if a firm employs more of every factor of production, leaving the relative proportions unchanged?

Bigness, or *mass production,* often enables a firm to reduce production costs per unit of output by, for example, quantity purchasing of materials, highly mechanized materials handling, effective use of special-purpose equipment, and greater specialization of labour. As the marginal cost of production falls, a firm's average variable cost curve (see Figure 12:1) and therefore also its average total cost curve will decline. Eventually, however, bigness of production will result in extra costs rather than economies, and the AVC and ATC curves will start to slope upwards to the right.

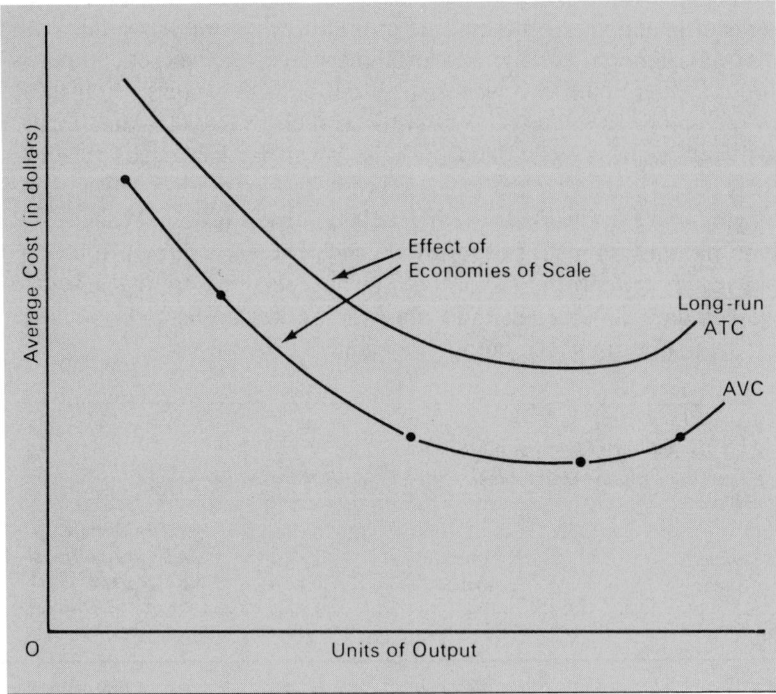

Figure 12:1 Economies of Scale Cause Declining AVC and ATC Curves

By increasing the amount employed of all the factors of production, a firm can obtain greater additional output from each factor than it would if that factor alone were increased. This greater output from the extra units of all the factors of production is described as *increasing returns to scale*. The more productive each factor of production is, because of mass production, the lower the cost of the product. And the lower the price, the bigger the demand for the product, and the bigger the demand for the factors that produce it.

12.4: FACTOR DEMAND UNDER PERFECT COMPETITION

We have noted that the demand for a factor of production is a derived one; that is, it will vary according to (a) the factor's productivity, and (b) the market value of the output which that factor helps to produce. Now, on the one hand, the market price of a product may remain the same whatever the amount produced. This is the case with perfect competition—a market structure in which the market price of the goods produced remains the same whatever the level of a firm's output. On the other hand, the market price of a product may fall as more is produced. This is the case of imperfect competition. Depending on which market structure we assume, the demand for a factor of production will be different. Consequently, even though imperfect competition is the typical market structure in modern society, we shall examine factor demand under the two possible situations.

Let us use a numerical example to explain how the demand for a factor of production is determined under perfect competition. In Table 12:2, we show, first of all, what might happen to output if more and more units of one factor, say factor A, are added to a fixed amount of other factors. In accordance with the law of diminishing marginal returns, we see that the additional output of, say, product X, from each extra unit of factor A becomes less and less as more of the variable

Table 12:2
Marginal Revenue Product Determines a Firm's Demand for a Factor of Production under Perfect Competition

Units of Variable Factor Input Combined with a Fixed Amount of Other Inputs	*Total Output (in units)*	*Marginal Physical Product (in units)*	*Marginal Revenue Product (in dollars)*
		30	60
1	30		
		28	56
2	58		
		26	52
3	84		
		24	48
4	108		
		21	42
5	129		
		18	36
6	147		
		15	30
7	162		
		11	22
8	173		
		7	14
9	180		
		3	6
10	183		

Note: It is assumed that market price remains the same at $2.00 per unit whatever the output under perfect competition.

factor is employed. Whereas the first unit of the variable factor increased output by 30 units, the tenth unit increased output by only 3 units. This additional output from each extra unit of the variable factor is called the *marginal physical product,* or *MPP*. The difference in total revenue, as a result of the employment of an additional unit of a factor of production, is called the *marginal revenue product*, or *MRP*. The MRP of factor A comprises two things: (a) the marginal physical product of that factor, and (b) the marginal revenue from the sale of product X. Algebraically, this can be stated as: $MRP_A = MPP_A \times MR_X$.

From the viewpoint of factor demand, a firm will employ additional units of a factor of production only so long as MRP exceeds the cost of the extra factor input. This extra cost we can call *marginal resource cost*, or *MRC*. A firm will stop hiring any more of a particular factor of production at the point where the MRP of that factor is equal to its MRC.

In Table 12:2, the firm would take on a tenth unit of the variable factor only if its cost were less than $6.00. If its cost were more, the firm would lose money by employing it—for the MRP is only $6.00. This same reasoning can be applied to every additional unit of the variable factor—only if the MRP is greater than the MRC will the firm hire it. The MRP schedule provides the information required to construct a firm's demand curve for a factor of production. Thus, from Table 12:2, we can see that at a factor price slightly less than $60.00, the firm will employ 1 unit. At a price slightly less than $56.00, it will employ 2 units. At a price slightly less than $48.00, it will employ 3 units, and so on. The demand curve, based on this data, is shown in Figure 12:2.

12.5: FACTOR DEMAND UNDER IMPERFECT COMPETITION

Unlike the situation under perfect competition, the market price for a firm's output under imperfect competition (that is to say, monopolistic competition, oligopoly, or pure monopoly) does not remain the same whatever the volume of sales. The market price will have to be reduced if a firm wishes to expand its sales. Previously, to obtain the MRP under perfect competition, we multiplied the marginal physical product of each additional factor input by one set market price. Under imperfect competition, however, we must multiply the MPP by the market price at that particular level of total output and subtract the reduction in market value of all the other units produced.

In Table 12:3. we retain the production data used previously. However, we illustrate, with different prices at different levels of output,

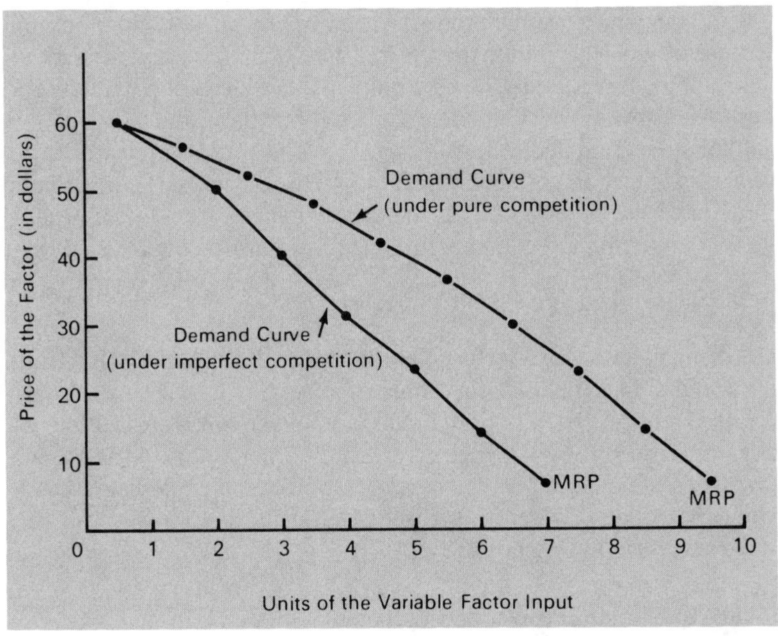

Figure 12:2 A Firm's Demand Curve for a Factor of Production.

Table 12:3
Marginal Revenue Product Determines a Firm's Demand for a Factor of Production under Imperfect Competition

Units of Variable Factor Input	*Total Output (in units)*	*Market Price per Unit*	*Total Revenue*	*Marginal Revenue Product*
1	30	$2.00	$ 60.00	$60.00
2	58	1.90	110.20	50.20
3	84	1.80	151.20	41.00
4	108	1.70	183.60	32.40
5	129	1.60	206.40	22.80
6	147	1.50	220.50	14.10
7	162	1.40	226.80	6.30
8	173	1.30	224.90	−1.90
9	180	1.20	216.00	−8.90
10	183	1.10	201.30	−14.70

Note: It is assumed that market price falls as output increases.

how the marginal revenue product would be altered with more output. Because of the decline in market price, the MRP of the seventh unit of factor input, for example, is now only $6.30, instead of $30.00 as before (see Table 12:2). This means, therefore, that if the MRC of the additional factor is about $6.00, only 7 units of factor input would be employed under imperfect competition. This compares with 10 units under perfect competition. A firm's demand curve for a factor of production under imperfect competition is also shown in Figure 12:2.

12.6: ELASTICITIES OF FACTOR DEMAND

The demand curve for a factor of production is downward-sloping from left to right. This indicates that more of a factor will be employed only at a lower price. But just how much is employment increased or decreased as a result of a change in price? In other words, what are the elasticities of demand for factor inputs? Obviously, empirical research would be needed to determine actual elasticities. However, we can make some useful generalizations.

Change in Marginal Revenue Product

We can begin by asking a question. If the price of a machine were to fall, how would this affect the amount employed? We have already seen that a factor will tend to be employed up to the point at which its marginal revenue product, or MRP, is equal to its marginal resource cost, or MRC. Now we have just said that the MRC has been reduced. Therefore, the answer to our question will be determined by what happens to the MRP. Perhaps the MRP will decline only very slowly as more of the factor is employed. This would be more likely in a situation in which a firm can sell more of its output at the existing price than one in which it would have to lower the price to sell more. It would also be more likely in a situation in which management can put the extra machines to most efficient use. If the MRP declines slowly, then the elasticity of demand for the factor of production would tend to be quite elastic. A reduction in its price would bring about a large increase in the amount employed. Conversely, if the MRP were to decline sharply as more of the factor is employed, it would not be long before the MRP had dropped to the same level as the MRC and no more of the factor would be employed. In such a situation, therefore, demand for the factor would be relatively inelastic.

We can also usefully ask another question. How would a rise in the price of labour affect the amount employed? This is the reverse of the previous case. Because of the increase in salaries or wages, the MRC is now greater than the MRP. A firm can consequently save money by employing less labour. If a reduction in the number of employees causes the MRP to rise quickly, the firm will soon be back to a position of equilibrium where, once again, MRP = MRC. In such a case, demand for labour is relatively inelastic. An increase in its price has caused a relatively small change in the amount employed. However, it is possible that the MRP of labour is reduced. It will therefore require a large reduction in the number of persons employed before the MRP of labour once more equals its MRC. In this case, the demand for the factor of production is relatively elastic. Consequently, a rise in the wage rate could eventually result in many workers losing their jobs.

Demand for the Product

The elasticity of demand for the product will be another important determinant of the elasticity of demand for the factors of production. Thus, if a reduction in the price of a product (caused by reduced factor prices) causes a large increase in the quantity demanded of that product, there will also be a large increase in the quantity demanded of the factors of production that are required to make that product. An elastic demand for the product will therefore tend to cause an elastic demand for the factors of production involved in its manufacture. Conversely, an inelastic demand for a product will tend to cause an inelastic demand for the various factor inputs required to produce it.

Substitutability

Another consideration that will affect the elasticity of demand for a factor of production is the degree to which a firm can substitute one factor for another in the production or marketing process. Technologically, at any particular point of time, there is only one method that is the most efficient for producing a good, given the relative costs of the various materials, parts, and factor inputs. But if the MRC of one factor changes relative to another, a different method of production (e.g., automatic tellers, industrial robots, word processors, etc.), involving less of the more expensive factor may now become the most efficient. In some cases, the degree of substitutability is very low; in others, it is very high. The higher it is, the more elastic will be the demand for that factor. Thus, if the price of factor A falls, more will be demanded not only because MRP now exceeds its MRC, but also because that factor can now be profitably substituted, to some extent, for factors B and C. Conversely, if the price of factor A rises, less will be demanded, not only because its MRP is now less than its MRC, but also because more units of factors B and C can be used instead. If factor A cannot be substituted at all for factors B and C, or vice versa, this will help to make the demand for factor A inelastic. Finally, we should note that a change in technology may in fact offset a change in relative factor prices.

Relative Importance of the Factor

If one factor accounts for only a small part of the total cost of production of a good, a change in the price of that factor will not greatly affect the price of that good. If, however, one factor (say, labour) accounts for most of the cost of a good, an increase in wage rates might cause a large increase in the price of the good. And this increase in the price of the product will, depending on the elasticity of demand for it, cause a large reduction in the amount sold. This will, in turn, cause a cutback in production and a fall in the amount of labour and other factors employed. The more important a factor is as a percentage of total cost, the greater therefore is the elasticity of the demand for that factor.

12.7: CHANGES IN A FIRM'S DEMAND FOR FACTORS OF PRODUCTION

We have just considered some of the forces that help determine the shape of the demand curve for a factor of production. Let us now consider what may cause a shift in this demand curve so that a firm instead of employing, say, 1000 workers at an average wage of $400 per week now wants to employ 1500 at the same price.

One reason for a change in factor demand would be a change in consumer demand for the product. If consumers decide that they want more of the product at the same price, there will also be an increase in demand for the factor inputs. Conversely, if consumers want, say, fewer North American-made cars (compared with foreign ones) at existing prices, there will be less demand for labour and other factors employed in the North American car industry.

A second reason for a change in factor demand is a change in the productivity of that factor, which would cause its MRP to become greater or less than its MRC. How would a factor be able to produce more units of output than before? There are several reasons. First, the proportion in which it is combined with other factors may be altered. Thus, if more capital is used, labour becomes more productive. A man with a forklift truck, for example, can move many more goods than a man without. Second, the quality of the factor may improve. Thus, an airline pilot trained recently might be considered to be more productive than a pilot trained twenty years ago; or a memory typewriter be considered more productive than a non-memory one. Third, technical know-how may enable factors to become more productive. Thus, without the discovery of the means of flight, labour, in the form of a pilot, would have been of little use. Improved technology has in fact greatly increased the productivity of all factors of production during the twentieth century.

A third reason for a change in the demand for a factor is a possible change in the price of other factors. Thus, if the price of labour rises, a firm will probably increase its demand for labour-saving machines. These machines, as well as being cheaper than labour (no wages or fringe benefits), may even be more hard-working (twenty-four hours a day, no coffee breaks), more loyal (never quitting and never answering back), and even more reliable (never going on strike, and rarely reporting sick). It is therefore not surprising that machines are rapidly being substituted for labour in so many industries in Canada. Fortunately, from the viewpoint of labour employment, machines cannot do everything that a person can.

12.8: INDUSTRY DEMAND FOR FACTORS OF PRODUCTION

So far, in our discussion, we have looked at factor demand by the individual firm. But if we are to go on in the next two chapters to look at the supply of each factor compared with demand, we must be able to talk in terms of total, or industry demand. To obtain the industry demand curve for a factor of production we might at first be tempted merely to add together the individual firms' factor demand curves. However, there is a serious complication. It is that, under every market structure except pure monopoly, a change in the price of a factor input would cause the whole industry, not just one firm, to alter its output to regain the position where MRP equals the MRC of the factor input. This increase in total output will cause the market price of the product to change, which will, in turn, cause a change in each firm's demand for factor inputs. The only way, in fact, to obtain the industry demand curve for a factor input is to determine, for each eventual market price, what amount of factor input each firm would demand to achieve its best-profit position. These individual firms' demands at each price could then be added together to form the industry demand curve. Obviously, this is a theoretical rather than a practical exercise.

"Eventually, we hope to do without people completely."

12.9: COMBINING THE FACTORS OF PRODUCTION

In deciding how to produce, every business firm is faced with the problem of how to combine the various factors of production in the most efficient way. The manager of a firm must decide how much of each factor of production to employ in order to produce the desired output. If a manager uses more of a factor than is really needed, he or she is being wasteful.

Least-Cost Combination

We have seen that a firm will employ more units of a variable factor of production as long as the benefit outweighs the cost. We have also seen that because of diminishing marginal returns, together with declining market price under imperfect competition, the marginal revenue product from the variable factor eventually declines. In practice, a firm is able, at least in the long run, to vary all the factors of production, not just one. The first question is, therefore, in what proportions should a firm employ all the various factors of production? Only by using the factors of production in the correct proportions will a firm be able to produce the desired output of a good at least cost. And only by achieving this least-cost combination will it maximize profit.

To achieve this least-cost combination, a firm will not only compare the expected benefit from an additional unit of a factor with that unit's cost, but will also compare the benefit that could be obtained by spending the same amount of money on alternative factors of production. Suppose for example, a firm believes that it can increase the monthly value of its output by $1000 by renting an additional machine for $600. Obviously, it will choose the extra machine. Because there is more benefit to be obtained by using more capital, it will increase the proportion of capital to labour. The least-cost combination of all factors of production will in fact, exist where the last dollar spent on each factor yields the same MPP. This combination may be summarized as follows:

$$\frac{\text{MPP of Factor A}}{\text{Price of Factor A}} = \frac{\text{MPP of Factor B}}{\text{Price of Factor B}}$$

The validity of this *least-cost rule* can easily be seen. If, for example, the MPP of a dollar's worth of factor A were greater than the MPP of a dollar's worth of factor B, then a firm's output could be increased at no extra cost by employing more of A and less of B. This switch in spending would go on until equality is achieved.

At any time, a firm may discover that because of, say, a new wage scale or a change in productivity or price of output, this equilibrium no longer exists. Therefore, the firm would have an incentive to alter the combination of its factors of production, for it may now be more profitable to use more machines and less labour. If there were complete mobility of resources, as under perfect competition, equilibrium would eventually be restored. This would be achieved, on the one hand, by an increase in the MPP of labour as less of it is used relative to capital and other factors; and, on the other hand, by a decrease in the MPP of capital as more of it is used relative to labour and other factors.

Optimum Size

We have seen how, in theory, the various factors of production can be combined in a firm in the best relative amounts—for example 3A to 1B. But just how many units of each factor should be used? 300A and 100B? 330A and 110B? Or some other combination? The answer is that a firm will continue to increase the absolute amount of each factor until the marginal revenue product of that factor is equal to its marginal revenue cost. So long as the additional benefit from employing more of a factor of production outweighs the additional cost, a firm will obviously go on increasing the amount used of that factor. Only when the additional cost threatens to equal or exceed the additional benefit will the firm call a halt. The overall equilibrium situation will be where:

$$\frac{\text{MRP of Factor A}}{\text{MRC of Factor A}} = \frac{\text{MRP of Factor B}}{\text{MRC of Factor B}} = 1$$

To check the validity of this statement, let us assume the following situation:

$$\frac{\text{MRP}_A\text{: 15}}{\text{MRC}_A\text{: 10}} \quad \text{and} \quad \frac{\text{MRP}_B\text{: 12}}{\text{MRC}_B\text{: 16}}$$

In other words, the marginal benefit of factor A exceeds its marginal cost, while the marginal cost of factor B exceeds its marginal benefit. Clearly, the firm can increase its profit by increasing the amount of factor A employed and reducing the amount of factor B. Equilibrium will be reached only when the MRP of each factor is equal to its cost.

Some Practical Considerations

To be realistic, we should remind ourselves that the theory of production that we have discussed depicts the optimum situation toward which a firm tends to gravitate. There are in practice many obstacles that can prevent this equilibrium from being achieved. First, a firm's knowledge of what an additional worker or machine will contribute is sometimes based more on hope than on fact. Second, in most firms it is impossible to add or subtract units of factor input at will. Since one factor, labour, is composed of human beings with feelings and family responsibilities, a firm cannot always be governed solely by financing considerations in reducing its labour force. Furthermore, a labour union often reduces the ease with which workers (and even machines) can be added or removed from a plant. Third, different units of the same factor are not equally productive—for example, one worker may do much more than another. Fourth, in the short run, a firm may not be willing to hire extra factors if it cannot be sure that demand for the product will continue at the same level. Despite all these reservations, the theory of production does provide a reasonable explanation of how firms, motivated mainly by profit, tend to decide how much of the various factors of production to employ and in what relative proportions. The theory does not, of course, attempt to explain the actual technology of production.

Summary

1. Industry's demand for the factors of production is said to be a *derived demand* because it depends on the demand for the goods and services that these factors help to produce. The demand for one factor compared with another will depend on (a) that factor's productivity, and (b) on the market value of the output which that factor helps to produce.
2. The *law of diminishing marginal returns* states that when the amount of one factor of production is increased relative to other fixed factors, the extra output or marginal return, from each additional unit of the variable factor may at first increase but will eventually decrease. The existence of diminishing marginal returns will influence the demand for that factor.
3. When a firm employs more of each factor, leaving the relative proportions unchanged, it may obtain *economies of scale* that will lower production costs per unit of output. These arise from such means as quantity purchasing, specialization of labour and equipment, and mechanized materials handling. By increasing the amount of each factor of production, a firm may therefore obtain a more than proportionate increase in output. This is called *increasing returns to scale*. The lower production costs can permit a lower

price, an increase in the quantity demanded of the product, and more demand for the factors of production involved in producing it.

4. Under perfect competition, a firm will continue to hire more of a factor of production so long as the marginal revenue product, or MRP, exceeds the marginal resource cost, or MRC. Equilibrium is where MRP = MRC.
5. Under imperfect competition, the market price of the good produced will have to be reduced if more of it is to be sold. Therefore, the marginal revenue product is the marginal physical product multiplied by the market price at that particular level of output *minus* the reduction in market value of all the other units produced. Equilibrium employment of the factor will also be where MRP = MRC.
6. Demand for a factor of production will be more elastic if the MRP declines only slowly as more of the factor is employed. Conversely, demand will be more inelastic if the MRP declines rapidly as more of the factor is employed. The elasticity of demand for the product also helps determine the elasticity of demand for the factors involved in its production. Other determinants are the degree to which a firm can substitute one factor for another in the production process; and the relative importance of the factor in the total cost of the good.
7. A shift in the demand curve for a factor of production can be caused by a shift in the demand for the final product; a change in the productivity of that factor; or a possible change in the price of other factors.
8. The only way to obtain the industry demand curve for a factor of production is to determine, for each eventual market price, what amount of factor input each firm would demand to achieve its best-profit position.
9. For a given level of output, a firm will achieve its least-cost combination of factor inputs when the last dollar spent on each factor yields the same marginal physical product.
10. To achieve its optimum size, a firm will continue to increase the absolute amount of each factor of production until the marginal revenue product of that factor is equal to its marginal resource cost.
11. There are some obstacles that may, in practice, prevent a firm achieving the equilibrium production situation that economic theory indicates. These obstacles include lack of knowledge as to marginal physical product; the indivisibility of factors of production;

the inclusion of social, as well as economic, criteria in increasing or reducing the use of a factor; variations in output between one unit and another of the same factor; and uncertainty as to the future level of demand for the final product.

Key Terms

Review Questions

1. The demand for the factors of production is said to be a "derived demand." Explain.
2. What is "productivity"? How does it help determine the demand for a factor of production? What other consideration is vital as a determinant of demand for a factor?
3. What is the law of diminishing marginal returns? How does it affect the demand for a factor of production?
4. What is meant by the economies of mass production? How do they arise?
5. What is meant by "increasing returns to scale"? What is their relationship to the economies of mass production? Why are they said to depend on the extent of the market?
6. Distinguish between the marginal physical product of a factor of production and the marginal revenue product.
7. A firm will stop hiring more of a particular factor of production at the point at which the MRP of that factor is equal to its MRC. Explain.
8. How is the MRP of a factor of production affected by imperfect competition?
9. How do changes in the MRP of a factor of production affect the amount employed of that factor?
10. How do changes in the MRC of a factor of production affect the amount employed of that factor?

11. How does the elasticity of demand for a product help determine the elasticity of demand for the factors involved in its production?
12. How does substitutability help determine the elasticity of demand for a factor of production?
13. How is the demand for a factor of production affected by the relative importance of that factor in the production process?
14. A shift in the demand curve for a factor of production can occur for any one of three reasons. What are they?
15. How can we obtain the industry demand curve for a factor of production?
16. How can a business firm theoretically achieve the least-cost combination of factors of production for a given level of output?
17. How can a business firm theoretically determine its optimum size?
18. What practical considerations limit the applicability of the economic theory of production?
19. Will the use of computers in various industries result in greater demand for labour or less (a) in the short run and (b) in the long run? Discuss.

13. WAGES: LABOUR'S SHARE OF INCOME

CHAPTER OBJECTIVES

A. To explain why wage rates differ from one occupation to another

B. To explain how wage rates are determined (a) when employers compete to seek workers and workers compete to obtain jobs; (b) when there is only competition among workers; (c) when there is only competition among employers; and (d) when there is no competition among employers or among workers

C. To discuss the effects on the labour market of government-set minimum wage rates

D. To emphasize how real wages today are much greater than in our ancestors' days

E. To point out how relative wage rates for different occupations can alter as the years go by

CHAPTER OUTLINE

How does a country share among its population the goods and services produced? In our modern society, this question is answered in terms of monetary income. The more money a person receives, the larger the amount and the better the quality of goods and services that he or she can buy.

A person's income is obtained mainly in the form of payment for the use of the productive resources (or factors of production) that such a person has at his or her command. The most obvious of these is the person's own time and efforts as a member of the labour force. However, additional sources of income, discussed in the next chapter, include rent from land and buildings; interest from the loan of money capital; and profit from the operation of a business.

13.1: WAGES DEFINED

The term *wages* is used in economics to embrace all the different types of payment—wages, salaries, commissions, bonuses, royalties, and fringe benefits—made to the various kinds of labour in exchange for their services. The *wage rate* is the price paid to a particular kind of labour for its services over a specific period of time. In practice, the wage rate is usually hourly for factory workers, shop assistants, and many clerical personnel; annually or monthly for professional and managerial staff.

The most important determinants of the standard wage rate for one type of employment compared with another are demand and supply—the number of job vacancies on the one hand and the number of workers seeking employment on the other.

13.2: DIFFERENT DEMAND/SUPPLY SITUATIONS

In economics, we talk about "labour" as a factor of production. In reality, labour is by no means homogeneous. No one worker is exactly the same as another. Consequently, we must recognize that at any one time there is not just one demand/supply situation for labour, but a whole series of them—as many, in fact, as there are different types of labour. The demand/supply situation for company presidents, for example, is different from that for company treasurers; and that of plant engineers different from that for plant supervisors. If, for example, the demand for company presidents falls relative to the supply, their salaries will drop, even though, at the same time, the salaries of executive secretaries may rise because of an increase in demand for them relative to their supply. Because of the existence of these different demand/supply situations, wage rates differ considerably from one job to another. They also differ for the same job, from one region to another and, even more, from one country to another. This is because physical distance causes separate labour markets even for the same type of worker.

Differences Between Workers

Although human beings are often said to be equal, in practice they differ greatly from each other in a variety of ways: in intelligence, ability to get along with others, willingness to accept responsibility, conscientiousness, ability to communicate, creativity, appearance, ability to withstand mental pressure, ability to organize, physical strength, attitude, skills, and dexterity—the list is almost endless. These differences mean, first, that some persons cannot perform certain jobs at all. For example, a successful bank manager might be a hopeless surgeon, even with the necessary medical training; or a skilled typist might be a hopeless bookkeeper. Second, some workers, although they may be able to perform the same job, may not be as efficient at it as some others.

Another important reason for differences between workers is the varying amounts and types of education, training, and experience that they have received. If it requires many years of academic and practical training to become, for example, a doctor, engineer, chemist, or accountant, it is to be expected that the number of such persons will be relatively small, particularly when compared with the number of unskilled workers.

There are also other differences between persons, such as personal appearance, that may be crucial when it comes to securing a particular job.

When we look at workers as a whole, we can see that they really consist of a number of *non-competing groups*. Plant managers form one group, geologists another, and so on. In the short run, a person's mobility between one group and another is usually very limited, which is why these groups are called "non-competing." Over time, some persons may be able to switch from one group to another—for example, a chemical engineer may become a college professor; or a lawyer, a politician. However, even in the long run, most groups remain largely non-competing. Few professional musicians will ever become accountants and few accountants will ever become professional musicians, even if comparative wage scales provided a financial incentive. In other words, each group represents a separate demand/supply situation, which accounts for the great differences in wage rates. Only if persons can easily switch from one occupation to another can such wage differences be

eliminated. Thus, only if a large number of persons had the ability, inclination, and opportunity to be successful television performers, for example, would wage rates for such performers drop to the level enjoyed by the vast majority of factory workers. But so long as only a limited number of people can perform certain jobs, disparities in wage rates will continue.

Hazardous or Unpleasant Jobs

All jobs do not exert the same appeal on prospective employees. Many people would not, for example, contemplate becoming police officers or firefighters because of the danger involved. Hardship, excessive travel, responsibility, and nervous tension are all examples of factors that tend to create separate demand/supply situations for particular types of jobs. In particularly demanding jobs, the wage rate resulting from the interaction of demand and supply will contain a premium—an equalizing difference—to offset these aspects. Thus, a police constable will receive more than a clerk; a garbage collector more than a street sweeper. Worker A, earning less at another, more pleasant job, will not attempt to compete with worker B, who is willing to perform a hazardous or unpleasant job for the extra money.

Geographical Immobility

Another reason for separate demand/supply situations, even for the same job, is that many people are reluctant to move from the area in which they have grown up. Such a move can mean that they must leave relatives, friends, and their old home, find a new school for any children, and adjust to a new community and even climate. Obviously the younger a person is and the fewer the family ties, the easier it is to move. Nevertheless, there are still many people in, say, the Maritime or Prairie provinces who would be reluctant to move to better-paying jobs in Calgary, Toronto or Vancouver, even if they were available. Geographical immobility is even greater, of course, between different countries—because of distance, immigration restrictions, cultural differences, etc.

The Multiplication Factor

This seemingly odd title refers to the fact that some employees are able, through the communications media, to multiply their services. Thus a television performer, although making only one personal performance, may be enjoyed at the same time, or even months or years later, by thousands or even millions of persons. Similarly, a successful novelist, although writing each book only once, can provide entertainment, through the printed word, to hundreds of thousands of interested readers. Because services can be multiplied in this way and therefore generate multiplied revenue, the person who provides them can command extremely high fees or salaries—for example, hundreds of thousands of dollars for ice-hockey and baseball stars.

Varying Degrees of Competition

In some employment situations, there is a high degree of competition among employers and employees. In others, there is relatively little. In the following pages, we analyze the various possible situations.

13.3: COMPETITIVE LABOUR MARKET

In this type of labour market, many different firms compete with one another to employ each particular kind of labour. Every firm has its own demand curve for each kind of labour, based on the expected monetary benefit (the marginal revenue) that additional units of that factor will confer. The industry demand curve for each kind of labour is the sum of these individual firms' demand curves, calculated at each particular wage rate.

In this labour market, workers also compete to obtain jobs. For every vacancy advertised, there are many applicants; and there is no union to restrict the number of workers entering a firm. It is possible to visualize the supply of each kind of labour, in these circumstances, as the number of workers willing to offer their services at each of a variety of wage rates. The lower the wage, the fewer the number of applicants—as workers will tend to remain at their present jobs or look for opportunities in other fields. The higher the wage, the larger the number of applicants.

In Table 13:1 we give an example of the demand for, and supply of, a particular kind of labour. We can see that the equilibrium wage rate is $10.00 per hour. This is the rate at which the industry's demand for this kind of labour (1000 workers) is equal to the supply (1000). The corresponding demand and supply curves are shown in Figure 13:1. Since the wage rate for labour is determined by the interaction of industry demand and market supply, no individual firm can exert any influence on this price.

For any individual firm, the price of each kind of labour is fixed and the supply unlimited. All the firm can do is to decide how much of this labour it will employ. It does this by comparing the extra financial benefit to be obtained from employing more workers (the marginal reve-

Table 13:1
Wage Determination in a Perfectly Competitive Labour Market

Wage Rate per Hour (in dollars)	Number of Workers Demanded by All Firms	Number of Workers Offering Their Services
6.00	2200	200
7.00	1800	400
8.00	1500	600
9.00	1200	800
10.00	1000	1000
11.00	800	1200
12.00	600	1400
13.00	450	1600
14.00	300	1800
15.00	150	2000

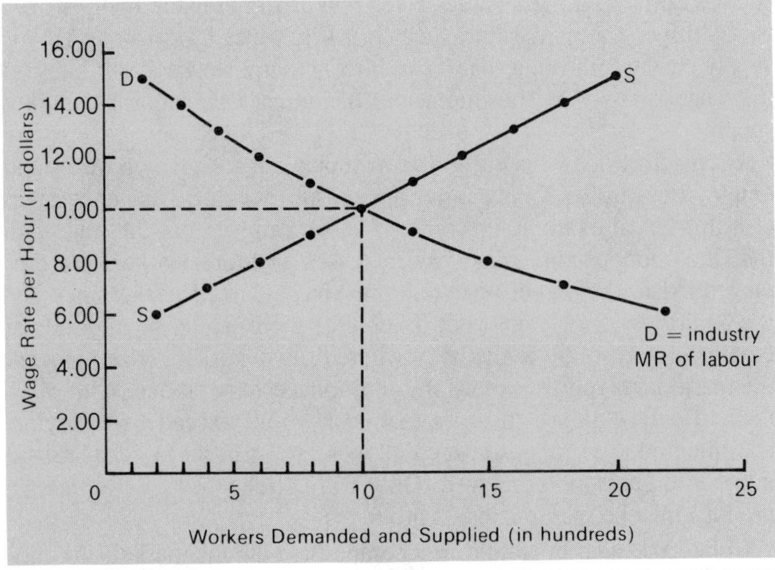

Note: One thousand workers are demanded and supplied at a wage rate of $10.00 per hour.

Figure 13:1 Demand for and Supply of Labour in a Perfectly Competitive Market nue) with the extra cost of employing them (the marginal cost). In a competitive labour market, the marginal cost is the same as the wage rate. If the marginal revenue exceeds the marginal cost, it will be profitable to hire more workers. If the marginal revenue is less than the marginal cost, it will be more profitable to employ fewer of them. Only when the marginal revenue equals the marginal cost will there be no incentive to alter the number of workers employed.

13.4: MONOPSONY

Another possible type of employment situation is monopsony—that is, a labour market in which there is only one firm recruiting labour, but competition among individuals to supply it. This is the exact opposite, incidentally, of a term we used earlier—monopoly, meaning only one seller.

Because the monopsonist is the only buyer of labour services, the labour supply curve that it faces will be the market supply curve that slopes upward from left to right, indicating that more labour will be supplied only at a higher wage rate. This is in complete contrast to a competitive labour market in which a firm faces a horizontal labour supply curve, indicating that it can hire as many workers as it likes, at the wage rate set by the interaction of industry demand and market supply.

What effect does this difference in supply curves have on wages and employment under monopsony? To explain, we make use once again of a numerical example. In Table 13:2, we can see that the wage rate that the monopsonist must pay increases as more workers are employed. Also, the higher wage rate must be paid to all workers, not just the additional ones employed; otherwise, there would be all kinds of employee unrest. Up to the point where fifteen workers are employed, the marginal revenue exceeds the additional cost of labour. With more than fifteen workers, the marginal cost would exceed the marginal revenue and the monopsonist could increase its profit by reducing the number of persons employed. Only with fifteen workers would the monopsonist be maximizing its profit.

Unlike the firm operating in a competitive labour market, the monopsonist's extra expenditure for each additional worker will be more than the going wage rate. This is because the wage rate, which has risen as more labour is demanded, is higher not just for the additional worker but for all the other workers already employed. Thus, for example, in hiring the fourteenth worker, the marginal cost, on an hourly basis is not $10.00 (the wage rate) but $23.00. This comprises $10.00

Table 13:2
Wage and Employment Determination under Monopsony

Number of Workers Employed	Wage Rate per Hour (in dollars)	Total Cost of Labour (in dollars)	Marginal Cost of Labour (MC) (in dollars)	Marginal Revenue of Labour (MR) (in dollars)	
10	6.00	60.00	— —	35.00	MC < MR
11	7.00	77.00	17.00	33.00	
12	8.00	96.00	19.00	31.00	
13	9.00	117.00	21.00	29.00	
14	10.00	140.00	23.00	27.00	
15	11.00	165.00	25.00	25.00	MC = MR
16	12.00	192.00	27.00	23.00	
17	13.00	221.00	29.00	21.00	
18	14.00	252.00	31.00	19.00	
19	15.00	285.00	33.00	17.00	
20	16.00	320.00	35.00	15.00	MC > MR

for the fourteenth worker plus $13.00 for the previous thirteen workers (an additional $1.00 each). Because of this fact, the wage rate and the amount of labour employed will both be less under monopsony than they would be in a competitive labour market. This can best be demonstrated by use of graphic analysis. In Figure 13:2 we can see that the monopsonist would hire fifteen workers (the point at which the marginal revenue curve intersects the marginal cost curve) compared with about nineteen workers in a competitive labour market. The monopsonist will also pay only about $11.00 per hour, compared with over $15.00 under pure competition.

We should, however, recognize the middle ground between monopsony on the one hand and a competitive labour market on the other. Thus, if only a few firms operate in a labour market, they may very well co-operate, formally or informally, to hold down the wage rate. This situation, in which there are just a few buyers in a labour market, is described as *oligopsony* (as contrasted with oligopoly which means just a few sellers). Where there are many buyers but the type of labour demanded is somewhat dissimilar and some firms prefer candidate A over candidate B or vice versa, the term used is *monopsonistic competition*. This latter market model is very close to the situation that exists in most labour markets.

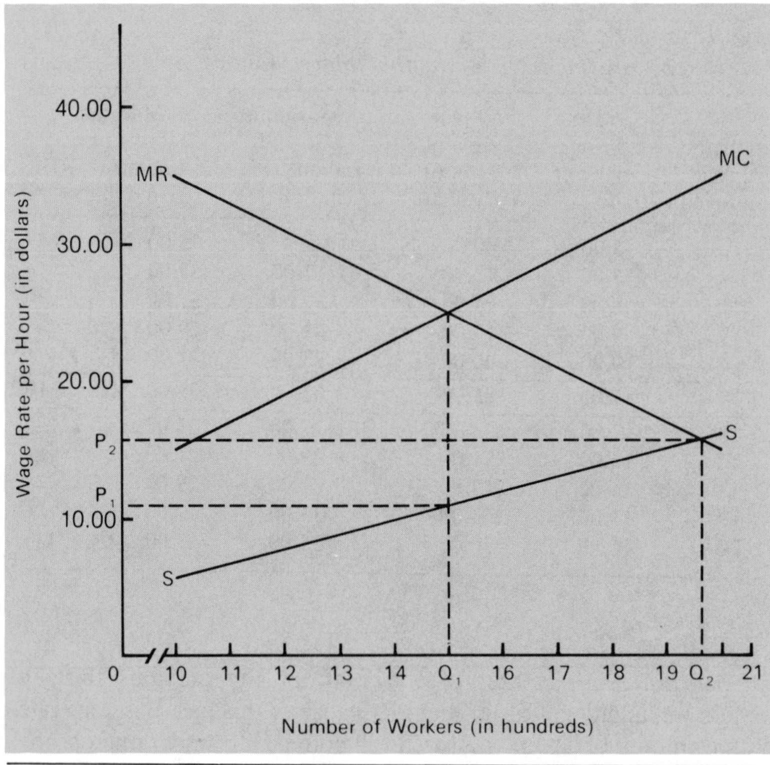

Note: The monopolist hires Q_1 workers (the labour force at which MR = MC) and pays a wage of P_1 dollars. Under pure competition, a firm would hire Q_2 workers and pay a wage rate of P_2 dollars.

Figure 13:2 A Monopsonistic Firm Will Pay a Lower Wage Rate and Hire Fewer Workers than Would a Firm Operating in a Perfectly Competitive Labour Market

13.5: LABOUR UNION MONOPOLY

In practice, not all individuals compete freely with each other in offering their services in the labour market. This lack of competition among workers comes about in the vast majority of cases through the existence of a strong *labour union*—an association of workers practising a similar trade or employed in the same company or industry.

A *craft union* is an association of workers practising the same trade—for example, the United Brotherhood of Carpenters and Joiners of America. An *industrial union* is an association of many different types of workers, but usually all employed in the same firm or industry—for example, the United Automobile, Aerospace, and Agricultural Implement Workers of America.

Restricting the Labour Supply

One way in which a labour union can affect wages and employment is by *restricting the labour supply*. Table 13:3 shows the demand for a particular type of worker at different wage rates. It also shows the supply of workers without a union and the supply of workers with a union. We can see from the Table that without any restriction of supply the wage rate would be $9.00 per hour; and the number of workers employed, 800. With a union, the supply of qualified workers, we assume, has been cut in half. As a result, the demand for and supply of workers are equal at a wage rate of $11.00 per hour—a point at which only 600 workers are employed. The effect of the labour union's action in restricting supply has been, therefore, to raise the wage rate by $2.00 per hour and reduce the number of persons employed by 200. The shift in the supply curve of labour and its effects on wages and employment are illustrated in Figure 13:3.

Table 13:3
A Labour Union May Restrict the Supply of Labour Causing a Higher Wage Rate and Less Employment

Wage Rate per Hour (in dollars)	Number of Workers Offering Their Services (without union)	Number of Workers Demanded	Number of Workers Offering Their Services (with union)
6.00	200	1100	100
7.00	400	1000	200
8.00	600	900	300
9.00	800	800	400
10.00	1000	700	500
11.00	1200	600	600
12.00	1400	500	700
13.00	1600	400	800
14.00	1800	300	900
15.00	2000	200	1000

Note: It is assumed that the existence of a craft union has reduced the available supply of qualified workers by half.

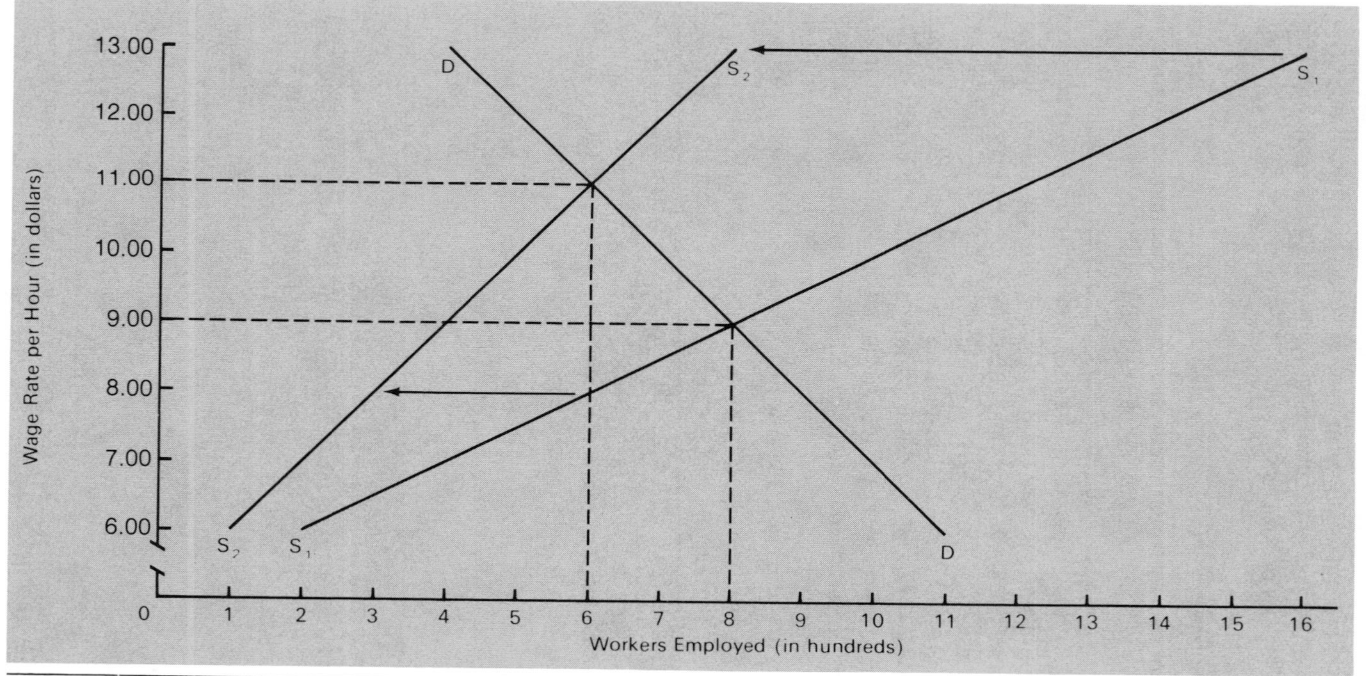

Figure 13:3 A 50 per cent Reduction in the Supply of Labour Causes the Wage Rate to Increase to $11.00 per hour (from $9.00) and the Number of Workers Employed to Decline to 600 (from 800).

Industrial unions, unlike the craft unions and professional associations, do not usually attempt to restrict the supply of labour. Since their membership consists of the unskilled and semi-skilled non-managerial workers in an industry, they are in no position to require long training periods, entrance examinations, and the like. Instead, their main concern is to try to ensure that every non-management worker in an industry is a dues-paying member of the union.

Although industrial unions are not greatly concerned with restricting the supply of workers, they are very much concerned with wage rates and conditions of work. In negotiating a labour contract with management, the union will try to obtain the best possible overall package of wages and fringe benefits. A high wage rate will obviously be the centrepiece of such a package.

A craft union will also be very much concerned with the rate of remuneration of its members. Thus, in a particular area, the craft unions—for example, in construction—will negotiate wage rates for the next one or two years with the employers. Also, professional associations will set a schedule of fees to which members are expected to adhere.

The ability of a craft union to enforce these negotiated wage rates is usually very great. If an employer tries to pay less, a strike will be called. However, the union's power extends only to those firms that have participated in the agreement. In construction, for example, the labour employed by most small builders is non-union. As far as professional associations are concerned, the policing of a fee schedule is often very difficult. That is why, for example, you will sometimes hear a lawyer quoting a fee at so much below "tariff". This tendency to charge less than the recommended fee will continue so long as the supply of lawyers tends to exceed the demand for them.

Increasing the Demand for Labour

A labour union may attempt to increase the wage rate and the number of union members employed by causing an increase in the "quantity" demanded—in other words, a movement along the demand curve for union labour. It may also try to achieve a shift of the demand curve to the right, meaning that more union labour is demanded at each wage rate than before. One way it can achieve these two aims is by trying to discourage employers from using non-union labour. Another way is to advertise products as being "union-made" in the hope that consumers will prefer such products over others. A third way is to include clauses in a labour contract that prevent an employer from substituting labour-saving machinery in the production process. A fourth way is to pressure Parliament for additional tariff or quota protection from foreign competition for the industry's products. At a more general level, a labour union can try to promote the demand for the industry's products by pressuring government to adopt a full-employment policy. It can also try to reduce competition for jobs by restrictions on immigration. Some of these policies—such as opposition to greater mechanization or automation—may eventually prove detrimental to labour's interest, particularly if they make an industry unable to compete with lower-priced imports. Figure 13:4 shows how an increase in the demand for labour may increase the wage rate and the number of workers employed.

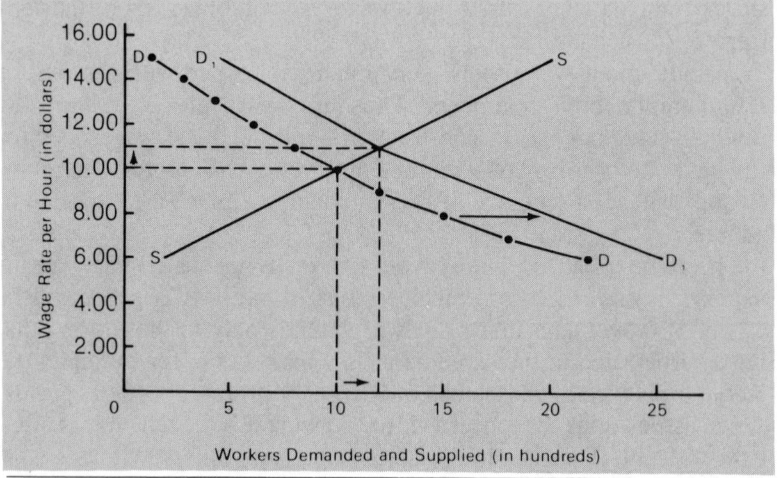

Note: An increase in the demand for labour causes the wage rate to increase to $11.00 per hour (from $10.00) and the number of workers employed to increase to 1200 (from 1000).

Figure 13:4 Effects of an Increase in the Demand for Labour on the Wage Rate and Number of Workers Employed

13.6: BILATERAL MONOPOLY

Sometimes a labour market lacks competition among both employers and employees—firms are not actively competing with each other to recruit employees and workers are not competing with each other in trying to obtain jobs. On the one side, there may be just one large firm or a few large firms acting jointly; on the other, there may be a large and powerful labour union. This situation is called *bilateral monopoly*. It combines a situation of monopsony (one buyer of labour services) with a situation of union monopoly (one seller of labour services).

To illustrate this type of labour market, Figure 13:5 combines the monopsony situation of Figure 13:2 with a labour union's desire for a wage rate of $14.00 per hour (the horizontal part of the supply curve S_1S). It is clear that no wage rate is logically acceptable to both parties. Therefore, the actual wage rate will be somewhere in between; its actual position will be determined by the relative bargaining strengths of management and labour.

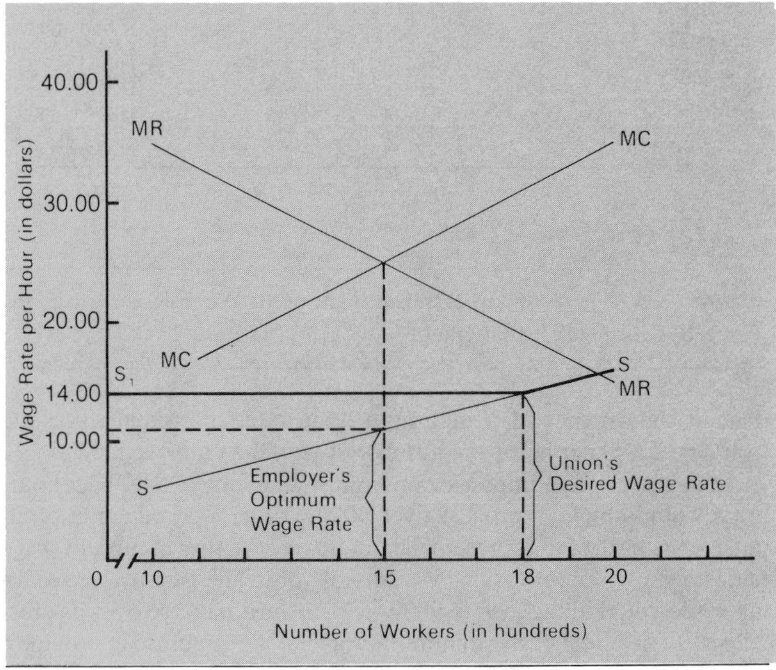

Note: The monopsonist seeks a wage rate of just over $10.00 per hour. But the labour union wants a wage rate of $14.00 per hour. The actual rate will be determined by relative bargaining strengths.

Figure 13:5 With Bilateral Monopoly, the Wage Rate Cannot Be Logically Determined

13.7: MINIMUM WAGE RATES

In many countries, the government sets a minimum wage rate for labour. In Canada, the federal and provincial governments carry out this task. The minimum wage rates are normally set above the level that would be established by the forces of demand and supply. How does this affect the number of workers employed? In Figure 13:6 we can see

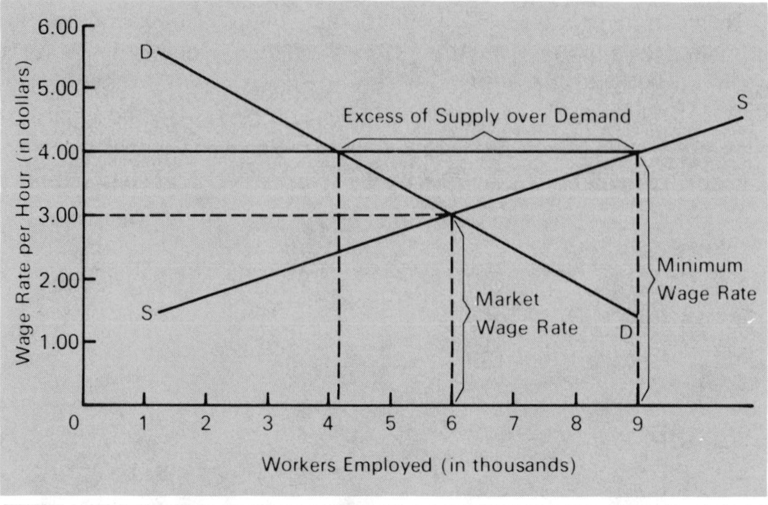

Figure 13:6 Government-Imposed Minimum Wage Rate Raises the Wage But Reduces Employment

that, in the absence of a minimum wage rate, the actual wage rate would be $3.00 per hour; the number of workers employed, 6000.

If the government imposes a minimum wage rate of $4.00 per hour, firms would employ only just over 4000 workers—a reduction of almost one-third of the present labour force. At this minimum wage rate, however, more workers would seek jobs. The labour force seeking work would in fact rise to 9000—a one-third increase over its present size. The effect of the minimum wage rate is therefore to provide a higher wage to those still employed, but to eliminate jobs for many others. The severity of unemployment will depend not only on the level of the minimum wage rate, but also on the elasticities of labour demand and supply.

The same result would occur from a union-negotiated minimum wage rate in a particular firm or industry. It is difficult for a labour union to gain the best of both worlds—higher wages and more employment. If it insists on a higher wage rate, it must usually accept less employment for its members. The only other way for a labour union to have both higher wages *and* more employment is if the marginal revenue of labour increases. This can be achieved by greater labour productivity, by an increase in the demand for the product causing the price to rise, or by both combined.

The possible unemployment of a number of its members will in theory have some moderating effect on a union's wage demands. The important consideration is the elasticity of demand for labour. Will the higher wage rate cause a large or a small reduction in the demand for labour? The more elastic the demand, the greater the reduction in the number of workers employed. This reduction may not take place immediately, but a firm will gradually substitute more and more labour-saving equipment and, in an assembly-type operation, use more and more parts manufactured more cheaply abroad. Even if it does not dismiss workers, it will achieve the same result by slowing the rate of recruitment of new workers. In practice, it appears that many labour unions believe that the sacrifice of some jobs, particularly those of future rather than present workers, is a necessary price for obtaining higher wages, better fringe benefits, and better working conditions for those union members who remain employed.

13.8: THEORY AND PRACTICE

There are in practice industries in which competition among employers to recruit new staff is considerable. There are also industries in which just a few firms—for example, car manufacturers—take a common hiring stand, particularly with regard to wage rates. On the employee side, there are industries in which employees have strong labour unions, and others—particularly industries comprising many small firms—in which competition among applicants for jobs is intense.

Most firms will hire an additional worker if his or her production is worth more than the wage and fringe benefits to be paid. However, it is by no means easy, in practice, to determine what exactly is an extra worker's productivity. Very often, additional hiring is based on a manager's opinion (possibly inaccurate) that an extra man or woman is needed. And since, according to one of Parkinson's Laws, work expands to fill idle hands, it soon becomes impossible to prove that the extra worker's tasks could perhaps have been done at no extra cost by someone else already on the payroll. Also, many employees, such as management trainees, may not be immediately productive.

Because of this lack of precise information about present or future worker productivity, hiring often tends to be done in an irregular fashion. In times of general economic expansion, a firm is fairly liberal in its hiring policy and the payroll is expanded. Conversely, in times of general economic contraction, even some of the supposedly "indispensables" may be fired and the payroll squeezed. The major variable is a company's sales prospects—how much can be sold and at what price. A worker's productivity may be the same, but a firm may believe rightly or wrongly that sales revenue will rise or decline. And revenue is just as important a part of labour's marginal revenue as is labour's marginal physical productivity. Furthermore, hiring to some extent reflect the subjective likes and dislikes of the recruiter. This means that a person may hire someone who is personally compatible, but who is not necessarily the most productive. In such a case, the extra labour cost may exceed the additional benefit received by the company.

In practice, labour is considerably immobile. Many workers are unaware of other suitable job opportunities. Also they are also often extremely reluctant, because of family, pension, and other ties, to change jobs. Furthermore, government intervenes in many labour markets by setting minimum wage rates, paid vacations, and other conditions of employment.

13.9: HIGHER REAL WAGES TODAY

In Canada today, a worker usually earns much more in real terms than did his or her parents and grandparents. Relatively abundant food, good clothing, free public education, medical care, automobiles, paid vacations, travel, household appliances, and even ownership of a home are all part of the good life that the average employed worker now enjoys. However, there is much more pollution of the land, the air, and the water than there was in our ancestors' days. And there still is, of course, much individual poverty that varies with the state of the economy and the level of unemployment.

The increase in real wages that has occurred over the years can be attributed in part to an improvement in the quality of labour. Generally speaking, we are healthier, better educated, better informed, and better trained than our ancestors. We may even claim to possess more entrepreneurial ability. Compared with our ancestors, we should therefore be able to produce more, even if our efforts were combined with only the same amount of land, capital, and technology as they possessed.

These other factors of production, however, have shown the most remarkable improvement over the years. Land, in its economic sense, means mineral resources as well as the soil. Discovery of major deposits of iron ore, nickel, and other minerals as well as vast resources of coal, oil and natural gas have contributed spectacularly to the increase in the Canadian worker's real wages. So also have the vast amounts of hydro-electric power that Canada's rivers and waterfalls have made possible, and the relatively easy transportation facilities provided by the St. Lawrence River and the Great Lakes. Even the soil itself has been transformed by fertilizer, drainage, and irrigation so that it can produce more. Also new crops such as rapeseed (or canola) have been successfully developed in Canada.

"I've just worked it out, Doris. At our rate of saving, I'll only need to work another ninety-three years to pay off our debts."

Another factor that has played an extremely important role in raising the Canadian worker's productivity is capital investment—the use of buildings, machinery and equipment in production. This normally requires the diversion of a part of a country's productive effort from the production of goods for consumption to the production of goods, such as factories and machines, that can produce other goods. In most countries, the desire to raise living standards quickly often means that capital formation is neglected. In a developing country, which has an abnormally large capital need because of its many resources waiting to be exploited, the local capital supply is usually insufficient. Also, in some relatively well-developed countries such as Canada the emphasis on a high standard of living means that a large part of the money to pay for major capital spending programs, both public and private, is often sought abroad. Whatever the source, this capital is indispensable in raising a country's productive capacity. And the large amounts of private industrial capital in Canada, as well as the vast amount of social capital, such as roads, railways, dams, hospitals, bridges, and so on, have meant that despite a larger labour force, the amount of capital per worker has greatly risen. This extra capital per worker, in large part due to investment from abroad, has greatly contributed to the rise in real wages of Canadian workers.

Another important reason for higher real wages in this country is the amazing growth in technology, much of it imported from the United States and elsewhere. Without this technical knowledge, most of our natural resources would still lie untapped as they did for so many hundreds and even thousands of years. Today, minerals, lumber, and other resources are made into usable products with the aid of electrically driven machines that multiply our power and dexterity many times over. Even the land, thanks to the development of more productive hybrid crops, now provides astonishing yields per acre. The "communications explosion" and transportation revolution have also meant that people are better informed and more widely travelled than was conceivable even only fifty years ago.

13.10: WAGE MOVEMENTS BETWEEN DIFFERENT OCCUPATIONS

If we look at economic history once more, we will observe that the difference in wage rates between one occupation and another has also changed over the years. This has been caused, as we should expect, by changes in demand and supply. Let us consider two examples.

At the beginning of this century, domestic servants were easy to obtain and cheap to employ. Nowadays, by contrast, the case is just the opposite. The reason for the increase in their wages relative to other occupations is twofold. First, the demand for domestic help is still quite high, despite the invention of labour-saving household devices: a large professional class, with both husband and wife at work, willing and able to hire domestic help, has emerged in Canada. Second, the supply of such labour has been reduced. This reduction has been caused by competition from alternative forms of employment such as retail stores and manufacturing firms; by the higher standard of education and training of the mass of the population who can therefore qualify for other forms of employment; by the widespread attitude that domestic service is degrading in a democratic society; and by the restrictions placed on the immigration of unskilled labour into Canada.

As another example, steelworkers used to work early in this century for 50 to 60 hours per week for an extremely low hourly wage. Nowadays, their wages compare favourably with accountants, lawyers, and teachers. On the demand side, there has been a growing need for steel in a new and developing country; consequently, more and more capital per worker, together with more sophisticated steel-making technology, has raised labour productivity. On the supply side, a strong labour union—the United Steelworkers of America—has emerged and has effectively insisted on a shorter work week, higher wage rates, and greater fringe benefits. Only now is the prosperity of Canada's steelworkers being adversely affected by cheaper foreign steel.

In our type of society, there is nothing static about relative wage scales. Over the past decade, for example, nurses, teachers, and lawyers have all known wide variations in the demand for their services. If demand for and supply of a particular type of labour alters, the wage rate will alter too. It is not surprising, therefore, that different groups of labour are constantly trying to expand demand for their services on the one hand and to restrict the supply and impose minimum pay rates on the other. The problem is, of course, that there is no objective measure to indicate what a particular kind of worker is worth; it is all a matter of supply and demand and sometimes government regulation.

Summary

1. The terms *wages* is used in economics to embrace all the different types of payment—wages, salaries, commissions, bonuses, royalties, and fringe benefits—that are made to the various kinds of labour in exchange for their services. The *wage rate* is the price

that is paid to a particular kind of labour for its services over a specific period of time. Wage rates vary considerably in Canada between different occupations and between different parts of the country because of different demand/supply situations.

2. Labour consists of a number of groups of individuals with different skills and abilities and with limited mobility from one group to another—hence the term "non-competing groups."
3. Sometimes the wages for a job will contain a premium to compensate for danger or unpleasantness.
4. Unwillingness to move from one part of a country to another, or from one country to another, helps create and perpetuate different demand/supply situations, even for the same job, and therefore different wage rates.
5. Some workers can multiply their services by use of TV, radio, or print.
6. Different degrees of competition, by firms seeking workers on the one hand, and workers seeking jobs on the other, also help create wage disparities. There are four theoretically possible basic situations: (a) the *competitive labour market*—with competition among firms to recruit employees and competition among workers to obtain jobs; (b) *monopsony*—with no competition among firms, but competition among workers; (c) *labour union monopoly*—with competition among firms but no competition among workers; and (d) *bilateral monopoly*—with no competition among firms and no competition among workers. A labour union can influence wages and employment by restricting the supply of labour; by direct negotiation; and by causing an increase in the demand for labour.
7. In many countries, the government sets a minimum wage rate for male and female labour. This can result in a higher wage to those still employed, but eliminate jobs for many others.
8. Today's workers usually earns much more in real terms than did his or her parents and grandparents.
9. Relative wage rates can vary over the years between different occupations.

Key Terms

Wages 232
Wage rate 232
Labour 233
Non-competing groups 233
Hazardous jobs 235
Monopsonistic competition 239
Labour union 240
Labour union monopoly 240
Craft union 240
Industrial union 240

Geographical immobility 235
Multiplication factor 235
Competitive labour market 236
Monopsony 238
Monopsonist 238
Bilateral monopoly 244
Minimum wage rate 245
Real wages 248
Wage movements 250

Review Questions

1. How is the term "wages" used in economics?
2. "Labour is by no means homogenous." Explain.
3. What are "non-competing groups"? How does their existence affect wage rates?
4. Give three examples of jobs which offer a danger, hardship, or isolation premium.
5. How does a person's reluctance to leave his or her home town affect wage rates?
6. What effect does immigration have on wage rates?
7. What are the characteristics of a competitive labour market?
8. What is monopsony? How does the supply curve of labour for a monopsonist differ from that for a firm operating in a competitive labour market?
9. What effect does the difference in the labour supply curve for a monopsonist have on wage and employment determination?
10. What is oligopsony? How does it differ from monopsonistic competition?
11. Distinguish between a craft union and an industrial union.
12. Why do labour unions and professional asociations restrict the supply of particular types of labour? What effect does this restriction have?
13. How can a labour union achieve higher wages and increased employment? What is the usual relationship between these two goals?
14. What is bilateral monopoly? Give two Canadian examples.
15. The amount of labour employed in a particular occupation is not, in practice, determined scientifically. Comment.
16. What are the possible economic and social effects of a government-set minimum wage rate?
17. Why are wages higher in real terms today than they were in the past?
18. Do wage rates for different occupations always bear the same relationship to each other? Answer, with examples.
19. What are the reasons for income inequalities in Canada?

20. How does a country share among its population the goods and services produced? Is this a satisfactory way? What alternatives, if any, exist?
21. Why are doctors, lawyers, and dentists among the highest-paid occupations in Canada? Will this increase the supply?
22. Why are self-employed entertainers and artists, employees, and people who fish, among the lowest paid? Will this decrease the supply?
23. "If I don't make it as a professional hockey player, I'll become a wildlife biologist!" Discuss.
24. Why is geography an important factor in explaining wage differences?
25. Competition in the labour market is against the workers' interests. Discuss.
26. The competitive labour market is the exception rather than the rule in Canada today. Discuss.
27. Profit-sharing, rather than the payment of wages, would reduce management-labour antagonisms and improve the allocation of a country's resources. Comment.
28. Explain and discuss how Canada's immigration policy affects the labour market in this country. What changes, if any, would you like to see? Why?
29. Marginal revenue and cost analysis does not really apply to labour. Discuss.
30. Today's Canadians are smarter than their parents and grandparents. Hence they are paid more. Discuss.
31. Plumbers now earn more but provide less service than their predecessors. Discuss.
32. In France, garbage is collected daily and letters are delivered six days a week. How does this compare with the situation in Canada, where jobs are hard to find? Discuss.
33. "In our type of society, there is nothing static about relative wage scales." How do you predict relative wage scales will change in the future for a variety of occupations? What trends are already apparent?

14. LABOUR UNIONS AND LABOUR LEGISLATION

CHAPTER OBJECTIVES

A. To indicate what exactly is a labour union
B. To explain the origins of labour unions in Canada
C. To examine the various types of labour unions
D. To indicate the political role of labour unions
E. To describe how workers bargain collectively for pay and other conditions of work
F. To explain how, during contract negotiations, conciliation is required by law before a firm may lock out its workers or the employees go on strike
G. To indicate how, during the life of a collective agreement, any grievances must ultimately be settled by arbitration
H. To outline the major types of labour laws in Canada

CHAPTER OUTLINE

14.1: LABOUR UNION DEFINED

A *labour union* or *trade union* is an association of workers, practising a similar trade or employed usually in the same company or industry. As we noted in the previous chapter, there are both craft unions and industrial unions. Whatever the case, the basic purpose of the union is to improve the economic welfare, including pay and job security, of its members through collective, rather than individual, bargaining of wage rates, hours of work, order of layoffs, and so on, with employers. Many labour unions use the term "union" in their official title, but many others use terms such as association, brotherhood, federation, alliance, or guild.

In the various Labour Relations Acts and Codes in Canada, the term "trade union" is used. In fact, the terms "trade union" and "labour union" are often used interchangeably. However, the term "trade union" is more commonly used with reference to a group of workers possessing a certain type of industrial skill or "trade" (in other words, a craft union), whereas the term "labour union" is more commonly used with reference to a group of unskilled and/or multi-skilled workers employed in a particular industry. Throughout this chapter, we use the term labour union.

There are, in addition to the labour unions referred to above, many employee associations that have not been officially recognized, under the term of a Labour Relations Act, as the bargaining agent for employees in a particular firm. Although without legal status, these unofficial or "quasi labour unions" are nevertheless recognized by the employer as the spokesman for its employees—bargaining on their behalf or at least presenting the employees' complaints to the employer.

Not all industries have the same degree of union membership. Thus, there is very little unionization so far among workers in agriculture, trade, finance, insurance, real estate, and service industries generally. However, this picture has been changing in recent years with, for example, nurses, teachers, and bank clerks joining the ranks of organized labour. In some industries—for example, railway transport, transportation equipment, leather, paper and allied industries—the degree of unionization is extremely high.

Certain persons are usually excluded from coverage under the federal and provincial Labour Relations Acts. This means that the employer has no legal obligation to recognize or bargain collectively with any unions representing such persons. In Ontario, for example, persons excluded from coverage under the Labour Relations Act include: domestics employed in a private home; persons employed in agriculture, hunting, or trapping; members of the police force; and full-time firefighters.

Public sector employees are covered by separate collective bargaining legislation.

14.2: HISTORY OF LABOUR UNIONS IN CANADA

Labour unions in Canada date from the early nineteenth century when the immigrant British began to organize associations of carpenters, printers, and shoemakers. However, geographical proximity and and financial and professional help from U.S. unions in establishing and expanding unions in Canada soon caused much closer ties to develop between organized labour in the two North American countries than between Canada and Britain. In the early part of the twentieth century, the Roman Catholic Church played an important role in organizing unions among French-speaking workers in Quebec.

During the nineteenth century, labour unions and their organizers had an extremely difficult time. First of all, they ran into bitter hostility from employers. Second, they could be prosecuted in the criminal courts for conspiring to restrain trade and, in the event of a strike, sued in the civil courts for losses caused to an employer. This situation continued until the beginning of the twentieth century when unions were given statutory protection from such actions.

14.3: TYPES OF LABOUR UNIONS

Until the 1930s, the craft union was the predominant type of labour union in Canada. However, the emergence of large mass-production industries employing vast numbers of unskilled and semi-skilled workers created a vacuum that the craft unions, with their rigorous entrance requirements, were neither able nor prepared to fill. Consequently, a new type of union, the industrial union, with membership open to almost all non-management workers, whatever the job, came into being. The exceptions include security personnel and persons employed in a confidential capacity.

Labour unions, as well as being divided into craft unions and industrial unions, differ in another way—the geographical scope of their membership. On this basis, labour unions can be classified as international, national, or local. *International unions* are unions with members in the United States and Canada that in practice have their head offices in the United States. An example of such a union is the International Chemical Workers' Union.

National unions are unions with totally Canadian membership—for example, the Canadian Union of Public employees.

Local unions are of two types. The *directly chartered local union* is organized by, and receives its charter from, a central labour congress and is not part of an international or national union. The *independent local union* is a local labour organization not formally connected to or affiliated with any other labour organization.

Table S.4
Union Membership in Canada, in thousands of persons, 1921-1986

Year	Union Membership	Total Non-Agricultural Paid Workers	Union Membership as a Percentage of Non-Agricultural Paid Workers	Union Membership as a Percentage of the Civilian Labour Force
1921	313	1 956	16.0	9.4
1926	275	2 299	12.0	7.5
1931	311	2 028	15.3	7.5
1936	323	1 994	16.2	7.2
1941	462	2 566	18.0	10.3
1946	832	2 986	27.9	17.1
1951	1 029	3 625	28.4	19.7
1956	1 352	4 058	33.3	24.5
1961	1 447	4 578	31.6	22.6
1966	1 736	5 658	30.7	24.5
1967	1 921	5 953	32.3	26.1
1968	2 010	6 068	33.1	26.6
1969	2 075	6 380	32.5	26.3
1970	2 173	6 465	33.6	27.2
1971	2 231	6 637	33.6	26.8
1972	2 388	6 893	34.6	27.8
1973	2 591	7 181	36.1	29.2
1974	2 732	7 637	35.8	29.4
1975	2 884	7 817	36.9	29.8
1976	3 042	8 158	37.3	30.6
1977	3 149	8 243	38.2	31.0
1978	3 278	8 413	39.0	31.3
1980	3 397	9 027	37.6	30.5
1981	3 487	9 330	37.4	30.6
1982	3 617	9 264	39.0	31.4
1983	3 563	8 901	40.0	30.6
1984	3 651	9 220	39.6	30.6
1985	3 666	9 404	39.0	30.2
1986	3 730	9 893	37.7	29.7

Source: Canada Department of Labour, *Directory of Labour Organizations in Canada, 1986,* Minister of Supply and Services Canada, Ottawa, 1986.

Note: The method of reporting was changed in 1980. Thus statistics up to and including 1978 are for Dec. 31 of each year. But statistics for 1980 are for Jan. 1 (i.e. — equivalent to Dec. 31, 1979). This explains the absence in the above Table of 1979 figures. Data for 1980 and subsequent years are as at Jan. 1.

Table S.5
Largest Unions in Canada, by Membership, 1986, in thousands

	Union	Membership
1.	Canadian Union of Public Employees	304.3
2.	National Union of Provincial Government Employees	254.3
3.	Public Service Alliance of Canada	182.0
4.	United Steelworkers of America	160.0
5.	United Food and Commercial Workers	156.0
6.	International Union, United Automobile, Aerospace & Agricultural Implement Workers of America	140.0
7.	Social Affairs Federation	93.0
8.	International Brotherhood of Teamsters, Chauffeurs, Warehousemen and Helpers of America	91.5
9.	School Boards Teachers' Commission	75.0
10.	Service Employees International Union	75.0
11.	International Brotherhood of Electrical Workers	68.6
12.	United Brotherhood of Carpenters and Joiners of America	68.0
13.	International Association of Machinists and Aerospace Workers	58.6
14.	Canadian Paperworkers Union	57.0
15.	International Woodworkers of America	48.0
16.	Labourers' International Union of North America	46.7
17.	Québec Government Employees' Union Inc.	44.0
18.	Ontario Nurses' Association (Ind.)	42.5
19.	United Association of Journeymen and Apprentices of the Plumbing and Pipe Fitting Industry of the United States and Canada	40.0
20.	Communications and Electrical Workers of Canada	40.0

Source: Labour Data Branch, Labour Canada, *Directory of Labour Organizations in Canada 1986*, Minister of Supply and Services Canada, Ottawa, 1986

14.4: LABOUR UNION ORGANIZATION

The basic unit of labour organization, formed in a particular plant or locality, is known as the "local". In the case of an industrial union, a local may consist of either the employees of several small firms in a given area or the employees of one large firm. In the case of a craft union, the membership usually consists of persons practising a common skill—for example, brick-laying—in a given area.

The internal organization of a typical local will vary considerably from one union to another. An example is shown in Figure 14:1.

The union local will have its own constitution, and will draw up its own by-laws governing the conduct of its officers and members. Power is usually exercised by an executive committee, comprising the president, vice-president, and business agent.

Union Officials

In the smaller locals, all the various executive positions are held on a voluntary part-time basis by working members. These persons are elected by the members of the local, for periods ranging from several months to several years. Only in the larger locals is there a full-time *business agent* whose salary is paid either by the local itself or by the national or international office. The part-time officials are reimbursed for time taken from work for union business. Where there is a business agent, he or she will handle much of the work of the union, helping perhaps in the enrolment of new members and in the representation of the union in grievance matters and in contract negotiations.

Part of the executive committee's work is delegated to the various other sub-committees: the organizing and membership committee (which is responsible for recruiting new members); the bargaining committee that looks after negotiations for a new collective agreement; the grievance committee (which is concerned with the processing of members' grievances with the employer); the recreation committee (which looks after dances, parties, excursions, and so on); and the education committee (which disseminates information about union aims and activities to present and prospective members and others).

In the plant itself, other union officials, the *shop stewards* or *zone representatives*, look after the interests of union members—for example, in handling complaints (e.g. incorrect pay) or in filing grievances. The senior steward for a particular area or division is known as the *chief steward*.

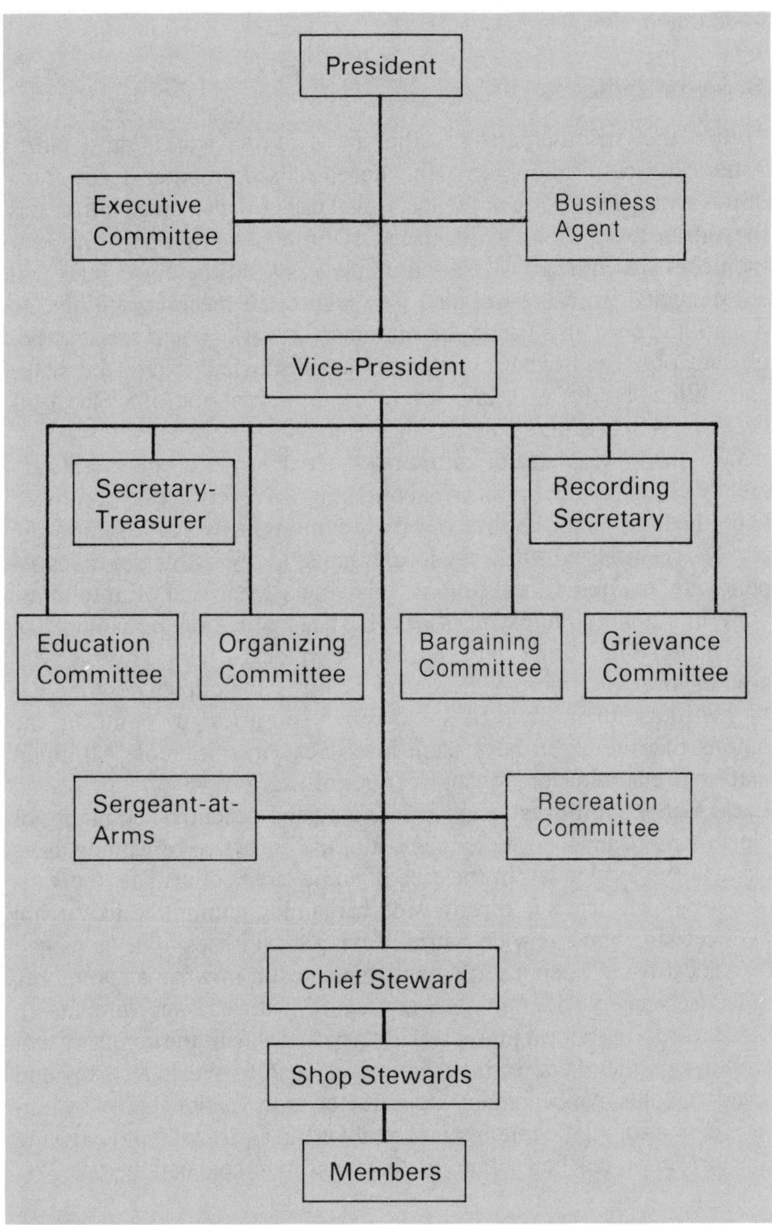

Figure 14:1 Internal Organization of a Typical Union Local

The powers of a union local can vary considerably according to the trade union of which it is a part.

Decentralization

Unlike their counterparts in other parts of the world, most North American labour unions are highly decentralized. In other words, most of the action takes place at the local level rather than at head office. It is the union local, close to the place of employment, where the new members are enlisted; where the employers send the union dues that are deducted from the worker's pay; where the meetings are held to discuss the problems facing the members at work; where social activities are organized; where grievances are discussed; where the strike committees are formed; and where the president and other local officers, as well as shop stewards, are elected.

Of course, the degree of autonomy that a union local enjoys will vary greatly from labour union to labour union. Nevertheless, compared with those in other countries, labour unions in North America are highly decentralized—with the local unions, to say nothing of the independently chartered local unions, enjoying a great deal of autonomy. Only in certain circumstances has the head office of the national or international union the right to interfere in local affairs. This high degree of local autonomy or decentralization is sometimes described as "grass-roots unionism". In some other countries, by contrast, the unions may not even have plant-level local organizations. All union matters are administered from a central office.

Local Collective Bargaining. In line with the decentralized nature of North American labour unions, most of the collective bargaining takes place at the local level. In the case of some large companies, the various locals will use a company-wide bargaining committee to bargain over certain company-wide issues, leaving local issues to be bargained on a local basis. Such a settlement might result in what is commonly called a company-wide "master agreement" with local supplements. In other words, each local union usually negotiates with the company that employs its members. In other countries such as West Germany and Sweden, collective bargaining is conducted at the national level by representatives of all the unions and employers in a particular industry and the agreement reached is binding on union members nation-wide.

14.5: POLITICAL ROLE OF LABOUR UNIONS

Labour unions, through the various provincial and national labour organizations, can exert pressure in municipal, provincial, and federal politics by offering support to political parties willing to help promote union aims. Labour unions also make direct representations to the provincial and federal governments on matter of urgent economic importance such as a high unemployment, high interest rates, or the need for price or profit controls.

Labour Councils

In Canada, the locals of many labour unions are affiliated with a Labour Council established by charter of the Canadian Labour Congress for their particular city or district—for example, The Toronto and District Labour Council (C.L.C.). The delegates from the various locals elect the council's officers, who are responsible for furthering the interests of the labour union movement at the community level—for example, by lobbying municipal governments or by organizing strike aid. These district councils are sometimes called joint boards or conference boards.

In industries organized along craft lines (such as painting and decorating), unions or union locals in a particular area may form a special council to co-ordinate members' activities and resolve jurisdictional problems. Such a council is sometimes called an Allied Trades Federation.

Labour Federations

Most provinces have a Federation of Labour, chartered by the Canadian Labour Congress, which acts as the central organization for the labour union movement in the province. The Federation holds annual conventions where delegates from the affiliated locals vote on policy matters and elect officers. The purpose of the Federation is to represent labour's interest at the provincial level, particularly in the establishment or amendment of labour legislation by the provincial government.

Canadian Labour Congress (CLC)

The major central organization for labour unions in Canada is the Canadian Labour Congress, with headquarters in Ottawa and regional offices in most of the provinces. Most international, national, and local unions, and all labour councils and federations are directly affiliated with the CLC and send delegates to its biennial conventions. The purpose of the CLC is primarily a political one: to act as the common spokesman, particularly in Ottawa, for organized labour throughout Canada. It is also active in helping to settle *jurisdictional disputes* among the affiliated unions. These are disputes in which two or more unions claim the right to be certified as the bargaining agent for the same group of employees—employees who may or may not already be represented by a union.

The primary goal of labour unions in Canada is to secure from employers greater economic benefits for their members. This includes better pay and fringe benefits as well as greater job security and improvement in working conditions, including occupational health and safety. This union philosophy, with its emphasis on economic rather than political goals, is sometimes called "business unionism". However, so far as most Canadian and American union leaders are concerned, North American style democracy and the private enterprise system, despite their faults, have provided their members with one of the highest material standards of living in the world.

14.6: COLLECTIVE BARGAINING

By belonging to a labour union, a worker not only feels psychologically more secure, but also receives the benefits of collective bargaining. Rather than bargain individually with the employer about wages, hours of work, holidays, and so on, the worker bargains as a member of a large group. This group, the union, is often able to employ professional negotiators to help obtain the most favourable terms for its members.

Occasionally, the management of a business firm will voluntarily recognize a labour union as the bargaining agent for the firm's employees. Usually, however, this recognition is that required by law once the union has satisfied the Labour Relations Board's requirements as to minimum employee support. A procedure for certification of the union as bargaining agent for a firm's employees is set out in each provincial Labour Relations Act. At the federal level, the procedure is set out in the Public Service Staff Relations Act and the Canada Labour Code—the former for federal government employees and the latter for other workers coming under federal labour jurisdiction such as airline, railway, and bank employees.

Once a labour union has been certified as the collective-bargaining agent for the workers in a particular plant, the employer is required to enter into negotiations and bargain "in good faith" with the union for a labour contract, setting out the rights and obligations of workers and management. Such a contract is usually for one, two, or three years' duration.

"Steady boys. Your jobs may be on the line next."

14.7: COMPULSORY CONCILIATION

If the employer and labour union are unable to negotiate a collective agreement, they must by law make use of a conciliator (a provincial government employee) who will try, by persuasion, to help them resolve their differences. If these new efforts are unsuccessful, management may try to enforce its point of view by methods such as a *lockout*—that is, closing the plant and "locking out" the employees. The employees, on the other hand, may go on *strike*—that is, withdraw their services and try to prevent management from hiring anyone else to take their place. To prevent striking employees from engaging in acts of personal intimidation or property damage, management may call on the police and private security services and ask one of the courts to issue a court order called an *injunction*, ordering a person or persons to stop doing something. If appropriate, use may also be made of the criminal law. As a last resort, if no agreement is reached, the government may intervene and, in the public interest, impose a settlement.

14.8: ARBITRATION

Every collective agreement must, by law, contain an arbitration clause. This means that if an employee grievance remains unresolved after having been considered at each of the steps of a clearly defined grievance procedure, it must be settled by *arbitration*—that is, by the decision of an outside person (or persons) who reviews the facts and make a decision legally binding on both management and labour. A *grievance* is an alleged violation of one or more terms of the labour contract or of customary practice in the firm.

14.9: LABOUR LEGISLATION

Under common law (the body of law that has developed over the centuries based on precedent, or prior judicial decision), an employer and an employee have a number of well-established obligations towards each other.

Thus management must, for example, provide the employee with a safe place in which to work; must employ reasonably careful and competent fellow workers; must fulfil any contractual agreements with the employee or the labour union that represents him or her; must reimburse the employee for any expenses properly incurred in the course of his or her duties; and must provide the employee with reasonable notice of dismissal, or wages instead.

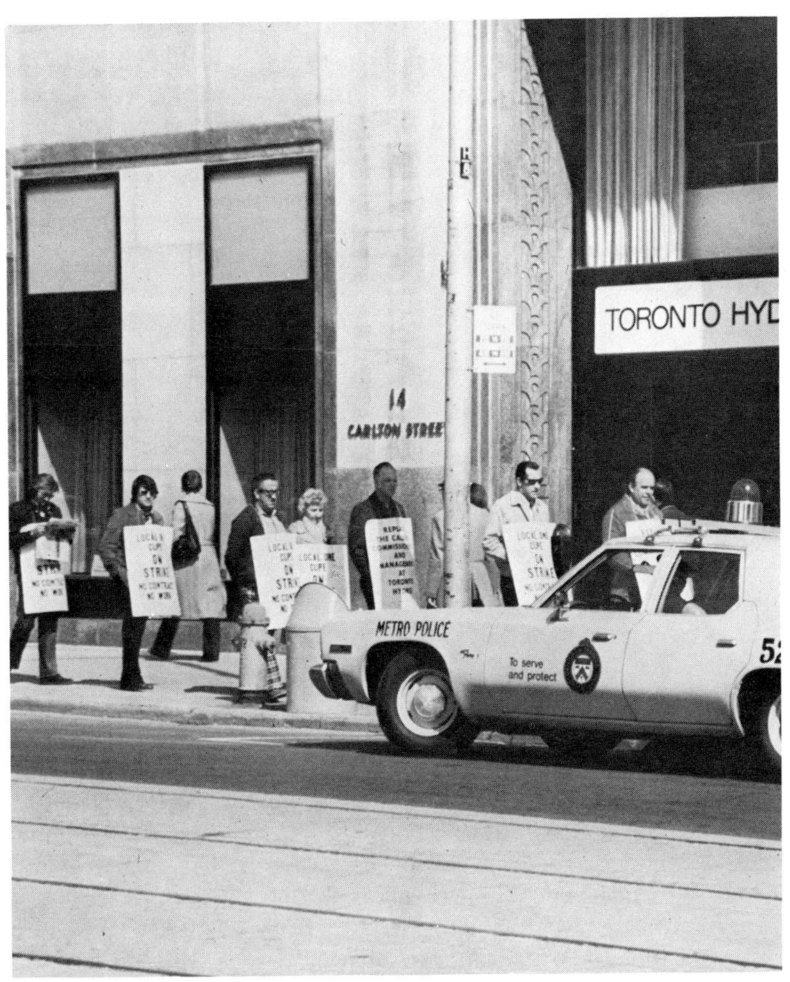
TORONTO HYD
14
METRO POLICE
To serve
and protect

The employee also has a number of obligations toward the employer. He or she should not be persistently late or absent without permission; should not disobey orders so long as they are reasonable and legal; should not be dishonest, disloyal, or clearly incompetent; should not be grossly immoral or habitually drunk at work or elsewhere; should not be habitually negligent or destructive at his or her job; and should not be chronically disabled, either because of accident or illness. Should the employee fail to fulfil any of these common law obligations, his or her employment may be terminated without notice.

Because of the Constitution Act, 1867, which gave the provincial governments the right to pass laws concerning "property and civil rights," most labour legislation in Canada is of provincial origin. The federal government is, however, empowered to pass labour laws with regard to industries specifically under its jurisdiction. These include: navigation, shipping, interprovincial railways, canals, telegraphs, steamship lines and ferries, airports, air transportation, radio stations, and works declared by Parliament to be for the general advantage of Canada or of two or more provinces. It also has jurisdiction over persons employed under federal government work contracts and on works partly financed by federal government funds. It also has the right to legislate on matters delegated to it by the provincial governments such as unemployment assistance and old age pensions.

Industries Under Federal Jurisdiction

Industries under federal jurisdiction, including firms employed under federal contract, are regulated by the terms of the *Canada Labour Code*. This Code, which came into force in July, 1971, consisted of five parts—each one absorbing a former Act. However, Part 1 (Fair Employment Practices) was subsequently replaced by the Canadian Human Rights Act and Part 2 (Female Employees' Equal Pay) was repealed.

Labour Standards

Part 3 of the Canada Labour Code requires that employers in industries under federal jurisdiction: (a) limit the hours of work of employees to a maximum of 8 hours per day and 40 per week; (b) pay one and one-half times the regular rate of wages for any hours in excess of the standard hours, if such hours are permitted by the Ministry of Labour; (c) pay a specified minimum hourly wage for all employees aged 17 and over, and a specified minimum wage for persons under 17; (d) provide each employee with a minumum of two weeks' vacation with vacation pay (4 per cent of the employee's annual wages) after every completed year of employment or, should the employee leave during a year, pay him or her the vacation pay for the completed portion of his or her year of employment; and (e) provide each employee a holiday with pay on each of the general holidays (New Year's Day, Good Friday, Victoria Day, Canada Day, Labour Day, Thanksgiving Day, Remembrance Day, Christmas Day, and Boxing Day) falling within the period of employment.

Safety of Employees

Part 4 of the Code tries to ensure safe working conditions for all employees in industries and undertakings under federal jurisdiction by: (a) specifying all the elements of a complete industrial safety program and the general obligation of employers and employees to perform their duties in a safe manner; (b) authorizing regulations to deal with problems of occupational safety; (c) authorizing the use of advisory committees and special task forces to assist in developing the industrial safety program, all to be accompanied by continuous consultation among federal and provincial government departments, industry and organized labour; (d) providing for research into causes and prevention of accidents; (e) authorizing an extended program of safety education; and (f) providing for regional safety officers and federally-authorized provincial inspectors to enforce the Code.

Industrial Relations

Part 5 of the Canada Labour Code regulates industrial relations in industries under federal jurisdiction. The Code recognizes the right of employees to organize and bargain collectively through trade unions. However, both employers and employees are required to bargain in good faith, and to include in the labour contract a provision for the arbitration of disputes. The Code prohibits unfair labour practices (such as discrimination and coercion) by both employers and employees, and provides for government conciliation officers or boards to help mediate differences between the two parties in contract negotiations. The administration of Part 5 of the Code is the responsibility of the federal Minister of Labour. Part of his or her authority—for example, the provisions covering the certification of bargaining agents—has been delegated to the Canada Labour Relations Board.

Fair Employment Practices

Under the Canadian Human Rights Act, discrimination is prohibited in any matter, including employment, on grounds of race, national or ethnic origin, colour, religion, age, sex, or marital status. However, exceptions are permitted for bona fide occupational reasons or if a person's employment is terminated at normal retirement age. The Act also prohibits pay differentials between male and female employees based on sex discrimination alone. Merit and/or seniority must be the only criteria for wage differentials. The Act is administered by the Canadian Human Rights Commission and heavy fines may be imposed for violations.

Provincial Labour Legislation

By virtue of their constitutional power, the provincial legislatures have enacted a large number of labour laws, many of which are frequently being revised. The most important of these provincial labour laws are reviewed in the following pages.

Minimum Wage Rates

All the provinces have legislation under which a provincial government board sets minimum wage rates for persons employed in industries in the province. This legislation is intended to ensure that a minimum standard of living is enjoyed by all employees and their families. For a few types of industrial employment, a higher minimum wage may be set under industrial standards laws. Provincially-set minimum wage rates now cover almost all employment except farm labour and domestic service.

Limited Working Hours

The number of hours of work which an employer may demand from an employee are limited by provincial statute in most provinces—for example, 8 hours per day and 40 hours per week. Many employees do, however, work more than this on a voluntary basis in which case they must be paid at one and one-half times the regular hourly rate for this "overtime". In many provinces, hours of work and wage rates in particular industries are regulated under the various Industrial Standards Acts or, in the case of Quebec, under the Quebec Collective Agreement Act. These Acts encourage conferences of employers and employees to discuss and recommend minimum wages and maximum hours of work for employees in their industries.

Annual Vacations with Pay

All the provinces have legislation providing for compulsory paid vacations for employees in most industries. Vacation pay stamps are used in some provinces. Vacation requirements, after a year of service, are normally two weeks' paid vacation.

Minimum Age

Every province has set a minimum age below which a person may not be employed. In Ontario, for example, this limit is fifteen for factory work, eighteen for mining below ground, and fourteen for work in shops, hotels, or restaurants. Persons under sixteen may not, however, work in Ontario during school hours unless they have been granted special permission, or unless they are on school holidays.

Fair Employment Practices

All provinces prohibit any discrimination by employer and labour union against new employees and new members by reason of race, colour, nationality, ethnic origin, or religion. Certain provinces also prohibit discrimination on the grounds of age or sex. The Acts expressly prohibit the publication of advertisements, use of application forms, and the making of inquiries in connection with the hiring of an employee by an employer, which express or imply discrimination on any of the forbidden grounds.

Equal Pay

Provincial legislation throughout Canada tries to ensure equal pay for men and women for the same or similar work.

Apprenticeship

Some provinces require that certain tradespeople—for example, plumbers, carpenters, electricians, and barbers—undergo a period of apprenticeship training and pass a test before being allowed to offer their services as qualified craftspersons.

Notice of Dismissal

In many provinces, an employer is required by law to give written notice of termination of employment in case of individual dismissal. In Ontario, the notice requirement also includes collective dismissal. In Quebec, notice must also be given in case of mass lay-off.

Accident Prevention

Most provinces have a Factory or Industrial Safety Act to help protect the health and safety of workers in factories and other workplaces. Matters covered include sanitation, heating, lighting, ventilation, and the guarding of dangerous machinery. There are also provincial laws regulating the design, construction, installation, and operation of mechanical equipment such as boilers and pressure vessels, elevators and lifts, and electrical installations; the use of gas- and oil-burning equipment and radiation-producing equipment such as laser sources; and the standards of qualification for workers who install, operate, or service such equipment.

Public Holidays

Most provinces, including Ontario, have legislation governing public holidays. In these provinces, an employee must receive the regular pay even though he or she does not work; if he or she does work, special overtime rates must be paid. The number of holidays named varies from seven to nine. The provisions for payment also vary slightly between provinces.

Labour Relations

There is a Labour Relations Act or Labour Code in every province which sets out the rights of employer and employees. Persons not usually covered by the Acts include domestic servants; persons employed in agriculture, horticulture, hunting, or trapping; police officers; firefighters; and teachers.

Some of the most important provisions of the Ontario Labour Relations Act are the following. Every persons is free to join a trade union of his or her own choice and to participate in its lawful activities. Similarly, a person is free to join any employers' organization and to take part in its lawful activities. Another provision of the Act is that the employer and the trade union which has been certified by the provincial Labour Relations Board as the bargaining agent for the employees, must bargain in good faith and make every reasonable effort to make a collective agreement. This collective agreement, or labour contract, lasting usually one, two, or three years, sets out in writing the rights and duties of employer and employee. Other provisions, such as compulsory conciliation and the inclusion of an arbitration clause in each collective agreement, were discussed earlier in this chapter.

Summary

1. A *labour union* (or *trade union*) is an association of workers, practising a similar trade or employed usually in the same company or industry whose main purpose is to improve the economic welfare of its members by collective rather than individual bargaining with employers.
2. Labour unions in Canada were started in the early nineteenth century. Although British immigrants helped start them, subsequent financial and other help from U.S. labour unions has been a stronger influence. Until the twentieth century, labour unions and their organizers could be prosecuted for conspiring to restrain trade.
3. Until the 1930s, the craft union was the predominant type of labour union in Canada. However, large mass-production factories created a need for a new type of union—the industrial union—with membership open to unskilled and semi-skilled workers.
4. Labour unions can also be divided according to geographical scope of membership. An *international union* has members in both Canada and the United States; a *national union* has only Canadian members; and a *local union* has only local membership within Canada.
5. The basic unit of organization of a labour union is the "local".
6. A Labour Council acts as the spokesperson for organized labour in each municipality. A Labour Federation represents labour unions in the province as a whole. The Canadian Labour Congress acts as a national spokesperson for organized labour. A second, but less powerful, central labour organization is the Confederation of National Trade Unions, with membership mainly in Quebec.
7. Employees who are members of a certified labour union bargain collectively (i.e., as one body) with employers as to the terms and conditions of employment, according to a procedure set out in the

relevant federal or provincial labour relations statute.

8. By law, an employer and a labour union must use the services of a conciliator (a person who tries, by persuasion to bring about an agreement) to negotiate a new collective agreement before the employer may "lock out" its employees or the union call a "strike".
9. An *injunction* is a court order that an employer may obtain instructing strikers to do or not to do something—for example, refraining from physical obstruction.
10. Every collective agreement must, by law, contain a clause whereby every grievance must eventually, if otherwise unresolved, be settled by arbitration.
11. Under common law, an employer and employee have a number of well-established obligations towards each other. Under the Constitution Act, 1867, the provincial governments have the major responsibility for labour laws in Canada. However, the federal government has the right to pass labour laws with regard to: (a) industries under federal jurisdiction; and (b) industries under federal contract. Provincial labour legislation relates to such matters as: minimum age for employment; minimum wage rates for male and female employees; maximum hours of work per week; annual paid vacations; public holidays; weekly rest day; equal pay; fair employment practices; apprenticeship training; workmen's compensation; and labour relations.

Key Terms

Labour union 255
International union 257
National union 257
Local union 257
Union local 260
Executive committee 260
Business agent 260
Shop steward 260
Decentralization 262
Labour council 263
Labour federation 263
CLC 263
Jurisdictional dispute 264
Business unionism 264
Collective bargaining 264
Compulsory conciliation 266
Lockout 266
Strike 266
Injunction 266
Arbitration 266
Grievance 266
Labour legislation 266
Labour standards 268
Safety of employees 269
Industrial relations 269
Fair employment practices 270

Review Questions

1. What is a labour union? What is its purpose?
2. How, why, and when did labour unions come into being in Canada?
3. Distinguish between craft unions and industrial unions. Which came first? Why?
4. What are international unions? Why do they exist? Why do Canadian workers belong to them?
5. Explain the typical organization of a labour union local.
6. Distinguish between the role of the business agent and that of the shop steward.
7. What external ties does a union local possess? Why?
8. What is meant by "business unionism"?
9. What is "collective bargaining"? What are its benefits for the employee?
10. How does a labour union become certified as a bargaining agent?
11. Explain the nature and purpose of compulsory conciliation.
12. How can (a) labour unions and (b) employers exert pressure on each other to arrive at a new labour agreement?
13. "Outstanding grievances must be settled by arbitration". Explain.
14. What are the common law obligations of the employer to the employee, and vice versa?
15. How is the responsibility for labour legislation divided in Canada between the federal and provincial governments?
16. What are the major areas covered by provincial labour legislation?

"How come you didn't make a profit last year?"

15. RENT, INTEREST, AND PROFIT

CHAPTER OBJECTIVES

A. To explain the economic meaning of "rent"
B. To distinguish between economic rent and "transfer earnings"
C. To indicate how economic rent occurs and how the concept applies to people and other resources as well as to land
D. To explain why interest rates (the payment for the use of borrowed funds) vary for different type of loans
E. To discuss the concept of profit as a reward for risk-taking by business firms

CHAPTER OUTLINE

15.1 Rent: The Return to Land and Other Resources
15.2 Interest: The Return to Capital
15.3 Profit: The Return to the Entrepreneur

15.1: RENT: THE RETURN TO LAND AND OTHER RESOURCES

In everyday conversation, we use the term "rent" to mean the price of using, for a certain period of time, a house, car, boat or other type of property owned by someone else.

Economic Rent and Transfer Earnings

In economics, rent has a different meaning. In fact, *economic rent*, as it is called, is the payment over and above that required to keep a factor of production, such as land, in its present use.

The most money that a factor of production can earn in alternative employment is called its *transfer earnings*. Thus, land on the outskirts of a town, now worth \$10000/ha for residential housing development, may only be worth \$2000/ha as farmland (the best-paid alternative employment). The implicit earnings of, say, \$1000 a year at a 10% annual rate of return would therefore comprise \$200 of transfer earnings and \$800 of economic rent. As another example, an accountant now employed for \$40000 a year may only be able to obtain an alternative position paying \$30000 a year. The present labour income would therefore comprise \$30000 of transfer earnings and \$10000 of economic rent. Economic rent is, in other words, that part of a factor's earnings that is surplus to its transfer earnings.

The more difficult it is for a factor of production to obtain alternative employment, the larger is the rent portion of its income. One of the chief characteristics of land, in the eyes of early economists, was precisely the fact that land, if not used for growing crops, could be used for little else. Consequently, since the transfer earnings were very small, most of the earnings of land comprised economic rent.

Relatively Fixed Supply of a Factor of Production

How does economic rent arise? In other words, why is a factor of production paid more than the maximum amount that it could secure in alternative use? The reason is that the factors of production are in relatively fixed supply: as demand increases for a factor with little change in its supply, the market price of the factor will rise. Thus, the value of land along the main street of a town will steadily increase (discounting the effects of inflation) because of the mounting pressure of demand.

The term *rent* was originally applied exclusively to land because of the very fact that its supply was fixed. It is true, of course, that land can be reclaimed from the sea and even deserts irrigated and made fertile. It is also true that land can be eroded, flooded, and otherwise destroyed. However, the amount of land involved is only a fraction of the total supply. The supply of land in any particular area is consequently almost completely inelastic. Whatever the price people are willing to pay, the supply of land cannot be increased. All that can happen is that the amount of land in the area may change hands. Because of this fixed supply, any increase in the demand for land will automatically cause a rise in its price. Thus, in Figure 15:1, an increase in demand, from D_1D_1 to D_2D_2, causes land rent to rise from OP_1 to OP_2.

Although the total amount of land is fixed, the supply of land for specific purposes is not. Any specific parcel of land can be used for several different purposes. Thus, the supply of building land in a particular suburban area can be increased (at the expense of the amount

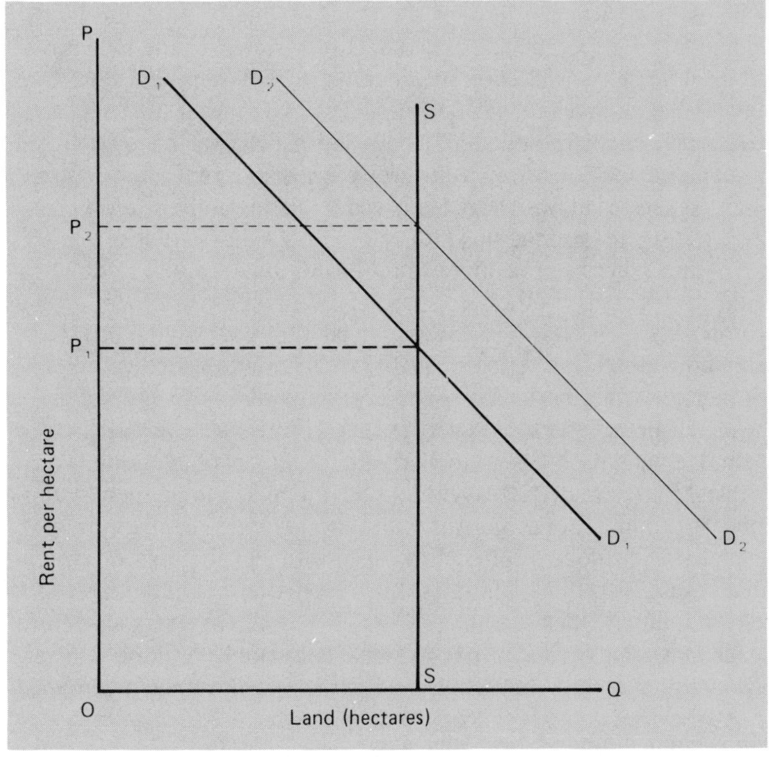

Figure 15:1 The Price (or Rent) of Land Is at the Point at which the Downward-Sloping Demand Curve Intersects the Vertical (Completely Inelastic) Supply Curve

of farmland) if the necessary water, road, sewer, and other services are installed. Often private developers will bear much of this cost. It is quite true to say, therefore, that the higher the price they can obtain per hectare of serviced land, the greater will be the supply. Because land can be used for many different purposes, the supply of land for any one particular purpose can be increased if a higher price is offered. The supply curve of such land, instead of being vertical, would be upward-sloping from left to right. Supply, in other words, would be relatively inelastic instead of completely inelastic. In such a case, the economic rent would be less than where the amount of land available for that particular purpose is absolutely fixed.

In the short run, other factors of production as well as land are relatively fixed in supply. These factors include, for example, shopping facilities in a particular locality. Only in the long run can the higher income to be earned in that area attract new stores. In the meantime, the existing stores will earn an economic rent. When new stores are built, this economic rent will decline and even disappear. Just like land, the other factors of production, labour and capital, which are also fixed in supply in the short run, will receive economic rent. At one time, when the term rent was restricted in economics to land, the term *quasi-rent* was used to describe this return to other factors.

Another example of economic rent relates to the earnings of highly-paid sports stars and other professional entertainers. In a year, such a person may earn, say, $500 000 of which $480 000 may be economic rent and $20 000 transfer earnings—what an entertainer could perhaps get in some other occupation. The economic rent is so large because the supply of such persons is very small compared with the demand for them. Demand itself has multiplied with the advent of television which enables, for example, a heavyweight boxing match to be seen by millions of people around the world and the reigning champion to earn several million dollars for each contest. Also, in the case of professional musicians, the invention of the record-player and the tape deck helped multiply their earnings. Only if every other person were a Beatle, a Rolling Stone, or a Who would pop stars be paid the same as, say, clerical workers—for supply would then have overtaken demand.

Some Applications of the Concept

The concept of economic rent has been used at various times as the basis for recommending:

1. A special land tax. Henry George, a printer in the U.S. in the nineteenth century, advocated in his book, *Progress and Poverty*, that a government's tax needs should be met by a single tax that would be levied on the unearned "surplus" on land.

2. Public confiscation and ownership of land. Whereas capital is accumulated in society only in response to a definite financial incentive, land and other natural resources have always been in existence. Whether a reward is paid for their use of not, so the argument runs, they would still be there. Also, unlike capital goods, land does not periodically have to be replaced. However, most of the present owners of land have purchased it from someone else. Why should they be penalized, the owners would argue, compared with people who have invested their savings in something else? Or compared with people who, instead of saving, used all their income for consumption?

3. The imposition of a capital gains tax—particularly on profits made from speculation in land. Because of a growing population, together with the benefit of the construction, mainly at public expense, of roads, sidewalks, sewers, and water mains, land appreciates in value without any effort on the owner's part. All or most of this increase in value should, it is argued, be taxed away for the benefit of the community as a whole. In fact, many municipal governments do already impose "lot levies" before approving new residential or other construction.

15.2: INTEREST: THE RETURN TO CAPITAL

Capital, in its real sense, consists of factory, commercial and office buildings, equipment, trucks, and other manufactured aids to production and marketing. These items are produced, at the expense of current consumption, because they enable business firms to have a larger output at lower per unit cost than if labour and land alone are used.

Real and Money Rates of Return

The extent to which capital, as a factor of production, increases output is called its *gross productivity*, or *real rate of return*. This amount, when calculated in monetary terms, minus an allowance for depreciation of the capital goods involved, constitutes the net productivity, or *marginal efficiency*, of that capital. Thus, the rate of return on a new piece of equipment, obtained by relating the increase in output (minus depreciation allowance) to the cost of the equipment, may work out at, say, 15 per cent a year.

Capital, in its monetary sense, is the money used by business firms to purchase capital goods and to help cover operating expenses. This money comes in part from lenders and in part from the owners of businesses themselves. The cost of the "borrowed capital" is called the *rate of interest*. So long as a business firm can use the money borrowed to earn a higher rate of return, it is worthwhile to borrow and pay this rate of interest. For the cost of money invested in a business by its owners (the "equity capital"), economists impute a rate of interest equal to its *opportunity cost*—in other words, what it would have cost the firm if the money had been borrowed instead of being supplied by the owners. This implicit cost is just as valid, from the economist's point of view, as the rate of interest paid for the use of other people's money.

Looked at from the lender's point of view, the rate of interest is the reward that the owner of money receives for temporarily giving up its use. Instead of lending it, a personal investor could, after all, have spent it. For abandoning this immediate pleasure, he or she is entitled to some recompense.

Different Rates of Interest

In practice, there are many different rates of interest, not just one. The rate that is charged will depend upon a number of factors, as listed below.

1. Risk involved. Part of the variation between interest rates is explained by the varying degrees of risk involved in obtaining repayment. Thus, if a person has a good *credit rating* (i.e. is considered to be trustworthy by lenders) and can offer stocks, bonds, accounts receivable, or other collateral as security for repayment of a loan, a bank will offer one of their lowest rates of interest. The lowest rate is called the *prime rate*, and is usually reserved for a bank's very best (least-risk) clients.

2. Length of time. Another part of the variation in rates is explained by the differences in length of time for which the money is borrowed. Thus, the rate of interest on short-term loans is usually lower than on long-term ones.

3. Size of loan. Another reason for some variation in interest rates is the size of the loan. Whatever the amount borrowed, the applicant must be interviewed and references checked. Also, instalments of principal and interest must be collected, and any delinquency followed up. Per dollar borrowed, the cost is higher for a small loan than for a large one, and this difference is reflected in the interest rates charged.

4. Geographical differences. Finally, between one part of the country and another, interest rates may vary to reflect local differences in the demand for and supply of funds. However, with branch banking and highly advanced means of communication, local differences are nowadays relatively slight. Even differences in rates of interest between different countries are now smoothed out by international flows of short and long-term funds.

15.3: PROFIT: THE RETURN TO THE ENTREPRENEUR

Business executives consider profit, or net income, to be the surplus of total revenue over total expenses. The more goods and services a firm can sell and the more it can charge for them, the greater will be its total revenue. The more efficiently a firm can produce and market its goods and services, the lower will be its total expenses. It is on this basis of total revenue minus total expenses that business firms calculate and report their profits or earnings.

Implicit Returns to Other Factors of Production

Because firms which have owner-managers do not always pay their managers a normal salary or even any salary at all, but give them a share of profit instead, part of the reported profits is really an implicit return to labour. This is particularly true of unincorporated businesses whose owners, even though running the business, are not permitted by law to pay themselves a salary. All they are allowed to do is take a drawing against future profits. Also, in businesses which own the land they use, the declared profit really contains an implicit rent. And for every business, there is an implicit return on that part of the capital which, instead of being borrowed at interest, is invested by the owners. This implicit return should at least be the same as the going rate of interest on borrowed capital. Business profit therefore contains implicit returns to labour, land, and capital, as well as a residual "economic" profit.

Pure Profit

Most economists consider profit to be an entrepreneur's reward for the acceptance of risk. *Pure* or *economic profit* is in fact the reward that the entrepreneur receives for undertaking the risk of establishing and operating a business. Practically every business-investment decision is accompanied by risk. This is because it is impossible to predict accurately, for example, how consumers will react to a new product; what competing firms will do; when and how governments will intervene; and how domestic and export markets will be affected by changes in the state of the economy. In return for his or her willingness to undertake the risk of losing money, both personal and borrowed funds, and wasting valuable personal time, the entrepreneur demands and merits a special reward. Without it, the entrepreneur would not undertake the risk; and the economy would forgo the income and jobs that could have been created.

Occasionally, a business enjoys some form of monopoly power which enables it to charge more for its products than it would in the presence of competition. Consequently, a *monopoly profit* may arise. Economists recognize that economic profit, although mainly a compensation for risk, may also contain such a monopoly profit.

Some economists, stressing the role of the entrepreneur as a fourth factor of production, consider profit to be the reward for entrepreneurial activity in general, not just risk taking. The more successful an entrepreneur is in combining resources to produce and market what the public wants, the greater will be the profit. Clearly, this concept of profit is very similar to the one already described, for risk and entrepreneurship are inextricably linked.

Whatever the approach used, one thing is clear. Since profit is a residual amount, over and above the explicit and implicit returns paid to labour, land, and capital, it may be positive or negative. The likelihood of making a profit is no greater than the risk of making a loss. Entrepreneurial ability or good management makes the difference.

Pure profit exists only in a dynamic situation, for, in the long run, other firms would move into an industry in pursuit of profit. And as they do, the effects of increased competition would be to reduce the profit earned by everyone. Of course, a certain minimum amount of profit must be earned by a firm, otherwise it would no longer continue to produce. This minimum amount, which is just sufficient to keep capital in a particular line of production, is known as *normal profit*. However, artificial barriers, such as brand advertising and other forms of product differentiation, help established firms to maintain some degree of additional profit by restricting newcomers.

The Purpose of Profit

The purpose of profit may be said to be that of motivating people to assume the risk of establishing and operating a business. Without the lure of profit, people would put their savings to a much safer use. Furthermore, only by producing what consumers want, is it normally possible for a firm to make a profit. Thus, the profit motive is instrumental in allocating a society's factors of production to the uses that society most wants. Of course, this profit motive should not be permitted unrestricted play; otherwise we might once again suffer the economic and social abuses of nineteenth-century *laissez faire*—or unrestricted free enterprise. Thus, as with the Combines Investigation Act, the government intervenes where necessary in the public interest.

The possibility of increased profit is also the most important motivating force for business firms to reduce costs and improve the efficiency of production. In communist countries, by way of contrast, production quotas assigned by regional-planning committees have long been used instead of profit as the motivating force. However, the result has been the output of many poor-quality goods which, although perhaps achieving the production quota, have often been relatively unsaleable. In non-communist countries, the profit motive has provided the incentive for business firms to emphasize not only quality but also the production of goods and services that consumers really want.

The more profit a firm makes, the more it can reinvest or pay out in dividends to its shareholders. In turn, shareholders have more money and a greater claim on the goods and services currently produced.

Profit Controls

Some people treat profit as a dirty word, synonymous with worker exploitation, ignoring its importance as a stimulus to saving, investment, risk-taking, innovation, sheer hard work, and an efficient allocation of a country's resources. As a result, governments have periodically restricted profits either generally by, for example, increased income taxes or price controls or selectively by, for example, rent controls. The economic effect of such restrictions is (a) to discourage investment by individuals and business firms; (b) to encourage them to invest in other more attractive countries; (c) to encourage individuals to increase their current consumption, rather than to save and invest part of their income; and (d) to distort the flow of public savings toward tax-incentive investment vehicles such as RRSPs, RHOSPs, MURBs, Canadian-produced feature films, etc.

In some cases, both past and present, business firms have earned extremely large profits. From the social point of view, excessively large profits, compared with the capital or entrepreneurial energy invested, may be considered undesirable. And most governments today redistribute part of this profit by taxation on the one hand and social security payments, etc. on the other. The question is, of course, just how much taxation and redistribution should there be if the "golden goose" is to survive?

Finally, we should not forget that so long as a competitive situation exists, new firms can enter an industry and thereby help eliminate excessive profits.

Summary

1. At one time, rent was considered by economists to be solely the return to land. Nowadays, in economics, rent is defined more broadly as the payment that any factor of production, not just land, receives over and above that required to keep it in its present use.
2. The most that a factor of production can earn in alternative employment is called its *transfer earnings*. Economic rent is, therefore, that part of a factor's earnings that is surplus to its transfer earnings.
3. Economic rent is caused by an increase in demand for a factor of production compared with a relatively fixed supply of it. The term "rent" was originally applied exclusively to land because of the

very fact that its total supply was fixed.

4. Although the total amount of land is fixed, the supply of land for specific purposes is not. This means that the supply of such land is relatively inelastic rather than completely inelastic, and its rent is correspondingly less.
5. In the short run, labour and capital are also relatively fixed in supply and therefore earn economic rent. Formerly, the term *quasi-rent* was used to describe this return to factors of production other than land.
6. The significance of the economic concept of rent is that society often pays far more than is necessary to keep a factor of production in its present use. The concept has also been used, at different times, and with varying response, as an argument in favour of a special land tax, the public confiscation and ownership of land, and the imposition of a capital gains tax.
7. Capital, in its real sense, consists of plant, equipment, trucks, and various other people-made aids to production. The extent to which capital causes output to increase is called its gross productivity, or real rate of return. Capital, in its monetary sense, is the money that is loaned by various financial institutions and the public to business firms.
8. The cost of borrowing capital is called the *rate of interest*. For money invested in a business by its owners, economists impute a rate of interest equal to its *opportunity cost*—that is to say, what it would have cost if borrowed. In practice, there are many different rates of interest because of differences in risk involved to the lender; length of time of the loan; size of the loan; and geographical location of the borrower. The money paid to a lender, after allowance for the factors just mentioned, constitutes the *pure rate of interest*.
9. The business concept of *profit* (the surplus of total revenue over total expenses) usually makes no allowance for implicit returns to land, labour, and capital. Most economists consider profit (a "residual" amount) to be a businessperson's reward for risk-taking; others consider it a reward for entrepreneurial activity in general, not just risk-taking.
10. In addition to this *pure*, or *economic profit*, there may also be an element of *monopoly profit*, depending upon the amount of competition in an industry.
11. The minimum amount of profit required to keep a firm in an industry is called *normal profit*.
12. The purpose of profit is to motivate people to assume the risk of

establishing and operating a business.

13. The actual amount of profit is determined by sales revenue (price, the attractiveness of a firm's products to consumers, the amount of competition, etc.) minus the costs of production and marketing.

Key Terms

Rent 277
Economic rent 277
Transfer earnings 277
Quasi-rent 280
Interest 281
Gross productivity 281
Real rate of return 281
Marginal efficiency of capital 281
Borrowed capital 281
Rate of interest 281
Equity capital 281
Implicit cost 281
Credit rating 282
Prime rate 282
Profit 282
Implicit return 282
Pure profit 283
Monopoly profit 283
Normal profit 284
Profit control 285

Review Questions

1. How is the term "rent" used in economics?
2. What are transfer earnings? What is their relationship to economic rent?
3. What gives rise to economic rent?
4. Why, at one time, was the term "rent" applied almost exclusively to land?
5. To what extent is the supply of land fixed?
6. In the short run, there are other factors of production, as well as land, that are relatively fixed in supply. Explain.
7. What is the meaning of the term "quasi-rent"?
8. What is the significance of the economic concept of rent?
9. Distinguish between real capital and money capital.
10. How can the rate of return be calculated on a new piece of industrial equipment?
11. What is the rate of interest? What significance does it have for business investment? Why does it fluctuate so much?
12. Why are there many different rates of interest, not just one? What is the pure rate of interest?
13. How does the business concept of profit differ from the economic one?

14. Distinguish between normal profit and monopoly profit.
15. What is the purpose of profit, from society's point of view?
16. What factors determine the level of a firm's profits?
17. How are profits controlled? What are the effects of such controls?
18. "Economic rent should be the subject of a special tax." Explain and discuss.
19. All interest rates should be the same and should not fluctuate over time. Discuss.
20. Interest rates are the main determinant of the level of business investment. Discuss.
21. Compare and discuss the following statements: (a) "There is no place for profit in a democratic society;" (b) "Profit may be termed the engine of economic growth".

16. POVERTY AMIDST PLENTY

CHAPTER OBJECTIVES

A. To explain what is meant by the term "poverty"
B. To indicate how many Canadians are considered to be poor
C. To distinguish between the various type of poor people in Canada
D. To identify the reasons for the existence of poverty in Canada
E. To outline the various government programs designed to help keep family income at a reasonable level
F. To explain the concept of a guaranteed annual income
G. To examine income inequality in Canada and the reasons for it

CHAPTER OUTLINE

16.1 Poverty in Canada
16.2 Types of Poor
16.3 Causes of Poverty
16.4 Government Income-Security Programs
16.5 Proposals for a Guaranteed Annual Income
16.6 Income Inequality

16.1: POVERTY IN CANADA

Canada, using a predominantly private-enterprise economic system, has been very successful over the years in raising its real GNP. And despite population growth, it has succeeded in achieving and maintaining (although it has slipped somewhat over the last 30 years) one of the highest standards of living in the world—now about fourteenth.

However, this same economic system has also meant great economic insecurity for the individual. Dependent primarily on the market place, a person can easily find (because of age, illness, accident, loss of a spouse, technological change, or general economic recession) that personal income can become very small or even cease altogether. This decline in income means, of course, a smaller share of the goods and services produced by society.

To ensure that every Canadian enjoys a reasonable minimum standard of living and has some protection against economic vicissitudes, the federal and provincial governments have adopted a variety of income-security programs. Unfortunately, these programs, although involving considerable government expenditure, have not been as successful as was originally hoped. Thus, although Canada is considered to be part of North America's "affluent society," Canadians do not have to look far to find evidence of poverty. As the Special Senate Committee on Poverty pointed out in 1971: "The grim fact is that one Canadian in four lacks sufficient income to maintain a basic standard of living."[1]

Poverty Defined

For many years, the term "poverty" was used to describe a situation in which a person or family was unable to afford a minimum level of physical subsistence. Thus, a poor person was one who was unable to pay for the food, clothing, and shelter needed to keep him or her alive and well.

Nowadays, poverty is more usually defined as a standard of living that is low relative to that enjoyed by most people in society. Thus, although a family in Canada may be reasonably well off when compared with the poor of many other countries, such as India or China, it may nevertheless be poor by Canadian standards. In accordance with this view, the Economic Council of Canada has defined *poverty* as:

> ... insufficient access to certain goods, services, and conditions of life which are available to everyone else and have come to be accepted as basic to a decent, minimum standard of living.[2]

In other words, poverty is a *relative* concept rather than an absolute one.

The Measurement of Poverty

One way of measuring poverty would be to compare the way that different people live and to award points for various factors. Thus a family that is under-fed, under-clothed, and badly housed, even though the parents earn a reasonable income (and spend it on other things), would still be considered poor. Obviously, however, the task of measurement would be immense, costly, and unpopular. Another and much simpler way is to use income as the measuring stick. A person earning $20000 a year under this system would be considered better off than one earning $10000.

A key consideration in defining poverty is the number of persons in a family. Thus a single person receiving $20000 a year is much better off than a family of ten, with the same total income.

Geographical location is another important factor. Thus, a person earning $10000 in, say, Ontario, may be worse off, because of differences in housing and other costs, than someone earning $8000 in Newfoundland. Similarly, someone earning $10000 in Toronto may be worse off than someone earning $7000 in a rural Ontario community.

Obviously, the level of income below which a family can be considered "poor" is a matter of opinion. However, the National Council of Welfare and other organizations commonly use as their poverty lines the "low income cut-offs" employed by Statistics Canada to produce data on Canada's low-income population.

Statistics Canada found, in a survey of family expenditure, that Canadian families spend, on average, 38.5 per cent of their income on food, clothing and shelter. Therefore, because poor families devote an above-average proportion of their limited income on the basic necessities, the low income cut-offs were set at the income level at which 58.5 per cent of income (that is 20 percentage points above the average) is spent on food, clothing and shelter. Consequently, any family or single person whose income is below this level is considered to be "low-income".

The income that is taken into account in the calculation is money income received by all family members aged 15 or over from: wages and salaries before deductions, net income from self-employment, investment income, government transfer payments such as Family Allowances and pensions, and other miscellaneous income.

Statistics Canada has taken into account the size of household by using seven categories of family size, ranging from a single person to seven or more persons. It takes into account place of residence by using five groups of communities: metropolitan areas with half a million or more people (Vancouver, Edmonton, Calgary, Winnipeg, Hamilton, Toronto, Ottawa-Hull, Montreal, and Quebec City); large cities (100000 to 499999); medium-sized cities (30000 to 99999); smaller centres (cities of 15000 to 29999 and small urban areas under 15000); and rural areas (both farm and non-farm).

Taking into consideration size of household and place of residence, Statistics Canada has produced a whole set of low income cut-offs for

Canada rather than just one. These low income cut-offs (See Table S.6) are then adjusted each year according to changes in the cost of living, as indicated by the Consumer Price Index.

Although the Statistics Canada low-income cut-offs are widely used as poverty guidelines, it should be pointed out that Statistics Canada itself states in its publication, *Income Distribution by Size in Canada*, that the cut-offs should not be interpreted as poverty lines as these involve a value judgment as to the minimum level of income below which an individual or family would generally be regarded as poor. As Michael Fraser, director of the Fraser Institute, has pointed out, a number of factors are ignored by the cut-off levels. First, they ignore an individual's personal wealth. Thus, a low income for a person who owns his or her home does not mean the same thing as for a person who is renting. A second factor that is ignored is the availability to many low-income persons, particularly senior citizens, of subsidized services such as free public transportation and reduced rate meals, pharmaceuticals, medical care, entertainment, and even travel. Third, statistics interpreted as poverty lines, ignore the fact that people, in their lifetime, pass through many different income stages. For example, is a person "poor" because he or she is working at a first job after leaving school and is perhaps still living at home or in shared accommodation? Within ten years, that person's income may have doubled, even in real terms. So, as well as taking into account place of residence and family size, Statistics Canada (and those who use low-income data) should perhaps include age as an important variable. Fourth, the composition of Canada's population should also be considered. Because of the passage of the baby boom through the population, Canada has a disproportionately large percentage of people at early and late stages in their earnings life cycle—when personal income is usually expected to be relatively low. And this should not be allowed to distort the average income so as to conclude that an extremely large segment of the Canadian population is poor—for example, the 3.5 millions suggested by the Canadian Council on Social Development.

Other groups that have put forward poverty lines for Canada include the Special Senate Committee on Poverty and the Canadian Council on Social Development. The poverty line suggested by the former is well above that obtained by using Statistics Canada's low income cut-off figures.

Health and Welfare Canada, from a national survey, concluded that single elderly persons required an after-tax income of $8722 in 1981 to cover essential needs, which was higher than what the Statistics Canada figures would suggest as the minimum income required.

Table S.6
Low Income Lines, Estimates for 1983

	Population of Area of Residence				
	500 000 and over	100 000 - 499 999	30 000 - 99 000	Less than 30 000	Rural
No. in Family					
1	$ 9 538	$ 9 058	$ 8 497	$ 7 856	$ 7 052
2	12 583	11 942	11 142	10 339	9 218
3	16 832	15 952	14 908	13 867	12 344
4	19 397	18 434	17 233	16 030	14 268
5	22 604	21 401	19 959	18 594	16 591
6	24 687	23 325	21 802	20 279	18 114
7 or more	27 172	25 729	24 047	22 363	19 959

Source: Statistics Canada

"According to the newspaper, we're just below the poverty line.."

The Poverty Rate

What percentage of Canada's population can be classified as poor? It depends, of course, on which poverty levels of income that we use and whether we consider them to be a true criterion of poverty, even in its relative sense. However, out of a total population of 25 millions, anywhere between one-tenth and one-fifth (that is, from 2.5 to 5 million persons) might be considered poor.

16.2: TYPES OF POOR

Those Canadians whose individual or family income today falls below the poverty line are by no means all the same. They include, in fact, many different types of poor people, each with problems of their own—problems that often require different solutions.

One useful division is between the *urban poor* and the *rural poor*. Another is between the *working poor* and the *welfare poor*. The poor can also be divided according to the principal cause of their poverty—for example, physical disability, old age, lack of a male family head, or unemployment. Furthermore, because of the cultural differences involved, special attention is frequently given to Canada's native peoples—the Indians, Métis, and Inuits—who together form about 2 per cent of Canada's total population.

The Urban Poor and the Rural Poor

How do the urban poor differ from the rural poor? The most important difference is that in the urban areas over half the poor are unattached individuals, whereas in the rural areas the bulk of the poor are families.[3]

In both urban and rural areas, poverty among the aged is high. However, in rural areas, a young family is just as likely to be poor as an old one. The poor in urban areas tend to earn more than the poor in rural areas. Furthermore, the difference in income between the poor and non-poor is much greater in urban areas than it is in rural areas.

The relatively large number of unattached individuals living in poverty in urban areas would seem to reflect the migration of young people from rural areas to the cities in hope of a more exciting time, if not a more worthwhile job. Although average income among the poor may be lower in rural areas, the cost of living (particularly accommodation) is normally much lower than in the urban areas. That is one of the reasons why many young families prefer to be poor in the country rather than in the city.

Among the rural poor are many farm families. Caught in a squeeze between slowly increasing prices of farm products on the one hand and quickly rising costs of production (hired labour, machinery, seed and fertilizer) on the other, the average small farmer in Canada has gradually found himself and his family working for a pittance wage. Only large-scale highly mechanized farming, including intensive factory-like chicken and hog production, seems to be profitable. But it is an option open to only a relative few. Among the rural non-farm poor, there are many Indians and Métis.

The Working Poor and the Welfare Poor

By far the largest group of poor persons in Canada is the *working poor*—people who work for very low rates of pay in such industries as laundries, textile mills, and retail stores, and as farm owners or employees. These are people who are able to find a job and prefer to work, even though they might be better off financially on welfare.

There are also many people in Canada, the *welfare poor*, who, for various reasons, are unable to work and rely on social assistance for all or part of their income. These welfare poor include: persons permanently disabled or ill; female heads of families; persons unemployed, aged, or temporarily disabled; and persons working but not earning sufficient to live on. Contrary to popular belief, studies in Canada and the United States suggest that only about 2 per cent of welfare recipients are people who prefer to receive welfare rather than work for a living.

Native Peoples

Living on 2 279 reserves, covering more than 6 million acres, Canada's Indian population totals over 300 000. As one Indian chief explained to the Special Senate Committee on Poverty, not all native people are poor, but those who are can be described as "the poorest of the poor." Most Indians, in fact, have considerably worse housing, sanitation, educational and health services than other poor people in Canada. Indian poverty, according to the Senate Committee, can be mainly attributed to "a basic misunderstanding and/or lack of appreciation of native cultures and the values on which they are based." A second factor, according to the committee, is "a paternalism that is blind to the rights of native peoples as people and to their need to preserve and develop their own identity and self-respect."[4] Others have argued that the average Indian lacks the inherent ability to cope with the demands of modern technological society. However, even when Indians possess the necessary skills or education for employment, they are widely discriminated against both by employers and fellow-employees—often because they are considered, rightly or wrongly, to be unsatisfactory workers.

Canada's Inuit, numbering about 25 000, live mainly in the Northwest Territories, Arctic Quebec, and Labrador. As the area is developed, notably in the pursuit of oil and natural gas, more and more Inuit are abandoning their previously independent fishing and trapping way of life to work as employees. Some have established their own production and marketing co-operatives, specializing in Arctic foods, parkas, sculptures, and other handicrafts. But, as with the Indians, considerable poverty continues to exist, even measured by local standards.

16.3: CAUSES OF POVERTY

There are many different reasons for poverty in Canada.

1. *The determination of salaries and wages by the market forces of supply and demand results in very high incomes for certain persons (see Table S. 7), but very low incomes for others.* A person employed at minimum wage-rates in certain areas can find that his or her income is insufficient to provide a decent standard of living. Only when both husband and wife work can many families in Canada make ends meet. Thus, a person, although employed full-time, can be poor because his or her abilities, education, training, character, age, and other characteristics are insufficient or unsuitable to secure or retain a higher-income job. People in this situation form Canada's "working-poor". In the case of many poor Canadian farmers and small-business owners, their way of life is bound up with their choice of occupation. Before switching occupations, even if jobs were available, such poor would need to be almost penniless.

2. *Many people who could perform a useful job are unable to find work.* The harsh winters in Canada have traditionally meant high seasonal unemployment. But more important in causing unemployment are such factors as the fluctuations of the business cycle, "stop-go" government monetary and fiscal policies, increased foreign competition, new capital-intensive manufacturing techniques, higher labour force participation rates by women, and a very high rate of other new entrants to the labour force. Others for whom job openings are available lack the necessary education and skills.

3. *Some people are unable to work because of old age, temporary or permanent illness, or physical disability, and the need (in the case of single-parent families) to stay home to look after young children.*

4. *Prejudice (because of ethnic origin, race, language, or sex) prevents*

Table S.7
Average Income in Different Occupations in Canada, 1984

Occupation	Number of Persons	Average Income ($)	Total Income ($ millions)	Occupational Share of Total Income (%)
S/e doctors & surgeons	33 329	95 597	3 186.2	1.12
S/e dentists	9 091	74 665	678.8	.24
S/e lawyers & notaries	20 678	65 167	1 347.5	.48
S/e accountants	11 338	55 519	629.5	.22
S/e engineers & architects	4 199	40 754	171.1	.06
Other s/e professionals	55 996	24 245	1 357.6	.48
Employees	10 312 882	21 118	217 790.9	76.77
Investors	1 041 401	19 713	20 529.5	7.24
Property owners	134 321	17 370	2 333.1	.82
S/e salesmen	35 784	17 537	627.6	.22
Farmers	271 740	15 855	4 308.4	1.52
Fishermen	35 439	14 487	513.4	.18
Business proprietors	521 641	13 534	7 060.0	2.49
S/e entertainers & artists	20 611	12 338	254.3	.09
Pensioners	1 185 578	12 553	14 882.6	5.25
Unclassified	1 858 153	4 309	8 005.9	2.82
Total	15 552 181	18 240	283 676.3	100.0
Business Proprietors				
Insurance agents	1 611	22 786	36.7	.01
Real estate	2 400	23 735	57.0	.02
Finance	5 591	18 540	103.7	.04
Wholesale trade	7 560	20 263	153.2	.05
Other business	9 920	15 913	157.9	.06
Forestry	7 763	18 798	145.9	.05
Recreation services	8 623	15 998	138.0	.05
Construction	82 848	14 506	1 201.8	.42
Manufacturing	17 607	17 718	312.0	.11
Utilities	61 737	13 592	839.1	.30
Retail trade	141 425	12 944	1 830.6	.65
Business services	16 287	13 105	213.4	.08
Other services	158 269	11 821	1 870.8	.66
Total	521 641	13 534	7 060.0	2.49

Source: Revenue Canada, *Taxation Statistics, 1986 Edition*
Note: Doctors, lawyers, and similar professional classifications shown above include only those earning the major part of their income as professional fees. Professionals whose principal source of income is in the form of salary are classified as employees

people from obtaining better jobs, or even jobs at all, despite human rights legislation.

5. *The children of poor people, through lack of educational and other opportunities, are often unable to break out of the "poverty circle"—a situation in which poor families, because of economic circumstances, are condemned to remain poor.*

6. *Some people are unwilling to accept a job that involves relocation, responsibility, strenuous mental or physical work, or other disagreeable conditions.* That is why, for example, labour sometimes has to be recruited in foreign countries for jobs that Canadians will not accept—such as fruit-picking, tobacco harvesting, and other agricultural work. However, it can also be argued that such jobs would be accepted by Canadians if the wage-rates were higher.

7. *The difficulty that many of Canada's native peoples have in accepting and adjusting to a different culture and the inability or unwillingness of the remainder of society to accept them as equals.*

16.4: GOVERNMENT INCOME-SECURITY PROGRAM

Today most Canadians recognize that they have a social obligation to help the less fortunate members of society. This recognition is expressed by donations to the various churches and church organizations such as the Salvation Army and to civil organizations such as the United Appeal. Much more important, though, are the contributions that most people make through taxes. This is because a large part of this tax revenue is used to help pay for a variety of government income-security programs all of which are designed to help people maintain a minimum, decent standard of living. Although most people object to paying so much in taxes, they nevertheless usually support the principle of collective social responsibility, a basic Christian ethic, whereby the economically strong help the economically weak.

Government income-security programs include unemployment insurance, the Canada and Quebec pension plans, old-age security, family allowances, youth allowances, workmen's compensation, and social assistance.

Unemployment Insurance

By the terms of the Unemployment Insurance Act, all regular members of the labour force in Canada are compulsorily insured against loss of wages through unemployment. In fact, about 95% of all employees are covered. The main exceptions are the self-employed, some part-time workers, and workers over 65 years of age. Both employers and employees pay contributions, with the employer collecting and remitting both to the government. Contributions are adjusted yearly. The government also makes a contribution. The program is administered by the Canada Employment and Immigration Commission, or CEIC.

Under the Act, a person can draw unemployment benefit for up to a certain number of weeks, so long as he or she has made a minimum number of recent contributions (depending on the economic region) and meets certain conditions of availability, capability, and searching for work. Persons who have made more contributions can claim a wider range of benefits. There is a two-week waiting period, once a claim has been accepted, before any benefit is paid. The benefit rate is 60% of average weekly insurable earnings, with a maximum benefit period. Persons collecting unemployment insurance benefits may work part-time and earn up to 25% of their weekly benefit rate before deductions. Any amount above that is deducted from the benefit cheque. Persons who have been dismissed for misconduct, quit their job voluntarily, or turned down a suitable job offer are disqualified from benefit for up to six weeks beyond the normal two-week waiting period.

The program is being constantly revised so current benefits and eligibility requirements should be checked at the local CEIC office. The current scale of benefits has been criticized by some (for example, the Canadian Federation of Independent Business) as being too generous and helping to destroy the work ethic. Others claim that it is not enough.

Canada Pension Plan

Every province except Quebec (which has its own comparable pension plan) participates in a federally-run pension plan. This plan, the Canada Pension Plan, began in 1966 and covers, on a compulsory basis, practically every employee, whatever his or her occupation, between the ages of 18 and 65 (or 70 if the person continues to work and does not apply for the retirement pension). It is financed by equal contributions from employee and employer.

The plan provides the following benefits: a retirement pension; a disability pension; benefits for the children of disabled employees; a widow's pension; benefits for the children of a deceased employee; benefits for disabled widowers; and a lump sum payment to a deceased employee's estate. A formal application must be made to receive them.

Benefits under the plan are portable. This means that if a person changes his or her job or place of residence, the pension rights remain the same. With a private plan, employees frequently lose all or part of the employer's contribution if they leave their jobs.

To take into account changes in the cost of living, all benefits under the plan are revalued annually so long as the Pension Index (which is, in turn, based on the Consumer Price Index) has increased by more than 1 per cent over that of the previous year. Thus, a person's benefits will not remain at a fixed dollar amount, but will increase each year as prices rise. This feature overcomes, to some extent, the common fear among pensioners that inflation will gradually wipe out the real value of their pensions.

Old Age Security

Under the Old Age Security Act, a person who is sixty-five or more and who has satisfied the Canadian residence requirements is entitled to receive an old-age pension in addition to any retirement pension under the Canada Pension Plan. A person receiving an old-age pension and living in Canada may also receive an additional monthly allowance, called a *guaranteed income supplement*, if he or she has little or no other income. There is also a special *spouse allowance* payable to the spouse of an OAS pensioner.

These three programs (the old age pension, the guaranteed income supplement, and the spouse allowance) all of which provide benefits for the elderly in Canada, are non-contributory. In other words, a person does not have to have paid contributions during past years (as with the Canada Pension Plan) to be eligible. The benefits are paid for from the government's general tax revenue. They are also indexed to the cost of living and adjusted each quarter.

Family Allowances

These are payments made by the federal government each month to supplement family income, for the benefit of each dependent child under 18 years of age. There is no limit on the number of children in a family who are eligible. The allowances are made on a *demogrant* basis—that is, every family, whatever the need, receives them so long as there are children of eligible ages. To help offset the fact that the allowance is paid, whatever the level of family income, such benefit is subject to income tax. Also, it has been proposed that benefits be made payable on a sliding scale, the actual amount of benefit depending on the size of family. The benefits are indexed to the cost of living and adjusted each January. Quebec has its own family allowance program. Alberta and Quebec vary the rate according to the child's age. And Quebec adds a provincial supplement.

Child Tax Credit

A person is entitled, under this Federal program that began in 1979, to receive a certain sum for each child under 18 years of age, additional to the Family Allowance. As net family income exceeds a stated exemption level, the credit is gradually reduced.

Workers' Compensation

In every province, a Workers' Compensation Act provides for the establishment of a fund, financed solely by employers, to pay compensation to an employee for industrial injury or disablement. An employee does not have to prove negligence on the part of his or her employer to obtain compensation. On the other hand, compensation may be withheld if the accident arose from the employee's gross misconduct—for example, being drunk on the job. If an employee is disabled, he or she may receive all necessary medical care and hospitalization; cash payments to compensate for loss of wages; a life pension for permanent disability; and rehabilitation services. If an employee dies as the result of an industrial accident or disease, his widow receives a monthly pension; a special lump sum payment; an allowance for funeral expenses; and a monthly allowance for each child below a certain age limit.

Social Assistance

Each province makes social assistance or "welfare" payments to families and individuals who can prove that they are in need. Half the money is provided by the federal government through the Canada Assistance Plan. Special allowances are also paid, after a means test, to blind and otherwise disabled persons. There are also war veterans' allowances for qualified veterans in need; and special federal social assistance to Indians and Inuit.

Under the Canada Assistance Plan, the federal government also shares the cost of various assistance and service programs administered by the provincial governments. These services include: (a) health care, including medical and surgical services, nursing, dental and optical care (including dentures and eye-glasses), drugs, and prosthetic appliances; (b) assistance to mothers with dependent children; (c) the maintenance of needy persons in such residential welfare institutions as home for the aged, nursing homes, homes for unmarried mothers, and child-care institutions; and (d) welfare services such as rehabilitation, casework, counselling and assessment, adoption, and homemaker and day-care services.

16.5: PROPOSALS FOR A GUARANTEED ANNUAL INCOME

Although Canada has a variety of income-security programs designed to help the needy, this whole welfare system, costing many billions of dollars a year, has been the subject of much criticism. One of the strongest condemnations was by the Special Senate Committee on Poverty, which stated:

> The social-welfare structure so laboriously and painstakingly erected in Canada over the past forty years has clearly outlived its usefulness. The social scientists who have studied it, the bureaucrats who have administered it, and the poor who have experienced it are of one mind that in today's swiftly-changing world, the welfare system is a hopeless failure. The matter is not even controversial; everybody's against it. But what is to take its place?[5]

The major criticism that is made of Canada's present welfare system is that it discourages the welfare recipient from trying to improve his or her position through employment. Any money that such a person earns is usually deducted from his or her welfare cheque. This system also encourages the welfare recipient to try to cheat the government by doing jobs on the side. A second important criticism is that the system creates dependence. The poor must ask for help if they are to obtain financial assistance. By doing so, they lose their sense of self-pride. A third important criticism is that it is unfair to the "working poor" who may work long hours at unpleasant jobs to earn the same amount of money, or just slightly more than someone living on welfare.

Obviously, the elimination of poverty in Canada is not just a matter of making payments to those in need. Sound government monetary and fiscal policies to promote economic growth are also needed to create jobs. So also are good trading relationships with foreign countries that provide important markets for our goods. There must also be suitable training and education for new entrants to the labour force and retraining opportunities for persons whose jobs may have disappeared because of technological change. Health care, education, and housing must be expanded and improved. However, government income-security payments can play an important part in eliminating poverty—certainly in helping those Canadians such as the old and disabled who are in no position to help themselves. The question is, therefore, how best to use the limited amount of money that the government is willing to spend on helping the poor?

A proposal that has been gaining some ground in Canada in recent years is that of a guaranteed annual income. This is a program whereby the federal government would pay everyone above a certain age an amount of money sufficient to bring that person's annual income up to a minimum guaranteed level. The usual method recommended for doing this is a "negative income tax". In other words, the government, instead of taking money in income tax from a person's pay packet every week or month, would, in the case of a poor person, *add* money, the actual amount depending on how low the level of earned income actually was.

The advantage of the negative income tax method is that it is selective: allowances are paid only to those who need them as established by a simple declaration of income. Such a system is considered to be more equitable and efficient than demogrant programs such as the old-age pension and family allowances which are paid to everyone with the required demographically measurable characteristic (age or family status) irrespective of financial need. The federal government has, in fact, turned, in its present welfare programs, more and more towards selective-type payments and away from demogrants. Thus, for example, instead of increasing the level of all old-age pensions, it has offered guaranteed income supplements to those old people who actually need the money.

The Special Senate Committee on Poverty, in its report, recommended, with respect to a guaranteed annual income, that:

> 1. The Government of Canada implement a Guaranteed Annual Income (G.A.I.) program using the Negative Income Tax (N.I.T.) method, on a uniform, national basis.
>
> 2. The proposed G.A.I. program be financed and administered by the Government of Canada.
>
> 3. The proposed G.A.I. plan be designed to cover all Canadians who need it. Initially, G.A.I. would not cover residents of Canada who are not Canadian citizens and Canadian citizens who are single, unattached individuals under forty years of age.
>
> 4. Basic Allowance Rates under the G.A.I. be set initially at 70 per cent of the poverty line for each family size as determined by the methods outlined in the report and raised progressively as quickly as possible.
>
> 5. The G.A.I. plan incorporate a work-incentive mechanism to ensure that those who work receive and keep more income than those who do not. It proposed that Basic Allowances initially be reduced at the rate of 70 cents for every dollar of other income.
>
> 6. Income-maintenance under the proposed G.A.I. plan be divorced from the provision of social services. The latter would remain the responsibility of the provincial governments.

7. The Canada Assistance Plan (C.A.P.) be retained and updated to serve as a vehicle for federal-provincial co-operation and cost-sharing in the delivery of social services. C.A.P. would also be used to cover, on a "needs" basis, those not covered initially by the G.A.I.

8. All existing federal income-maintenance legislation be progressively repealed. Social-insurance programs such as Unemployment Insurance, and the Canada Pension Plan, would be retained, as would certain contractual programs related to Canada's native peoples. The G.A.I. would immediately replace the Family Allowance, Youth Allowance, and Old Age Security programs, operated by the Federal Government.

9. The G.A.I. program be based on the principle that no one would receive less income under the G.A.I. than he or she now receives from other federal programs such as Old Age Security and income supplements. Other allowances or insurance payments would be treated as "other income" and augmented through the G.A.I. program where they are less than the G.A.I. allowances.

10. Income tax exemption levels be raised so that no Canadian whose income is below the "poverty line" would be subject to income tax.[6]

Under the plan recommended by the Senate Committee, income floors would be set for a single person, for a family of four, and for a family of ten. Others have recommended that the government set two basic floor levels. Thus, people who are able to work might be guaranteed an income set at 70 per cent of the poverty level. Those who are unable to work might be guaranteed 100 per cent.

The federal government, after considering the possibility of a guaranteed income plan, reached the conclusion that it would be too costly for the country, at least at the present time.[7] The government also decided that some joint federal-provincial pilot studies employing the G.A.I. technique should first be carried out. So far, therefore, the government has preferred to revise existing programs rather than launch a national guaranteed annual income plan. However, it has allocated some money for experimental guaranteed income projects.

The pilot projects, first undertaken in Manitoba, seek the answers to a variety of questions. For example: will G.A.I. aid encourage recipients to work and earn more than those on regular welfare? Will it discourage husbands from deserting their families so that dependants will receive welfare? Will it help lower the school drop-out rate of children from welfare families? Will it depress local wages for the unskilled because people cannot afford to work for uneconomic wages? Will it cause rents and prices to rise in low-income communities because more money is available? Above all, will G.A.I. aid be cheaper and simpler to operate than conventional welfare?

16.6: INCOME INEQUALITY

Throughout history, people have been arguing about the way in which a country's wealth should be divided. Why should a peasant slaving away in the master's fields from dawn to dusk earn a pittance while the absentee landlord, with money to burn, lives it up in town? This simple line of reasoning has brought about many political upheavals over the years. The French revolution of 1789 and the Russian revolution of 1917 are two of the most dramatic. But revolutions sparked by economic injustice, alleged or real, are still continuing throughout the world.

Before the widespread use of money, the problem of sharing a country's economic wealth was one of physically allocating the produce of the land. With the use of money, the actual division of wealth came to be decided in terms of purchasing power. Today, as a result, the question "for whom to produce?" is answered in terms of income. The larger a person's income, the greater his or her ability to buy the various goods and services produced.

Personal incomes (as Table S.8 confirms) vary greatly in Canada. Some people earned little or no income at all, while others received extremely large incomes.

The Lorenz Curve

Another way of measuring income inequality is to consider how *total* income is shared. Thus, if each 1 per cent of the population received 1 per cent of the total income, there would be complete income equality between each 1 per cent of the population. This can be shown graphically (Figure 16:1) by what is known as a Lorenz chart—named after M.O. Lorenz, a German statistician of the 1900s. Such a chart measures, on the vertical axis, the percentage of total income received, and, on the horizontal axis, the percentage of persons receiving that income.

If there were complete equality of income distribution, then 10 per cent of total income would be received by 10 per cent of the population; 20 per cent of the total income by 20 per cent of the population; 30 per cent by 30 per cent; and so on. This situation would be depicted in the Lorenz chart by a straight diagonal line called a Lorenz curve,

Table S.8
Income Inequality in Canada, 1984

Income Class (Dollars)	Number of Persons	% of Grand Total Cumulative	Total Income in $ millions	% of Grand Total Cumulative
Loss and Nil	786 502	5.06	399.0	.14
1 to 1 000	566 917	8.70	270.6	.05
1 to 2 000	434 098	11.49	645.5	.18
2 to 3 000	425 988	14.23	1 062.5	.56
3 to 4 000	484 432	17.35	1 693.2	1.15
4 to 5 000	472 794	20.39	2 129.0	1.90
5 to 6 000	517 519	23.72	2 848.1	2.91
6 to 7 000	561 698	27.33	3 649.1	4.19
7 to 8 000	550 631	30.87	4 128.7	5.65
8 to 9 000	515 866	34.18	4 386.7	7.20
9 to 10 000	509 204	37.46	4 835.1	8.90
10 to 11 000	488 361	40.60	5 126.0	10.71
11 to 12 000	466 203	43.60	5 359.6	12.60
12 to 13 000	453 018	46.51	5 660.0	14.59
13 to 14 000	432 829	49.29	5 838.5	16.65
14 to 15 000	417 643	51.98	6 052.5	18.78
15 to 16 000	407 784	54.60	6 318.1	21.01
16 to 17 000	401 066	57.18	6 615.6	23.34
17 to 18 000	388 532	59.68	6 799.0	25.74
18 to 19 000	374 901	62.09	6 933.5	28.18
19 to 20 000	352 348	64.35	6 866.0	30.60
20 to 22 000	646 628	68.51	13 560.2	35.38
22 to 24 000	588 024	72.29	13 517.7	40.15
24 to 26 000	546 100	75.80	13 643.4	44.96
26 to 28 000	498 788	79.01	13 463.9	49.71
28 to 30 000	465 630	82.00	13 497.9	54.46
30 to 32 000	419 149	84.70	12 983.6	59.04
32 to 34 000	346 832	86.93	11 435.3	63.07
34 to 35 000	159 582	87.96	5 504.2	65.01
35 to 37 500	360 756	90.28	13 064.7	69.62
37.5 to 40 000	289 452	92.14	11 207.7	73.57
40 to 45 000	415 674	94.81	17 575.4	79.76
45 to 50 000	251 621	96.43	11 896.6	83.96
50 to 60 000	247 210	98.02	13 421.2	88.69
60 to 70 000	107 577	98.71	6 934.2	91.13
70 to 100 000	116 503	99.46	9 509.4	94.49
100 to 250 000	73 542	99.93	10 265.2	98.10
250 000 and over	10 779	100.00	5 377.6	100.00

Source: Revenue Canada, *Taxation Statistics, 1986 Edition*
Note: Income class based on a person's total income.

rising from left to right. Usually, however, this line is bent rather than straight. The greater the curvature of the Lorenz curve, the greater the inequality of distribution. The flatter the curve, the more equal the distribution of income.

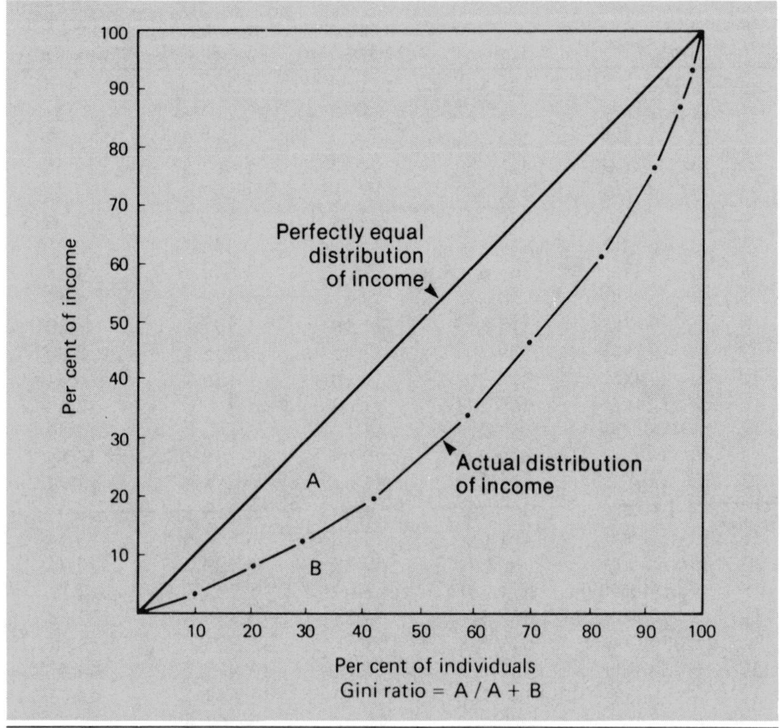

Figure 16:1 Lorenz Curve

Since most married couples pool their incomes, Lorenz curves can also be constructed showing the distribution of income among families and unattached individuals. They can also be plotted to show the distribution of wealth rather than income. However, such data, for Canada, is still hard to obtain.

Reasons for Income Inequality

There are two basic types of income that a person can receive: employment income and investment income. Let us briefly consider why one person may have higher employment or investment income than another.

Employment Income

One reason for inequality of employment income is that human beings are different physically, mentally, and emotionally. This means that some people can do things better than others. It also means that some people, given the right motivation, work harder than others, accept more responsibility, and take more risks. Whatever type of society exists, some people emerge as leaders and others as followers. These differences in physical, mental, and emotional abilities between different people are often inherited traits. However, a good family life, education, training, and a good general environment can help a person to make the most of what he or she has.

Another important reason for inequalities in employment income in Canada is the difference in education, training, and experience of different members of the labour force. Some people are better qualified than others to hold down a higher-paying job. If it requires many years of academic and practical training to become, for example, a doctor, lawyer, engineer, or accountant, it is to be expected that such a person's income will be greater than that of an unskilled worker. Even in socialist countries, persons with highly skilled jobs receive larger incomes than the semi-skilled and unskilled.

Inequalities of employment income are also attributed to differences of social and ethnic background. Native-born white Anglo-Saxon Protestants (or WASPs), so it is said, are assured of economic success. However, compared with many other countries, merit is much more important in Canada as a determinant of economic success than social background. And in most provinces, a human rights code legally forbids discrimination in employment on grounds of race, colour, nationality, ethnic origin, or religion. However, the very existence of such a code implies that discrimination did, and still continues to, exist.

Sex and age are also responsible for differences in rates of pay, despite equal pay legislation. They can also even determine whether a person obtains a job or not.

Finally, looking at Canada as a whole, differences in employment income between equally able and qualified persons can arise because of geographical location.

Investment Income

Investment income consists mainly of income derived from the ownership of savings deposits, stocks, bonds, and real estate. Why might one person have a larger investment income than another? One important reason is that many people are able and willing to save and invest part of their current income. Another is that some people are shrewder investors than others. This means that, over a period of years, people gradually accumulate varying amounts of wealth in its different forms. This accumulated wealth, through both investment return and the realization of *capital gain* (the profit on resale of an asset) provides investment income. Of course, in old age, this investment income, together with pensions, may form the only income. However, for many people, investment income does provide an additional source of income even during their working lifetime. And the larger the amount of wealth, and the shrewder the form and timing of the investment, the greater this income is.

Some people inherit wealth from parents and relatives. This can, depending on the temperament of the recipient, form a large windfall income for a few years or, if invested wisely, a continuing source of investment income. In the past, it was relatively easy to pass wealth from one generation to the next. Nowadays, government-imposed death duties make it more difficult. Nevertheless, through trusts and other means, considerable sums are still passed in Canada from parents to children and grandchildren.

Income Inequality: Good or Bad?

Should everyone receive the same income?

In practically every type of society, one of the most important human motivating forces is the acquisitive instinct. In order to make money, people have taken all manner of risks, worked all kinds of hours, and endured all kinds of hardships. Without this driving force, Canada would not be as developed a land as it is today.

Of course, this motive is not the only one for human activity. But it is, for most people, the most important. Consequently, if the opportunity to earn an above-average income is removed, some other motivating force must be found. In wartime, it is often a sense of patriotism. In peace-time, nationalism, religion, political creed, may all inspire men and women in their work.

However, the experience of most communist, or socialist countries is that where the profit motive does not exist, compulsion must take its place. People must be told where to work, for how long, and at what wages. So long, therefore, as Canadians are unwilling for government to control every aspect of their economic life, they must be assured of the possibility of additional reward for additional effort. The need for above-average earnings does not mean, however, that there should be be no effort to help people whose income, often through no fault of their own, is unusually low.

Summary

1. Canada's economic system, although providing one of the highest standards of living in the world, has meant great economic insecurity for the individual. Consequently, the federal and provincial governments have adopted a variety of income-security programs. However, these programs have not always lived up to expectations. And perhaps one in four Canadians can be classified as poor.
2. Nowadays, poverty is usually defined as a standard of living that is low relative to that enjoyed by most people in the society. It is a *relative* concept rather than an absolute one.
3. There are various ways of measuring poverty. The most usual is to establish a "poverty line" level of income and classify anyone receiving income below this level, as poor.
4. There are many different types of poor people, and each group has problems of its own. One useful division is between the urban poor and the rural poor. Another is between the working poor and the welfare poor. Canada's native peoples are usually the subject of special attention.
5. There are many different reasons for poverty in Canada: income inequality, unemployment, old age, illness, physical disability, prejudice, lack of education, unwillingness to relocate, and in the case of native peoples, difficulty in adjusting to a different type of society.
6. Government income-security programs include unemployment insurance, the Canada and Quebec pension plans, old-age security, family allowances, youth allowances, workmen's compensation, and social assistance.
7. A guaranteed annual income has been proposed as a good replacement for the present system of income-security programs. Under it, the government would pay everyone above a certain age an amount of money sufficient to bring that person's annual income up to a minimum guaranteed level.
8. Incomes vary greatly in Canada. A Lorenz curve is a useful means of depicting this graphically.
9. Reasons for inequality of employment income include differences in physical, mental, and emotional abilities; difference in education, training, and experience; differences in social and ethnic background; sex; age; and geographical location.

10. Reasons for inequality of investment income include differences in willingness to save and invest, differences in shrewdness of investments, and differences in inherited wealth.
11. One of the most important human motivating forces is the average person's acquisitive instinct. If the opportunity to earn an above-average income is removed, some other motivation to work must be found. Compulsion has not proven very effective.

Key Terms

Poverty 290
Poverty line 291
Poverty rate 295
Urban poor 295
Rural poor 295
Working poor 296
Welfare poor 296
Poverty circle 299
Unemployment insurance 299
Canada pension plan 300
Old age security 301
Family allowance 301
Child tax credit 302
Workers' Compensation 302
Social assistance 302
Guaranteed annual income 303
Negative income tax 304
Income inequality 306
Lorenz curve 306
Employment income 309
Investment income 309

Review Questions

1. What is meant by "poverty"? Compare poverty in Canada with that in one or more economically underdeveloped countries.
2. How is poverty measured in Canada?
3. What are the "low income cut-offs" used by Statistics Canada?
4. What are the main criticisms of using the low income cut-offs as poverty lines?
5. What has been the poverty rate in Canada in recent years?How realistic is it?
6. In what ways do the urban poor differ from the rural poor?
7. Who are the "working poor"?
8. What are the main reasons why many people require welfare assistance in Canada?
9. What are the various causes of poverty in Canada?
10. How do governments in Canada try to reduce income insecurity for the individual?
11. Explain how a guaranteed annual income could be implemented.

What could be its advantages and disadvantages?

12. To what extent do personal incomes vary in Canada?
13. What is a Lorenz curve? What purpose does it serve?
14. Give five reasons for income inequality in Canada.
15. To what extent is income inequality desirable?
16. Without adequate motivation, people would lose interest in their work and the economy would suffer. Discuss.

References

1. Special Senate Committee on Poverty, *Poverty in Canada* (Ottawa: Information Canada, 1971), p. vii.
2. Economic Council of Canada, *Fifth Annual Review* (Ottawa: Queen's Printer, 1969), pp. 104-5.
3. N.H. Lithwick, *Urban Poverty*, Research Monograph No. 1, in *Urban Canada: Problems and Pospects* (Ottawa: Central Mortgage and Housing Corporation, 1971).
4. *Poverty in Canada*, p. 35.
5. *Poverty in Canada*, p. vii.
6. *Poverty in Canada*, pp. xv and xvi
7. Department of National Health and Welfare, *Income Security for Canadians* (Ottawa: Information Canada, 1970), pp. 26-27.

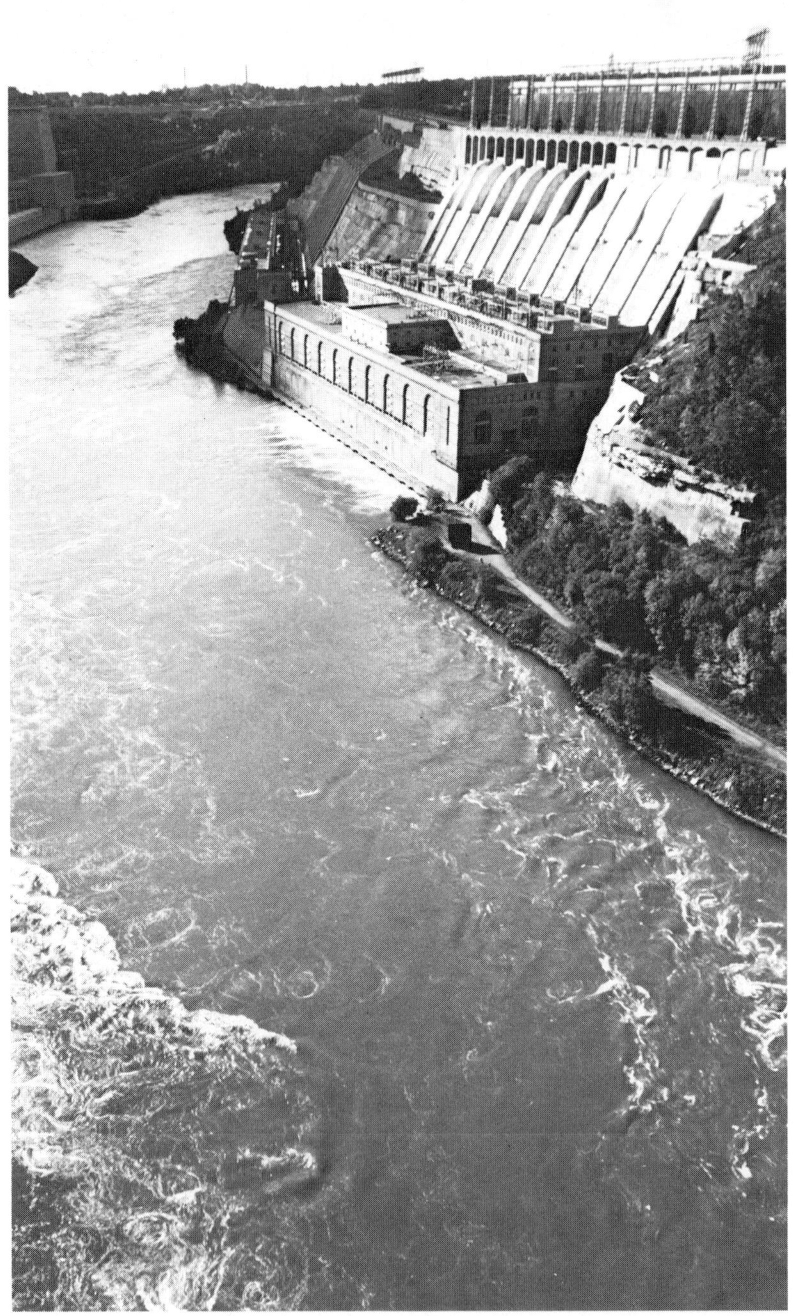

17. CANADIAN MANUFACTURING, MINING, AND ENERGY

CHAPTER OBJECTIVES

A. To examine the nature of Canadian manufacturing and the problems that face it
B. To examine the state of Canada's mining industry
C. To review Canada's energy supplies and discuss the federal government's energy policy

CHAPTER OUTLINE

In the nineteenth century, Canada was a predominantly agricultural country with most families making their living by raising crops and tending livestock. But today the main sources of income and employment for Canadians are industrial ones—manufacturing, mining, power, construction, transportation, communications, wholesale and retail trade, and other services. Government is also an employment and income sector of growing importance.

17.1: MANUFACTURING

Originally, the term "manufacturing" meant making a product by hand. Nowadays, however, manufacturing means the production of goods by people using power-driven machinery. For purposes of analysis, manufacturing industries can be classified as primary or secondary.

Primary manufacturing is the processing of basic raw materials such as metal ores and crude lumber. Industries of this type, which have existed for many years in Canada, now sell their output primarily to markets in Canada, the United States, Western Europe, and Japan. *Secondary manufacturing* is the production of finished goods and parts from processed raw materials. Many industries produce the parts that are used by other industries for assembly into a finished product, such as farm machinery or an automobile. A major part of this secondary manufacturing emerged during and after World War II. It has been aided in its growth, since the late nineteenth century, by tariff protection from lower-priced imports. This has not only encouraged domestic manufacturers to expand, but also foreign, mainly U.S., producers to set up branch plants in Canada for manufacturing or assembly. However, since World War II, tariff protection has been gradually reduced and Canadian manufacturing firms have had to overcome stiffer competition or go under.

Much of the output of Canada's secondary manufacturing industries is sold in the Canadian market. However, export sales, particularly to the United States, are growing in importance. The Canada-United States automotive products agreement, signed in 1965, has resulted in a tremendous expansion in bilateral trade in vehicles and parts. But foreign competition, particularly from S.E. Asia, has become more intense.

Types and Location

The various types of manufacturing being carried on in this country are shown in Table S.9. The most important industries, in term of value added, are foods and beverages, transportation equipment, petroleum and coal products, paper and allied products, and primary metals.

Most of Canada's secondary manufacturing industry is to be found in a few key areas, notably southern Ontario, southern Quebec, and the Vancouver area of the West Coast. Primary manufacturing is much more widespread.

Manufacturing Processes

Many different processes are used to manufacture finished and semi-finished products from raw materials and parts. One classification is as follows:

1. Extractive. This is the process of extracting materials and products from land, sea, and air—for example, iron, copper, and nickel from the land, salt from the sea, and oxygen from the air.

2. Conditioning. This occurs when a raw material is changed into a

Table S.9
Canadian Manufacturing Shipments, by Industry, in millions of dollars, 1985

Industry		
Non-durable goods		% of total
Food	32 414	13.3
Beverage	4 784	2.0
Tobacco products	1 645	0.7
Rubber products	2 540	1.0
Plastics products	3 688	1.5
Leather and allied products	1 284	0.5
Primary textile	2 701	1.1
Textile products	2 602	1.1
Clothing	5 394	2.2
Paper and allied products	18 192	7.5
Printing, publishing and allied	9 176	3.8
Refined petroleum & coal products	25 740	10.5
Chemical and chemical products	17 572	7.2
Sub-total	127 730	52.3
Durable goods		
Wood	10 689	4.4
Furniture and fixture	3 234	1.3
Primary metal	16 478	6.8
Fabricated metal products	13 584	5.6
Machinery	7 408	3.0
Transportation equipment	42 364	17.4
Electrical & electronic products	12 324	5.0
Non-metallic mineral products	5 783	2.4
Other manufacturing	4 517	1.9
Sub-total	116 380	47.7
Total shipments	244 110	100.0

Source: Statistics Canada, *Inventories, Shipments and Orders in Manufacturing Industries,* Cat. 31-001.

more valuable form—for example, wool into cloth, and hides into leather.

3. Analytical. This is the process of breaking down a raw material into a number of different products—for example, petroleum into gasoline, fuel oils, lubricating oils, and paraffin.

4. Synthetic. In this process, various raw materials are combined into a finished product—for example, flour, salt, and yeast into bread.

5. Assembly. Here, a number of component parts and materials are put together (i.e., assembled) to form a finished product—for example, a telephone. Sub-assembly is the same process, except that the product—for example, a loudspeaker—will be used as a component part of the final product, the television set.

Characteristics of Manufacturing

Modern manufacturing is characterized by a high level of mechanization and, to a lesser extent, automation; it makes use of electric power to drive the production machinery and conveyor systems; it employs a high degree of specialization, both of workers (division of labour) and machines; it uses mass-production techniques and standardization whenever advantageous; it requires common timing, or "synchronization," of deliveries, manufacturing, assembly and sub-assembly operations; and it employs highly sophisticated production technology. Because of these facts, production costs per unit of output are much lower than under the earlier handicraft system. In other words, the same number of workers and capital can, in the same amount of time, produce much more than previously.

Let us now look at these characteristics of modern manufacturing a little more closely.

1. Mechanization. When machines are used to perform work previously done by hand (usually with relatively unsophisticated tools), the system of production is said to be *mechanized*. Most manufacturing industry in Canada is now highly mechanized. First, it has been possible to invent machines to perform most routine tasks more efficiently than the average worker, equipped only with hand tools, can. Second, as labour costs have risen and machines have become relatively cheaper, more and more of them have been purchased and relatively fewer workers hired. As a result, each worker now usually operates and controls a larger amount of machinery. The modern manufacturing process has, in other words, become more and more *capital-intensive* and less and less *labour-intensive*. This is also true of the handling and transporting of raw materials, parts, and finished products from one

place to another within the modern manufacturing plant.

2. Automation. It was only a matter of time before machines were invented to control other machines. This process of *automation* has meant that even fewer workers are required relative to a given amount of capital. Their job is primarily one of control, maintenance, and "trouble-shooting" in the event of a mechanical breakdown. Fortunately, from the labour-employment point of view, automation has by no means become as widespread as mechanization. A familiar example of automation is the thermostat in the home, which switches the furnace on and off according to the temperature. Another is the computer-controlled office elevator system. But many manufacturing processes have now been automated.

3. Electric power. We tend to take electric power for granted, but it is only an invention of the last century. Previously, manufacturing had to rely on steam-power (a nineteenth-century invention) and before that on water-power, wind-power, animal-power, and human-power. Without the existence of electricity and electric motors, manufacturing would have been stunted in its growth, and the key modern tool, the electronic computer, would have been impossible.

4. Specialization. The great increase in output per worker that specialization in manufacturing affords has long been pointed out by economists. Thus Adam Smith, the eighteenth-century Scottish economist, used the example of a nail factory to point out the economic benefits of the "division of labour". By specializing in the performance of one or two tasks, rather than trying to make a complete good, a worker can become highly proficient in his or her work. Consequently, a group of workers, each performing his or her own specialized tasks at great speed, can produce much more than if each were to work as an independent craftsperson. This principle of specialization, or *division of labour*, and the benefits it affords, have also been extended to machines and manufacturing plants. However, a prerequisite for specialization is a large enough market to enable all the output to be sold. If the scale of production is small, the scope for specialization is more limited.

5. Mass production. Many goods are now produced in great quantities at one large factory rather than at many small plants or workshops. By concentrating production in this way, a manufacturer is best able to make use of power-driven production machinery and materials-handling equipment. The large volume of output also enables the firm to enjoy the benefits of specialization of labour and machines; to obtain quantity discounts for purchases; and to spread its relatively fixed costs of production and marketing—for example, administrative salaries, factory rent, research and development, advertising, and marketing organization—as widely as possible. Long production runs, in other words, mean lower per unit costs of production and marketing. The only limit to these economies of scale is the volume of output which, in turn, is limited by the extent of the market.

6. Standardization. Each material and part used in the manufacturing process must conform to strict standards of size, shape, strength, and quality. Only in this way can a manufacturer make use of machines tooled to handle certain size materials and parts, and ensure that the product meets the desired performance and safety requirements. Work methods are also standardized, after careful time and motion studies, to ensure that plant employees work in the most efficient way.

7. Synchronization. Modern manufacturing operations are usually quite complex, involving large numbers of workers, a vast array of machines, and a continuous inflow of materials and component parts to be assembled or otherwise made into finished goods. Therefore, precise timing of the various manufacturing and assembly operations is critical. Also, one of the ways in which Japanese automobile manufacturers have been able to cut costs is by keeping inventories of materials and parts to an unprecedented minimum, by exact timing of deliveries from locally situated suppliers. And North American car manufacturers are now switching to "just in time" inventory control. Nowadays, in many manufacturing plants, a delay in a sub-assembly or other manufacturing operation, or in delivery of materials or parts, can easily hold up a whole production line. Because of this need for synchronization, each worker must keep up a certain pace in his or her work or else delay the work of many others.

8. Technology. The technical knowledge employed to produce and market goods has increased at a fantastic rate in the twentieth century. In fact, most of the goods purchased today were not available two or three generations ago. Compared with the nineteenth century, it takes a much shorter time between the invention of a new material, product, machine, or method and its commercial application.

9. CAD/CAM. With the lower price and increased sophistication of modern electronic computers, more and more firms in Canada and elsewhere are turning to computer-assisted design and computer-assisted manufacturing, or CAD/CAM for short. Experience so far shows that the use of computers in designing products and manufacturing processes, as well as in planning and controlling production, can greatly improve productivity—that is, a greater value of output per person employed.

10. Robotics. Already in Canadian auto plants, industrial robots are busy welding and painting cars. These robots operate under the instructions of built-in microcomputers and can be programmed for a variety of repetitive manufacturing tasks. Unlike earlier robots, they are not built to perform only one task. By changing the program (a quite simple task), the plant supervisor can easily switch the modern industrial robot from one task to another, as called for by changes in production plans.

Problems of Canadian Manufacturing

Canada, with just over 25.5 million persons, is a relatively small market for manufactured goods compared with the United States or the European Economic Community. Long production runs are only possible, therefore, if there is a substantial export market as well as the local Canadian one. This has been achieved in some industries—for example, cars and trucks—by integrating the production plans of Canadian-located plants with sister plants south of the border. In some other industries, exports, particularly to the United States, have also enabled firms to achieve economies of mass production. However, in many industries, dependence on the relatively small home market has stunted growth. Furthermore, the existence of a large number of firms within the same industry, each differentiating their product by advertising and other means, has limited the individual firm's growth even more. Of course, not all goods can be mass produced. That is why we still have so many small business firms in Canada—in manufacturing as well as in service industries.

Another serious concern at the present time, as discussed in Chapter 20, is the slow rate of increase in Canada's industrial productivity compared with other countries.

The large sales that Canadian manufacturers make to the U.S. market, although highly beneficial in terms of income and employment for Canadians, do have some dangers. If the United States adopts a more protectionist attitude, as it has in recent years, U.S. imports of manufactured goods from Canada can be severely affected. Consequently, the greater the dependence on the U.S. market, the more vulnerable Canadian manufacturers (and their employees) become. However, attempts to diversify Canada's exports of manufactured goods geographically have not been very successful. In recent years, for example, the value of Canadian goods exported to the European Economic Community, or EEC, our second biggest market, has gradually declined, whereas the value of our exports to the United States has continued to edge up.This trend is expected to continue as the foreign exchange rate for the Canadian dollar remains relatively stable compared with the U.S. dollar but continues to strengthen against the European and other foreign currencies, making Canadian goods more expensive in non-U.S. markets.

Canadian manufacturers also have to worry about foreign competition, both in their export markets and in the Canadian market itself. Other countries such as South Korea, Taiwan, Malaysia, Singapore, Hong Kong, and Japan, with lower labour costs, fewer strikes, and equal or better technology for the production of many goods, provide formidable competition. Only the transportation costs involved in bringing the goods to North America and government pressure to obtain "voluntary" restrictions of exports from these countries for certain goods have prevented even deeper inroads. Nevertheless, Canadian manufacturers have in recent years stopped production of certain product lines such as television sets. Also, following the old adage of "if you can't beat them, join them," many Canadian manufacturers have been forced to switch their production of parts and certain finished goods from Canada to the Far East, at the expense of Canadian income and employment.

Investment capital is not short in Canada. However, funds have not easily been available for new business ventures where the element of risk is high. The difficulty of obtaining such funds has often inhibited a firm's growth and even led to the sale of all or a controlling percentage of the firm's common shares to U.S. or other foreign investors.

As in many other countries, labour strikes have increasingly disrupted Canadian manufacturing industry. Although conciliation is compulsory under provincial labour legislation, management and labour often find it difficult to reach a negotiated agreement. Prolonged strikes, with all their harmful effects on the public as well as on the parties directly involved, seem to be a necessary prelude to a new labour-management contract. Also, wage settlements in certain industries have been so high that the resultant higher prices for the goods produced have impaired their competitive effectiveness, particularly abroad.

17.2: MINING

The Canadian mining industry has been an important source of income and jobs for Canadians since the earliest days of Confederation. Iron, copper, nickel, zinc, and coal are the "big five" in production value, followed by potash, gold, uranium, cement, and sulphur (see Table S.10). In the 1980s, Canada's mining industry has been generally depressed as a result of a drop in world demand for mineral products and the emergence of lower-cost Third World suppliers.

Table S.10
Canada's Principal Mineral Products, 1984

	$ millions	Per cent of total
A. *Metals*		
Antimony	3.2	0.0
Bismuth	2.0	0.0
Cadmium	7.8	0.0
Cobalt	61.1	0.1
Columbium	18.8	0.0
Copper	1 365.7	3.1
Gold	1 252.3	2.9
Iron ore	1 482.4	3.4
Iron remelt	134.8	0.3
Lead	195.3	0.5
Molybdenum	106.2	0.2
Nickel	1 166.1	2.7
Platinum group	—	—
Selenium	11.9	0.0
Silver	461.9	1.1
Tantalum	—	—
Tellurium	0.5	0.0
Tin	3.8	0.0
Tungsten	—	—
Uranium	901.6	2.1
Zinc	1 495.2	3.4
Sub-total	*8 670.4*	*19.8*
B. *Non-Metals*		
Asbestos	379.3	0.9
Barite	7.0	0.0
Gemstones	1.1	0.0
Gypsum	61.6	0.1
Magnestic dolomite & brucite	8.1	0.0
Nepheline syenite	17.9	0.0
Peat	51.8	0.1
Potash	867.5	2.0
Quartz	40.8	0.1
Salt	210.2	0.5
Soapstone, talc pyrophyllite	11.2	0.0
Sodium sulphate	37.7	0.1
Sulphur, in smelter gas	63.2	0.1
Sulphur, elemental	609.1	1.4
Sub-total	*2 366.5*	*5.4*
C. *Fuels*		
Coal	1 794.6	4.1
Natural gas	7 940.9	18.1
Natural gas by products	2 849.8	6.5
Petroleum, conde	17 813.9	40.7
Sub-total	*30 399.2*	*69.4*
D. *Structural Materials*		
Clay products	136.8	0.3
Cement	717.3	1.6
Lime	157.6	0.4
Sand and gravel	546.3	1.3
Stone	393.4	0.9
Sub-total	*1 951.5*	*4.5*
E. *Other minerals*	*401.4*	*0.9*
Grand Total	*43 789.0*	*100.0*

Source: Statistics Canada, Cat. 26-202.

Foreign Sales

Much of the capital used to develop Canada's mines has come from abroad; and much of the output is shipped to the United States rather than processed and used in Canada. This has led to a continuing argument that Canada is being stripped of its natural resources to feed the mineral-hungry industries of countries such as the United States and now, to an increasing degree, Japan.

Certainly, Canada would be better off, in terms of income and employment, if it had the manufacturing industry that could profitably utilize these raw materials. But with a market of only about 25 million people at home, and limited ability to compete abroad with other more efficient manufacturing countries, there seems little hope for many years that Canada can make use of all the minerals that are at present mined. And certainly, according to the doctrine of comparative advantage, Canada should be prepared to export minerals in exchange for other products.

The argument has also been advanced that these minerals should be left in the ground until Canadian industry needs them. But this would mean abandoning Canada's present mining industry, and all the employment and income that it generates, for the sake of retaining mineral stockpiles that may in the future be replaced in industry by something else, or by minerals found elsewhere. A saner argument would seem to be to encourage as much processing as possible of these minerals in Canada before they are shipped abroad (perhaps by means of an export tax on unprocessed minerals), and gradually to develop efficient Canadian manufacturing industries to use as many of these minerals as possible.

However, if Canada is to obtain access to the large United States market for its manufactured products, it must also be willing to sell at least part of its minerals.

Tax Incentives

A controversy that has surrounded the Canadian mining industry for many years is whether it should receive special tax concessions. Until 1971, mining firms, and also oil and gas firms, were permitted to write off almost all their exploration, development, drilling, and property acquisition costs before paying any income tax. Furthermore, the income from new mines, or from abandoned mines that were reopened, was exempt from income tax for the first three years of operation. Combined with the previous concession, this meant that a mine was free of tax for six or seven years, during which time the firm would often try to extract as much ore as possible, often with little regard for the ecology. Some mines might even be closed at the end of the tax-holiday period.

Mining, oil, and gas firms were also given a special "depletion allowance" to compensate them for the fact that their wealth—the mineral resources—was being used up in the process of earning income. This concession was a deduction of one-third from their taxable incomes each year. Shareholders of mining companies were also permitted a depletion allowance on their dividend income in calculating their personal income tax.

Just like any other firm, a mining company was allowed to depreciate assets, such as machinery, that gradually wear out. However, the rate of depreciation was an attractive 30 per cent per annum, based on a diminishing balance. Mine shafts and haulage ways built after a mine had begun operation could be written off completely in one year. Also, certain provincial taxes could be included as expenses for income tax purposes. There were also other benefits.

In 1971, the federal government, as part of its overall tax reform, made a number of changes in the tax treatment of mining companies. However, it continued the general direction of its previous tax policy. As the Minister of Finance stated: "Substantial tax incentives are maintained to recognize the risks involved in exploration and development, the international competition for capital, and the levels of incentives available in other companies."[1] Amongst the changes, the three-year income tax exemption on new mines was withdrawn after 1973, and replaced by an accelerated write-off of capital equipment and on-site facilities, including townsite facilities. Also, the system of automatic depletion for mining and petroleum corporations was replaced in 1976 by a new system by which only one-third of actual expenditures can be deducted. Shareholders' depletion allowances on dividends from mining and petroleum corporations were abolished in 1971.

These tax concessions have in the past undoubtedly spurred the development of Canada's mineral resources. However, critics such as Eric Kierans charge that this is just the problem; federal taxation and incentive programs place too much emphasis on the development of natural resources at the expense of manufacturing, a sector which creates many more jobs. Furthermore, these tax concessions, the critics say, are made even worse by the fact that they stimulate a boom in mining investment and the funds that flow in from abroad drive up the foreign exchange rate of the Canadian dollar. This makes Canadian manufactured goods more expensive abroad and so retards the growth of this important job-creating sector. Another sore point is the fact that such a large portion of Canada's extractive industries is still foreign-owned. The tax concessions, it is argued, mean that the Canadian government is providing foreigners with money to help buy more of Canada. In the 1980s, this same criticism is being made with regard to the tax concessions provided under the National Energy Program for oil and gas exploration in Canada's "frontier" lands.

Mineral Policy

Amongst the federal government's plans for the future is a national advisory committee on the mineral industry made up of industry representatives. This committee would advise the government on such matters as mining economics, mineral exports, and environmental problems. Another initiative is the development of a mineral resource policy for Canada.

A set of fifteen guidelines for such a policy was outlined by Mr. Jack Austin, the federal Deputy Energy Minister, in March, 1971.[2] These were as follows: (1) maintenance of an adequate domestic mineral supply at reasonable prices so that shortages or uneconomic prices do not impede the development of secondary industry in Canada; (2) standards established within which the public and private sectors, whether Canadian or foreign-owned, are expected to operate with respect to land tenure, pricing and marketing, operating practices, further processing, the degree of domestic ownership and control, employment practices, land conservation and reclamation, and integration of land and resource development; (3) to encourage an increasing degree of domestic mineral processing and mineral-based manufacturing instead of exporting raw or lightly processed products, and to optimize the return from mineral exports in term of price and value in relation to tonnage; (4) the expansion of Canadian ownership and control over mineral resources, while taking appropriate account of a continuing need for foreign capital and achieving maximum benefit from foreign capital invested in the mineral industry; (5) to maintain and improve Canada's competitive position in world mineral markets; (6) to establish an infrastructure by either government or industry to include power, transportation, communication, education, community facilities, and other factors necessary for rational mineral exploitation; (7) to ensure that technical and economic information systems are set up to disseminate data such as geological and mineral maps and reports, statistics, and technical information; (8) to alleviate regional economic disparities through optimum exploitation of mineral potential in "disadvantaged regions"; (9) to forecast problems related to mineral depletion and declining regions in order to cushion the effect of impending mine closings; (10) to conserve mineral resources through optimum recovery of minerals from deposits; (11) to establish pollution-control standards and to minimize costs external to the mineral project itself; (12) maximum reduction possible in foreign "discriminatory actions" such as tariffs and non-tariff barriers that affect Canada's mineral trade; (13) to ensure that mineral exploitation contributes an equitable share of the tax revenue to the nation; (14) an increase in the development and application of domestic skills in mining; and, (15) overall development of Canadian mineral resources in a manner that contributes to, and reflects, general government policies.

Provincial Incentives

In Canada there are provincial as well as federal incentives to mining. Thus, for example, the Ontario government has an incentive plan to aid mineral exploration in designated parts of the province. Under the plan, the government pays one-third of the cost of an approved exploration program up to a stated maximum for each project.

17.3: ENERGY

Canada is blessed with an abundant supply of oil, natural gas, coal, and electric power (see Table S.11). However, much of the crude oil is in presently unaccessible form or geographical location.

Oil and Natural Gas

Canada's present large oil industry began in 1947 with the discovery of the Leduc oilfield in Alberta. Previous discoveries of significance had been made at Petrolia, in south-western Ontario, in the 1850s, and at Turner Valley, near Calgary, Alberta, in 1913. Nowadays, Alberta is by far and away the leading oil-producing province, followed by Saskatchewan and British Columbia. Alberta is also the leading producer of natural gas, followed by British Columbia. Oil and natural gas are shipped by pipeline from Alberta to markets in the United States and central Canada.

The discovery, in the late 1960s, of vast quantities of oil and natural gas in Prudhoe Bay, on Alaska's north shore, meant that a large new U.S. source of supply was found for the United States market. It has also meant a difficult environmental problem for Canadians. Since the oil and gas are brought overland to Alaska's south shore and then shipped by ocean tanker to Seattle, or ports further South, there is grave risk of pollution to Canada's West Coast should a mishap occur in, for example, the foggy waters of Juan de Fuca Strait. Discoveries of

Table S.11
Electric Power in Canada, 1985

	Thousands of megawatt hours	Per Cent of total
A. *Total Generation*		
Hydro	300 736	67.4
Steam conventional	85 323	19.1
Steam nuclear	57 095	12.8
Internal combustion	734	0.2
Gas turbine	2 524	0.6
Total	446 412	100.0
Utility generation	408 643	91.5
Industry generation	37 769	8.5
Total	446 412	100.0
Deliveries to the U.S.	43 016	
Total available	406 089	
B. *Electric Power Available by Province*		
Newfoundland	9 551	2.4
Prince Edward Island	576	0.1
Nova Scotia	7 662	1.9
New Brunswick	10 441	2.6
Quebec	144 534	35.6
Ontario	122 386	30.1
Manitoba	15 840	3.9
Saskatchewan	12 067	3.0
Alberta	33 290	8.2
British Columbia	48 975	12.1
Yukon	257	0.1
N.W.T.	509	0.1
Canada	406 089	100.0

Source: Statistics Canada, *Electric Power Statistics*, Cat. 57-001.

natural gas on King Christian Island, as well as of oil and natural gas on Canada's Arctic north slope make the problem of transportation—overland to Alberta or by tanker to the Atlantic Ocean—an urgent, and environmentally very hazardous, problem. If a pipeline is built in the Canadian North, this will involve an investment of many billions of dollars—far more than was involved in the construction of the St. Lawrence Seaway project. Because much of this money would have to come from the United States, the undertaking of such a project would inevitably cause an appreciation of the foreign exchange value of the Canadian dollar. This, in turn, would make it harder for Canadian firms to export their goods and services, and so, it is feared, create another economic problem for Canada. However, on the positive side, the sale of Arctic oil and natural gas would be a welcome new source of income for Canada and a welcome replacement for costly imported oil.

On Canada's east coast, oil and gas have been discovered in economic quantities off Nova Scotia and Newfoundland as a result of off-shore drilling. This, it is hoped, will provide the Atlantic provinces with the same economic stimulus received by Alberta in the late 1940s.

The National Energy Program

In 1980, the federal government announced a National Energy Program (or NEP) with the aim of ensuring by 1990 oil supply security for Canada and substantial Canadianization of the petroleum industry. And the NEP, spearheaded by Petrocan, a new Crown corporation, endowed with immense financial assets, gave considerable impetus to oil and gas exploration throughout the country. For example, gas from the Scotia Shelf was expected to be brought ashore by 1987. Although less accessible, the Hibernia field in the Grand Banks off Newfoundland, which is estimated to contain 1.8 billion barrels of recoverable oil, making it the largest oil pool in Canada, is also being developed. One problem that has slowed development has been the need to secure federal-provincial agreement over the resources. In Nova Scotia's case, such agreement has already been reached, with revenues to be divided about 42 per cent to the industry, 30 per cent to the Nova Scotia government, and 14 per cent to the federal government. Newfoundland is still negotiating.

Under the National Energy Program, to help offset the high cost of off-shore exploration (more than $300 000 a day to operate a rig off the East Coast) the federal government gave to the oil companies, on the basis of their degree of Canadian ownership, what are called Petroleum Incentive Program (PIP) grants.

Companies with a 75% Canadian Ownership Ratio (or COR) received the maximum grants, which covered 80% of their direct exploration spending. Foreign-owned companies were eligible for grants covering 25% of their direct exploration costs. In addition, there were tax write-offs for all companies, whatever the degree of foreign ownership. However, as from 1983, to curb the increasingly high cost of frontier oil exploration, written permission had first to be obtained from the federal Energy Minister for wells costing $50 million or more, in order to qualify for the full benefit offered by federal grants.

A factor that hampered oil and gas development in Western Canada was the 1981 two-tier oil pricing agreement between the Alberta and federal governments. Under this agreement, increases in the price of Western oil from wells discovered prior to the end of 1980 were restricted to a fixed percentage of the world price, with a maximum of 75 per cent of the average imported price in Montreal. Oil discovered subsequently could be sold at the world price. At the present time, this means that about 85% of Canadian oil is sold at the Special Old Oil Price (SOOP) and the other 15% at the New Oil Reference Price, or NORP, equivalent to the world price. Under the agreement, the price of natural gas is also restricted, with a maximum of 65 per cent of the wholesale price of oil in Toronto.

According to Western critics, Canadian oil prices were held below world prices to please voters in Central and Eastern Canada. This in turn discouraged investment in Canada's oil industry (for example, the Alsands and Cold Lake oil sands projects) and resulted in Canada moving from a substantial surplus in oil trade with other countries to a substantial deficit. Although Canadians would have paid more for their oil, Canada would now be self-sufficient and the economy much better off—especially as the federal government has had to subsidize the importation of foreign oil to keep Eastern Canadian oil prices below world prices. Politically, the Alberta government had championed the cause of a world price for its oil production whereas the federal government had tried to keep its 1980 election promise to consumers to keep Canadian oil prices below world levels.

In 1985, the Conservative federal government replaced the National Energy Program with a program of its own. This policy included the deregulation of oil prices, the removal of various export charges on oil and petroleum products, and the phasing out of various tax incentives for oil and gas exploration and development. Whereas the NEP had severely discriminated against foreign companies, the new energy policy was to be non-discriminatory with regard to both ownership and location.

One factor bedevilling oil exploration and development in Canada has been the world price of oil. Since most of Canada's oil is costly to extract and bring to market, a drop in the world price can easily make a project uneconomic. Thus, to be economically viable, Hibernia oil (from offshore Newfoundland) would, at the present time, have to sell for at least $25 to $27 U.S. per barrel; output from the Alsands project for at least $30 U.S.; and Sable Island (Nova Scotia) natural gas for an oil equivalent of $16 to $18 per barrel. In other words, Canada is a high marginal cost oil and gas producer that requires relatively high and rising world prices to make investment attractive, even with government incentives. Now that the world price of oil has dropped substantially (from $30 U.S. to $15 U.S.), the development of Canadian resources has become less profitable at the present time. Already in 1982, the $13.5 billion Alsands project in Northern Alberta was halted because of unwillingness of the last two private-sector participants (Shell Canada and Gulf Canada) to proceed. Also, plans for an Alaska Highway natural gas pipeline were further delayed. To encourage oil development and conservation, the Canadian government (whatever the political party) is expected in the future to move away more quickly from a "made-in-Canada" oil price towards world prices for all oil sold in Canada—whether produced in Canada or purchased from abroad. Even with world prices and government exploration incentives, no frontier oil is expected before 1990. Although progress is being made in the Grand Banks, the other frontier hope (the Beaufort Sea and the Arctic Islands) is still doubtful—because of conflicting reports of actual oil and gas reserves and the problem of transportation to market (tanker or a revived Mackenzie Valley pipeline?). In the West, of the several oil megaprojects that have already bitten the dust, only Imperial Oil's Cold Lake heavy-oil project is likely to be revived, and then on a reduced scale and with special tax and other concessions from the federal and provincial governments.

Coal

After World War II, oil and natural gas began to replace coal as a fuel for heating and transportation, both in Canada and abroad. As a result, Canada's coal industry entered a period of decline. In Nova Scotia, the long-established coal industry was squeezed between falling demand on the one hand and rising costs and shrinking reserves on the other. In the West, however, low-cost, open-pit mines in Alberta and Saskatchewan have been able to supply, at reasonable profit, the increasing fuel needs of thermal-electric power plants. Mines in Alberta and British Columbia have also, in recent years, begun to export metallurgical coal to Japan and make a significant contribution to Canada's balance of payments. However, in the early 1980s a world coal glut and increased Australian competition, made the prospects for Canadian Western coal producers less rosy.

Electricity

By 1985, Canada's electric-power generating capacity totalled almost 90 000 electrical megawatts, practically all of it built in this century. As most parts of Canada are rich in water-power, hydro-electricity has been the main type of electricity generated. Amongst the various provinces, Quebec is the most richly endowed, with over 40 per cent of Canada's water-power resources and the largest amount of developed capacity. British Columbia is the second most energy-wealthy province. Ontario, although a large producer of hydro-electricity, also makes substantial use of conventional and nuclear thermal-electric power. However, a decline in electricity demand in the early 1980s has slowed the development of the nuclear energy industry. Newfoundland, by contrast, still has a rich, relatively untapped hydro-electric potential. However, exploitation has been hindered by disagreement between Newfoundland and Quebec as to the terms on which electricity may be transmitted across Quebec territory to U.S. export markets. In the Maritimes, plans for a massive Nova Scotia tidal-power development, harnessing the Bay of Fundy, are still awaiting funds.

Summary

1. Industry, rather than agriculture, is now Canada's main source of income and employment.
2. Manufacturing, in its modern sense, means the production of goods by people using power-driven machinery. *Primary manufacturing* is the processing of basic raw materials. *Secondary manufacturing* is the production of finished goods and parts from processed raw materials.
3. Canada's most important manufacturing industries, in term of value added, are food, beverages, primary metals, paper and allied products, and transportation equipment.
4. Manufacturing can be divided into the following processes: extractive, conditioning, analytical, synthetic, and assembly.

5. The most important characteristics of modern manufacturing are: mechanization, automation, use of electric power, specialization of labour and equipment, mass production, standardization, synchronization, and advanced technology, including CAD/CAM and robotics.
6. Problems that face Canadian manufacturing include the relatively small domestic market (just 25.5 million people); dangers from excessive dependence on the U.S. market; the existence of a relatively large number of firms in many Canadian industries, which helps to prevent long production runs; foreign competition at home and abroad; appreciation in the foreign exchange rate for the Canadian dollar; difficulties in obtaining additional capital; and uneasy labour-management relations.
7. In Canada's mining production, nickel, copper, iron, zinc, and asbestos are the "big five," followed by lead, potash, gold, silver, and coal.
8. Much of the capital to develop Canada's mines has come from abroad, and much of the output is shipped to the United States rather than processed and used in Canada. Although mineral exports constitute an important source of national income, it would be preferable to have more of these minerals processed in Canada or, even better, to have them used by Canadian manufacturing industry and exported as finished or semi-finished goods.
9. A controversy that has surrounded the Canadian mining industry for many years is whether it should receive special income tax concessions as an incentive to the development of the country's mineral resources.
10. Guidelines for a Canadian mineral resource policy have been set out by the Federal Government.
11. Provincial governments also provide financial incentives for mineral exploration.
12. Canada's present large oil industry began in 1947 with the discovery of the Leduc oilfield in Alberta. This province is now Canada's leading producer of both oil and natural gas. However, large oil and gas fields have been discovered in the Canadian Arctic and in the off-shore Atlantic.
13. In 1985, Canada's National Energy Program, designed to ensure national oil self-sufficiency by 1990 and substantial Canadianization of the petroleum industry was replaced by a new, less nationalistic energy policy.
14. After years of decline, Canada's coal industry, now centred in Alberta and British Columbia, has begun to revive, supplying both

thermal-electric power plants in Canada and markets in Japan.

15. At the present time, Canada has almost 90 000 megawatts of electric-power generating capacity, predominantly hydro-electric. Quebec is Canada's most richly endowed province as regards water-power resources and developed electricity generating capacity.

Key Terms

Manufacturing 315
Primary manufacturing 316
Secondary manufacturing 316
Extractive process 316
Conditioning process 316
Analytical process 318
Synthetic process 318
Assembly process 318
Mechanization 318
Capital-intensive 318
Labour-intensive 318
Automation 320
Division of labour 320
Mass production 320
Standardization 321
Technology 321
Synchronization 321
CAD/CAM 321
Robotics 321
Mining 323
Tax incentives 325
Depletion allowance 326
Depreciation allowance 326
Mineral policy 327
National energy program 330

Review Questions

1. What is manufacturing? Distinguish, in your answer, between primary and secondary manufacturing.
2. What are the most important types of manufacturing industry in Canada? Which are the country's key manufacturing centres?
3. What are the five basic types of manufacturing processes?
4. Distinguish between mechanization and automation. What are the implications for employment in Canada of the growing use of capital-intensive methods of production?
5. What is the significance of electric power in manufacturing growth?
6. What is the nature of specialization in industry? How does it contribute to industrial productivity?
7. What is mass production? Why is its use restricted to certain kinds of products? Why does it require standardization and synchronization?

8. What is technology? Why is it so important to Canada's economic and social future?
9. Explain the terms CAD/CAM and robotics. What impact are these items expected to have on Canadian manufacturing industry?
10. What are the major problems facing Canadian manufacturing industry today?
11. What are the principal types of ore obtained from Canada's mines? Why is it that such a large proportion of the output is exported? How beneficial is this to Canada?
12. The Canadian mining industry has for a long time received special tax concessions. What is their purpose? How justified are they?
13. What are the key features of the federal government's mineral policy? How suitable a policy does it seem for Canada?
14. Where are Canada's oil and natural gas deposits to be found? What are the principal markets? What transportation problems face the development of newly discovered deposits?
15. What has been the history of Canada's coal industry?
16. How great is Canada's capacity to generate electric power? Where is this capacity located?
17. What is the federal government's energy policy? Discuss.

References

1. The Hon. E.J. Benson, Minister of Finance, *Summary of 1971 Tax Reform Legislation* (Ottawa: The Queen's Printer, 1971), p.45.
2. *The Globe and Mail,* Toronto, March 26, 1971.

18. CANADIAN AGRICULTURE

CHAPTER OBJECTIVES

A. To highlight the two basic economic problems that face most Canadian farmers
B. To discuss government price-support programs
C. To review the role of agricultural marketing boards
D. To examine crop insurance as an income-stabilization device
E. To review the various types of farm credit programs
F. To explain the effect of transportation subsidies
G. To discuss the future role of government in assisting Canadian agriculture

CHAPTER OUTLINE

18.1 Basic Economic Problems
18.2 Government Assistance
18.3 Price Supports
18.4 The Canadian Wheat Board
18.5 The Canadian Dairy Commission
18.6 Other Marketing Boards
18.7 Disposal of Surpluses
18.8 Crop Insurance
18.9 Agricultural and Rural Development
18.10 Farm Credit
18.11 Transportation Subsidies
18.12 Future Role of Government

In Canada, as well as in the U.S., Western Europe, and other countries of the world, agriculture is considered to be part of the social as well as economic fabric of society. In other words, farming communities, spread across the country, as well as being an important source of jobs and income outside the urban, industrial areas, help provide political and social stability. In Canada's case, with the vastness of its territory and the scantiness of its population, a prosperous agricultural industry give incentive to settlement and development. Also, from the economic point of view, Canadian agriculture makes a substantial contribution to the country's GDP (gross domestic product) and to its balance of international payments.

18.1: BASIC ECONOMIC PROBLEMS

Over the years, Canadian agriculture has suffered from the fact that the Canadian farmers' average income has been both relatively small and dangerously unstable. To help alleviate this situation, the federal and, to a lesser extent, the provincial governments have introduced a variety of programs of financial and other assistance. However, by helping to overcome one problem, government is seen by many critics to have created another. Canadian agriculture, it is alleged, now depends for its continued existence on a government paternalism that stifles any attempt by farmers to solve their own economic problems. Furthermore, the taxpayer at large is required each year to help pay for farm surpluses that cannot be sold and to maintain in use substandard farmland that is not really needed. But this is only one side of the story.

Low Average Income

For many years, the average income of farmers, relative to that of workers in other occupations, has steadily declined. Also, farming is one of the hardest forms of physical work. And, today, with the high degree of farm mechanization, the scientific approach to farming, and the amount of government regulation, a good farmer needs to be a labourer, mechanic, manager, bookkeeper, and veterinarian, all wrapped into one. It is not surprising, therefore, that the sons and daughters of farm families are moving to the cities where incomes are usually higher and the jobs less physically demanding. Of course, not all farmers suffer from low income; as in any occupation, incomes vary greatly. There are, for example, many prosperous wheat farmers in the Prairie provinces, but there are also many poor ones. Throughout Canada, many farmers are struggling along at a subsistence level, trying to make a living from relatively unproductive, marginal land.

The causes of this relative decline in average farm income are not hard to find. Basically, the demand for Canada's agricultural output has failed to increase as fast as the supply. On the demand side, people can only eat a limited amount. The demand for food is, as economists would say, relatively income-elastic. Thus, a doubling of a person's income does not mean a doubling of that person's expenditure on food. Spending on food must compete, in priority, with spending on transportation, housing, home furnishings, entertainment, travel, and many other non-food items. Once people are reasonably well fed, they tend to spend any additional income on these other items. Of course, many people in this country and abroad go short of food, but demand, as we saw earlier, implies the ability to pay as well as the desire to have. Unfortunately, without money, many people cannot obtain all the goods, including food, that they would like to have.

The demand for Canada's agricultural output is also affected by competition from farmers in other countries. Within Canada, for example, fruit and vegetable farmers find that much of their market is taken by imports from Florida and California. And recently farmers have complained, to no avail, to the Anti-Dumping Tribunal about the import of subsidized Italian wines and canned tomatoes. However, trade works both ways. Thus, the demand for Canadian beef has been greatly increased by export sales to the United States. Similarly, the demand for Canadian wheat has been greatly increased by sales to the Soviet Union and China. However, the signing in 1983 of a new five-year U.S.-Soviet grain agreement, has meant extra competition for Canada. Under the agreement, the annual minimum Soviet grain purchase from the U.S. will be 9 million tons, out of a total Soviet import requirement of 30 million tons or more, in a bad Soviet harvest year. On the whole, Canadian farm exports exceed imports by about $4 billion each year, and provide about one quarter of Canada's trade surplus. Key products are wheat, barley, and other grains; meat products, especially fresh and frozen pork; and fishery products.

On the supply side, Canadian agriculture has been characterized by a dramatic rise in output per acre. New and improved strains of high-yield crops, improved methods of cultivation, new chemical fertilizers and insecticides, and farm machinery of all kinds have been the principal causes. This increase in the supply of farm products has far exceeded the increase in demand. As a result, the prices received by farmers and ranchers for their products have declined over the years relative to the prices received by manufacturing and service industries. A farmer's net income consists of the gross income from the sale of the output minus expenses. But, whereas the price paid for the output has not increased greatly despite inflation, the prices of the inputs have increased tremendously. The wages for hired help are one of these

"The trouble is, the public's just not eating the right foods.."

expenses, but just as important has been the increase in the price of the other inputs such as farm machinery, seed, and fertilizers. Unlike the manufacturer, the farmer is not easily able to pass on these higher costs to the consumer in the form of higher prices. As a result, the profit margin, even for the most efficient farms, has gradually decreased.

Unstable Income

It is bad enough for farmers that their average income is relatively low, but, even worse, that this income is unstable. The most important cause of this instability is changes in supply. Good weather can mean bumper harvests, but it can also mean a drastic fall in market price; bad weather can mean small harvests and high prices. In addition, all kinds of diseases and pests can affect crop and livestock output. Also, a few good years usually encourage an expansion in output; and this overproduction in turn depresses market prices and farm incomes. Canadian producers of eggs, chickens, and hogs are all examples of farmers who have suffered badly in the past from an excess of supply in relation to demand. Only government price supports, which we will discuss later in this chapter, have prevented other farmers from sharing this fate.

Changes in demand are also responsible for unstable farm income. The prices of farm products tend to decline much more when demand falls than do the prices of non-farm products. This is because the supply of farm products is much more inelastic than the supply of other products. A farmer with land, buildings, and equipment is committed to farming. If the price of the farm output falls, the farmer cannot easily switch to the production of something else. Also, in the export market, competition from foreign producers of wheat and other farm products can cause sudden changes in demand.

In the case of Western grain farmers, another problem has been the closing down of West coast ports by grain workers' strikes. Normally, the West Coast grain terminals run at full capacity all year round. Therefore a strike or lockout can severely disrupt Canada's $5 billion grain export trade. The West Coast ports of Vancouver and Prince Rupert handle about 45 per cent of prairie grain exports.

18.2: GOVERNMENT ASSISTANCE

The decline in prosperity of Canadian agriculture relative to other sectors of the economy and the instability that has characterized agricultural prices and incomes over the years, have resulted in a variety of federal and provincial government programs to assist farmers.

Government became involved in agriculture as far back as the early days of Confederation, with grants and sales of land to prospective settlers. However, until the 1930s, government activities were confined mainly to land conservation and rehabilitation. In the 1930s, however, government intervention took an additional dimension—that of income assistance. Thus, in 1935, the federal government passed the Prairie Farm Rehabilitation Act to help farmers in Alberta, Manitoba, and Saskatchewan develop water supplies and otherwise rehabilitate farms which had suffered badly from prolonged drought and soil drifting. It also passed the Canadian Wheat Board Act to provide farmers with stable minimum prices for their wheat. Furthermore, in 1939, the federal government passed the Prairie Farm Assistance Act to provide indemnities to farmers whose crops might be damaged or destroyed by various natural hazards, and who are not covered by a provincial government crop insurance plan.

Early in World War II, the federal government imposed price ceilings on agricultural products so that the public would not face steeply rising food prices. To compensate farmers for their loss in potential income, the government made cash payments to them and subsidized the purchase of feed, seed, fertilizer, limestone, machinery, and other agricultural inputs. After the War, the price controls were gradually removed and most of the subsidies eliminated. However, the continued relative deterioration of the agricultural sector of the economy, the economic and social importance for Canada of a healthy farming industry, and the political value of the farm vote (one-third of federal M.P.s are from rural areas) have led to successive Canadian governments providing more and more assistance. One extremely important form of this government assistance has been price-support programs.

18.3: PRICE SUPPORTS

A *price support* is an undertaking by the government that a farmer will receive a minimum price per unit for all or a specified amount of his or her output. Since the purpose of the price support is to keep up the level of a farmer's income, this minimum price is usually higher than the one that would be set by the normal interaction of market demand and farm supply.

Price-Support Methods

How can a government implement a price-support program? Basically, there are three ways: (a) by buying up surplus output at the floor price; (b) by leaving output unrestricted, but enabling producers to sell all their output by subsidizing the price to consumers; and (c) by paying farmers to restrict output or by penalizing them if they produce more than their allocated quota.

The first of these methods, buying up any surplus, prevents competition among sellers faced with a limited demand which would force the market price down. Thus, in Figure 18:1, the government will have to purchase the amount Q_2Q_3. The total revenue received by producers would be the minimum price, OP_2, times the quantity, OQ_3. This is equal to the rectangle OP_2AQ_3. Of this sum, conumers would pay an amount equal to the rectangle OP_2EQ_2, and the government would pay the remainder, equal to the rectangle Q_2EAQ_3. The federal government uses this approach, for example, to ensure that Canadian dairy

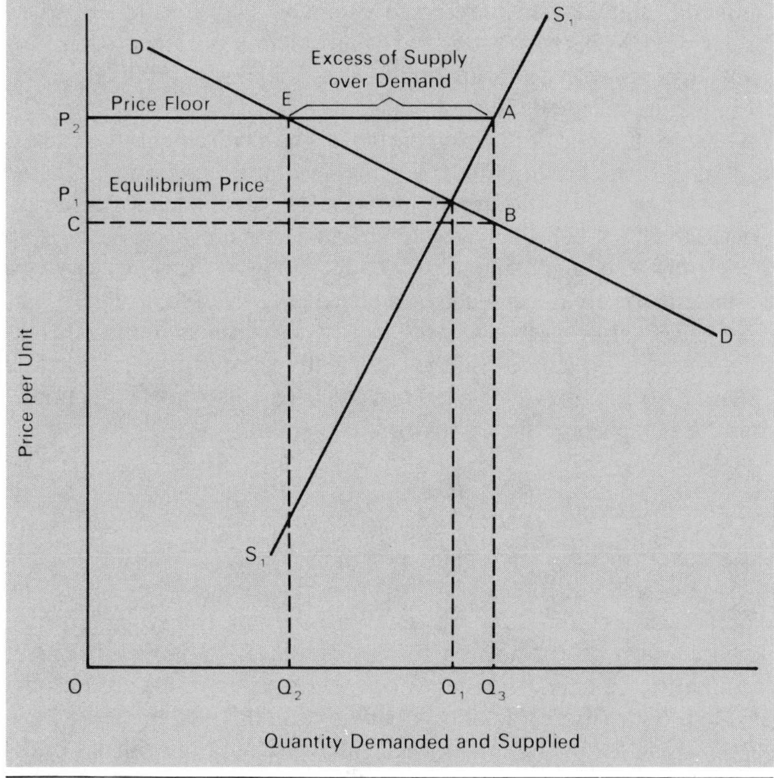

Note: Without a price floor, the equilibrium market price is OP_1, and the quantity demanded and supplied are equal at OQ_1.

With a minimum price of OP_2, the quantity demanded, OQ_2, is much less than the quantity supplied, OQ_3.

Figure 18:1 A Price Floor Causes Supply to Exceed Demand

farmers achieve the Target Returns level—a fair return on their labour and investment based on a cost of production formula.

The second way in which a government can implement a price-support program is by making deficiency payments to farmers. Thus, in Figure 18:1, a government could ensure that producers sell all the output, OQ_3, that they would produce at the floor price, OP_2, by enabling producers to sell it at a price OC. At this price, the amount demanded would be as large as the amount supplied—namely OQ_3. The producers would receive a total price per unit of OP_2, of which the part OC would come from the consumer and the part CP_2 from the government. The total revenue received by producers would be equal to the rectangle OP_2AQ_3. Of this amount, $OCBQ_3$ would come from the public, and CP_2AB from the government. This technique is used, for example, as part of the federal government's support program for dairy farmers—with a subsidy paid on each 100 litres of milk produced for industrial milk and cream production.

The third method of price support is for the government to persuade farmers to restrict their output. Thus, as we can see in Figure 18:2, the quantity supplied at the minimum price, OP_2, would have to be restricted to OQ_2. Such a policy would mean a new supply curve, S_2S_2, to the left of the original supply curve S_1S_1. However, it is not easy in a democratic society to persuade farmers voluntarily to reduce their output. Consequently, cash payments are often given as an incentive. This system is used in Canada and the U.S., with regard to grain production. Canada also imposes levies (or penalty payments) on, for example, dairy farmers who produce above quota.

Resource Allocation

Since government price-support programs interfere with the normal working of market forces and the price mechanism, they affect the allocation of a country's resources. With the first two types of price-support programs (buying up surplus output at the government-set minimum price or making deficiency payments) farmers are encouraged to produce more than they otherwise would. Thus, in Figure 18:1, output is OQ_3, not the amount OQ_1 that it would be with no price-support programs. Also, under these conditions, consumers must pay considerably more.

In economic theory, we tend to assume that if output is reduced, the human and other resources that are consequently freed can gradually be diverted to other uses that are more highly prized by consumers. In practice, there is great immobility of farm resources. Crops, livestock,

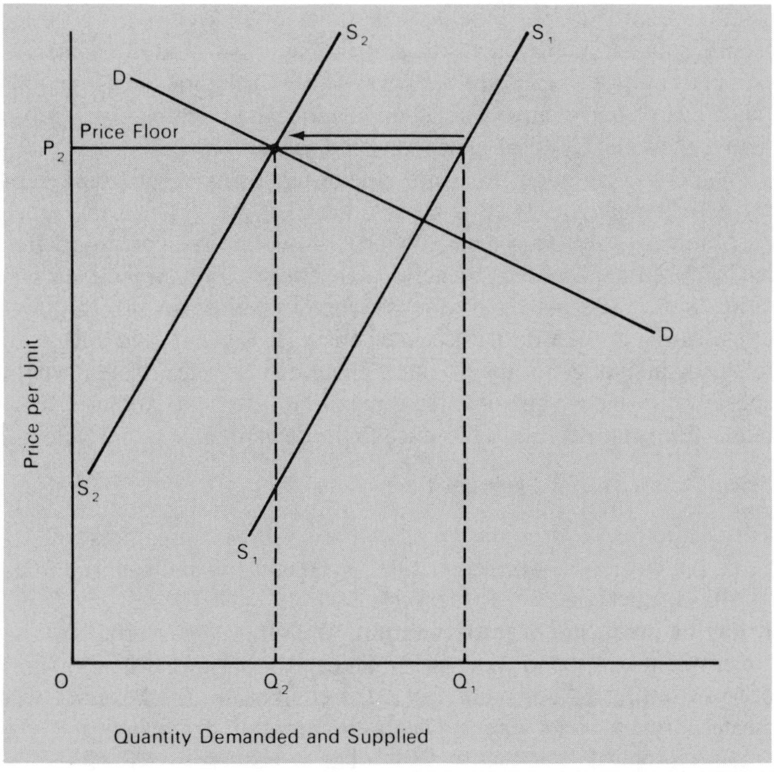

Note: Before the crop restriction program, the quantity supplied, OQ_1, at the minimum price, OP_2, exceeded the quantity demanded.

With crop restriction, a new supply curve, S_2S_2, intersects the demand curve, DD, at the minimum price. Since no surplus or shortage exists at this price, there is a state of market equilibrium. This will continue so long as individual farmers adhere to their production quotas and so long as demand remains unchanged.

Figure 18:2 Crop Restriction Means a Shift in the Supply Curve

and other farm products can be varied, it is true, in response to changing consumer demand. However, there is no way that a country's farms can be converted into manufacturing or service industries, except in a relatively minor way—for example, by "dude" ranches. Consequently, most price-support programs are adopted for political and social reasons to help prevent the economic decay of whole rural areas.

If farms rate low in consumer priority compared with, say, beauty parlours this will be reflected, by means of the price mechanism, in Canada's resource allocation. However, our governments have long acted in accordance with the view that they often know what is better for the national interest than the consuming public; and the preservation of a country's farms and rural way of life, including the geographical spread of our relatively small population, may well be worth more than a theoretically ideal allocation of resources.

With crop restriction, the third type of price-support program, supply is deliberately reduced to keep up market price. Thus, in Figure 18:2, output is only OQ_2 instead of OQ_1. Although keeping productive land unused appears less wasteful than burning or dumping surplus production, it still makes little sense when viewed against the amount of starvation in the world. Also, the consumer is still required to pay a relatively high price for the product. Therefore, the ideal system would appear to be one which encourages maximum effective land use, a fair return to the farmer, and a fair price to the consumer.

Price-Elasticity and Program Costs

The cost to the government of various price-support programs will depend to a large extent on the nature of the demand and supply curves for the product concerned (see Table 18:1).

1. Paying producers to restrict output. With this type of program; the government will spend more if demand and supply are elastic. This is because setting a floor price above the equilibrium market price will create a much wider gap between the amount demanded and the amount supplied (see Figure 18:1). The larger the excess of supply over demand, the more the government will have to pay producers to cut back output to the same amount as the quantity demanded. The more price-inelastic are demand and supply, the smaller the cost of such a program.

2. Buying up surplus output. As with the first method, the cost of the program will be larger, the more price-elastic are demand and supply. Instead of paying producers not to produce, the government purchases the surplus. The wider the gap between market demand and industry supply, the more the government has to buy.

3. Subsidizing the price to consumers. With this method, the cost of the program will be larger if demand is inelastic rather than elastic. This is because the surplus output would have to be sold to consumers at a price considerably less than the floor price. The more inelastic the demand, the more the price would have to be reduced to increase the quantity demanded. This means that the more inelastic the demand, the greater the difference between the floor price guaranteed to the producer and the price paid by the consumer. The difference is the government subsidy. On the supply side, the more elastic the supply, the greater the cost of the program. This is exactly the same as with the

Table 18:1
How Elasticity of Demand and Supply Affects the Cost to the Government of a Price-Support Program

Government Cost of Price-Support Program	Type of Price-Support Program: Paying Producers to Restrict Output	Buying up Surplus Output	Subsidizing the Price to Consumers
Cost of program will be larger if *demand* is:	elastic	elastic	inelastic
Cost of program will be larger if *supply* is:	elastic	elastic	elastic
Cost of program will be smaller if *demand* is:	inelastic	inelastic	elastic
Cost of program will be smaller if *supply* is:	inelastic	inelastic	inelastic

two previous methods of price support.

Canadian Government Policy

In 1944, the federal government passed an Agricultural Prices Support Act that empowered a Prices Support Board to set minimum prices for any agricultural product that it saw fit. To prevent the market price falling below this floor, the Board was authorized under the Act to purchase the product at the minimum price. In practice, the Board provided temporary emergency help for a variety of products including apples, beans, and turkeys. Two products, eggs and butter, received continuous price support.

The Agricultural Prices Support Act, designed to help farmers adjust from conditions of war to those of peace, continued in force until 1958. During its period of operation, the Board spent about $100 million in price supports. However, it was replaced in 1958 by a new and more ambitious measure, the Agricultural Stabilization Act. Under this Act, the federal government, by means of an Agricultural Stabilization Board, committed itself to support, at not less than 80 per cent of the previous ten-year average market or base price, the prices of nine commodities: cattle, hogs, and sheep, butter, cheese, and eggs; and Eastern wheat, oats, and barley. The government also gave itself the discretionary right to support the prices of other agricultural products.

Because of the large surpluses of hogs and eggs that developed in the 1950s, the federal government later altered its price-support program for those products. Instead of offering to purchase any amounts of hogs and eggs that could not be sold at the floor price, the government decided to let farmers sell these surpluses in the market place at whatever price they would bring. The Board would then pay farmers the difference between the government-set floor price and the national average market price. It should be noted that these *deficiency payments* are not paid on all of a farmer's output, only on a set amount, or quota, established for each farm. In this way, additional output is discouraged, and the total amount of farm subsidies held down. The deficiency payment method was also later used to support the price of sheep, soybeans, sugar beets, wool, honey, cattle, and tobacco.

18.4: THE CANADIAN WHEAT BOARD

Wheat, oats, and barley produced in Western Canada are products not included within the scope of the Agricultural Stabilization Act because they are the subject of special legislation. Under the Canadian Wheat Board Act of 1935, the federal government established a crown corporation, the Canadian Wheat Board, for the purpose of "the marketing in an orderly manner, in interprovincial and export trade, of grain grown in Canada." For many years the Board concerned itself only with the marketing of wheat. However, in 1949, it extended its control to oats and barley. Today, the Board has extensive control over the marketing of Western wheat and more limited control over the marketing of Western oats and barley.

How is wheat actually marketed? Each farmer is allowed to deliver a certain quota of wheat to the local elevator, the owner of which acts as an agent for the Wheat Board. The wheat is then sold by the board either at home or abroad. The farmer is paid an "initial price" for his or her wheat that is set by the federal government at the start of each crop year, on the basis of the expected selling price. This initial price is, in effect, a guaranteed floor price. In recent years, however, the actual price at which the Wheat Board has sold the wheat has usually exceeded this floor price. The difference is then paid to the farmers. However, they are charged a certain amount per bushel for elevator and freight costs.

Canadian wheat, although considered one of the best hard wheats in the world, has for many years faced a difficult market situation abroad. Internationally, Canada has co-operated with other major wheat producers to ensure the orderly marketing of wheat. Thus it was a member until 1969 of the International Grain Agreement that went into operation in 1949-50; and, since 1969, has been a member of the International Grains Arrangement. However, the selling prices established for different types of wheat under the International Grains Arrangement have been repeatedly undercut as a result of an excess supply of wheat in relation to demand. Only large sales of wheat to the Soviet Union and China have enabled Canadian wheat farmers to earn as much as they have without the need for government subsidy. However, diplomatic recognition of China by other wheat-producing countries such as Australia and the United States has resulted in more competition for Canada in that market. Also, Britain's entry into the Common Market has reduced Canada's wheat exports to that country as Britain now purchases more European wheat. Clearly, if Canadian wheat is to continue to be sold in substantial quantities abroad, the Canadian Wheat Board will have to reduce its export price. This will become even more necessary if importing countries continue the present trend of using softer, less expensive wheat for baking. In the future, therefore, Canadian wheat farmers may well have to rely on the Wheat Board's floor price for a reasonable income.

Until 1970, the Canadian Wheat Board placed no restriction on the amount of land planted to wheat. However, a growing wheat surplus led the federal government to introduce a program to reduce the amount of land used for growing wheat. And this program has effectively curtailed production.

After World War II, oats and barley were once more sold on the open market. However, in 1949, the marketing of these coarse grains was also put under the control of the Canadian Wheat Board. Each farmer is given a quota of grain that can be sold to the Board at an established price. Since this price usually exceeds the price elsewhere, the floor price provides substantial aid to the farmer. Unlike wheat, oats, and barley, Prairie rye and oilseeds are still sold on the open market.

18.5: THE CANADIAN DAIRY COMMISSION

Since the 1930s, the marketing of fluid milk in Canada has been regulated, for public health as well as economic reasons, by provincial governments. Each province has its own milk control board that sets minimum prices at which fluid milk may be sold. In 1967, however, a Canadian Dairy Commission was established by the federal government to complement the activities of the provincial boards. Specifically, the commission's purpose was to regulate the production and marketing, including pricing, of milk and milk products entering into interprovincial and international trade. More broadly, the Commission aimed "to provide efficient producers of milk and cream with the opportunity of obtaining a fair return for their labour and investment and to provide consumers with a continuous and adequate supply of dairy products of high quality." To achieve this aim, the Commission offers to purchase creamery butter, the two top grades of cheddar cheese, and dry skim milk at officially-set floor prices. It also provides subsidies to producers of industrial milk and cream, based on assigned output quotas. Despite these quotas, which determine a dairy producer's eligibility for subsidy, Canadian farmers still produce large surpluses of dairy products. Some of these, such as evaporated milk and skim-milk powder, are sold abroad, usually at a loss. Like other marketing boards, the CDC is criticized by consumer groups for unnecessarily raising the price of dairy products to the Canadian public.

18.6: OTHER MARKETING BOARDS

In an attempt to obtain better prices for their products, Canadian farmers began many years ago to establish marketing cooperatives. Although these organizations enabled farmers to ensure better grading and packing of their products, develop a common brand image, and negotiate sales from a position of collective strength, they suffered from the fact that membership was purely voluntary. As a result, most have now been replaced by farmer-controlled marketing boards, imposed by provincial statute, which have control over the entire production and marketing of a particular product in each particular province. Canada now has over 120 such government-authorized but producer-controlled and managed boards, together accounting for about one-quarter of the total value of all farm product sales. A board may be established under provincial law once a majority of the farmers producing a particular product have voted in favour.

Marketing boards operate in different ways to achieve their basic objectives of raising farmers' income and eliminating wide fluctuations in it. Some boards limit themselves to promoting their product by advertising and other means. Others have also undertaken to improve transportation, assembly, storage, market research, and other marketing functions for their product. Another tool used by some marketing boards is the two-price system under which a board sells its product at a higher price in one market than another, or charges a higher price for one use rather than another. Thus, wheat may be sold at a lower price abroad than at home, or milk sold at a lower price for industrial use than for domestic consumption. Like the early co-operatives, marketing boards try to obtain the full benefits of collective bargaining in negotiating sale orders for their products. Because of compulsory

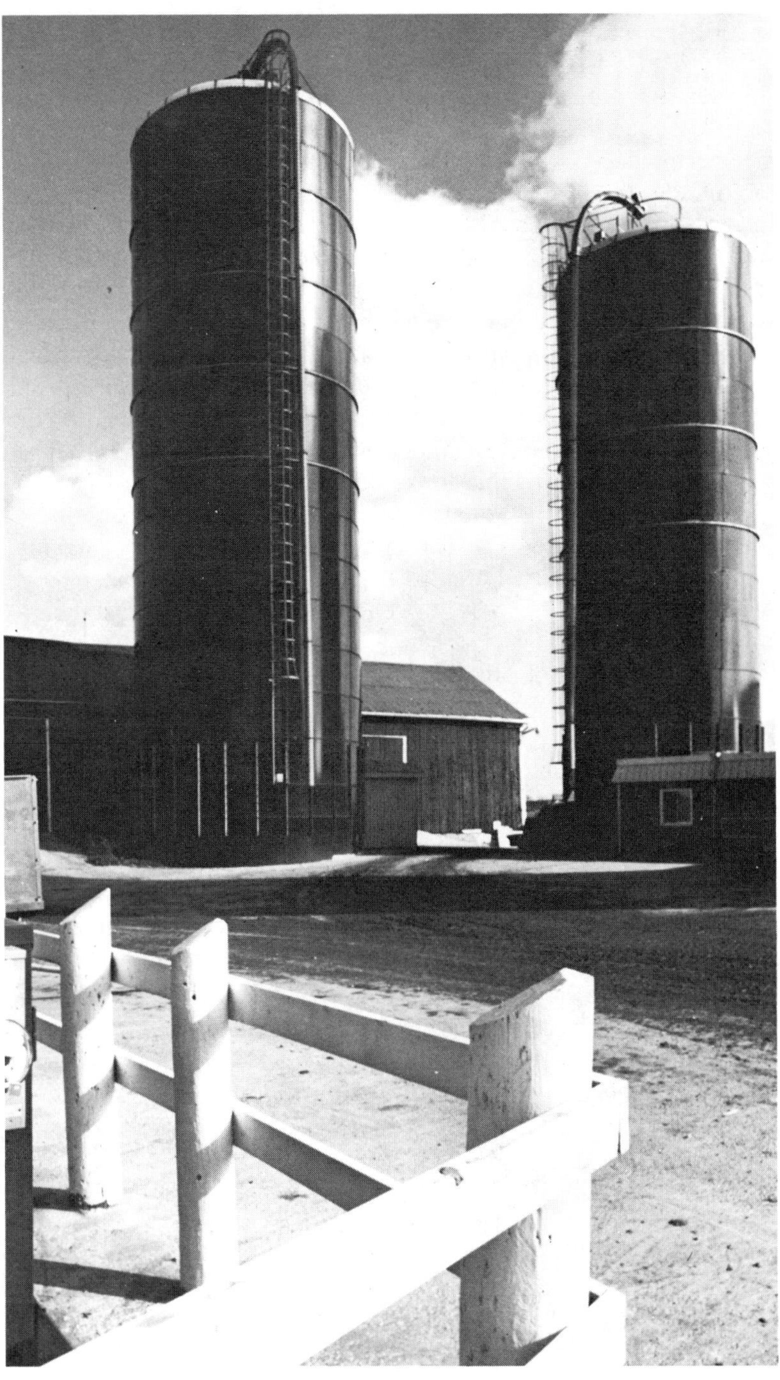

membership and compliance with the regulations, no farmer within the same province is free to undercut the price offered by the board. Another important tool for maintaining prices at a reasonable level has been the establishment of input quotas by various boards for their member producers. Thus, for example, the Ontario Fine-Cured Tobacco Growers Marketing Board allocates acreage rights to members, and the British Columbia Broiler Growers Marketing Board allocates broiler floorspace rights. Other boards such as the milk marketing boards use sales quotas instead, whereby each producer is permitted to sell only a specified amount of the product.

One of the biggest problems that faced marketing boards for many years was that most of them, except for the Canadian Wheat Board, were provincial in scope. That is, the efforts of one board could be undone by competition from another board in another province. The "chicken and egg war" that broke out between several provinces in 1971 was a case in point. Obviously, national marketing boards were needed, except for products such as tobacco that are produced in only one province. This need was partly met in 1972 with the federal government's Farm Products Marketing Act, which authorized the establishment of a national marketing board for poultry and eggs and permitted producers of other commodities to establish national marketing boards. Canada now has four federal marketing boards—one each for eggs, milk, chickens, and turkeys.

Supply-management marketing boards have been criticized for some years by consumer and industry groups in Canada such as the Grocery Products Manufacturers of Canada who claim that they give farmers too much control over the price of chickens, eggs, milk and turkeys in Canada. And there is serious concern that new marketing boards may be set up in the future for beef, hogs, and potatoes. The major criticisms are that such marketing boards restrict the supply of the product, artificially drive up prices, permit inefficiencies, and disallow economies of scale. It has been suggested that, to prevent abuse, the power to fix prices should be transferred from the marketing boards to a quasi-judicial board similar in nature to the Canadian Transport Commission or the CRTC.

18.7: DISPOSAL OF SURPLUSES

If a government adopts a policy of buying up surplus output at the minimum price, it faces the problem of handling, storing, and disposing of this food or other product. Obviously, it cannot sell this surplus output in the domestic market because this would depress the market price to the level at which it would have been without the government price-support program and thus make nonsense of the price floor. It might, however, give some of the surplus away to needy people who would not otherwise have provided part of the demand. This would prevent any interference with the floor price, but the government would have to ensure that none of the food disposed of in this manner finds its way to the normal market.

In practice, most governments try to dispose of surpluses abroad, sometimes in the form of gifts. For example, U.S. dried eggs and bottled orange juice concentrate became something of an institution in Britain during World War II. Canada, too, has made gifts of food at various times in recent years, normally in response to a particular disaster such as earthquake, famine, or disease. Canada has also provided gifts of food that can be sold locally to raise funds for economic development projects.

Instead of giving surpluses away, governments often try to sell them to foreign countries. Canada's wheat sales to China and the Soviet Union are a successful example of this policy. However, a government does not always have a free hand in this matter. If it sells surplus products abroad at a price less than that charged in its own country, it can be accused of "dumping." This means that, in many countries, local producers can successfully appeal to their governments to raise import tariffs on such goods to bring their price up to the level charged at home. This, in turn, may make it unprofitable for foreign importers to buy such surplus products. Sometimes, a government can sell its surplus abroad for more than it paid for it at home, but this is unusual.

Another difficulty in selling surpluses abroad is that the world market may be the main market for a country's product. In these circumstances, a government may buy up surplus output in order to keep up the price in the international market. This is the policy that Brazil, Colombia, and other major coffee producers follow. Disposing of surpluses then becomes a real problem. It was solved in Brazil's case for many years, to the horror and chagrin of coffee drinkers the world over, by dumping coffee into the Atlantic Ocean or by just burning it. In recent years, however, Brazil has switched its price-support program to one that requires coffee producers to restrict output.

Sometimes world producers will agree, in order to avoid disastrous price competition, to limit exports to commonly agreed-on quotas. This was the arrangement, for example, under the International Coffee Agreement, the International Sugar Agreement, and the International Grain Agreement. However, it is difficult to enforce the quotas assigned to member countries, to say nothing of the problem posed by producing countries who are unwilling to participate. It was this prob-

"You boys figure it out. We'd be a lot better off producing less, but selling it for more.."

lem of member and nonmember countries selling below the agreed world floor price that caused Canada to abandon the International Grain Agreement in 1969.

18.8: CROP INSURANCE

One of the problems that has always bedevilled Canadian farmers is the risk of loss from natural hazards such as drought, floods, hailstorms, frost, rust, and insects. Unfortunately, private insurance companies have found from sad experience that crop insurance is too risky a business to be profitable. Consequently, farmers have had to turn to the government for help of this kind. The Prairie Farm Assistance Act, passed by the federal government in 1939, was designed to meet this need. Under the Act, farmers marketing grain through the Canadian Wheat Board are required to pay a levy of 1 per cent of the value of sales. In return, they are paid an indemnity if the crop is damaged or destroyed. In practice, total indemnities have considerably exceeded total levies, the difference being paid by the federal government.

In 1959, the federal government went a step further in crop insurance. In that year, it passed the Crop Insurance Act, which gave provincial governments the necessary authorization to set up crop insurance programs of their own. It also provided for the federal government to pay part of the cost. The provincial crop insurance programs, covering practically all crops, including fruit trees, instead of just a few, are now considered to have made the Prairie Farm Assistance Act redundant.

18.9: AGRICULTURAL AND RURAL DEVELOPMENT

In 1966, the federal government passed an Agricultural and Rural Development Act (ARDA), replacing the Agricultural Rehabilitation and Development Act of 1961. The purpose of the new Act was to help people living in rural areas adjust to a changing social, economic, and technological environment. This was to be achieved by means of federal-provincial shared-cost programs covering land use, soil and water conservation, development of rural income and employment opportunities, and all necessary research. Federal money for the programs was provided under a special Fund for Rural Economic Development Act (FRED), also passed in 1966. Both the Act and the Fund were terminated in 1969 when the Department for Regional Economic Expansion (DREE), now replaced by the Department for Regional and Industrial Expansion (DRIE), was established to promote rural and other types of regional economic development.

18.10: FARM CREDIT

To make a reasonable living from the land, the modern Canadian farmer has to combine large amounts of machinery with a relatively small amount of labour. This machinery is, of course, expensive. Also, the need to reorganize farms into larger, more economical units to operate requires considerable financing. As well, short-term financing is customarily required to bridge the gap between the time at which a crop is planted and the time at which cash is received from its sale.

Although most farmers traditionally save a large part of their net income, outside financing is virtually indispensable to help meet their purchasing needs. A great deal of the money required, particularly short and medium-term financing, is obtained from private individuals, chartered banks, farm supply companies, and credit unions. However, the federal and provincial governments have also provided help in a variety of ways. We shall now briefly describe the most important of these government financing programs.

Farm Credit Corporation

In 1959, the federal government passed the Farm Credit Act. This Act established a federal government agency, the Farm Credit Corporation, to make long-term mortgage loans to farmers. Previously, only a limited amount of long-term financial help had been available from a Canadian Farm Loan Board established in 1929. For some loans, the security is land alone; for others, it is land, livestock, and machinery. The rate of interest charged to farmers is very close to that which the corporation itself pays for its funds. The Farm Credit Corporation is now the most important source of long-term loans for farmers. Other sources of long-term mortgage loans are the loan corporations set up by various provincial governments.

The Canadian Federation of Agriculture, on behalf of Canadian farmers, has frequently complained that funds available to farmers through the Farm Credit Corporation are insufficient. Another complaint has centred on the fact that, after government-supplied funds were quickly used up by farmers trying to refinance their operations to stay in business, the Department of Finance restricted FCC borrowing in foreign money markets to less than half the amount desired.

Farm Syndicates Credit Act

By this Act, effective from 1965, the federal government authorized the Farm Credit Corporation to make loans to syndicates of three or more farmers for the purchase of farm machinery, buildings, and installed equipment. These loans are for up to 80 per cent of the value of the machinery, with a maximum total amount.

Animal Disease Eradication

The federal government compensates herd owners when their animals have to be put away because of disease. The compensation is usually their market value.

Farm Improvement Loans Act

This Act, passed in 1944, encourages the chartered banks to make short and medium-term loans to farmers by providing a federal government guarantee for such loans. Bank financing under the Act, with a maximum amount per farmer, has been used predominantly for the purchase of farm machinery and equipment, livestock, and farm improvement.

Prairie Grain Advance Payments Act

Under this Act, the Canadian Wheat Board is authorized by the federal government to make interest-free advance payments to Prairie grain farmers who are prevented from delivering their grain because of insufficient elevator space.

Federal Business Development Bank

This government-owned bank makes mortgage loans to new and existing agricultural enterprises when the funds cannot be obtained on reasonable terms and conditions elsewhere. There is no fixed maximum amount.

Provincial Aid

Most provincial governments have established programs of financial aid to farmers. In Alberta, for example, a farmer may borrow funds from the government, under the Farm Purchase Credit Act, to help buy a farm. In British Columbia, as another example, loans are available to farmers, under the Farmers' Land Clearing Assistance Act, to finance the clearing and breaking of land.

18.11: TRANSPORTATION SUBSIDIES

One of the ways in which the Federal Government helps farmers is by transportation subsidies.

Livestock Feed Assistance Act

Under this Act, the federal government helps pay the cost of transporting feed grains from the Prairie provinces to Eastern Canada and to British Columbia. The purpose of the Act is to ensure that feed-grain prices remain relatively stable without great differences between one part of Canada and another. A special Board administers the freight and storage assistance programs involved.

Crow's Nest Pass Agreement

By this agreement, made between the federal government and Canadian Pacific Railway in 1897, railway freight rates for grain being shipped from the Prairie provinces to Thunder Bay ports were held at the 1898 level. This was in return for substantial federal subsidies to build a 300-mile rail line through the Crow's Nest Pass in the Rockies. Later, in 1925, the fixed rate was legislated—for the Canadian National as well as the C.P.R. and extended to all Prairie delivery points and to West Coast ports. Farmers, so it is estimated, now pay about one-fifth of the actual cost to the railways of shipping the grain. This transportation subsidy to farmers is met by the federal government which, under the National Transportation Act of 1967, reimburses the railway companies for the revenue loss incurred. However, because of the low rates, the C.P.R. has not found it worthwhile to invest in new track and rolling stock and this has hampered Canadian grain exports. Whereas Canada now exports about 31 million tonnes of grain a year, it could, with better transportation, export 40 million tonnes by 1990. In 1982, the federal government abolished the special railway freight rates for grain shipments and undertook to pay a subsidy instead to the railways and farmers. In return, the railway companies undertook to improve their grain handling facilities.

18.12: FUTURE ROLE OF GOVERNMENT

One important conclusion of the Federal Task Force on Agriculture some years ago was that government should reduce its direct involvement in agriculture. To achieve this, the Task Force recommended a number of measures. They included: (a) the control and reduction of farm surpluses to manageable proportions by switching production to

Table S.12
Canadian Farm Cash Receipts, by Source, in millions of dollars, 1985

Source	$ millions	Per cent of total
Crops		
Wheat	2 505	12.6
Wheat C.W.B. participation payments	570	2.9
Oats	54	0.3
Oats C.W.B. participation payments	1	0.0
Barley	533	2.7
Barley C.W.B. participation payments	145	0.7
C.W.B. net cash advance payments	128	0.6
Rye	30	0.2
Flaxseed	194	1.0
Rapeseed	906	4.5
Soybeans	230	1.2
Corn	575	2.9
Sugar beets	12	0.0
Potatoes	273	1.4
Fruits	289	1.5
Vegetables	549	2.8
Floriculture and nursery	384	1.9
Tobacco	158	0.8
Other crops	443	2.2
Deferred grain receipts	-496	-2.5
Liquidation of deferred grain receipts	792	4.0
Western grain stabilization payments	—	—
Sub-total	9 401	47.2
Livestock and Products		
Cattle	3 263	16.4
Calves	327	1.6
Hogs	1 822	9.1
Sheep	3	0.0
Lambs	26	0.1
Dairy products	2 716	13.6
Poultry	901	4.5
Eggs	509	2.6
Other	185	0.9
Sub-total	9 752	49.0
Forest and maple products	116	0.6
Dairy supplementary payments	282	1.4
Deficiency payments	16	0.1
Provincial income stabilization program	196	1.0
Total cash receipts	19 913	100.0

Source: Statistics Canada, *Farm Cash Receipts,* Cat. 21-001.

other agricultural products in greater demand or by taking land out of production; (b) the phasing out of certain agricultural subsidies and price supports; and (c) the improvement of farm management. Financial assistance would be provided temporarily to facilitate crop switching and land retirement; educational and other assistance would be provided to younger farmers switching to other occupations; and financial assistance would be provided to older farmers.

These recommendations undoubtedly sound harsh to people who make their living from the land, particularly when they see that many people living in urban areas receive their income from tariff-protected manufacturing industries or from tax-supported government departments. Nevertheless, the question remains: to what extent should Canadian agriculture stand on its own feet?

From the purely economic point of view, there is the question of the most efficient allocation of Canada's resources. Should the federal and provincial governments try, at considerable public expenses, to keep in use farmland that is only marginally productive? Is money well spent, in social as much as economic terms, in trying to slow the present drift from the land? Is it worth spending large sums of public money to reclaim marshland in certain parts of the country when more than enough good farmland is unused elsewhere?

Also, the public may well ask, just how effective has government aid been in solving the farmers' twin problems of low and unstable income? As regards low income, most government payments, because they are usually geared to assigned production quotas or existing farm sizes, help the rich farmer just as much as the poor one. In other words, financial assistance is not being given to farmers selectively. It is not being directed where the need is most urgent or where the benefits are likely to be greatest. Also, in the case of farm loans, the farmer who often needs the greatest help, very often does not possess the land, buildings, and other collateral to qualify for a loan. Those who do receive farm credit are often the ones who could obtain loans in competition with other business borrowers and who could afford to pay the normal rate of interest. The same criticism may be applied to transportation subsidies that benefit all farmers, not just the poorer ones. However, this brings us to another question. Are the poorer farmers poorer because their farms are inherently inefficient? If this is the case, then financial aid may well be like pouring water (the taxpayers') into a bottomless well.

With regard to income stability, government price-support programs have meant that farmers can now count on a much more stable income than was previously the case. However, because the government is unwilling to sell farm surpluses in the domestic market when the market price is reasonably high, these surpluses, purchased with the taxpayers' money, must be held in storage—eventually to be sold abroad, often at ridiculously low prices, to be given away, or even to be destroyed. Certainly, the government has not attempted to follow the more reasonable policy of buying up farm surpluses in good crop years and reselling them in bad ones. Instead, it has held the floor price at a level higher than would be the case if surpluses were resold at home over a period of years. In other words, it has provided incomes to farmers which are not only stable but also higher. But this may well be in the national interest.

Income Stabilization Policy

At the present time in Canada, income stabilization is being achieved by both marketing boards and price-support programs. However, many people believe that the latter are preferable because they do not involve any attempt to control supply, fix prices, or otherwise interfere with the free market. In 1983, the Ministers of Agriculture for all provinces except Newfoundland set up a task force to develop a national price support program for farmers that would replace the present hodge-podge of schemes.

All Canadian farmers would be eligible to participate in such a scheme except those already protected by supply-management marketing boards. The scheme would be funded equally by the federal and provincial governments on the one hand and by participating farmers on the other. Although requiring a government subsidy, this could be much less than under equivalent programs in the U.S. and the European Economic Community. The price-support levels would be kept below the cost of production to ensure that market forces, not subsidies, control the supply and prices of agricultural products. Others suggest a higher support price based on a cost-of-production formula.

Agricultural Exports

A more controversial issue in the area of government support for agriculture was the federal government's decision to create a Crown corporation, Canagrex, to expand Canada's exports of agricultural products.

Summary

1. Over the years, the Canadian farmer's average income has usually

been both relatively small and highly unstable. Consequently, governments have introduced various programs of financial and other assistance which have in turn led to allegations of excessive government paternalism and an undue tax burden on the nation.

2. The two main reasons for the relative decline in average farm income are (a) the failure of demand for agricultural output to increase as fast as supply; and (b) the increase in the cost of agricultural inputs.
3. The two main causes of unstable farm income are changes in the weather (affecting supply) and changes in demand.
4. Until the 1930s, government assistance to farmers was confined mainly to land conservation and rehabilitation. Thereafter, it also included income assistance.
5. One government measure to keep up farm income has been price supports. This has taken three forms: buying up surplus output at the government-set floor price; subsidizing the price to the consumer; and persuading farmers, with cash incentives, to restrict output.
6. Government price-support programs, since they interfere with the normal working of market forces and the price mechanism, affect the allocation of a country's resources.
7. The cost to the government of the various price-support programs will depend to a large extent on the elasticities of demand and supply of the products involved.
8. Canada now has a Wheat Board, Dairy Commission, and other federal and provincial marketing boards to control the production and marketing of various farm products.
9. Provincial governments, through crop insurance programs, provide a vital service to farmers, not available from the private insurance companies.
10. Another important form of government assistance to agriculture is the provision of a variety of farm credit programs.
11. The provision of government-subsidized railway freight rates, under the Crow's Nest Pass Agreement and other later legislation, was to be reduced or eliminated in the 1980s.
12. Although controversial, government is expected to continue its income-stabilization efforts for farmers.
13. The federal government also intended, through a new Crown corporation, Canagrex, to try to increase Canadian exports of agricultural products.

Key Terms

Price support 342
Deficiency payment 344
Crop restriction 344
Initial price 348
Grain quota 349
Surplus 350
Marketing board 350
Dumping 353
Crop insurance 355
Farm credit 356
Transportation subsidy 358
Canagrex 361

Review Questions

1. Why is average farm income relatively small compared with that of other sectors of the economy?
2. Why has farm income been relatively unstable?
3. What new dimension did government assistance to Canadian farmers take in the 1930s? What was its significance?
4. What are the main types of government price-support programs? What is their purpose?
5. How do price-support programs affect the allocation of a country's resources?
6. How do the elasticities of demand and supply affect the cost to the government of price-support programs?
7. Explain the nature and purpose of the 1944 Agricultural Price Support Act. How did the 1958 Agricultural Stabilization Act change government assistance to farmers?
8. Explain the nature and purpose of the Canadian Wheat Board.
9. How is wheat now marketed in Canada?
10. How is milk marketed in Canada?
11. Why do farm surpluses occur? Why does their disposal seem to be such a problem?
12. Explain the nature, purpose, methods, and limitations of marketing boards in Canada.
13. Why is crop insurance an important form of government assistance to agriculture?
14. What was the purpose of the 1966 Agricultural and Rural Development Act (ARDA)? How was it financed? What agency now performs this work?
15. What are the ways in which government helps provide credit and loans to farmers?
16. What types of transportation subsidy does the Canadian government provide to farmers?

17. What were the recommendations of the Federal Task Force on Agriculture with regard to the future role of government in Canadian agriculture?
18. Why can't farmers manage on their own? Discuss.
19. What is the most efficient type of agricultural price-support program from society's point of view?
20. "Canada should be the breadbasket of the world." Discuss.
21. "Paying farmers not to produce is as sinful as throwing coffee into the sea." Discuss.
22. "Canada should follow the example of the oil-producing countries by forming an international wheat cartel and raising the price of wheat." Discuss.
23. "If marketing boards are permitted in agriculture, they should be permitted in other industries." Comment.
24. "There seem to be many prosperous farmers in Canada." Discuss.
25. "It is against Canada's national interest to let people build houses on good farmland, wherever it may be." Discuss.

19. BUSINESS ORGANIZATION

CHAPTER OBJECTIVES

A. To explain how persons organize their business activities from the ownership point of view
B. To describe the nature, advantages, and disadvantages of the sole proprietorship form of business ownership
C. To explain the partnership form of ownership, including the differences between a general partnership and a limited partnership
D. To analyze the corporate form of business ownership, including a discussion of common and preferred shares, and the nature and role of the multinational corporation
E. To describe the co-operative form of ownership
F. To examine the various forms of government enterprise

CHAPTER OUTLINE

19.1 The Sole Proprietorship
19.2 The Partnership
19.3 The Business Corporation
19.4 The Multinational Corporation
19.5 The Co-operative
19.6 Government Enterprises

The business firm is the unit of ownership that people use to pool their funds and/or abilities for business purposes. It usually has, as its principal long-term aim, the maximization of profit by producing and marketing the goods and services that society wants. It can be set up as a sole proprietorship, a partnership, a corporation, or a co-operative. Each form of business ownership has its own characteristics, as summarized in Table 19:1. Also, in the last thirty years, there has been a tremendous expansion in the number of multinational corporations, mainly U.S.owned, in Canada. There is also in Canada a great number of business enterprises owned and operated by the federal, provincial, and municipal governments.

Table 19:1

Characteristics of the Various Types of Business Ownership (A = good; B = fair; C = poor)

	Sole Proprietorship	General Partnership	Limited Partnership	Business Corporation (Private)	Business Corporation (Public)
Ease and cost of establishment	A	B	B	C	C
High personal motivation	A	A	A	A	A,B
Quickness and freedom of action	A	B	B	A,B	A,B
Privacy	A	B	B	B	B,C
Possible management disputes	A	B	B	A,B	B
Ease of dissolution	A	B	B	C	C
Availability of capital	C	B	B	B	A
Professional management	C	C	C	B,C	A,B
Easy transferability of ownership	A	C	C	B	A
Continuity of existence	C	B	B	A	A
Personal liability for business debts	C	C	A,C	A	A
Relatively frozen investment	B	B	B	B	A
Legal restrictions	A	B	B	C	C
Income tax	B,C	B,C	B,C	A,B	A,B

19.1: SOLE PROPRIETORSHIP

A sole proprietorship is a business owned by one person. Although the owner may employ other people, the owner alone is responsible for its debts.

Advantages

The most important advantages of this form of business organization are: ease of establishment, high personal motivation, quickness and freedom of action, privacy, and ease of termination.

The legal requirements for starting a small business are minimal. Only certain types of business require a municipal licence or a provincial vendor's permit. And only if the owner wishes to use a name for the business other than his or her own, does the name and other particulars of the business need to be registered with the provincial government.

The proprietor is highly motivated because he or she receives all the profits, has pride of ownership, and meets a personal challenge. Being the boss, the owner is free to make business decisions without the approval of someone else. The owner is able to maintain privacy about the financial affairs of the business and is in a good position to keep secret any special processes, formulas, recipes, or business contacts. Also, the owner can legally terminate the business merely by closing its doors.

Disadvantages

The sole proprietorship form of ownership also has some disadvantages. These include: unlimited personal liability, limited talent, limited capital, lack of continuity, and possibly heavier income taxation than if the business were incorporated.

Unlimited personal liability means that a sole proprietor's personal assets can be seized, if necessary, to pay outstanding business debts. Thus, a person's life savings could be wiped out by a business failure. The sole proprietor usually has no one else on whom to rely to run the business. Good assistants are difficult to find and expensive to retain. The owner will also find it more difficult to borrow money than if there were business partners to whom the lender could also turn. If the sole proprietor becomes ill or dies, the business can easily come to a halt. Depending upon his or her level of business and other personal income, the sole proprietor may pay more income tax than under the corporate form of business organization This is because the personal income tax is at a progressive rather than a flat rate.

19.2: THE PARTNERSHIP

A partnership is a business firm that has two or more owners who pool their talents and/or their funds, but which is not incorporated. It can be either a general or a limited partnership.

In a *general partnership*, all the partners, called general partners, may take part in the management of the business and all have unlimited personal liability for business losses. In a *limited partnership*, there are both limited partners and at least one general partner. The limited partner is liable for business debts only up to the amount of his or her investment. However, in return, that partner (or partners) must not take part in the management of the business. Otherwise, he or she may be considered by the courts to have been a general partner. Usually a written partnership agreement is drawn up to govern the conduct of the partners. An example of such an agreement is shown below. There is no set form prescribed by law.

PARTNERSHIP AGREEMENT

AGREEMENT made this 15th day of December 19--

BETWEEN Lorne Park, of 7 Curlew Drive, Mississauga, Ontario and T.L. Kennedy, of 3572 Ashbury Road, Burlington, Ontario.

IN CONSIDERATION of the sum of One Dollar paid by each party to the other (the receipt whereof is hereby acknowledged) the parties do hereby mutually covenant and agree as follows:

1. That the said parties will, as partners, engage in and conduct the business of a hardware store.
2. That the name of the firm shall be Mississauga Hardware.
3. That the term of the partnership shall commence on the 1st day of January, 19--, and shall continue until one month after one partner has notified the other partner in writing of his intention to withdraw from the partnership.
4. That the place of business shall be Sherwood Mall, Mississauga, Ontario.
5. (a) That the capital of the firm shall be $50 000, to be contributed in equal cash amounts of $25 000 each on the signing of the Agreement.

   (b) That neither party's contribution to the partnership shall bear him interest.
6. That the partnership capital and all other partnership monies shall be deposited in the Sherwood Mall branch of the Bank of Nova Scotia, from which all withdrawals shall be made only by cheques

signed jointly by both partners.

7. (a) That books of accounts be kept in accordance with standard accounting procedures.
   (b) That these books be kept on the premises and open to the inspection of either partner.
8. That each partner shall be entitled to draw 500 dollars per week from the funds of the partnership on account of his profits.
9. (a) That at the end of June of every year, an inventory shall be taken and the assets, liabilities, and gross and net income of the business ascertained.
10. That neither partner shall, without the written consent of the other, draw, accept, sign, or endorse any bill of exchange, promissory note, or cheque, or contract any debt on account of, or in the name of the partnership, except in the normal course of business and up to the amount of $500.
11. That each partner shall devote his whole time and attention to the partnership business, and shall not, during the term of the partnership, engage in any other business.
12. That should one of the partners die, his executors shall be entitled to receive the value of his share of the partnership property at the time of his death, together with 1 per cent interest a month in lieu of profit from that day on until final settlement of the property.
13. That on termination or dissolution of the partnership, other than by the death of a partner, an audit shall immediately be made of the firm's assets and liabilities and the balance be divided equally between the partners.
14. (a) That in the event of a disagreement between the partners as to the conduct of the business, as to its dissolution, or as to any other matter concerning the business, the same shall be referred to arbitration within 10 days of written notice being served by one partner on the other.
    (b) That each partner shall appoint one arbitrator, who shall in turn appoint a third arbitrator.
    (c) That the matter referred to arbitration shall be decided by simple majority of the arbitrators.

IN WITNESS WHEREOF, the parties hereto set their hands and seals, the day and year first above written.

Witnesses: *David Bell* — *Lorne Park*

David Bell — Lorne Park

Pauline Gloucester — *T.L. Kennedy*

Pauline Gloucester — T.L. Kennedy

Advantages

The most important advantages of the partnership form of business organization are: more capital, more talent, high personal motivation, and relatively few legal restrictions.

1. More capital. A partnership pools the funds of a number of people, whereas a sole proprietorship has only the one owner's money. Also, an individual with a good business idea, talent, or experience but no money can often establish a business only by joining with someone else who does have capital to invest. It is also normally easier for a partnership to obtain credit from suppliers or borrow money from a bank than it is for a sole proprietor. This is because the creditor or lender can have the security of the business and personal assets of several persons for repayment rather than those of just one person.

2. More talent. Not everyone feels competent to run a business on his or her own. Two or more partners, by combining their energies and talents, can often make a success of a business whereas one person alone might fail. This is particularly true when a business demands a variety of talents such as technical knowledge, financial skill, and sales ability. The partnership also offers the means of retaining valuable employees by making them partners in the business.

3. High personal motivation. As with the sole proprietorship, the owners of a partnership business know that all the profits (less the government's share) will go to them. Consequently, they have every motivation to make it successful. This is in addition to the pride of ownership and personal satisfaction that comes from being self-employed.

4. Few legal restrictions. To set up a partnership, legal fees may be incurred in preparing a written partnership agreement, if the partners do not wish to rely on their own wisdom alone. Also, the partnership must be registered. Once this is done, however, the only legal requirements are a municipal business permit, if necessary, and observance of tax, labour, fire, and other regulations.

Disadvantages

The main disadvantages of the partnership type of business ownership are: possibly higher income tax; unlimited personal liability; possible management disputes; limited capital (compared with a public business corporation); relatively frozen investment; and possible lack of continuity.

1. Possibly higher income tax. Like a sole proprietor, a partner must pay personal income tax on any business income. Because the personal income tax is graduated, the rate of tax constantly increases. However, if the business is set up as a corporation, any income earned by the business would be subject to a flat (not graduated) rate of income tax, with a special deduction if the business is small (i.e. has a maximum annual income of $200000) and Canadian-controlled. Thus a Canadian-controlled private corporation (or CCPC) enjoys, in Ontario, a special 24% corporate income tax rate on active income (as distinct from investment income). Once a small business starts to prosper, the tax advantages of incorporation can be substantial. However, this special tax rate does not apply to a firm that provides medical, legal, or other personal services.

2. Unlimited personal liability. In both a general and a limited partnership, the general partner can be forced to sell his or her personal assets to pay any outstanding business debts. This liability is both joint and several. This means, first, that all the partners are together liable for the debts of the partnership; second, that one partner may be required to pay *all* the debts of the business if the other partners fail to pay their shares. If a person is unwilling to assume this risk, he or she can become a limited partner, with liability only up to the amount of his or her investment.

3. Possible management disputes. Because more than one person manages the business, occasional disputes will inevitably arise. If the disputes are serious, they may cause the partnership to terminate. Unfortunately, it is not easy to foresee whether the personalities of the partners will clash. This can be a real disadvantage to a partnership, particularly if one of the partners has formerly operated alone and is not accustomed to collective decision-making.

4. Limited capital. A partnership has more capital at its disposal than a sole proprietorship, but less than a business corporation, particularly a public one. Most large enterprises today require greater sums than can be obtained from a few investors alone. Unlike a public business corporation, the general partnership cannot solicit funds from the general public by selling shares or bonds. Additional long-term funds can, however, be arranged by mortgaging fixed assets. The need for long-term funds can be substantially reduced by leasing buildings, equipment, and vehicles, rather than buying them. A corporation can raise long-term funds by selling shares of capital stock to the limit authorized in its charter. It can also borrow long-term funds by issuing a bond. The partnership, with its unlimited personal liability for general partners and difficult transfer of ownership (as explained next), cannot usually attract large amounts of capital.

5. Relatively frozen investment. It is not easy for a partner to sell his or her share of the partnership to obtain cash to meet some sudden need. The partner must first obtain the approval of the other partners for the transfer of ownership to a new partner. If approval is not forthcoming, the other partners must usually buy out the retiring partner's share, depending on the partnership agreement. However, this process is slow.

6. Lack of continuity. A partnership legally terminates if one of the partners dies, becomes insolvent, incapacitated, or insane; commits a breach of the partnership agreement; acts against the best interests of the business—for example, by being constantly absent; or, if the partnership is for an indefinite period, gives notice of his or her intention to dissolve the partnership. The need for terminating the business is usually overcome in practice by the inclusion in the partnership agreement of a clause providing for the purchase of that partner's share of the business should any of these events take place. The money to purchase a partner's share is often provided for by a term-insurance policy on the life of each partner with the partnership as the beneficiary. However, a partnership certainly does not have the continuity of a business corporation which continues to exist whatever the fate of its owners.

19.3: THE BUSINESS CORPORATION

A business corporation (or limited company as it used to be called) is a business firm that is a legal person in its own right. As such, the corporation has its own name, its own address, its own capital, and its own life. Because of its separate legal existence, any debts incurred by it can be repaid only out of its assets. There is no recourse to its shareholders. This is completely different from the sole proprietorship and general partnership, in which the owners are legally responsible for all the obligations of the business and must therefore, satisfy any outstanding claims by creditors of the business from their own personal funds.

Private or Public

Business corporations can be either private or public. In a private business corporation, the transfer of shares of ownership requires the approval of the corporation's board of directors; and the shares or bonds must be sold privately. A public business corporation, conversely, is a one that can transfer its shares of ownership freely. This means that it can sell its stocks and bonds to the general public, using advertisng where necessary to do so, so long as it has the approval of the provincial securities commission. The term public corporation is also sometimes used in practice to mean a government-owned or Crown corporation.

Federal or Provincial Incorporation

A business corporation may be established on the authorization of either the federal or the provincial government. Federal incorporation is considered most appropriate when a firm expects to do business in a number of provinces. This is cheaper and more effective than incorporating in each of the various provinces in which business is to be undertaken. Also, it provides the firm with protection against discriminatory provincial legislation. Provincial incorporation is quite adequate, as well as being cheaper, if business is to be transacted in one province alone. All laws of general application such as income, sales, and property taxes, business licences, and compulsory annual statistical returns apply equally to both types of business corporation.

To establish a corporation in Ontario, for instance, there need be only one applicant who must be eighteen or more years of age. Also, the name of the proposed corporation must not be the same or similar to the name of a known corporation, association, partnership, individual, or business, if its use would be likely to deceive, unless consent has been given by the party concerned. The corporation must include the word "Limited," "Incorporated," or "Corporation," or the abbreviation "Ltd.," "Inc.," or "Corp." as the last word of its name.

Capital Stock

The ownership of a corporation is represented by its *capital stock*. This consists of common shares and, in many cases, preferred (or preference) shares. The holders of these shares are known as *shareholders* or *stockholders*. Authorization to issue shares is obtained from the government concerned in the articles of incorporation (or, depending upon the province, the charter or memorandum of association) that establishes the corporation. The shares are issued as and when funds are required. Most corporations now issue their common shares at no-par value. The term *par value* means that a corporation has placed a definite monetary value on the share, usually stated on the *stock certificate* (the written evidence of ownership) at the time of issuance. *No-par value*, or *without par value*, means that no price is stated. Preferred shares have a par value since it is usually the basis on which their fixed dividend is calculated. The actual price or value of any share at any particular moment is what it will fetch in the market. This is known as the market price or *market value* of the share.

Trans Code	Line No	Stat	Comp Type	Method Incorp
A	0	0	A	3
18	20	28	29	30

Share	Notice Req'd	Jurisdiction
S	N	ONTARIO
31	32	33 – 47

Form 1
Business Corporations Act 1982

Formule numéro 1
Loi de 1982 sur les compagnies

ARTICLES OF INCORPORATION
STATUTS CONSTITUTIFS

1. The name of the corporation is: *Dénomination sociale de la compagnie:*

A B C T O Y S I N C O R P O R A T E D

2. The address of the registered office is: *Adresse du siège social:*

1284 Ontario Street

(Street & Number or R.R. Number & if Multi-Office Building give Room No.)
(Rue et numéro ou numéro de la R.R. et, s'il s'agit d'un édifice à bureaux, numéro du bureau)

Toronto, Ontario — M 5 H 3 H 1

(Name of Municipality or Post Office) *(Nom de la municipalité ou du bureau de poste)* — (Postal Code) *(Code postal)*

City of Toronto in the *dans le/la* Municipality of Metropolitan Toronto

(Name of Municipality, Geographical Township) *(Nom de la municipalité, du canton)* — (County, District, Regional Municipality) *(Comté, district, municipalité régionale)*

3. Number (or minimum and maximum number) of directors is: One (1) *Nombre (ou nombres minimal et maximal) d'administrateurs:* Five (5)

4. The first director(s) is/are: *Premier(s) administrateur(s):*

First name, initials and surname *Prénom, initiales et nom de famille*	Residence address, giving street & No. or R.R. No. or municipality and postal code. *Adresse personnelle, y compris la rue et le numéro, le numéro de la R.R. ou, le nom de la municipalité et le code postal*	Resident Canadian State Yes or No *Résident Canadien Oui/Non*
Mr. John Smith	456 Anywhere Street Toronto, Ontario M5H 3L1	Yes

The *book value* of a share is the value, as shown in the company books or accounts, at which it was originally issued. The *asset value* is each share's portion of the corporation's assets. It is calculated by dividing the *net worth* of the corporation (total assets minus total liabilities) by the number of shares that have been issued.

Common Shares

Each common share of a corporation's capital stock entitles the owner to certain benefits: to vote at shareholders' meetings; to share in the profits of the corporation; and to share in the assets of the corporation should it be liquidated.

1. Voting rights. Normally, each common share entitles the owner to one vote at the shareholders' meetings. In some companies, two classes of common stock, A and B, are issued, with the class A shares carrying the voting rights. Any person or group owning a majority of the voting common shares, or even sometimes just a substantial percentage, can appoint the board of directors and thereby control the management of the corporation. In raising additional long-term capital by selling more common shares, the directors must therefore always take into account how these new shares may affect voting control.

The term *holding company* is used to describe a firm that exercises control over a number of subsidiary companies by means of ownership of all, a majority, or, in some cases, just a substantial proportion of the voting shares of these companies. The holding company and its subsidiaries are known as a *conglomerate* or *group*.

2. Share of profits. The common shareholders of a corporation have the right to any profits that remain after preferred shareholders have received their fixed rate of dividend. This right does not mean, however, that the profits have to be paid out to them. *Dividends* are in fact that part of a corporation's profits which the board of directors decides to pay to the shareholders. One of the duties of a corporation's board of directors is to decide how much of the profits is to be distributed to shareholders in the form of dividends and how much is to be kept in the business as retained earnings. If the dividend policy is unsatisfactory, the shareholders can change it only by replacing or influencing the board of directors.

One of the most important reasons why directors retain earnings in the business is to provide additional long-term equity capital. From the shareholder's point of view, a conservative dividend policy is not entirely unfavourable. In the first place, the corporation will be in a stronger financial position, and this should be reflected in increased earnings. Secondly, the extra assets usually cause the market price of the shares to rise in anticipation of an increase in dividends. This increase can result, when the shares are sold, in a capital gain for the seller.

In many instances, business corporations which have built up a substantial amount of retained earnings (or *earned surplus*) will declare a *stock dividend.* This is a distribution of additional shares to existing shareholders. Since the net worth of the company is now divided among a larger number of shares, the asset value of each share is reduced. The shareholder will benefit if the decline in market value of his or her shares is not as great as the reduction in asset value. The shareholder may also benefit by having lower-priced, and possibly more marketable shares. The corporation itself has benefited by distributing stock rather than cash, which it can retain for company use.

Another device, somewhat similar to a stock dividend, is a *stock split.* In this case, a company does not issue new stock backed by retained earnings; it merely splits existing shares into several new ones. Of course, each new share has a smaller amount of company assets behind it. For example, a four-for-one-split reduces the assets behind each share to a quarter of the amount behind each old share. A stock split is often made when the market price of the present shares is too high to make them easily marketable—for example, $500 each. Often, when the stock is split, the market price of each new share may be more than the exact proportionate amount of each old share. This is because the new lower-priced shares are more attractive to investors.

When additional capital stock is to be issued, a corporation may give its existing shareholders the opportunity to buy new stock at less than the current market price, before offering the stock for sale to the general public. These privileges, which lapse within a short period of time, are called *rights*, and are usually in proportion to the amount of stock that each shareholder now owns. The number of rights granted to a shareholder are stated on a certificate called a *warrant.* These rights can be traded in the securities market. The term *warrant* is also used to describe a certificate which gives its holder an option to buy a certain number of shares of a company over many months or even years at successively higher prices. Such a warrant is sometimes attached to bonds and preferred shares as a promotional feature. Like a right, a warrant may be traded.

3. Share of assets. Usually the least important benefit to a shareholder is the right to share in the assets of the corporation on its liquidation. Normally a corporation is terminated because it is unprofitable; as a result, little money is usually left for shareholders from the sale of the company's assets, once the various tax collectors, bondholders, and other creditors have been paid—especially when a corporation is forced into bankruptcy by its creditors.

Preferred Shares

The capital stock of a corporation may consist of preferred or preference shares as well as common shares. Where this is the case, the preferred shares, as the name implies, enjoy a favoured or "preferred" position with regard to profits and assets.

1. Voting rights. The right to vote is normally withheld from the holders of preferred shares in exchange for the preferences given. However, the right to vote at the shareholders' meetings may become effective if preferred dividends have not been paid for a certain number of months or years. In this way, the preferred shareholders are given the opportunity to influence management, usually by having a representative on the board of directors.

2. Share of profits. Preferred shareholders are entitled to receive from the profits of the corporation a fixed dividend on their shares before anything is distributed to the common shareholders. This fixed annual rate of dividend is set as a percentage of the par value of the share or as a specific amount per share.

The right to a preference in receiving profits applies, it should be noted, only to distributed profits. A company is not contractually obliged to pay a preferred dividend each year: the profits may be retained as additional long-term capital. However, preferred shares are normally cumulative, unless otherwise specifically stated. Therefore, any dividend withheld in one year must be paid in subsequent years, before any dividend can be paid on the common shares. Where a preferred share does not have this right, it is described as *non-cumulative*.

In paying dividends, some corporations give a preference to one preferred share over another. Where this is done, the different types of preferred shares are ranked Preferred A, Preferred B, and so on.

3. Share of assets. Should the assets of a corporation be sold—for example, on voluntary liquidation—preferred shareholders rank before common shareholders in their claim to a share of the proceeds. They are, however, only entitled to receive the sum stated on the preferred share certificate. The common shareholders are entitled to receive all the remainder.

4. Other features: redeemability, convertibility, participation. Preferred shares, in addition to their other characteristics, may also be *redeemable*, or *callable*. By making the preferred shares redeemable, management gives itself the option of repaying this type of equity capital at a pre-set price whenever it finds it advisable—for example, to replace an issue carrying a higher dividend rate with one carrying a lower rate. The holder of the redeemable preferred share must, however, be given due notice and be paid a prescribed premium.

Another feature sometimes added to a preferred share is that of *convertibility*. A convertible preferred share is one that is convertible at the option of the owner into common stock at a fixed price or at a set ratio—for example, one preferred share for every two common shares. This option is given for a fixed number of years, or for as long as the shares are outstanding. The purpose of making preferred shares convertible into common shares is to add a speculative element to them. A preferred share may also be *participating*. This means that once the preferred shares have received their fixed dividend, and once the common shares have received a stated amount—for example, $1.00 per share in any one year—the preferred shares are entitled to receive a predetermined part of the remaining profits.

Advantages of the Corporate Form of Ownership

The main advantages that the corporate type of business ownership can offer are: limited liability for the owners; possibly lower income tax; continuity of existence of the firm; relatively easy transferability of ownership; professional management for the owner's investment; and more capital.

1. Limited personal liability. Unlike the sole proprietor and the general partner who stand to lose part or all of their personal assets if their business fails, the shareholder of a corporation can only lose the investment that he or she has made in purchasing the shares.

2. Possibly lower income tax. Canadian-controlled private corporations or CCPCs, need pay a rate of only 25 per cent (in provinces with a 10 per cent provincial tax rate) on the first $200 000 of active annual business income. In Ontario, the rate is 24 per cent. This compares with the graduated personal income-tax rates that a sole proprietor or partner must pay, rising to as much as 55 per cent on taxable income over $62 657. Once a corporation has earned $1 000 000 of business income, it is no longer eligible for the reduced rate. The general rate of corporation income tax is 46 per cent. However, profits from manufacturing and processing are taxed at a flat rate of about 40 per cent.

3. Continuity of existence. Because the corporation is itself a legal person, separate and distinct from its shareholders, its life is unaffected by the death or other personal misfortunes that may befall any of its owners. The corporation's existence can be brought to an end only by the vote of its shareholders to dissolve it.

4. Transferability of ownership. It is very easy to transfer shares of ownership of a public business corporation from one party to another. All that is required is to find a buyer and record that buyer's name in the stock register. And stock exchanges, stock brokers, and trust companies exist to facilitate this task. With the private business corporation, however, the transfer of shares must first be approved by the board of directors.

5. Professional management. In many private business corporations, the major shareholders are usually actively engaged in the management of the business. Therefore there is no gap between owners and managers. However, the structure of the business corporation, in which a board of directors is empowered to set basic business policies and appoint a president to carry them out, permits people to invest their money in a business without themselves becoming involved in its management. This feature is taken full advantage of in the public business corporation whereby many large businesses are now operated with predominantly professional, hired management.

6. More capital. An extremely important advantage of the corporate form of ownership is its suitability for raising large amounts of capital. This is particularly true of the public business corporation which can have an unlimited number of shareholders and can advertise the sale of its stocks and bonds to the public. An investor's liability is limited to the amount invested whatever happens to the corporation; the firm (and the investment) will continue whatever happens to the investor; the investor can easily sell his or her shares of ownership for cash should the need arise; and the investor does not need to spend time in the management of the business.

A private business corporation is, however, relatively handicapped in its ability to raise long-term funds. First, it may not advertise the sale of its shares of capital stock to the general public, or otherwise solicit funds from them. Second, the ownership of the shares is not easily transferred once they have been initially sold—for the approval of the board of directors must be obtained and existing shareholders must usually be given the first right to purchase the shares. Private business corporations, often family-owned businesses, consequently tend to rely heavily on reinvested profits for their capital expansion.

Disadvantages

Compared with the sole proprietorship and partnership, the corporate form of business ownership has the following main disadvantages: the initial cost; more government regulation; less privacy; and possibly less personal incentive.

1. Initial cost. To set up a corporation, it is necessary to pay a fee to the government. This fee will vary in size according to the amount of capital stock authorized. Usually, also, it is prudent to pay for a lawyer's services in handling the incorporation. To set up a provincially incorporated private business corporation, the total initial cost, including legal fees, the corporate seal, and shareholders' registers, can easily range from $500 to $1000.

2. Government regulation. A number of government regulations are directed specifically at business corporations. Corporations must, for example, maintain a set of books specifying shareholders, directors, capital, and so on; keep certain books of accounts; have annual shareholders' meetings; and file annual tax returns with the federal and provincial governments. Corporations must also limit their transactions to those specified in their charter, articles of incorporation, or memorandum of association (depending on the province) or permitted generally by the Act under which they were incorporated. These powers can be amended only by the issue by the government of supplementary articles, or other similar document of authorization.

3. Less privacy. The Business Corporations Act requires that a business corporation furnish its shareholders with an annual income statement and balance sheet. Many firms believe that this information helps their competitors and consider it highly detrimental to have to reveal anything at all. A private business corporation offers greater privacy because its financial statements do not have to be published. The subsidiaries of many foreign firms in Canada are in fact set up as private business corporations to help safeguard their privacy. The same applies to many Canadian firms.

4. Possibly less personal incentive. In most private corporations, particularly the small ones, the managers of the business are also the major shareholders. Their personal desire to perform well is, like that of the sole proprietor or partner, highly motivated by the fact that all the profits earned will be theirs.

In the public business corporation, which is often quite large, the president and the department managers, or vice-presidents, are usually paid employees. Although they may have great personal ambition and dedication to the business, their personal incentive and loyalty are rarely as strong as that of an owner. This is partly overcome in some firms by stock options, profit-sharing plans and annual performance bonuses.

19.4: THE MULTINATIONAL CORPORATION

Many firms sell part of their output abroad, license foreign companies to use their manufacturing processes, or even establish their own overseas manufacturing plants. Many firms also import goods from abroad. Because of their involvement with foreign countries, these firms are sometimes called international. However, in many international firms, manufacturing involvement abroad has become so great that head office management now makes marketing, production, financial, and investment decisions on a global rather than domestic or national basis. Where this is the case, the term *multinational corporation* is used.

Existence in Canada

Multinational companies have existed for many years: the Hudson's Bay Company in Canada was one of the first. Nevertheless, only since World War II and more specifically since the 1950s, has the number and size of these enterprises increased tremendously. Because of American managerial ability, technological know-how, and financial resources, most of these multinational firms are U.S. owned. Because Canada is geographically so close, has abundant resources, has well-developed markets in certain areas, and is politically stable, much U.S. investment has been directed towards this country. Furthermore, an increasingly large proportion of this investment has been direct rather than portfolio. In other words, it has involved mainly the purchase of shares of ownership rather than the straight lending of money. As a result, more and more business firms in this country have become subsidiaries of U.S. multinational corporations. That is why Canada is sometimes said to have a "branch-plant economy." In 1974, the federal government established a Foreign Investment Review Agency, or FIRA, to screen all foreign investment to help ensure that it would provide significant benefit for Canada, particularly in terms of employment and income. This agency was replaced in 1985 by the Investment Canada Agency (ICA) which reviews only major acquisitions by foreigners. Canada also has many multinational corporations of its own, with subsidiaries in other countries.

Reasons for Growth

The main reason that a domestic or national corporation becomes multinational is financial: it hopes to increase or maintain sales revenue, reduce or hold down costs, and thereby improve its profitability and financial solvency. Revenue is often threatened when a country imposes tariffs, quotas and other barriers on imports. By establishing manufacturing facilities within the country, a firm can retain its hold on the foreign market, even though its exports are restricted. Also, more positively, the establishment of overseas manufacturing facilities offers new sales prospects, even to firms which have not previously exported to that country. Furthermore, a foreign subsidiary, as well as producing and selling profitably in the local or regional market, may well buy parts and equipment from plants located in the home country that are also owned by the multinational corporation. On the cost side, lower local costs for raw materials and labour are a great attraction to overseas manufacturing. This is so even after allowance for differences in labour productivity. Often special tax concessions and development grants are also available from foreign governments. Thus a Canadian or U.S. multinational may produce parts or finished products in its plants abroad for shipment and sale in the home country—hence the accusation by Canadian or U.S. workers and their unions that such companies are "exporting jobs".

As regards financial solvency, control over foreign sources of raw materials helps ensure that production in the home country will not be held up. The financial stability of an enterprise is also enhanced by having plants in a number of countries. Political upheavals and wars usually affect some countries but not others. By geographical diversification, a business firm is hedging its bets.

Internal Organization

The internal organization of the multinational corporation is quite diverse. Usually, key decisions such as new capital investment and new labour contracts are made at head office in the home country, usually the United States. Other powers are delegated to regional and country offices. The usual organization is a blend of functions (marketing, production, finance) and geographical areas. Research and new product development, an extremely important activity in the typical multinational corporation, is usually controlled and integrated by head office even though parcelled out among research laboratories in various countries.

19.5: THE CO-OPERATIVE

Another type of business organization is the co-operative.

Characteristics

One main characteristic is that each member, whatever his or her investment, is entitled to only one vote at members' meetings. This is the opposite of the business corporation where a shareholder has as many votes as common shares. Also, no voting by proxy is permitted in a co-operative—a person must be present at the annual meeting in order to cast a vote. Second, a fixed rate of interest is paid on capital invested by the members. And, third, profits not retained in the business are paid out to members in the form of patronage returns which vary with the amount of business transacted. If, for example, a member has bought one per cent of the goods sold, that member receives one per cent of the profit paid out.

Incorporation

Co-operatives are permitted to incorporate under the Corporations Act of their province, and many have in fact done so. By incorporating, the co-operative retains its essential co-operative features of democratic control (one member, one vote), fixed interest on capital, and patronage returns, yet also enjoys the benefits of limited personal liability for its members and continuity of existence for itself.

Origin

Co-operatives are believed to have originated in England in the first half of the nineteenth century. Specifically, a retail co-operative was established in Rochdale, Lancashire, in 1844. In Canada, the co-operative movement has been most popular in the Western provinces.

Types

The principal types of co-operative business in Canada are: consumer (or retail) co-operatives which specialize in retailing goods; marketing co-operatives which engage in the marketing of members' fruit, milk, and other farm products, and in the purchasing of seed and fertilizer for them; financial co-operatives (also called credit unions or *caisses populaires*) which borrow from some members and lend to others; insurance co-operatives which supply members with fire, life, hail, and public-liability insurance; and service co-operatives which supply members with such services as housing, rural electrification, medical insurance, transportation, recreational facilities, rental of machinery, and even funerals.

Purpose

The main purpose of the co-operative enterprise, whatever its specialization, is to provide members with goods or services at a lower price than that normally charged. This lower price may be offered immediately when the goods or services are bought, later in the form of a patronage return, or in both ways combined. Marketing co-operatives enable growers to establish common processing, grading, packaging, and advertising facilities, and to use a common brand name for their products.

Advantages

From a member's point of view, the co-operative has several advantages: first, the member can buy goods and services more cheaply or sell goods more profitably; second, the member can always have a say in its management because of the "one member, one-vote" stipulation; and, third, the member can enjoy limited personal liability and know that the business has continuity of existence, so long as the co-operative is incorporated.

Disadvantages

The disadvantages of the co-operative include: first, its limited ability to raise capital; and, second, the possibility that the democratic control may prevent good management.

19.6: GOVERNMENT ENTERPRISES

Governments own and operate many businesses in Canada and, even though there is not the same degree of public ownership as in many countries of Western Europe, the number is steadily increasing. Nevertheless, Canada still remains vastly different from the communist countries where ownership and operation of industry is almost entirely in the hands of the state.

Federal

At the federal level, certain government-owned businesses are run by regular government departments. However, most federally-owned businesses are operated by *Crown corporations*, which are recognized in the eyes of the law as independent legal persons. Unlike ordinary business corporations, all or most of the shares of capital stock are owned by the federal government rather than by private individuals. Also, they are ultimately accountable to Parliament, through a minister, for the conduct of their affairs.

Most government-owned businesses are run by a special type of Crown corporation, known as a *proprietary corporation*. Such Crown corporations are engaged in lending and other financial operations, as well as in the production and marketing of goods and services to the public. They include Air Canada, The Canada Post Corporation, the Canada Development Corporation, the Canadian Broadcasting Corporation, the Canada Mortgage and Housing Corporation, the Canadian National Railways, and Polysar Corporation Limited. Unlike other Crown corporations, they do not usually require parliamentary appropriation of funds to finance their operations.

Another type of Crown corporation is the *agency corporation*. Such a corporation manages trading or service operations of a quasi-commercial nature and the procurement, construction, and disposal activities of the federal government. Examples of this type of crown corporation include Atomic energy of Canada Limited, Canadian Patents and Development Limited, Crown Assets Disposal Corporation, and the National Harbours Board.

A third type of crown corporation, though less of a business, is the *departmental corporation*. These are responsible for government administrative, supervisory, and regulatory services. Such corporations include the Agricultural Stabilization Board, the Economic Council of Canada, the National Research Council, and the Canada Employment and Immigration Commission.

Provincial

At the provincial and municipal level, government-owned and operated public utilities supply electricity and water; provincial boards retail liquor; development corporations provide grants and loans; and housing corporations provide shelter. Also, a number of provincial governments have become partners in manufacturing operations usually to attract industry to slow-growth areas. All these various enterprises are operated by corporations with all or part of the shares of ownership held by the provincial or municipal governments. Sometimes the enterprise is called a "Board" or "Commission," according to whether a Board of Directors or a Commission (of Commissioners) is entrusted with its management. Thus, there are liquor boards and hydroelectric commissions.

Summary

1. The business firm, organized as a sole proprietorship, partnership, corporation, or co-operative, is the unit of ownership that people use to pool their funds and/or abilities for business purposes.
2. A *sole proprietorship* is a business owned by one person who alone is responsible for its debts. The most important advantages of this form of business organization are: ease of establishment, high personal motivation, quickness and freedom of action, privacy, and ease of termination. The disadvantages include unlimited personal liability, limited talent, limited capital, lack of continuity, and possibly heavier income taxation. Unlimited personal liability means that a sole proprietor's personal assets can be seized, if necessary, to pay outstanding business debts.
3. A *partnership* is a business firm that has two or more owners who pool their talents and/or their funds, but which is not incorporated. In a *general partnership*, all the partners, called *general partners*, take part in the management of the business and all have unlimited personal liability for outstanding business debts. In a *limited partnership*, there are both limited partners and at least one general partner. The limited partner is liable for business debts only up to the amount of his or her investment. However, in return, the partner must not take part in the management of the business. The most important advantages of the partnership form of business organization are: more capital, more talent, high personal motivation, and relatively few legal restrictions. The main disadvantages are: possibly higher income tax, unlimited personal liability, possible management disputes, limited capital (compared with a public business corporation), relatively frozen investment, and possible lack of continuity.
4. A *corporation*, or *limited company*, is a business firm which is a legal person in its own right. A *private business corporation* is one which has restrictions placed on its right to sell shares of its capital stock. A *public business corporation* has no such restrictions and can advertise the sale of its shares and bonds to the general public, if approved by the provincial securities commission. A business corporation may be established under the authority of either the federal or the provincial government.
5. The ownership of a corporation is represented by its *capital stock*, comprising common shares and, in many cases, preferred, or preference, shares. Most common shares are issued with *no-par value*. Each common share entitles the owner to vote at shareholders'

meetings on a one-vote-per-share basis, to share in the profits of the corporation, and to share in the assets of the corporation should it be liquidated. The board of directors of the corporation, as one of its basic policy decisions, decides on the dividends to be paid to the common shareholders. Sometimes a *stock dividend* will be declared, or a *stock split* made. A corporation may also make a rights issue to its shareholders. Preferred shares do not usually confer voting rights on their owners. They do, however, confer a right to a fixed dividend, based on the par value of the stock, before any dividends are paid to common shareholders. Preferred shares may be cumulative or non-cumulative. They may also be redeemable, convertible, or participating.

6. The *advantages* of the corporate form of business ownership, from the owners' point of view, are: limited personal liability for the shareholders, possibly lower income tax, continuity of existence, easier transfer of ownership, professional management, and more capital. *Disadvantages* include the high initial cost, government regulation, less privacy, and possibly less personal incentive.
7. In recent years, there has been a tremendous expansion in the number and size of *multinational corporations*. These are international firms that have manufacturing operations in various countries and make marketing, production, financial, investment, and other major business decisions on a global rather than purely domestic basis. For various reasons, more and more business firms in Canada have become subsidiaries of U.S. multinational corporations. Hence the label sometimes applied to Canada of a "branch-plant economy." However, the Investment Canada Agency tries to ensure that major foreign acquisitions are of net benefit to Canada. Canada also has multinationals of its own.
8. A *co-operative* is a business firm in which each owner or member has only one vote and in which profits are distributed according to the amount of business the member has transacted with the co-operative. Co-operatives are permitted to incorporate under the Corporations Act of their province. In Canada, there are consumer co-operatives, marketing co-operatives, insurance co-operatives, and service co-operatives. The main purpose of the co-operative enterprise is to provide members with goods or services at a lower cost than would otherwise be possible.
9. There are many government-owned and operated businesses in Canada. The federally-owned ones are usually run by Crown corporations. At the provincial and municipal level, boards and com-

missions supply, for example, electricity, public transit, and liquor.

Key Terms

Sole proprietorship 366
Unlimited personal liability 367
Partnership 368
General partnership 368
Limited partnership 368
Partnership agreement 368
Business corporation 372
Capital stock 373
Shareholder 373
Par value 373
No-par value 373
Stock certificate 373
Market value 373
Book value 375
Net worth 375
Common share 375
Holding company 375
Conglomerate 375
Dividends 375
Stock dividend 376
Stock split 376
Rights 376
Warrants 376
Preferred shares 377
Non-cumulative 377
Redeemability 377
Convertibility 378
Participation 378
Corporate income tax 378
Multinational corporation 381
Direct investment 381
Portfolio investment 381
Co-operative 382
Crown corporation 384

Review Questions

1. Explain briefly the nature and purpose of the business firm.
2. What is a sole proprietorship? What are the advantages of this form of business ownership?
3. What is unlimited liability? Why is it considered a disadvantage of the sole proprietorship form of business ownership? What other disadvantages exist?
4. Distinguish between a general partnership and a limited partnership.
5. What are the most important advantages of the partnership form of ownership?
6. What are the most important disadvantages of the partnership form of ownership?
7. What is a business corporation? Distinguish between a private and a public one.
8. Why might federal incorporation be preferred to provincial incorporation? And vice versa?

9. What is the requirement for establishing a corporation in your province?
10. What is capital stock? Distinguish between par value and no-par value shares. Why are shares issued without a par value?
11. Distinguish between the market value, the book value, and the asset value of a share.
12. What are the privileges of a common shareholder?
13. What is a holding company? A conglomerate?
14. Distinguish between a stock dividend and a stock split.
15. Distinguish between a right and a warrant.
16. What are the privileges of a preferred shareholder?
17. Distinguish between cumulative and non-cumulatve preferred shares. What is a redeemable preferred share?
18. A preferred share can be convertible and/or participating. Explain.
19. What are the advantages of the corporate form of business ownership?
20. What are the disadvantages of the corporate form of ownership?
21. What is a multinational corporation? What encourages a domestic or national business corporation to become a multinational one?
22. Explain the nature and purpose of the co-operative form of business ownership.
23. What is a crown corporation?
24. How do provincial and municipal governments organize public utilities and other government-owned business enterprises?
25. Why do most business firms start out as sole proprietorships? Discuss.
26. Why would an entrepreneur operating as a sole proprietor decide to take in partners? Discuss.
27. In a limited partnership, all the partners have limited liability. Discuss.
28. Why might a sole proprietor decide to incorporate his or her business? Explain and discuss.

"Guys, I've called this meeting because there seems to be something wrong with our productivity.."

20. CANADIAN PRODUCTIVITY

CHAPTER OBJECTIVES

A. To explain what is meant by the term "productivity"
B. To emphasize the fact that a country's productivity determines the standard of living of its people
C. To show how Canadian productivity is lagging behind that of other nations
D. To identify the reasons for slow productivity growth in Canada
E. To explain how poor productivity makes Canadian firms more vulnerable to foreign competition
F. To indicate why S.E. Asian goods are usually cheaper and often better-made than many Canadian ones
G. To examine the research and development efforts that are now being undertaken in Canada
H. To review government efforts to assist the growth of Canadian productivity
I. To emphasize the vital role of both management and labour in improving Canadian productivity
J. To discuss the federal government's industrial strategy

CHAPTER OUTLINE

20.1: PRODUCTIVITY DEFINED

In the 1980s, a critical economic concern for Canada is productivity. The term *productivity* is normally used in the sense of *labour productivity*—meaning the value of the average output per person employed over a given period of time such as an hour, a week, or a year. Logically, however, we can also talk about the productivity of the other main factors of production: land and capital. In fact, land varies greatly in productivity throughout Canada and the world. And capital also varies in its productivity, depending on whether the machines being used in a manufacturing plant are new or old, and on the way in which they are maintained. We can also talk about *total factor productivity*—the output of all the factors of production combined.

20.2: CANADA'S PRODUCTIVITY RECORD

Canadian productivity, defined as real GNP per employed person, has deteriorated significantly since 1973. After increasing at an annual rate of 2.5 per cent between 1966 and 1973, productivity declined 0.1 per cent a year from 1974 to 1981. Other studies show that from 1973 to 1981, productivity in Japan grew at an annual rate of 6.8 per cent, in France 4.6 per cent, in West Germany, 4.5 per cent, and in Canada 1.6 per cent, just less than in the U.S. According to the European Management Forum, an independent organization that evaluates the international competitiveness of 22 industrial nations, Canada ranked thirteenth in ability of companies to produce goods at competitive prices; twenty-second in productivity trends; twentieth in the introduction of labour-saving technology; and nineteenth in employee turnover. According to another source, the OECD, Canada's annual productivity growth over the period 1960-1980 was 2.4 per cent, compared with an average of 3.9 per cent for 16 OECD countries. The only country with a lower productivity growth rate was Britain, with 2.3 per cent.

In recent years, the productivity growth rate has risen quickly in many countries. Unfortunately, Canada has lagged well behind. For example, U.S. Department of Labour figures show that, in the period 1950-1981, manufacturing productivity increased by 110 per cent in

Table S.13
Growth of Productivity, Average Annual Percentage, 1966-1984

	1966-1973	1974-1979	1980-1984	1980	1981	1982	1983	1984
Canada	2.5	0.3	0.4	-1.9	0.5	-1.2	2.4	2.1
United States	1.5	0.3	0.8	-0.8	1.4	-1.3	2.4	2.5
Japan	8.6	3.0	3.2	3.8	3.2	2.2	1.3	5.3
Germany	4.1	3.0	1.7	1.0	0.6	0.7	3.1	3.0
France	4.8	3.0	1.7	1.1	1.0	1.8	1.5	2.8
United Kingdom	3.1	1.2	1.9	-1.0	2.0	4.1	3.6	1.0
Italy	5.6	1.5	0.8	2.5	-0.3	0.0	-1.3	3.0
Seven major countries	3.9	1.5	1.5	0.5	1.6	0.1	2.2	3.2

Source: OECD, *Economic Outlook*, December 1984, *Main Economic Indicators* the U.S., 194 per cent in Canada, 267 per cent in Sweden, 341 per cent in Denmark, 350 per cent in France, 414 per cent in West Germany, 462 per cent in Netherlands, 470 per cent in Italy, and by 1334 per cent in Japan. Although Canadian productivity increased faster than in the U.S., this position has been reversed in more recent years.

All the statistics show, in other words, that Canada's labour productivity growth is now one of the slowest in the non-communist industrialized world. This conclusion also applies to total factor productivity. This characteristic of our economy—ailing productivity—has even been called the "Canadian disease". And forecasts by the Economic Council of Canada and the Conference Board of Canada for the 1980s, estimate productivity growth, in the event of no major change, at no more than one per cent a year.

20.3: PRODUCTIVITY AND THE STANDARD OF LIVING

A person living in one country may work much harder than a person living in another, yet receive much lower real wages—that is, the goods and services that he or she obtains in exchange for the money wages received. As we become well aware, when travelling abroad, the material standard of living that the average person enjoys varies greatly between different parts of the world.

The basic reason for this disparity in living standards is the difference in productivity. This may be caused by differences in the persons themselves. For example, a farmer in country A may be physically weaker, less knowledgeable, less determined, etc. than a farmer in country B—which would help account for part of the lower productivity in country A. But there are other important considerations. The farmer in country A may have very little farm equipment or other capital goods. Also what he has may be out-dated or in poor state of repair. And this would also help keep his output low relative to the farmer in country B. Furthermore, the land that he works may be rocky, dry, and otherwise infertile, compared with that in country B. Consequently, the farmer in country A may never achieve the standard of living that is enjoyed by the farmer in country B, even though he or she may work harder.

Even though the farmer in country B may now enjoy a high standard of living (due in part to a large amount of capital per worker and abundant natural resources), his standard of living may deteriorate as the years go by. This would be the case if the farmer in country B let his capital goods deteriorate or grow out-of-date; if he neglected his resources; and/or worked less hard and less skillfully. The situation could become even worse if the goods produced by the farmer in country B become so expensive or so poor in quality that consumers, not only in other countries but in country B as well, prefer to buy the goods produced by the farmer in country A.

In summary, as a country's productivity rises, so normally does the standard of living of its people. Conversely, as a country's productivity declines, so does the standard of living. Britain is considered to be a good example of a country whose productivity and standard of living have declined in modern times. Japan, West Germany and other West European countries are examples of countries whose productivity and standard of living have substantially increased. Canada's productivity and standard of living were rising for many years after World War II. However, since the mid-1970s, the rates of increase of both have been slipping compared with those of many other countries. Whereas at the end of World War II, Canadians had the fourth highest standard of living in the world. Now it is about the fourteenth.

The implications of a declining rate of increase in productivity are several. Because the amount of goods and services being produced is increasing relatively slowly, money wages, which are increasing more quickly, will buy less. Also, the government will not be able to afford to provide as many social services for the public. There will be increasing social hostility between the "haves" and the "have-nots"; labour-management relations may worsen; and the country's goods will become less competitive with those of other countries, both at home and abroad, because they now cost more to produce and must therefore be higher priced.

20.4: PRODUCTIVITY AND WAGES IN CANADA

Whereas the growth of labour productivity has been relatively slow in Canada in recent years, real wages per worker have increased faster. In other words, higher wages have not been matched by higher productivity. This widening gap between productivity and wages has not only reduced the international competitiveness of Canadian goods but has also increased inflationary pressures in Canada. This is because the money earned is chasing relatively fewer goods and services. Also, although productivity in Canada is lower than in the U.S., our principal export market, average wages in Canada are higher—a fact which is gradually making it more and more difficult for Canadian manufacturers and other producers to compete in the U.S. market and elsewhere. Only if the exchange rate for the Canadian dollar sinks even further can Canadian export prices remain competitive—but this means that Canada would have to pay more for its imports and for the servicing and repayment of its large foreign debt which is denominated in U.S. dollars and other hard currencies.

20.5: REASONS FOR THE DECLINING RATE OF INCREASE IN PRODUCTIVITY IN CANADA

Many different factors have been blamed for the declining rate of increase in productivity in Canada. The only agreement among economists and others in this matter is that there is not just one cause but many together that are to blame. These various possible causes are listed below, in no particular order.

1. There has been a reduction in the amount of capital employed per worker. However, Canadian industry is much more capital intensive than that of the U.S., yet Canadian productivity is lower. Nevertheless, more investment in new products and new production processes could have been made in Canada.

2. There has been a gradual shifting of workers away from sectors of the economy such as manufacturing that have a high measured productivity (partly because of more capital per worker) to service industries in which productivity, as well as being hard to measure, appears to increase only very slowly.

3. A large number of women and young persons entered the Canadian labour force in the 1970s as a result of changing attitudes and the post-war baby boom which, according to some analysts, means a less experienced work force.

4. The increase in energy prices adversely affected the use of capital.

5. Relations between management and labour in many firms, particularly large ones, have continued to be antagonistic, with resultant strikes, walkouts, and low worker morale, and an attitude by many union leaders that improvement in productivity is not the proper concern of a labour union.

6. Too many people have been educated for the wrong jobs.

7. There is insufficient competition in Canada—due to weak anti-monopoly legislation and the existence of too many government-protected monopolies and oligopolies.

8. The highly graduated rates of personal income tax in Canada discourage a person from working harder and undertaking business risk.

9. The fact that Canada's manufacturing sector (in which productivity gains can be most spectacular) is so small.

10. There has not been enough spent on research and development aimed at improving production.

11. There has been an undue emphasis over the last two decades in Canada on the redistribution of wealth to the detriment of the rate of creation of new wealth.

12. The Canadian market is so small that it prevents long production

runs, with corresponding economies of scale, unless substantial quantities of the product can be exported—and relatively few Canadian firms are good at exporting, even to the U.S. market.

13. A labour union complaint: the failure of the Canadian government to insist on greater Canadian content in imported goods or on other restrictions on imports.

14. Canada's cold climate.

15. Canada's small population being spread over such a wide country, causing high transportation costs.

16. Government safety and pollution requirements that require nonproductive expenditure from the GNP point of view.

17. Foreign ownership of so much Canadian industry.

18. Shipping of so many resources abroad without sufficient processing in Canada.

19. Poor business management.

20. Insufficient tax incentives to industrial investment.

21. Insufficient tax incentives for the export of manufactured goods.

22. Insufficient savings and investment in Canada compared with consumption. We should consume less out of current production and save and invest more, government tax incentives or not.

23. Lack of a coherent industrial strategy by the federal government.

20.6: VULNERABILITY OF CANADIAN FIRMS

Many Canadian firms have already succumbed to foreign competition as a result of their inability to compete at home or abroad on the basis of price, product quality, or both. And many other firms now import component parts and even complete products that were formerly manufactured in Canada. The most vulnerable Canadian firms, now and in the future, are of two basic kinds. The first are those that produce a good that can be manufactured more cheaply in lower-cost countries and can be economically transported to Canada and other world markets. Some examples are textiles, clothing, shoes, home entertainment equipment, business office equipment, cars, motorcycles, bicycles, and base metals. In the last instance, the production of base metals such as manganese, the ore-producing countries now do their own refining instead of just exporting the ore.

The second kind of vulnerable Canadian firms are those that produce a good or service that will be made obsolete by technological change. For example, Canadian copper producers who see their product being replaced in power transmission by aluminum, and in communications by fibre optics; or metal manufacturers who have already seen many of their markets taken over by plastics. The Swiss watch industry fell into both categories of vulnerability when it was devastated in the 1970s by, first, the competition of S.E. Asian low-cost producers and, second, by the invention and manufacture of quartz and digital watches in North America.

In the future, as another example of the changes in store for us, automobiles are expected to become completely non-metallic; and high-performance toughened adhesives, or industrial "superglues", are expected to transform basic manufacturing methods for just about everything from washtubs to machine tools to aircraft. At least one pundit has forecast that in the next few decades, Canada and the U.S. will gradually witness the disappearance of such traditional industries as automobiles, clothing, appliances, steel, and a host of others—and that a massive structural change is already taking place in the North American economy as S.E. Asian manufacturers increase their penetration of the world market. The salvation of Canadians, so it is suggested, is to concentrate on resource-based "high-tech" industries. A report by the Science Council of Canada has suggested that Canada is already falling behind in the race to exploit the new computer technology. For example, Canada is now a major net importer of computers and automated office systems. However, a recent report by the Economic Council of Canada is more optimistic.

A particularly significant trend that is emerging in modern industry is the application of labour-saving computerized technology. Sometimes called CAD/CAM (Computer-Assisted Design/Computer-Assisted Manufacture), this approach has already received much attention in Canada. Nevertheless, Canada is still in the early stages compared with Japan where so-called "manless" plants, with numerous programmable robots, already produce a variety of high-quality products in the auto, steel, electronics, and machine-tool industries. In these new plants, computer equipment and special programming are combined with traditional mechanical automation, in a process called "mechatronics". This trend has been called the "second industrial revolution" and by Alvin Toffler, the "Third Wave" and promises to change the manufacturing process and the industrial workplace as drastically as did steam-power in the nineteenth century, and mass-production techniques in the early twentieth century. A key characteristic of these new manufacturing plants is the use of a central computer linked to satellite computers. Electronic instructions are given to the various robots which then act accordingly. The satellite computers monitor the work being done and make adjustments as and when necessary.

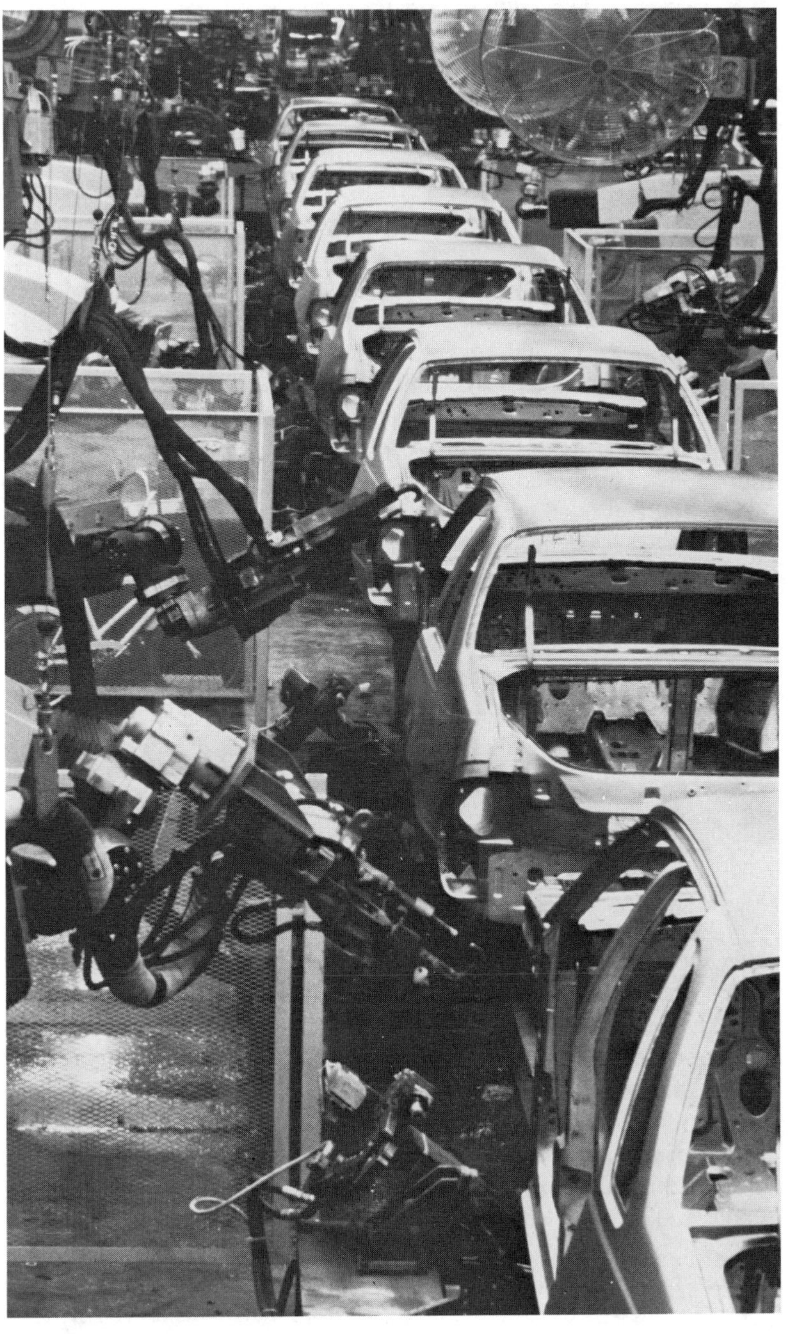

20.7: COMPETITION FROM S.E. ASIA

For many years, goods made in Japan and other S.E. Asian countries were considered to be cheap but shoddy imitations of those made in North America and Western Europe. However, in the last few decades the picture has completely changed. Now, many Western consumers buy the S.E. Asian product for quality as well as price. And this dramatic change has threatened the existence of many traditional Western industries—automobiles, watches, steel, ships, toys, calculators, TV sets, motor cycles, bicycles, pens, clothing, textiles, etc. and, before long, so it is anticipated, computers and pharmaceuticals.

The easy explanation for the inability of many Canadian or U.S. firms to compete effectively with the S.E. Asian product (from Japan, South Korea, Hong Kong, Taiwan, Singapore, Malaysia, and now mainland China) is the lower cost of labour in those countries. This is estimated at about one-third of the North American wage—with Japan now a relatively-high-labour-cost country in the S.E. Asia region. However, the S.E. Asian producers have several other advantages. First, they have adopted and, where necessary, adapted the latest Western industrial technology, as well as developed new technology of their own. Second, they have invested large sums of money in modern plant and equipment so that (a) the amount of capital per worker in many industries is extremely high and (b) the condition and technological efficiency of that capital is excellent. Thus, for example, Japan now has more industrial robots than all the other countries of the world combined. Third, the quality control standards for materials, components, and finished products are usually more demanding than in the West where product testing is often done on a sample basis. Fourth, the quality of labour (dedication, intelligence, trainability, manual dexterity, patience etc.) is high. Fifth, the motivation of the worker and management is generally greater—the "have nots" struggling to improve their lot, unspoilt by the commonplace luxuries of the West. Sixth, their business management is often more efficient—whether it be in the area of labour relations (the Theory Z style of participative management), marketing, finance, or production planning and control. Seventh, there is much closer co-operation between government and business than there is in Canada and the U.S. This involves joint planning and implementing, often with government financial assistance for research and development, of an industrial strategy for the country. All these factors, when taken together, mean that S.E. Asian productivity is often higher than Canadian productivity and provides a sharp competitive edge that has already sliced through many world markets.

20.8: INDUSTRIAL RESEARCH AND DEVELOPMENT

Innovation—the invention of new products or production processes—is one acknowledged key to productivity growth. And innovation usually requires, as a prerequisite, a serious and sustained industrial research and development effort. Unfortunately in Canada, private sector R & D has not been impressive. Most large firms, usually Canadian subsidiaries of U.S. multinationals, have been content to borrow any new technology from their parent companies abroad and pay a licensing fee for its use in Canada. And the U.S. parent companies, for obvious reasons, are usually inclined to concentrate their R & D centres in the U.S. However, despite what has just been said, there are a number of large and small Canadian firms that are leaders in innovation (Northern Telecom, Mitel, etc.) and who even sell successfully in the Japanese market—considered to be one of the hardest for a foreign firm to crack.

At the present time, Canada is spending about 1.2 per cent of its GNP on research and development with the federal government hoping to raise that figure to 1.5 per cent. By contrast, the U.S., West Germany, and Japan already each spend about 2 per cent of their GNP on R & D.

20.9: GOVERNMENT ASSISTANCE

Oddly enough, governments in Canada have a better reputation for R & D support than do private business firms, although it is the latter who will go under if they do not keep ahead in the technology race. Nevertheless, even in the public sector, federal expenditures—through tax incentives and grants—have declined (in constant 1971 dollars) since their peak in fiscal year 1973-74. Also, since the early 1970s, federal expenditure on R & D, as a percentage of Canada's GNP, has steadily slipped. However, in the federal budget of April 1983, new government proposals for R & D support in Canada were announced. Specifically, the income tax credit for R & D expenditures by business firms was increased by 10 per cent and more government money was to be made available in R & D grants. The federal government also asked for submissions from the private sector on a government R & D paper. One suggestion, already made, was that the government broaden the application of the R & D tax incentives to include "technological development" rather than the narrower and pure-research oriented "scientific research".

At the federal level, most of the programs of assistance for industrial research and development are now administered by the Department of Regional and Industrial Expansion. Previously, they were under the Department of Science and Technology which is now responsible for advising on science policy for Canada.

In 1983, the federal government proposed the establishment of a National Centre for Productivity and Employment Growth, with financing of $5 million a year. The centre's main function would be to bring together management, labour, and government to work on the problem of improving productivity, to distribute information on methods for improving productivity, and to act in an advisory capacity to help the government formulate productivity policies.

The federal government has also during the 1980s given a great deal of thought to the development of a technology strategy for Canada. Suggestions include: the establishment of R & D income tax shelters for individuals; the establishment of national technology centres across Canada—for example, a biotechnology centre in Saskatoon, a manufacturing technology centre in Winnipeg, and a food-processing technology centre somewhere in New Brunswick; a stronger Buy Canadian policy; and encouragement of foreign multinationals to do more R & D and manufacturing in Canada.

At the provincial level, Ontario as one example, has set up six technology centres around the province—for example, the Ontario Centre for Microelectronics in Ottawa that plans to help small and medium-sized businesses to develop new electronic products and to use microelectronics to solve manufacturing problems and the Ontario Centre for Automotive Parts Technology in St. Catherines.

20.10: THE ROLE OF MANAGEMENT AND LABOUR

If Canada is to remain competitive both at home and abroad it must raise labour productivity by applying the latest computer-assisted manufacturing technology. However, labour unions in Canada have in the past been reluctant to accept such changes without adequate safeguards for the livelihood of their members.

In Japan, by contrast, workers have been extremely willing and able to accept this new manufacturing technology even though it is labour-saving. This seems to be the result of three factors. First, the system of life-time employment used by most large Japanese companies which assures the worker of a new job if his or her old one disappears. Second, the fact that the average Japanese worker has a relatively high level of technical education and training. And, third, the much more co-operative attitude between management and labour, based on dedication to employer and country.

It should be noted here that labour productivity depends only partly on the persons employed. Thus the slow improvement in productivity in Canada cannot be blamed solely on the Canadian worker's alleged lack of effort, lack of skill, hostility towards management, unwillingness to accept new technology, lack of pride in his or her work, etc., although these must share some of the blame. Just as important is the way in which production is organized and the employees managed (including the way in which the workers are motivated).

An essential prerequisite of the acceptance of rapid technological change in Canada is therefore an improvement in labour-management relations.

In the vast majority of North American companies, management treats the average employee as if he or she is basically lazy, dull, unambitious, selfish and resistant to change. This conventional approach was labelled by Professor Douglas McGregor in 1957, in his book, *The Human Side of Enterprise*, as the Theory X style of management. Other companies adopt a more positive attitude towards their employees, giving them more training and responsibility whenever possible, and treating them more like human beings than mere cogs in a vast production machine. McGregor labelled this approach "Theory Y". Nevertheless, even with the Theory Y approach, the company always comes first, and if sales drop, heads soon start to roll. In Japan, by contrast, a somewhat different system of management seems to exist—one that blends discipline, loyalty, employee participation, quality circles, greater mutual trust, greater openness and exchange between employer and employee, job security and other elements, into a more fruitful whole. This style of management has been called by W.G. Ouchi, in a book about it, "Theory Z".

A *quality circle* is a group of employees who meet together, on a regular basis, with or without a member of supervisory management, to discuss ways in which work methods, manufacturing or assembly operations, and the quality of the product can be improved. Although the idea originated in the U.S., it seems to have been applied more extensively, and with perhaps better results, by the Japanese. However, more and more Canadian companies are making use of quality circles and other ways of improving worker motivation and productivity such as by profit-sharing and employee stock-ownership plans.

At the national level, the federal government, organized labour, and private business are now starting to co-operate again—for example, in a proposed Canadian Labour Market and Productivity Centre.

"You mean, we should have been following Theory Z, not Theory Y?!"

20.11: CANADA'S INDUSTRIAL STRATEGY

The long-term program that a government adopts toward its country's industrial sector is known as its *industrial strategy*. Thus, for example, in 1879, the Canadian government greatly increased the level of tariffs on imported manufactured goods as a deliberate policy of protecting and thereby promoting local manufacturing industry. Although tariff protection in Canada and other countries has since declined as a result of multilateral trade agreements, other tools are nowadays being used to encourage manufacturing growth. The Federal Business Development Bank, the Canada Development Corporation, and the Department of Regional and Industrial Expansion all provide federal financial assistance to industry. There are also financial incentives and technical assistance to undertake research and development and to promote exports of manufactured and other goods. Industry in general, and small businesses in particular, have benefited in recent years from reductions in corporate income taxation. At the individual industry level, federal government initiatives have led to the auto pact with the United States (which gave a powerful boost to car, truck, and parts production in Canada), the development of Arctic oil and gas fields, and the establishment of a computer industry. At the regional level, provincial governments, usually through development corporations, have also tried to promote industrial growth by loans and equity participation. Also, joint federal-provincial initiatives have led to new enterprises being started in Canada—such as the helicopter manufacturing plants now scheduled for Ontario and Quebec.

As the years go by, changes in demand, production, technology, and overseas sources of supply cause changes in the relative prosperity of different industries. Therefore, unless an industry can adjust, it may soon become stagnant. Already in Canada and other countries there are such pockets of industrial depression. Consequently, a country's industrial strategy, as well as needing to be clear and internally consistent, should be flexible. It is not surprising, therefore, that there has been much talk in Canada in recent years of the need for a new industrial strategy to cope with changing times. Let us now consider some of the factors that such a new strategy must take into account.

1. Employment. Canada has a high rate of unemployment. Should only industries that are labour-intensive be encouraged? Should industrial growth be artificially encouraged in otherwise slow-growth regions of the country?

2. Productivity. Productivity per worker varies greatly from one industry to another. It is greater in the capital-intensive, high-technology industries such as oil and chemicals than in, say, the leather and clothing industries. Should only high-productivity industries be encouraged despite the fact that they are capital-intensive rather than labour-intensive?

3. Growth. The long-term growth prospects for some industries (for example, electronics) are better than for others. Should the emphasis of government assistance be placed only on industries with above-average growth prospects? Should traditional, but ailing industries such as textiles and footwear be encouraged to survive?

4. Resources. Large quantities of Canada's raw materials are now exported with relatively little processing. Should there be incentives to encourage greater processing in this country, and thus increase income and employment opportunities for Canadians from resources that are gradually being depleted?

5. Imports. Apart from automobiles, much of Canada's exports consists of food and raw materials, while most of its imports are manufactured goods. Should imports of manufactured goods be discouraged by means other than tariffs—a policy followed by, for example, Japan and many Latin American countries?

6. Market size. Countries throughout the world are entering into regional free-trade arrangements. Canada, if it is to maintain or improve the average standard of living of its 25 million people, cannot be self-sufficient. And, despite political misgivings, Canada cannot turn away from the large, rich U.S. market just across the border. The automobile pact, by treating the North American market as one, and by dividing production between Canadian and U.S. plants, has increased prosperity all round by taking better advantage of the economies of mass production. Should Canada try to arrange similar pacts for other products, and even with other countries—for example, with the European Common Market countries?

Industrial and Regional Development Program (IRDP)

In 1983, a new program for Canadian national economic development was announced by the federal government. This program, to be administered by the Department of Regional and Industrial Expansion (DRIE), will provide substantial government financial assistance in the form of grants, loans, and loan-guarantees, to Canadian businesses. It applies to six separate phases of the corporate and product life cycle, as follows: industrial infrastructure; industrial innovation; plant establishment; modernization and expansion; marketing; and industrial renewal. The basic purpose of the program is to make Canadian industry more competitive so as to maximize its sales potential in both the domestic and foreign markets. An Industrial and Regional Development Board, with both business and labour representatives from across Canada, is to advise the government on overall industrial policies and strategies. Also, task forces are to be assembled for key industrial sectors (such as the aeronautics and automotive industries) to advise on specific development programs for those sectors.

How the new program will work out is uncertain. Some critics argue that it is nothing more than a spruced-up package containing almost the same kinds of industrial development assistance already available for years. The only new additions are funding for new product research and development, marketing studies, the application of new manufacturing technology, and tourism projects. On the other hand, there will now be one standardized instrument for basic industrial development rather than a bewildering variety of programs. In fact, the IRDP replaces nearly 80 industrial development programs previously offered by ITC and DREE. Also, the budget has been increased.

One problem with IRDP is the need to reconcile, in the allocation of funds, the aims of developing a more productive industrial base in Canada (the philosophy of ITC) with the aim of assisting the economically disadvantaged regions of Canada (the philosophy of DREE). This is to be attempted by dividing Canada's 260 census districts into four economic groups, ranging from the poorest 5% of its population (tier IV) to the most affluent 50% (tier I). Project funding varies according to tier group—with a firm in a tier IV district receiving a larger percentage of assistance than a firm in a tier I district. Furthermore, funding assistance to establish a new plant is not available to firms in tier I districts.

The program is to be administered in a decentralized way, with most applications for assistance being processed locally by DRIE staff. Also, regional executive directors are to orient the focus of the IRDP to the specific development needs of their province.

Summary

1. *Productivity* is the value of the average output per person employed over a given period of time.
2. According to the statistics, productivity has been increasing more slowly in Canada than in most other industrial countries.
3. If productivity declines, so does a country's standard of living.
4. Wages in Canada have been increasing faster than labour productivity.

"Russ, I want you to fit some 'quality circles' into our organization.."

5. Many reasons (as listed in the Chapter) have been put forward for Canada's slow productivity increase. The only consensus is that it is not just one factor, but many combined, that are the cause.
6. Canadian firms are vulnerable in two ways: to lower-cost imports and to changes in technology.
7. S.E. Asian firms, notably in Japan, not only have the competitive advantage of lower labour costs but also seem able to apply new technology faster in manufacturing production, seem willing to invest the large sums of money required, and enjoy greater management-labour co-operation.
8. Spending on research and development in Canada is considered to be inadequate.
9. Canada's federal and provincial governments are now taking steps to help encourage productivity in Canada.
10. A critical issue in Canada, in any discussion of productivity, is Canada's adversary system of management-labour relations as compared with Japan's "Theory Z" style of management.
11. Federal and provincial governments have assisted Canadian industry in various ways. However, it is argued that Canada badly needs a more definite *industrial strategy*—that is to say, a long-term government program to promote industry. Some of the considerations that such a strategy must take into account are: employment opportunities, productivity, growth prospects, use of natural resources, competition of imports, and market size, including export opportunities.
12. In 1983, the federal government announced a new Industrial and Regional Development Program for Canada.

Key Terms

Productivity 392
Labour productivity 392
Total factor productivity 392
Standard of living 394
High-tech industry 398
Labour-saving computerized technology 398
CAD/CAM 398
Mechatronics 398
Second industrial revolution 398
R & D 401
Innovation 401
Government assistance 401
Theory Z management 403
Industrial strategy 405
IRDP 406

Review Questions

1. What exactly is "productivity"?
2. How successful has Canada been in raising productivity? How does our record compare with that of other industrial countries?
3. The standard of living is higher in Canada than in the Third World countries because Canadians work harder. Discuss.
4. Explain, in terms of productivity, the fact that the standard of living has declined in Britain since World War II but risen in such countries as Switzerland, Denmark, West Germany and Japan.
5. To what extent does productivity explain regional differences of living standards within Canada?
6. What are the economic implications of the fact that wages have been increasing faster in Canada than productivity?
7. Many reasons have been suggested for slow productivity growth in Canada. Which do you consider to be the five most important reasons. Why?
8. "Labour productivity depends only partly on the person employed". Explain and discuss, with reference to Canada and Japan.
9. What types of Canadian firms have gone out of business in recent years because of low-cost foreign competition?
10. What types of Canadian firms have gone out of business in recent years because their products have become obsolete?
11. What has been called the "second industrial revolution"? What was the "first"?
12. What is CAD/CAM? Why is it attracting so much business and government attention in Canada?
13. "The reason that imports from S.E. Asia are cheaper than Canadian-made goods is mainly lower labour costs". Discuss.
14. What is industrial "innovation". Explain, with examples.
15. What are our federal and provincial governments doing to encourage R & D?
16. "Japan's biggest competitive advantage over Canada is the attitude of its labour force". Discuss.
17. How have the federal and provincial governments assisted manufacturing industry in Canada?
18. What is an industrial strategy? What problems could such a strategy help Canadian manufacturers solve?
19. Explain the nature and purpose of the IRDP.

Index

LIST OF STATISTICAL TABLES